ASP.NET Core 2.2 MVC, Razor Pages, API, JSON Web Tokens & HttpClient

How to Build a Video Course Website

ASP.NET Core 2.2 MVC, Razor Pages, API, JSON Web Tokens & HttpClient

Overview 1
   Setup 2
   Book Version 2
   Source Code 2
   Other Books by the Author 3
   Online Courses and Free Content by the Author 3
   Disclaimer – Who Is This Book for? 4
   Rights 4
   About the Author 4
Part 1: MVC How to Build a Video Course Website 7
1. The Use Case 9
   Introduction 9
   The Use Case 9
      The User Interface (MVC) 10
      Login and Register User 10
      The Administrator Interface (Razor Pages) 10
   Conclusion 11
      Login and Register 11
      The User Dashboard View 11
      The Course View 12
      The Video View 15
      The Administrator Dashboard Razor Page 16
      A Typical Administrator Index Razor Page 16
      A Typical Administrator Create Razor Page 17
      A Typical Administrator Edit Razor Page 18
      A Typical Administrator Delete Razor Page 19

2. Setting Up the Solution 21
Introduction 21
Technologies Used in This Chapter 21
Overview 21
Creating the Solution 21
Installing AutoMapper 26
Creating the Database 27
Adding the Common and Database Projects 28
Adding Entity Framework Core to the Database Project 29
Adding the VODUser Class 30
Adding the Database Context 31
Creating the First Migration and the Database 32
Summary 34

3. Login 35
Introduction 35
Technologies Used in This Chapter 35
Redirecting to the Login Page 35
Styling the Login Page 37
Adding the login.css Stylesheet 38
Scaffolding the Login and Register Pages 38
Changing the Layout of the Login Page 40
Styling the Login Page 42
Summary 44

4. Register User 45
Introduction 45
Technologies Used in This Chapter 45
Overview 45

Index

Changing the Layout of the Register Page 46
    Styling the Register Page 47
    Testing the Registration and Login Forms 47
Summary 49

5. Modifying the Navigation Bar 51
Introduction 51
    Technologies Used in This Chapter 51
Overview 51
Adding a Logo to the Navigation Bar 52
Add the Drop-Down Menu 52
Summary 55

6. Data Transfer Objects 57
Introduction 57
    Technologies Used in This Chapter 57
Overview 57
The DTOs 57
    Adding the DTOs 62
The View Models 64
    Adding the View Models 65
Summary 66

7. Entity Classes 67
Introduction 67
    Technologies Used in This Chapter 67
Overview 67
The Entities 67
    The Video Entity 67
    The Download Entity 68

    The Instructor Entity 69

    The Course Entity 69

    The Module Entity 70

    The UserCourse Entity 71

  Adding the Entity Classes 71

  Summary 75

8. Creating the Database Tables 77

  Introduction 77

    Technologies Used in This Chapter 77

  Overview 77

  Adding the Tables 77

    Adding the Entity Classes to the VODContext 78

    Creating the Tables 79

    Adding Seed Data 79

  Summary 87

9. The Database Read Service 89

  Introduction 89

    Technologies Used in This Chapter 89

  Overview 89

  Adding the DbReadService Service 89

    Adding the Service Interface and Class 90

    Fetching All Records in a Table (GetAsync) 91

    Fetching Records Using a Predicate Function (GetAsync) 92

    Fetching a Single Record Using a Predicate Function (SingleAsync) 93

    Finding Out if an Item Exists (AnyAsync) 95

    Including an Entity's Navigation Properties (Include) 96

    Converting an Entity Collection to a List of SelectList Items (ToSelectList) 98

Index

    Adding the Service and Testing the Read Methods 100

    Summary.. 101

10. The UI Data Service... 103

    Introduction.. 103

        Technologies Used in This Chapter... 103

    Overview... 103

    Adding the IUIReadService Interface... 103

    Adding the UIReadService Class 104

    Injecting the IUIReadService into the HomeController's Constructor 106

    Implementing the GetCourses Method.. 107

    Implementing the GetCourse Method 108

    Implementing the GetVideo Method 109

    Implementing the GetVideos Method 110

    Removing the Injected Service From the HomeController 112

    Summary.. 112

11. The Membership Controller and AutoMapper... 113

    Introduction.. 113

        Technologies Used in This Chapter... 113

    Overview... 113

    Adding the Membership Controller 114

        Adding the Membership Controller 114

    Configuring AutoMapper.. 116

    Implementing Action Methods 118

        The Dashboard Action Method 118

        The Course Action Method... 122

        The Video Action Method 127

    Summary.. 132

12. The Dashboard View 133

Introduction 133

Technologies Used in This Chapter 133

Overview 133

Implementing the Dashboard View 134

Adding the membership.css Style Sheet 134

Adding the Dashboard View 137

Iterate Over the Courses in the Dashboard View 138

Creating the _CourseCardPartial Partial View 140

Summary 143

13. The Course View 145

Introduction 145

Technologies Used in This Chapter 145

Overview 145

Adding the Course View 147

Adding the Back to Dashboard Button 148

Adding the Course Information to the View 150

Styling the Course Information Section 152

Adding Columns for the Modules and the Instructor Bio 153

Adding the Modules 153

Adding the Videos 155

Styling the _ModuleVideosPartial View 159

Adding the Downloads 160

Styling the _ModuleDownloadsPartial View 163

Adding the Instructor Bio 164

Styling the _InstructorBioPartial Partial View 166

Summary 166

Index

14. The Video View 167
Introduction 167
Technologies Used in This Chapter 167
Overview 167
Adding the Video View 169
Adding the Back to Course Button 171
Adding Row and Columns for the Video View Content 172
Adding the _VideoPlayerPartial Partial View 173
Styling the _VideoPlayerPartial Partial View 177
Adding Properties to the LessonInfoDTO Class 178
Adding the _VideoComingUpPartial Partial View 179
Styling the _VideoComingUpPartial Partial View 184
Adding the _InstructorBioPartial Partial View 185
Summary 187

Part 2: Razor Pages How to Build the Administrator Website 189

15. Adding the Admin Project 191
Overview 191
Technologies Used in This Chapter 192
Creating the Admin Solution 192
Summary 198

16. The Administrator Dashboard 199
Introduction 199
Technologies Used in This Chapter 199
Modifying the Navigation Menu 200
Creating the Dashboard 201
Adding the Count Method to the DbReadService 202
Adding the CardViewModel Class 203

Adding the _CardPartial Partial View 204
Calling the Count Method From the Index Razor Page 205
Styling the _CardPartial View 208
Modifying the Index Razor Page 211
Summary 212

17. The Admin Menu 213
Introduction 213
Technologies Used in This Chapter 213
Overview 213
Adding the _AdminMenuPartial Partial View 214
Summary 216

18. Custom Button Tag Helper 217
Introduction 217
Technologies Used in This Chapter 217
Overview 217
Implementing the Btn Tag Helper 218
Creating the Tag Helper 218
Turn the Anchor Tag into a Bootstrap Button 221
Adding an Icon and Styling the Button 225
Summary 229

19. The Database Write Service 231
Introduction 231
Technologies Used in This Chapter 231
Overview 231
Adding the DbWriteService Service 231
Adding the Service Interface and Class 231
The SaveChangesAsync Method 233

Index

    The Add Method 234

    The Delete Method 235

    The Update Method 237

  Summary 239

20. The User Service 241

  Introduction 241

    Technologies Used in This Chapter 241

  Overview 241

  Adding the UserService Service 241

  The UserDTO Class 241

    Adding the ButtonDTO Class 242

    Adding the UserDTO Class 243

    Adding the Service Interface and Class 244

    The GetUsersAsync Method 245

    The GetUserAsync Method 247

    The GetUserByEmailAsync Method 248

    The RegisterUserDTO Class 250

    The LoginUserDTO Class 251

    The AddUserAsync Method 251

    The UpdateUserAsync Method 253

    The DeleteUserAsync Method 256

    The Truncate and IsNullOrEmptyOrWhiteSpace Extension Methods 258

    The GetUserAsync Method 260

  Summary 263

21. The User Razor Pages 265

  Technologies Used in This Chapter 265

  Overview 265

The [TempData] Attribute 266

The Users/Index Razor Page 266

    Altering the IndexModel Class 267

    Creating Button Partial Views 269

    Altering the Index Razor Page 271

The Users/Create Razor Page 275

    Altering the Razor Page CreateModel Class 276

    Altering the Create Razor Page 280

The Users/Edit Razor Page 285

    Altering the Razor Page EditModel class 285

    Altering the Edit Razor Page 287

The Users/Delete Razor Page 289

    Altering the DeleteModel Class 289

    Altering the Delete Razor Page 291

The Users/Details Razor Page 293

    Adding the Details Razor Page 293

    Altering the Razor Page DetailsModel Class 294

    Altering the Details Razor Page 300

Summary 306

22. The Alert Tag Helper 307

Introduction 307

    Technologies Used in This Chapter 307

    Adding the Alert Tag Helper Class 308

Summary 312

23. The AdminEFService 313

Overview 313

    Technologies Used in This Chapter 313

Index

The IAdminService Interface	313
The AdminEFService Class	315
The DTO Classes	321
The Course DTO	321
The Module DTO	322
The Download DTO	322
The Video DTO	323
The Instructor DTO	324
AutoMapper Mappings	324
Summary	327
24. The Remaining Razor Pages	**329**
Overview	329
Technologies Used in This Chapter	329
Example of Typical Razor Pages	329
The _DeletePageButtons Partial Razor View	333
The Instructors Razor Pages	333
The IndexModel Class	334
The Index Razor Page	336
The CreateModel Class	337
The Create Razor Page	339
The EditModel Class	341
The Edit Razor Page	343
The DeleteModel Class	345
The Delete Razor Page	348
The Courses Razor Pages	349
The IndexModel Class	349
The Index Razor Page	350

- The CreateModel Class 352
- The Create Razor Page 355
- The EditModel Class 357
- The Edit Razor Page 359
- The DeleteModel Class 361
- The Delete Razor Page 363

The Modules Razor Pages 364
- The IndexModel Class 365
- The Index Razor Page 366
- The CreateModel Class 367
- The Create Razor Page 369
- The EditModel Class 371
- The Edit Razor Page 373
- The DeleteModel Class 374
- The Delete Razor Page 376

The Video Razor Pages 377
- The IndexModel Class 378
- The Index Razor Page 379
- The CreateModel Class 380
- The Create Razor Page 382
- The EditModel Class 384
- The Edit Razor Page 387
- The DeleteModel Class 389
- The Delete Razor Page 391

The Downloads Razor Pages 393
- The IndexModel Class 393
- The Index Razor Page 394

Index

    The CreateModel Class 396

    The Create Razor Page 397

    The EditModel Class 399

    The Edit Razor Page 401

    The DeleteModel Class 402

    The Delete Razor Page 404

Summary 406

Part 3: API, HttpClient & JWT How to Build and Secure an API 407

25. The API Project 409

Overview 409

    Technologies Used in This Chapter 409

    What Is HTTP, Response and Request? 409

    Status Codes 411

    What Is REST? 414

    Designing URIs 414

    The LinkGenerator Class 415

    Postman 416

Adding the API Project 417

Adding the Instructors Controller 420

    Adding the Get Action Method 421

    Adding the Get Action Method for a Single Instructor 423

    Adding the Post Action Method 424

    Adding the Put Action Method 427

    Adding the Delete Action Method 429

Adding the Courses Controller 431

    Modifying the Action Methods 431

Adding the Modules Controller 438

Modifying the Action Methods 439
Adding the Videos Controller 448
Modifying the Action Methods 448
Adding the Downloads Controller 457
Modifying the Action Methods 458
Summary... 465

26. Calling the API With HttpClient 467
Overview... 467
Technologies Used in This Chapter.. 467
What is HttpClient? 468
HTTP Headers 470
Using Streams to Improve Performance and Memory Usage.................. 472
Supporting Cancellation 477
Using a HttpClientFactory... 479
Handling Errors 481
Adding the AdminAPIService and HttpClientFactoryService Classes 483
Adding the HttpResponseException class 487
Adding the StreamExtensions Class 488
Serialize a JSON Object... 488
Deserialize From JSON to an Object of Generic Type............................... 490
Deserialize From JSON to an Object Instance 491
Adding the HttpClientExtensions Class 492
Create an Extension Method That Adds Request Headers 493
Create an Extension Method That Serializes the Request Content 494
Create an Extension Method That Creates Request Content 495
Create an Extension Method That Deserializes Response Data.............. 496

Index

Create an Extension Method That Throws an Exception Based on the Response Status Code 497

Implementing the GetAsync Method 499

Find Id Properties From a Generic Type with Reflection.. 499

Create a URI with the Generic Type and the Ids in the _properties Collection 501

Calling the API.. 503

Adding the GetListAsync Extension Method in the HttpClientExtensions Class . 503

Adding the GetListAsync Method to the HttpClientFactoryService Class 505

Adding the GetAsync Method to the AdminAPIService Class 506

Implementing the SingleAsync Method 507

The GetExpressionProperties Method 511

The ResolveExpression Method 513

The GetProperties<TSource> Method for Lambda Expressions 514

The SingleAsync<TSource, TDestination> Method.. 516

The FormatUriWithIds<TSource> Method 517

The GetAsync<TResponse, TRequest> Extension Method in the HttpClientExtensions Class 519

The GetAsync<TSource> Method in the HttpClientFactoryService Class................ 520

Calling the API.. 521

Implementing the PostAsync Method 522

The PostAsync<TRequest, TResponse> Extension Method in the HttpClientExtensions Class 522

The PostAsync<TRequest, TResponse> Method in the HttpClientFactoryService Class 524

The GetProperties<TSource>(TSource source) Method for Objects........................ 525

Calling the API.. 527

Implementing the UpdateAsync Method 528

The PutAsync<TRequest , TResponse> Extension Method in the
HttpClientExtensions Class 528

The PutAsync<TRequest, TResponse> Method in the HttpClientFactoryService Class
.... 529

Calling the API... 530

Implementing the DeleteAsync Method 531

The DeleteAsync Extension Method in the HttpClientExtensions Class 531

The DeleteAsync Method in the HttpClientFactoryService Class............................ 532

Calling the API... 534

Summary.. 535

27. JSON Web Tokens (JWT).. 537

Overview... 537

Technologies Used in This Chapter... 537

The JWT Structure 537

Creating the JWT 539

Adding the TokenDTO Class 539

Adding the TokenService Service 540

Adding the ITokenService Interface 541

Adding the TokenService Class 541

Fetching the User's Claims 542

Creating the Token 544

Update the UserService to Handle Claims 546

Adding the Token to the User 552

Generate the Token and Add It to the User 553

Fetching a User's Token... 554

Adding the TokenController Class 555

Adding the GenerateToken Action 556

Index

    Adding the GetToken Action 557

    Testing the TokenController 558

Securing the API 559

    Adding Authorization with Claims and Policies 559

    Adding JWT Authentication 562

Adding the JWT Token to the HttpClient API Calls 564

    Adding the CreateTokenAsync Method to the HttpClientFactoryService 565

    Adding the GetTokenAsync Method to the HttpClientFactoryService 566

    Adding the IJwtTokenService Interface 566

    Adding the JwtTokenService Class 567

        Implementing the CreateTokenAsync Method 568

        Implementing the GetTokenAsync Method 570

        Implementing the CheckTokenAsync Method 571

        Adding the Token to the AdminAPIService 572

Summary 573

Other Books and Courses by the Author 575

Online Courses and Free Content by the Author 575

ASP.NET Core 2.2 MVC, Razor Pages, API, JSON Web Tokens & HttpClient

This page has been intentinally left empty.

Overview

I want to welcome you to *ASP.NET Core 2.2 MVC, Razor Pages, API, JSON Web Tokens & HttpClient*. This book will guide you through creating a video course membership site secured with JSON Web Tokens.

This book's target audience is developers who want to learn how to build ASP.NET Core 2.2 MVC, Razor Page, and API applications. The API has JSON Web Token (JWT) authentication and authorization, and the Razor Pages calls the API with HttpClient. You should be an intermediate level C# developer with some experience in MVC, Entity Framework, HTML5, and CSS3. The book presupposes that you have a solid C# foundation with good knowledge in OOP, Linq/Lambda, generics, and asynchronous calls; this is not a book about the C# language.

You will learn ASP.NET Core 2.2 by building three applications in five projects. The first application is a UI for users registered with the membership site built with the MVC template; the second is an administration UI built with Razor Pages; the third is an API secured with JSON Web Token authentication and authorization that the administration application calls with HttpClient. All three applications use several services with differing purposes. Apart from the three application projects, a project for shared resources is created as well as a database project with the sole purpose of handling the shared Entity Framework Core 2.2 database. When finished, you will have created a fully functioning video course website, where users can register to get access to video content, and administrators can add and modify course content and users.

You should already be familiar with MVC 5 or ASP.NET Core to get the most from this book; it delivers the content in a fast, no-fluff way. The book is practical and tactical, where you will learn as you progress through the modules and build real web applications in the process. To spare you countless pages of fluff (filler material), only valuable information, pertinent to the task at hand, is discussed. The benefit is a shorter and more condensed book, which will save you time and give you a more enjoyable experience.

The goal is to learn ASP.NET Core 2.2 by building web projects: an experience that you can put in your CV when applying for a job or a consultant position, or when negotiating a higher salary.

By the end of this book, you will be able to create ASP.NET Core 2.2 applications on your own, which can create, edit, delete, and view data in a database.

…ok, you will be using C#, HTML, and Razor with Visual Studio 2019 version 16.0.0 or later. You can even use Visual Studio Community 2019, which you can download for free from www.visualstudio.com/downloads.

You can develop ASP.NET Core 2.2 applications on Mac OS X and Linux, but then you are restricted to the ASP.NET Core libraries that don't depend on .NET Framework, which requires Windows.

The applications in this book will be built using ASP.NET 2.2 without .NET Framework.

You will install additional libraries using NuGet packages when necessary, throughout the book.

The complete code for all applications is available on GitHub with a commit for each task.

https://github.com/csharpschool/VideoOnDemand22

Book Version

The current version of this book: 1.1

Errata: https://github.com/csharpschool/VideoOnDemand22/issues

Contact: csharpschoolonline@gmail.com

Source Code

The source code accompanying this book is shared under the MIT License and can be downloaded on GitHub, with a commit for each task.

https://github.com/csharpschool/VideoOnDemand22

Other Books by the Author

The author has written other books and produced video courses that you might find helpful.

Below is a list of the most recent books by the author. The books are available on Amazon.

 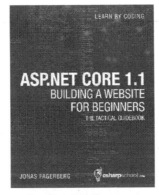 

ASP.NET Core 2.0 – MVC & Razor Pages

ASP.NET Core 1.1 – Building a Website

ASP.NET Core 1.1 – Building a Web API

ASP.NET MVC 5 – Building a Website

C# for Beginners

Online Courses and Free Content by the Author
You can find online courses and free content at https://www.csharpschool.com.

Disclaimer – Who Is This Book for?

It's important to mention that this book is not meant to be a *get-to-know-it-all* book; it's more on the practical and tactical side, where you will learn as you progress through the exercises and build real applications in the process. Because I dislike reading hundreds upon hundreds of pages of irrelevant fluff (filler material) and view it as a disservice to the readers, I will only include important information pertinent for the tasks at hand, thus making the book both shorter and more condensed and also saving you time and effort in the process. Don't get me wrong: I will describe the important things in detail, leaving out only the things that are not directly relevant to your experience with ASP.NET Core 2.2 web applications. The goal is for you to have created one working MVC application, one Razor Page application, and an API application upon finishing this book. ***If you prefer encyclopedic books describing everything in minute detail with short examples, and value a book by how many pages it has, rather than its content, then this book is NOT for you***.

The examples in this book are presented using the free Visual Studio 2019 (version 16.0.0) Community version and ASP.NET Core 2.2. You can download Visual Studio 2019 (version 16.0.0) here: www.visualstudio.com/downloads

Rights

All rights reserved. The content is presented as is and the publisher and author assume no responsibility for errors or omissions. Nor is any liability assumed for damages resulting from the use of the information in the book or the accompanying source code.

It is strictly prohibited to reproduce or transmit the whole book, or any part of the book, in any form or by any means without the prior written permission of the author.

You can reach the author at csharpschoolonline@gmail.com.

Copyright © 2019 by Jonas Fagerberg. All rights reserved.

About the Author

Jonas started a company back in 1994 focusing on teaching Microsoft Office and the Microsoft operating systems. While still studying at the University of Skovde in 1995, he wrote his first book about Windows 95, as well as several course materials.

In the year 2000, after working as a Microsoft Office developer consultant for a couple of years, he wrote his second book about Visual Basic 6.0.

From 2000 to 2004, he worked as a Microsoft instructor with two of the largest educational companies in Sweden teaching Visual Basic 6.0. When Visual Basic.NET and C# were released, he started teaching those languages, as well as the .NET Framework. He was also involved in teaching classes at all levels, from beginner to advanced developers.

In 2005, Jonas shifted his career toward consulting once again, working hands-on with the languages and framework he taught.

Jonas wrote his third book, *C# Programming*, aimed at beginner to intermediate developers in 2013, and in 2015 his fourth book, *C# for Beginners – The Tactical Guide*, was published. Shortly after that his fifth book, *ASP.NET MVC 5 – Building a Website: The Tactical Guidebook*, was published. In 2017 he wrote three more books: *ASP.NET Core 1.1 Web Applications*, *ASP.NET Core 1.1 Web API*, and *ASP.NET Core 2.0 Web Applications*. In 2019 he wrote the book *ASP.NET Core 2.2 MVC, Razor Pages, API, JSON Web Tokens & HttpClient*.

Jonas specifically writes all books and video courses with the student in mind.

ASP.NET Core 2.2 MVC, Razor Pages, API, JSON Web Tokens & HttpClient

Part 1:
MVC
How to Build a Video Course Website

1. The Use Case

Introduction
In this book, you will learn how to build ASP.NET Core 2.2 MVC, Razor Page, and API Web Applications. Entity Framework Core 2.2 handles the data. The views and pages of the projects use Custom Tag Helpers, HTML, and CSS to display their content. AutoMapper will convert between entities and Data Transfer Objects (DTOs). JSON Web Tokens will be used to authenticate and authorize users in the API.

The Use Case
The customer has ordered a Video on Demand (VOD) application and requests that the newest technologies are used building the solution. The application should be able to run in the cloud, be web-based, and run on any device. They have specifically asked that Microsoft technologies are the core of the solution. Avoid deviations from that path.

As a first step, they would like a demo version using dummy data to get a feel for the application. The dummy data can be seeded into the tables when creating the SQL Server database.

YouTube should be used to store the videos, to keep costs down. No API or functionality for uploading videos is necessary for the final application. It is enough for the administrator to be able to paste in a link to a video stored in a YouTube account when adding a new video with the admin user interface.

The finished solution should contain five projects: The first is called **VOD.Common**, and will contains all entity classes, DTOs, and a couple of services as well as other classes shared between the projects. The second is the **VOD.Database** project that contains services for data manipulation and CRUD operations as well as the database context and the database migrations. The third is a user interface for regular users called **VOD.UI**. The fourth application is named **VOD.Admin** and is used by administrators to perform CRUD operations on the tables in the database. The fifth is named **VOD.API** and is used to perform CRUD operations in the database as well as create JSON Web Tokens.

ASP.NET Core 2.2 MVC, Razor Pages, API, JSON Web Tokens & HttpClient

The User Interface (MVC)

This web application should be created using the MVC project template. Users should be able to register and log in to the web application. Automatically redirect the user to the membership site upon successful login or registration.

The first view after login should be a dashboard, displaying the courses available to the user. When clicking on a course, display the course curriculum in a list below a marquee and some information about the course. Each course can have multiple modules, which can have multiple videos and downloadable content. Downloadable content should open in a separate browser tab.

When the user clicks on a video listing, open a new view, where the video player contains video, but the automatic play is disabled. Display information about the course and a description of the video below the video player. To the right of the video player, a thumbnail image for the next video in the module should be displayed, as well as buttons to the previous and next video. Disable the buttons if no video is available.

Display an instructor bio in the **Course**, **Detail**, and **Video** views.

The menu should have a logo on the far left and a settings menu to the far right.

Don't use the database entity classes as view models; instead, each view should use a view model, which contains the necessary Data Transfer Objects (DTOs) and other properties. Convert entities to DTO objects with AutoMapper and send them to the views.

Login and Register User

When an anonymous user visits the site, the **Login** page should be displayed. From that page, the visitor will be able to register with the site by clicking on a **Register as a new user** link; here, on the **Register** page, the visitor creates the new user account.

When these pages are displayed, a menu with a **Home** link should be available (takes the visitor to the login page).

The Administrator Interface (Razor Pages)

Create this web application with Razor Pages. Each table should have four Razor Pages for adding and modifying data: **Index**, **Create**, **Edit**, **Delete**. Send a collection of **SelectList** items to the Razor Page from its code-behind file using the dynamic **ViewData** object to display the data in a drop-down with a <select> element. Data stored using the **ViewData** object in C# can be retrieved and displayed in HTML with the same **ViewData** object.

1. The Use Case

If the logged in user is an administrator, a drop-down menu should appear to the right of the logo, containing links to views for CRUD operations in the database connected to the site. There should also be a dashboard on the main **Index** page where the admin can click to open the **Index** pages associated with the different tables in the database and perform CRUD operations (the same links as in the menu).

Conclusion

After careful consideration, these are the views and controls necessary for the application to work properly.

Login and Register

You can reuse the default Razor Pages; they only need some styling. Remove the default links for registering and logging in a user in the navigation bar, and the **Home** controller's **Index** action will reroute to the **Login** page instead of displaying the **Index** view, which will ensure that the login panel is displayed when the application starts.

Below is a mock-up image of the **Login** and **Create** views. Note the icons in the text boxes; icons from Google's Material Icons will represent them.

The application will collect the user's email and password when registering with the site, and that information will be requested of the visitor when logging in. There will also be a checkbox asking if the user wants to remain logged in when visiting the site, the next time.

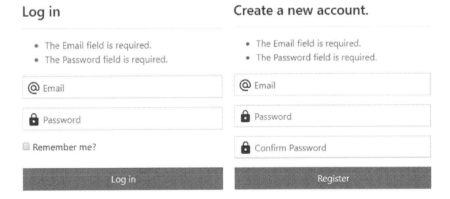

The User Dashboard View

By analyzing the use case, you can surmise that the dashboard's course cards should be loaded dynamically, based on the user's access to courses. The courses will be displayed three to a row, to make them large enough, which means that the view model must contain a collection of collections, defined by a course DTO.

Each course DTO should contain properties for the course id, course title, description, a course image, and a marquee image. Display each course as a card with the course image, title, description, and a button leading to the course view.

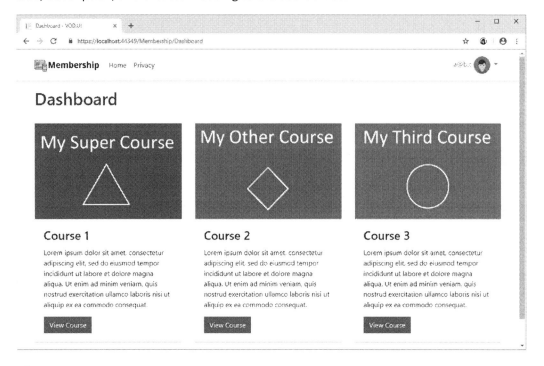

The Course View

The course view should have a button at the top, leading back to the dashboard. Below the button, there should be three sections: an overview, the course modules, and an instructor bio.

The marquee image, the course image (as a thumbnail in the marquee), the title, and description should be in the top card.

Below the top card to the left, the course modules and their content should be listed. Note that there are two possible types of content in a module: videos and downloads. Each video should display a thumbnail, title, description, and the length of the video (duration). List the downloads as links with a descriptive title.

To the right of the list of modules is the instructor bio, which contains a thumbnail, name, and description of the instructor.

To pull this off, the course view model needs to have a Course DTO, an Instructor DTO, and a list of Module DTOs. Each Instructor DTO should contain the avatar, name, and description of the instructor teaching a course. The Module DTO should contain the module id, title, and lists of Video DTOs and Download DTOs.

A Video DTO should contain the video id, title, description, duration, a thumbnail, and the URL to the video. Clicking a video will load the video into the **Video** view. Autoplay should be disabled.

A Download DTO should contain a title and the URL to the content. When clicking the link, the content should open in a new browser tab.

ASP.NET Core 2.2 MVC, Razor Pages, API, JSON Web Tokens & HttpClient

1. The Use Case

The Video View

There should be three sections in the **Video** view, below the button leading back to the **Course** view. Displayed to the left is a large video card containing the video, course, and video information. To the top right is a card displaying the image and title of the next video in the current module, along with **Previous** and **Next** buttons.

Below the *next video* card is the *Instructor* card.

To pull this off, the video view model must contain a **VideoDTO**, an **InstructorDTO**, a **CourseDTO**, and a **LessonInfoDTO**. The **LessonInfoDTO** contains properties for lesson number, number of lessons, video id, title, and thumbnail properties for the previous and next videos in the module.

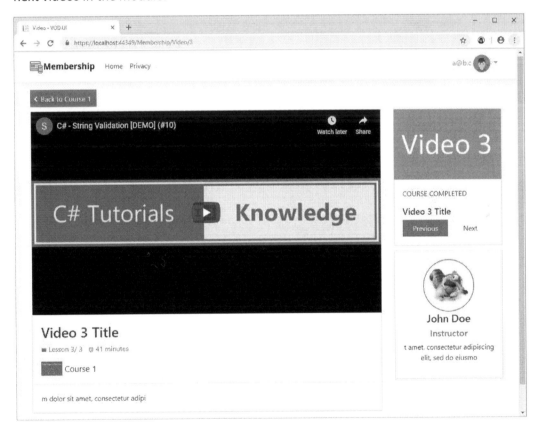

ASP.NET Core 2.2 MVC, Razor Pages, API, JSON Web Tokens & HttpClient

The Administrator Dashboard Razor Page

The administrator dashboard page should have links, displayed as cards, to the different **Index** Razor Pages representing the tables in the database. A menu should also be available for navigating the Razor Pages.

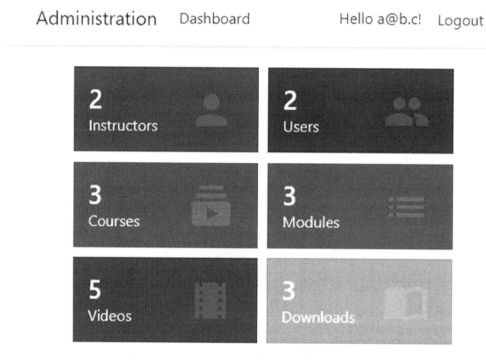

A Typical Administrator Index Razor Page

A typical **Index** page contains a title and two buttons at the top – **Create New** and **Dashboard** – a table with information about the entity, and two buttons for editing and deleting information about the entity. A custom Tag Helper will be used to render the buttons.

1. The Use Case

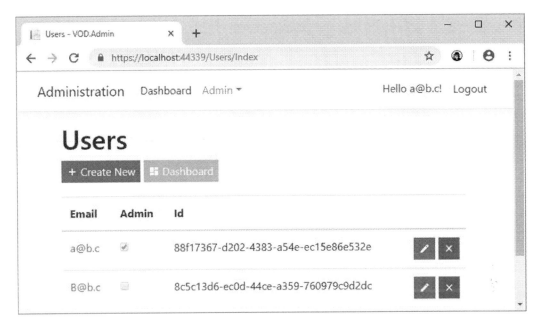

A Typical Administrator Create Razor Page

A typical **Create** Razor Page has labels and input fields for data needed to create a new record in the database.

The Razor Page should have a **Create** button that posts the data to the server, a **Back to List** button that takes the user back to the **Index** page, and a **Dashboard** button that takes the user back to the main **Index** page.

ASP.NET Core 2.2 MVC, Razor Pages, API, JSON Web Tokens & HttpClient

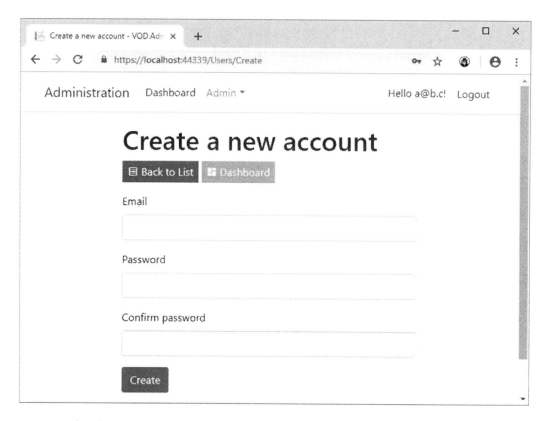

A Typical Administrator Edit Razor Page

A typical **Edit** Razor Page has labels and input fields for the data needed to update a record in the database.

The Razor Page also has a **Save** button that posts the data to the server, a **Back to List** button that takes the user back to the **Index** page, and a **Dashboard** button that takes the user back to the main **Index** page.

1. The Use Case

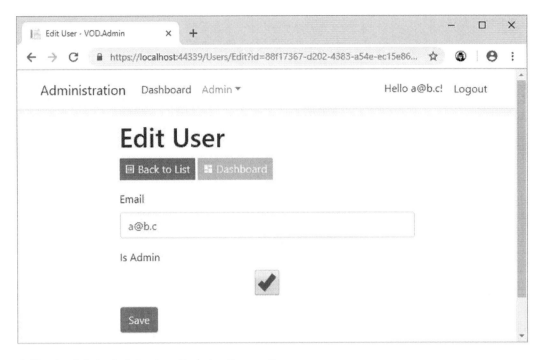

A Typical Administrator Delete Razor Page

A typical **Delete** Razor Page has labels for the entity data, a **Delete** button prompting the server to delete the entity from the database, a **Back to List** button that takes the user back to the **Index** page, and a **Dashboard** button that takes the user back to the main **Index** page.

ASP.NET Core 2.2 MVC, Razor Pages, API, JSON Web Tokens & HttpClient

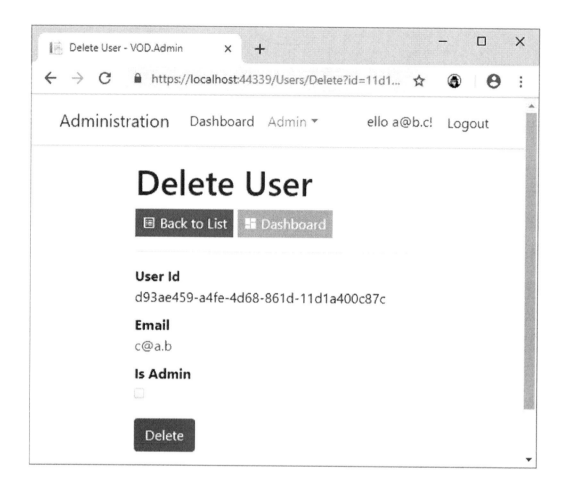

2. Setting Up the Solution

Introduction
In this chapter, you will create the solution and install the necessary NuGet packages for it in Visual Studio 2019.

Technologies Used in This Chapter
- **Web Application (Model-View-Controller)** – The template used to create the **UI** and **Admin** projects.
- **Web API** – The template used to create the Web Service project for CRUD operations in the database. It will use JSON Web Token authentication and authorization.
- **Class Library** – The template used to create the **Database** and **Common** projects.
- **MVC** and **Razor Pages** – To build the Web Application and Web API projects.
- **AutoMapper** – A NuGet package that, when installed, will map objects from one type to another. Will be used to map entity objects to DTOs.

Overview
The customer wants you to build the solution with Visual Studio 2019, ASP.NET Core 2.2, and the **ASP.NET Core Web Application** template. The first step will be to create the solution and install all the necessary NuGet packages not installed with the project template. The template will install the basic MVC plumbing and a **Home** controller with **Index** and **Policy** action methods, and their corresponding views.

Creating the Solution
If you haven't already installed Visual Studio 2019 version 16.0.0 or later, you can download a free copy here: www.visualstudio.com/downloads.

1. Open Visual Studio 2019 and click the **Create a new project** button in the wizard.
2. Select **ASP.NET Core Web Application** in the template list and click the **Next** button (see image below).
3. Name the project *VOD.UI* in the **Name** field.

4. Name the solution *VideoOnDemand* in the **Solution name** field. It should not end with *.UI*.
5. Click the **OK** button.
6. Select **.NET Core** and **ASP.NET Core 2.2** in the drop-downs.
7. Select **Web Application (Model-View-Controller)** in the template list.
8. Click the **Change Authentication** button and select **Individual User Accounts** in the pop-up dialog; this will make it possible for visitors to register and log in with your site using an email and a password (see image below).
    a. Select the **Individual User Accounts** radio button.
    b. Select **Store user account in-app** in the drop-down.
    c. Click the **OK** button in the pop-up dialog.
9. Click the **Create** button in the wizard dialog.
10. Open *appsettings.json* and add the following connection string. It's important to add the connection string as a single line of code.

```
"ConnectionStrings": {
    "DefaultConnection": "Server=(localdb)\\mssqllocaldb;
        Database=VOD;Trusted_Connection=True;
        MultipleActiveResultSets=true"
}
```

2. Setting Up the Solution

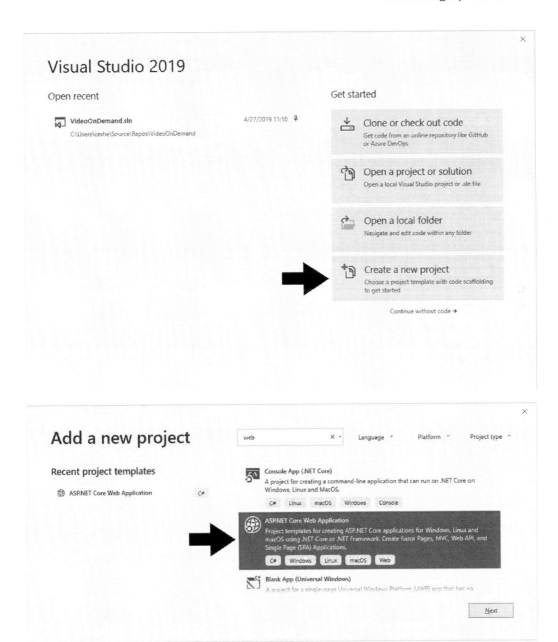

ASP.NET Core 2.2 MVC, Razor Pages, API, JSON Web Tokens & HttpClient

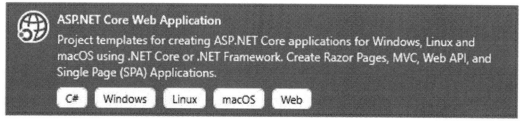

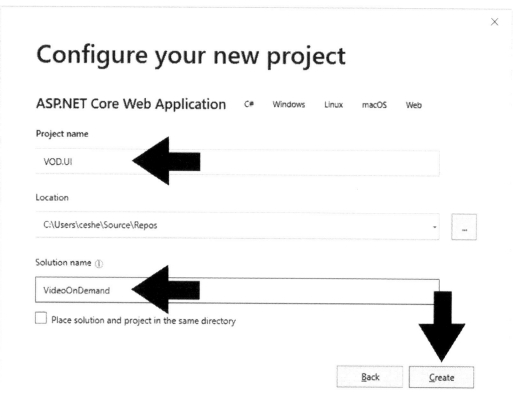

2. Setting Up the Solution

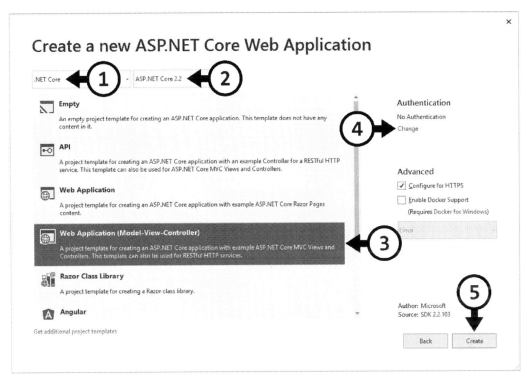

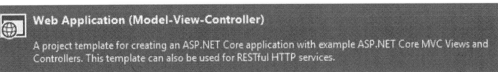

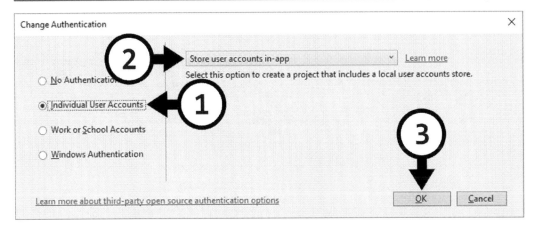

ASP.NET Core 2.2 MVC, Razor Pages, API, JSON Web Tokens & HttpClient

It is no longer possible to manage NuGet packages with a *project.json* file. That is handled by the *.csproj* file, which can be edited directly from the IDE.

It is also important to understand the concept of Dependency Injection since it is used to make object instances available throughout the application. If a resource is needed, it can be injected into the constructor and saved to a private class-level variable. No objects are created in the class itself; instead, request them through DI.

Installing AutoMapper

AutoMapper will be used to map an entity (database table) object to a Data Transfer Object (DTO), which is used to transport data to the views. You can either add the following row to the <ItemGroup> node in the *.csproj* file manually and save the file or use the NuGet manager to add AutoMapper.

```
<PackageReference Include=
"AutoMapper.Extensions.Microsoft.DependencyInjection" Version="6.1.0" />
```

The following listing shows you how to use the NuGet manager to install packages.

1. Right click on the **Dependencies** node in the Solution Explorer and select **Manage NuGet Packages** in the context menu.

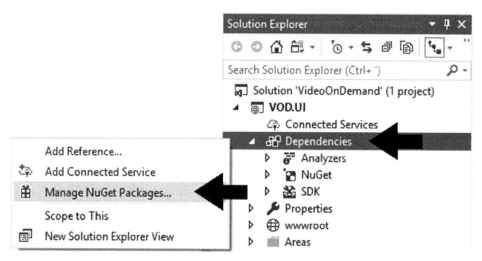

2. Click on the **Browse** link at the top of the dialog.
3. Select **nuget.org** in the drop-down to the far right in the dialog.
4. Type *AutoMapper.Extensions.Microsoft.DependencyInjection* in the textbox.

2. Setting Up the Solution

5. Select the package in the list; it will probably be the first package in the list.
6. Make sure that you use the latest stable version (6.1.0).
7. Click the **Install** button.

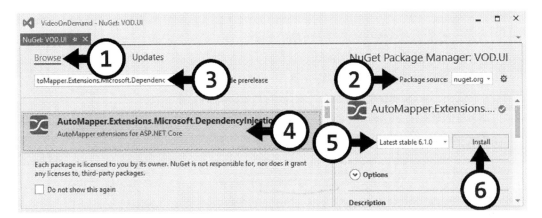

To verify the installed package, you can open the *.csproj* file by right-clicking on the project node and selecting **Edit VOD.UI.csproj**, or you can expand the *Dependencies -NuGet* folder in the Solution Explorer.

Creating the Database

There are only a few steps to creating a database that will enable users to register and log in. In a later chapter, you will expand the database by adding tables to store application data.

To create the database, you must create an initial migration to tell Entity Framework how the database should be set up. You do this by executing the **add-migration** command in the *Package Manager Console*.

After a successfully created migration, you execute the **update-database** command in the same console to create the database. After creating the database, you can view it in the *SQL Server Object Explorer*, available in the **View** menu.

Add a separate project called **VOD.Common** for the entity and context database classes shared by all projects. Reference this project from the other projects.

ASP.NET Core 2.2 MVC, Razor Pages, API, JSON Web Tokens & HttpClient

Adding the Common and Database Projects

The **Common** project you will create should contain all classes shared among the projects, such as entity and service classes that support the database. The **Database** project should contain Entity Framework Core and all database-related code.

1. Right click on the **VideoOnDemand** solution in the Solution Explorer and select **Add-New Project** in the menu.
2. Select **Class Library (.NET Core)** in the template list and click the **Next** button.
3. Name the project **VOD.Common** and click the **Create** button.
4. Remove the file *Class1.cs*.
5. Repeat step 1 through 4 and name the project **VOD.Database**.
6. Add a reference to the **Common** project in the **Database** project.
    a. Right click on the *Dependencies* node in the **Database** project and select **Add Reference** in the context menu.
    b. Check the checkbox for the **VOD.Common** project and click the **OK** button.

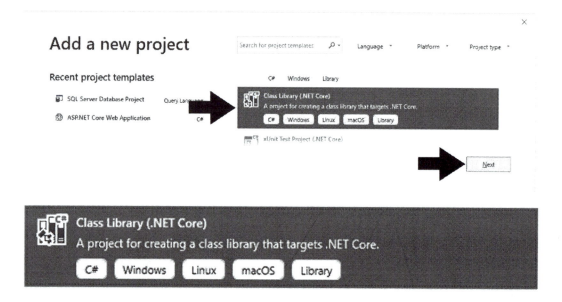

2. Setting Up the Solution

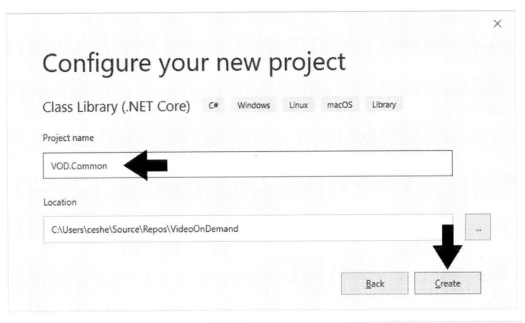

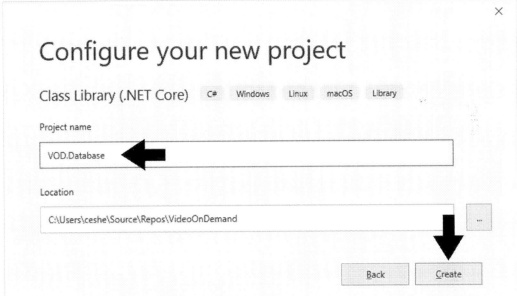

Adding Entity Framework Core to the Database Project
1. Open the Package Manager Console from the View menu.
2. Select the **VOD.Database** project in the drop-down menu in the console.

ASP.NET Core 2.2 MVC, Razor Pages, API, JSON Web Tokens & HttpClient

To Database

3. Install the latest stable version (2.2.2) of the **Microsoft.EntityFrameworkCore.SqlServer** package by executing the following command in the Package Manager Console window:
   `Install-Package Microsoft.EntityFrameworkCore.SqlServer -Version 2.2.4`
4. Install the latest version of the **Microsoft.EntityFrameworkCore.Tools** NuGet package in the Package Manager Console window:
   `Install-Package Microsoft.EntityFrameworkCore.Tools -Version 2.2.4`
5. Install the latest stable version (2.2.0) of the **Microsoft.Extensions.Identity.Stores** package by executing the following command in the Package Manager Console window:
   `Install-Package Microsoft.Extensions.Identity.Stores -Version 2.2.0`

Adding the VODUser Class

1. Add a folder named *Entities* to the **VOD.Common** project.
2. Add a **public** class called **VODUser** to the *Entities* folder; this class is the user identity class that handles users for both the administration and user websites.
3. Add a **string** property named **Token** that will be used to store a JWT Token in an upcoming chapter. Properties added to the **VODUser** class are used by EF to create corresponding columns in the **AspNetUser** table.
4. Add a **DateTime** property named **TokenExpires** that will be used to store the expiration date and time for the JWT Token.
5. Add an **IList<Claim>** named **Claims** collection that isn't mapped to the database and instantiate it with an empty list; EF ignores non-mapped properties when creating columns in the table. This collection will be used to store the logged-in user's authentication claims in an upcoming chapter; the claims are used to authenticate the user when calling an API to perform CRUD operations.
   `[NotMapped]`
   `public IList<Claim> Claims { get; set; } = new List<Claim>();`
6. Inherit the **IdentityUser** class in the **VODUser** class to add the basic user functionality to it. The **VODUser** class handles users in the database and EF uses it when creating the database. You need to add a reference to the **Microsoft.Extensions.Identity.stores.dll** assembly to resolve the **Microsoft.AspNetCore.Identity** namespace that gives access to the **IdentityUser** class.

30

2. Setting Up the Solution

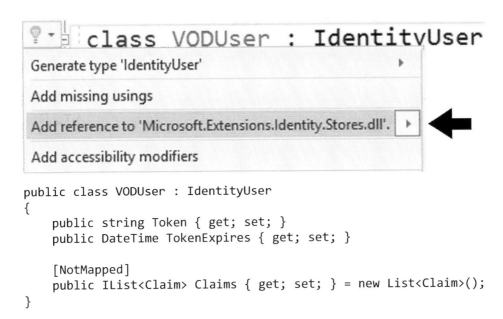

```
public class VODUser : IdentityUser
{
    public string Token { get; set; }
    public DateTime TokenExpires { get; set; }

    [NotMapped]
    public IList<Claim> Claims { get; set; } = new List<Claim>();
}
```

Adding the Database Context

1. Add a folder called *Contexts* to the **Database** project.
2. Add a **public** class called **VODContext** to the *Contexts* folder and inherit the **IdentityDbContext<VODUser>** class. This database context will be used to add entity classes that represent tables in the database, and to call the database from the other projects. You need to resolve the **Microsoft.AspNetCore.Identity.EntityFrameworkCore** namespace to get access to EF Core identity. You also need to resolve the **VOD.Common.Entities** namespace to get access to the **VODUser** class.

   ```
   public class VODContext : IdentityDbContext<VODUser>
   {
   }
   ```

3. Add a constructor that has a parameter of type **DbContextOptions<VODContext>** called **options**.

   ```
   public VODContext(DbContextOptions<VODContext> options)
       : base(options)
   {
   }
   ```

4. Override the method called **OnModelCreating** and have it call the same method on the base class. You will later use this method to configure certain features of the database.

```
protected override void OnModelCreating(ModelBuilder builder)
{
    base.OnModelCreating(builder);
}
```

Creating the First Migration and the Database

1. Add references to the **VOD.Common** and **VOD.Database** projects in the **VOD.UI** project to gain access to the **VODUser** and **VODContext** classes.
2. Open the *Startup.cs* file and locate the **ConfigureServices** method.
3. Change the **IdentityUser** class to **VODUser** in the **AddDefaultIdentity** method call. You need to resolve the **VOD.Common.Entities** namespace.
4. Change the **ApplicationDbContext** class to **VODContext** in the **AddDbContext**, and **AddEntityFrameworkStores** methods call. You need to resolve the **VOD.Database.Contexts** namespace.
5. Add a **using** statement to the *Entities* folder in the **_ViewImports** view in the *Views* folder to make the namespace available globally in the project.
   ```
   @using VOD.Common.Entities
   ```
6. Change the **IdentityUser** class to **VODUser** in the **_LoginPartial** view to match the user defined for the database.
   ```
   @inject SignInManager<VODUser> SignInManager
   @inject UserManager<VODUser> UserManager
   ```
7. Delete the *Data* folder and all its content from the **VOD.UI** project.
8. Remove the **VOD.UI.Data using** statement in the *Startup.cs* file.
9. Make sure that **VOD.UI** is the startup project.
10. Open the *Package Manager Console* by selecting **View-Other Windows-Package Manager Console** in the main menu.
11. Select **VOD.Database** in the right drop-down to select the correct project.
12. Type in *add-migration Initial* and press **Enter** on the keyboard to create a first migration called *Initial* in a new folder called *Migrations* in the **Database** project.
13. Type in *update-database* and press **Enter** to create the database.
14. Open the *SQL Server Object Explorer* from the **View** menu and make sure that the database was successfully created (see image on the next page).
15. Open the **AspNetRoles** table and add a role named **Admin** that can be used to distinguish regular users from administrators. Assign *1* to the record's **Id** column,

Admin to its **Name** column, and *ADMIN* to its **NormalizedName** column. Right click on the table node and select **View Data** to open the table.

It may take a second or two for the SQL Server node to populate in the SQL Server Object Explorer. When it has, expand the server named **MSSQLLocalDB** and then the **VOD** database, where you find the new tables. The tables prefixed with **AspNet** stores user account information, and EF uses them when a user registers and logs in. In this course, you will use the **AspNetUsers**, **AspNetRoles**, **AspNetUserClaims**, and **AspNetUserRoles** tables when implementing registration and login for your users, and to determine if a user is an administrator.

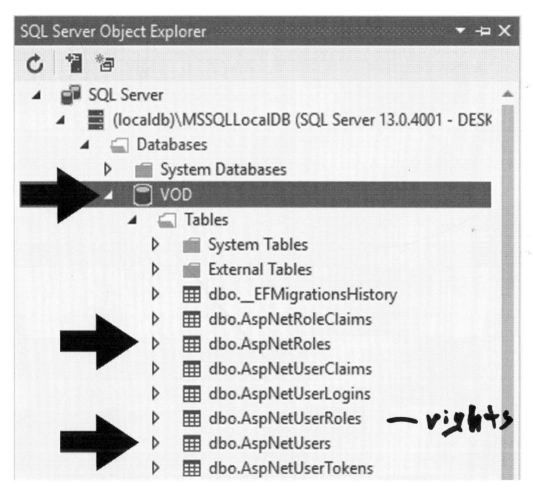

Summary

In this chapter, you created the three initial projects that will be used throughout the remainder of this book to create a user interface (UI), share resources, and communicate with the database. You also installed the AutoMapper NuGet package, which later will be used to map database entity objects to Data Transfer Objects (DTOs), which provide the views with data.

Next, you will redirect the **Home/Index** action to display the **Account/Login** page; this will display the login form when the application starts. Then you will style the login form, making it look more professional.

3. Login

Introduction

In this chapter, you will make the login page available as soon as a visitor navigates to the web application. To achieve this, you will redirect from the **Home/Index** action to the **Account/Login** action.

Because the login page only should be displayed to visitors who haven't already logged in, you will use Dependency Injection to make the **SignInManager** available from the controller, making it possible to check if the user is logged in.

Technologies Used in This Chapter
1. **Dependency Injection** – To inject objects into a controller's constructor.
2. **C#** – For writing code in the controller's actions and constructor.
3. **Razor** – To incorporate C# in the views and pages where necessary.
4. **HTML 5** – To build the views and the pages.
5. **Bootstrap and CSS** – To style the HTML 5 elements.
6. **Tag Helpers** – To add HTML 5 elements and their attributes.

Redirecting to the Login Page

ASP.NET Core is designed from the ground up to support and leverage Dependency Injection (DI). Dependency Injection is a way to let the framework automatically create instances of services (classes) and inject them into constructors. Why is this important? Well, it creates loose couplings between objects and their collaborators; this means that the framework injects objects into the collaborators so that they don't need any hard-coded instances.

Not only can built-in framework services be injected, but you can configure your classes and interfaces for DI in the **Startup** class.

Now, you will use DI to pass in the **SignInManager** to a constructor in the **HomeController** class and store it in a private variable. The **SignInManager** and its **User** type need two **using** statements: **Microsoft.AspNetCore.Identity** and **VOD.Common.Entities**.

ASP.NET Core 2.2 MVC, Razor Pages, API, JSON Web Tokens & HttpClient

1. Open the **HomeController** class located in the *Controllers* folder in the **UI** project.
2. Add the following **using** statements if they don't already exist.
   ```
   using Microsoft.AspNetCore.Identity;
   using VOD.Common.Entities;
   using VOD.UI.Models;
   ```
3. Add a constructor that receives the **SignInManager** through dependency injection and stores it in a private class-level variable.
   ```
   private SignInManager<VODUser> _signInManager;
   public HomeController(SignInManager<VODUser> signInMgr)
   {
       _signInManager = signInMgr;
   }
   ```
4. Check if the user is signed in using the class-level variable you just added and redirect to the **Login** Razor Page in the *Areas/Identity/Pages/Account* folder if it's an anonymous user. Otherwise open the default **Index** view, for now. You will change this in a later chapter.
   ```
   public IActionResult Index()
   {
       if (!_signInManager.IsSignedIn(User))
           return RedirectToPage("/Account/Login",
               new { Area = "Identity" });

       return View();
   }
   ```
5. Run the application by pressing F5 or Ctrl+F5 (without debugging) on the keyboard.
6. The login page should be displayed. If you look at the URL, it should point to */Identity/Account/login* on the localhost (your local IIS server) because of the **RedirectToPage** method call.

3. Login

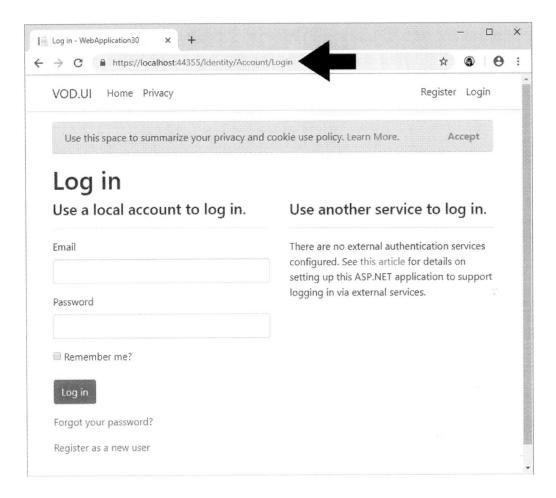

Styling the Login Page

As you can see in the image above, the **Login** Page isn't very pleasing to the eye. Let's change that by styling it with CSS, Bootstrap, and Material Icons. After styling the page, it should look something like this.

ASP.NET Core 2.2 MVC, Razor Pages, API, JSON Web Tokens & HttpClient

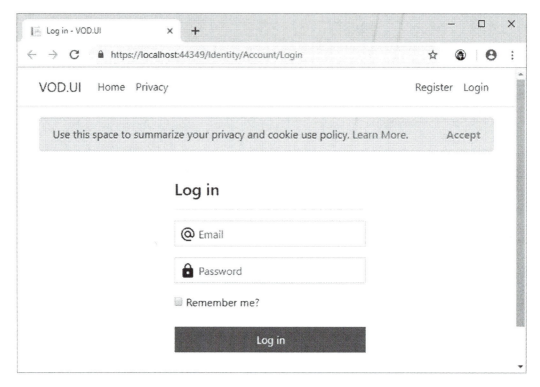

Adding the login.css Stylesheet

1. Stop the application in Visual Studio.
2. Add a new style sheet file called *login-register.css* to the *wwwroot/css* folder in the Solution Explorer. Right click on the folder and select **Add-New Item**.
3. Select the **Style Sheet** template in the list, name it *login-register.css*, and click the **Add** button.
4. Remove the **Body** selector from the file.
5. Open the **_Layout** view in the *Views/Shared* folder.
6. Add a link to the *login-register.css* below the *site.css* file or drag the file from the Solution Explorer and drop it in the **_Layout** view.
   ```
   <link rel="stylesheet" href="~/css/login-register.css" />
   ```
7. Save all files.

Scaffolding the Login and Register Pages

Scaffolding these pages to the *Areas/Identity/Pages/Account* folder will make it possible to modify and style them.

3. Login

1. Right click on the **Areas** folder and select **Add-New Scaffolded Item** in the menu.
2. Select the **Identity** option in the dialog's left menu.
3. Select the **Identity** template in the template list.
4. Click the **Add** button.

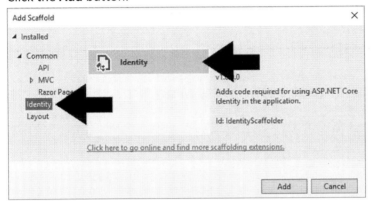

5. Check the **Account/Login** and **Account/Register** checkboxes.
6. Select the **VODContext** class in the **Data context class** drop-down.
7. Click the **Add** button.

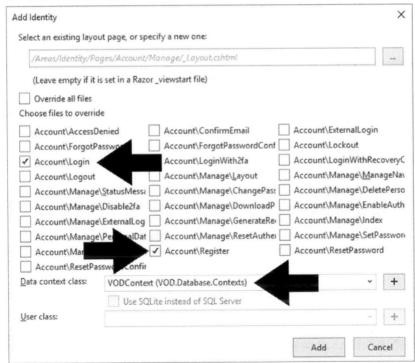

ASP.NET Core 2.2 MVC, Razor Pages, API, JSON Web Tokens & HttpClient

Changing the Layout of the Login Page

These changes will prepare the form for its much-needed styling.

1. Open the **_Layout** view and add a link to Google's **Material Icons** library to both `<environment>` elements inside the `<head>` element. You can read more about it here: https://google.github.io/material-design-icons/
   ```
   <environment include="Development">
       ...
       <link href="https://fonts.googleapis.com/icon?
           family=Material+Icons" rel="stylesheet">
   </environment>
   ```
2. Open the **Login** page in the *Areas/Identity/Pages/Account* folder.
3. Remove the `<h1>` title element.
4. Add the class **login-register** to the `<div>` with the **row** class. Later, you will add the CSS selector to the *login-register.css* file.
5. Add the class **offset-md-4** to the `<div>` with the **col-md-4**.
6. Replace the **Email** `<label>` element with an `<i>` element for the **alternate_email** icon from the *Material icons* library.
   Replace: `<label asp-for="Input.Email"></label>`
   With: `<i class="material-icons">alternate_email</i>`
7. Repeat step 6 for the **Password** `<label>` but change the icon from **alternate_email** to **lock** inside the `<i>` element.
8. Add the **placeholder** attribute with the text *Email* to the **Email** `<input>` element. The placeholder is instructional text displayed inside the textbox that is removed when the user types in the control.
   ```
   <input asp-for="Input.Email" class="form-control"
   placeholder="Email" />
   ```
9. Remove the validation `<span>` elements below the two `<input>` elements.
10. Add the **placeholder** attribute with the text *Password* to the **Password** `<input>` element.
11. Remove the form-group containing the *Register a new user* and *Forgot your Password?* `<p>` elements and all its content.
12. Remove the `<div>` with the **col-md-6** and **offset-md-2** classes and all its content.

3. Login

The form should look like this after the layout change.

Log in

Email

Password

☐ Remember me?

[Log in]

The complete code for the **Login** page:

```
@page
@model LoginModel

@{
    ViewData["Title"] = "Log in";
}

<div class="row login-register">
    <div class="offset-md-4 col-md-4">
        <section>
            <form id="account" method="post">
                <h4>Log in</h4>
                <hr />
                <div asp-validation-summary="All"
                    class="text-danger"></div>
                <div class="form-group">
                    <i class="material-icons">alternate_email</i>
                    <input asp-for="Input.Email" class="form-control"
                        placeholder="Email" />
                </div>
                <div class="form-group">
                    <i class="material-icons">lock</i>
                    <input asp-for="Input.Password" class="form-control"
                        placeholder="Password" />
                </div>
                <div class="form-group">
```

```
                        <div class="checkbox">
                            <label asp-for="Input.RememberMe">
                                <input asp-for="Input.RememberMe" />
                                @Html.DisplayNameFor(m =>
                                    m.Input.RememberMe)
                            </label>
                        </div>
                    </div>
                    <div class="form-group">
                        <button type="submit" class="btn btn-primary">
                            Log in</button>
                    </div>
                </form>
            </section>
        </div>
    </div>

    @section Scripts {
        <partial name="_ValidationScriptsPartial" />
    }
```

Styling the Login Page

Now that you have altered the Login page's layout, it's time to style it using CSS. Add the CSS selector one at a time to the *login-register.css* file, save the file, and observe the changes in the browser.

Note that you might have to clear the browser history for the changes to be applied.

Add a 40px top margin to the row, to push it down a little from the navigation bar.

```
.login-register {
    margin-top: 40px;
}
```

Next, add 35px left padding to all the form controls, and remove the border radius to give the textboxes sharp corners.

```
.login-register .form-control {
    Padding-left: 35px;
    border-radius: 0;
}
```

Next, position the icons absolute and give them 8px padding to align them nicely with the textboxes.

```
.login-register .material-icons {
    position: absolute;
    padding: 8px;
}
```

Next, change the color of the icon and the placeholder text to a light blue when hovering over the textboxes. Some browsers dim the color on hover; use opacity to show full color.

```
.login-register .form-group:hover .material-icons,
.login-register .form-group:hover ::placeholder {
    color: #2580db;
    /* Some browsers dim the color on hover,
        use opacity to show full color */
    opacity: 1;
}
```

The last thing to style is the **submit** button. Make the button take up the entire width of its container and remove the border-radius to give it sharp corners.

```
.login-register button {
    width: 100%;
    border-radius: 0;
}
```

Log in

- The Email field is required.
- The Password field is required.

@ Email

🔒 Password

☐ Remember me?

Log in

ASP.NET Core 2.2 MVC, Razor Pages, API, JSON Web Tokens & HttpClient

Summary

In this chapter, you learned how to scaffold **Login** and **Register** Razor Pages and how to redirect to a Razor Page from an MVC controller action.

Then, you changed the layout of the **Login** page, and applied CSS and Bootstrap classes to its elements, to make it look nicer to the user.

Next, you will change the layout of the **Account/Register** page and apply CSS and Bootstrap classes to its elements.

4. Register User

Introduction
In this chapter, you will alter the layout of the **Account/Register** page and style it with CSS and Bootstrap. You can reach the page from a link in the navigation bar.

Technologies Used in This Chapter
1. **Razor** – To incorporate C# in the pages where necessary.
2. **HTML 5** – To build the pages.
3. **Bootstrap and CSS** – To style the HTML 5 elements.

Overview
The task appointed to you by the company is to make sure that visitors have a nice user experience when registering with the site, using the **Account/Register** page. The finished **Register** page should look like the image below.

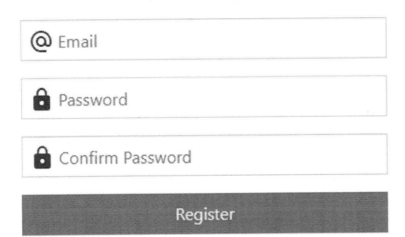

ASP.NET Core 2.2 MVC, Razor Pages, API, JSON Web Tokens & HttpClient

Changing the Layout of the Register Page

These changes will prepare the form for its much-needed styling.

1. Open the **Register** page in the *Areas/Identity/Pages/Account* folder.
2. Remove the <h1> title element.
3. Add the class **login-register** to the <div> with the **row** class. Later, you will add the CSS selector to the *login-register.css* file.
4. Add the class **offset-md-4** to the <div> with the **col-md-4**.
5. Replace the **Email** <label> element with an <i> element for the **alternate_email** icon from the *Material icons* library.
   Replace: `<label asp-for="Input.Email"></label>`
   With: `<i class="material-icons">alternate_email</i>`
6. Repeat step 5 for the two **Password** <label> elements but change the icon from **alternate_email** to **lock** inside the <i> element.
7. Add a **placeholder** attribute with the text *Email* to the **Email** <input> element. The placeholder is instructional text displayed inside the textbox that is removed when the user types in the control.
   `<input asp-for="Input.Email" class="form-control" placeholder="Email" />`
8. Remove the validation <span> elements below all <input> elements.
9. Add the **placeholder** attribute with the text *Password* to the **Password** <input> element.
10. Add the **placeholder** attribute with the text *Confirm Password* to the **ConfirmPassword** <input> element.

The complete markup for the **Register** page:

```
@page
@model RegisterModel
@{
    ViewData["Title"] = "Register";
}

<div class="row login-register">
    <div class="offset-md-4 col-md-4">
        <form asp-route-returnUrl="@Model.ReturnUrl" method="post">
            <h4>Create a new account.</h4>
```

4. Register User

```html
            <hr />
            <div asp-validation-summary="All" class="text-danger"></div>
            <div class="form-group">
                <i class="material-icons">alternate_email</i>
                <input asp-for="Input.Email" class="form-control"
                    placeholder="Email" />
            </div>
            <div class="form-group">
                <i class="material-icons">lock</i>
                <input asp-for="Input.Password" class="form-control"
                    placeholder="Password" />
            </div>
            <div class="form-group">
                <i class="material-icons">lock</i>
                <input asp-for="Input.ConfirmPassword"
                    class="form-control"
                    placeholder="Confirm Password" />
            </div>
            <button type="submit" class="btn btn-primary">
                Register</button>
        </form>
    </div>
</div>

@section Scripts {
    <partial name="_ValidationScriptsPartial" />
}
```

Styling the Register Page

Because the Register page uses the same CSS styles as the **Login** page, reuse the selectors and properties in the *login-register.css* file. No new selectors are needed if you have added the **login-register** selector to the row <div> in the Razor Page markup.

Testing the Registration and Login Forms

1. Start the application.
2. Click the **Register** link in the navigation bar.
3. Fill in an email address and a password and click the **Register** button. It can be a fake email address if you like. I usually use an easy-to-remember email address, like *a@b.c*, when testing.
4. If the registration succeeded, the **Home/Index** view should be displayed, and the email should be visible to the right in the navigation bar.

5. Click the **Logout** link to the far right in the navigation bar. The login form should be displayed.
6. Try to log in to the site with the email you just registered. The application should redirect you to the **Home/Index** view.
7. Close the application from Visual Studio.
8. Open the *SQL Server Object Explorer* from the **View** menu.
9. Expand the **MSSQLLocalDB** node, and then your database.
10. Expand the **Tables** node and right click on the **AspNetUsers** table. See image below.
11. Right click on the table and select **View Data** to open the table in Visual Studio.
12. The table should contain the user you added. See image below.

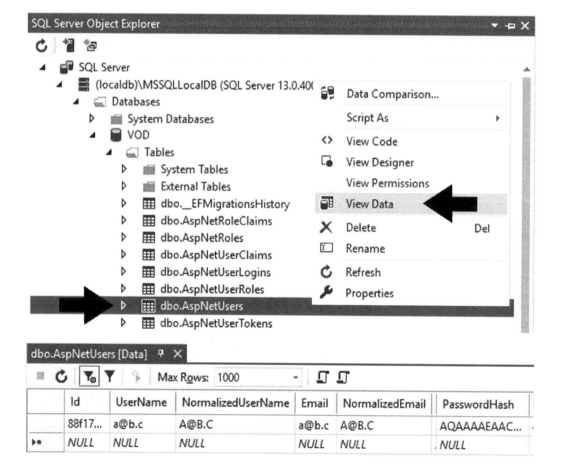

Summary

In this chapter, you changed the layout of the **Register** page and applied CSS and Bootstrap classes to spruce up its elements. You also registered a user and logged in using the account.

Next, you will change the layout of the navigation bar, and style it with CSS and Bootstrap classes. You will also create a drop-down menu for logout and settings options and remove their links from the navigation bar.

Lastly, you will add a logotype to the navigation bar.

ASP.NET Core 2.2 MVC, Razor Pages, API, JSON Web Tokens & HttpClient

5. Modifying the Navigation Bar

Introduction
The layout and styling of the navigation bar can be improved. In this chapter, you will alter the layout of the navigation bar, only displaying certain links when the user is logged out and creating a drop-down menu for the **Logout** and **Settings** options. You will also add a logo to the navigation bar.

Technologies Used in This Chapter
1. **Razor** – To incorporate C# in the views where necessary.
2. **HTML 5** – To build the views.
3. **Bootstrap and CSS** – To style the HTML 5 elements.

Overview
Your task is to change the appearance of the navigation bar. It should be white with a logo to the far left. The **Home** and **Privacy** links should be visible to the left in the navigation bar and the drop-down menu to the far right, which should be visible when the user is logged in.

To control when the links are displayed, you need to inject the **SignInManager** and **User-Manager** to the **_LoginPartial** view.

```
@inject SignInManager<VODUser> SignInManager
@inject UserManager<VODUser> UserManager
```

To achieve this, you will have to alter the **_Layout** and **_LoginPartial** views.

Current navigation bar when logged out

VOD.UI   Home   Privacy   Register   Login

Current navigation bar when logged in

VOD.UI   Home   Privacy   Hello a@b.c!   Logout

ASP.NET Core 2.2 MVC, Razor Pages, API, JSON Web Tokens & HttpClient

Altered navigation bar when logged out

Altered navigation bar when logged in

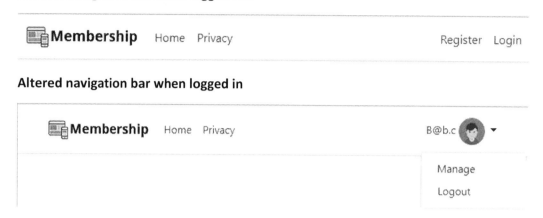

Adding a Logo to the Navigation Bar

1. Add a new folder named *images* to the *wwwroot* node.
2. Add the logo image to the *wwwroot/images* folder. You can find all the images used in this book in the GitHub repository for this book or use other images.
3. To replace the brand text (*VOD.UI*) with a logo, you delete the text in the <a> tag decorated with the **navbar-brand** class in the **_Layout** view and add the logo image in its place. You can drag the image from the *wwwroot/images* folder.
4. Add the **alt** tag with the text *Brand* to the <img> element you added to the <a> tag.

   ```
   <a class="navbar-brand" asp-area="" asp-controller="Home"
     asp-action="Index">
       <img src="~/images/Logos/membership-logo.png" alt="Brand" />
   </a>
   ```
5. Run the application and verify that the logo is visible when logged in and logged out.

Add the Drop-Down Menu

To give the navigation bar a cleaner look, you will remove the **Logout** and **Manage** links (the email greeting link) and add a drop-down link with an avatar and the email address.

1. Right click on the *wwwroot/css* folder and select **Add-New Item** in the context menu.
2. Select the **Style Sheet** template and name the file *navigation.css*.

5. Modifying the Navigation Bar

3. Remove the **body** selector.
4. Add a <link> to the *navigation.css* file below the *login-register.css* file in the **_Layout** view.
5. Open the **_LoginPartial** view located in the *Views/Shared* folder.
6. Add an <li> element above the first <li> element in the if-block and decorate it with the **drop-down** and **nav-item** Bootstrap classes; this will be the container for a drop-down menu item, to which you will add options.
   `<li class="nav-item dropdown"></li>`
7. Add an <a> element inside the previous <li> element; this will be the link to open the menu. Decorate it with the **nav-link** and **drop-down-toggle** classes and give it the id **user-drop-down**. Also add the **data-toggle** attribute set to **drop-down**, the attribute **role** set to **button**, the **aria-haspopup** attribute to **true**, and the **aria-expanded** attribute set to **false**. These settings will ensure that the menu begins collapsed and that the anchor tag will act as the menu's open/close button.
   a. Add the logged-in user's username (which is the email by default) followed by a space ( ) inside the <a> tag.
   `@User.Identity.Name `
   b. Add the avatar image to the right of the username inside the <a> tag and decorate the <img> element with the classes **img-circle** and **avatar**. Set the image height to 40.

```
<li class="nav-item dropdown">
    <a class="nav-link dropdown-toggle" href="#"
     id="user-drop-down" role="button" data-toggle="dropdown"
     aria-haspopup="true" aria-expanded="false">
        @User.Identity.Name <img src="~/images/avatar.png"
            class="img-circle avatar" height="40" />
    </a>
</li>
```

8. Add a <div> element decorated with the **dropdown-menu** class below the <a> element you just added. This will be the container for the menu options.

9. Move the <a> element below the drop-down menu into the <div> decorated with the **dropdown-menu** class. Add the **dropdown-item** class to the <a> element to transform it into a menu item. Remove the **nav-link** and **text-dark** classes. Change the text to *Manage*.
```
<a class="dropdown-item" asp-area="Identity"
asp-page="/Account/Manage/Index" title="Manage">Manage</a>
```

10. Move the <form> element below the drop-down menu into the <div> decorated with the **dropdown-menu** class. Add the **dropdown-item** class to the <form> element to transform it into a menu item. Add the id **logout-menu-button** to the <button> element inside the <form> element; you will use it to target the button with CSS.
```
<form class="dropdown-item form-inline" asp-area="Identity" asp-
page="/Account/Logout" asp-route-returnUrl="@Url.Action("Index",
"Home", new { area = "" })">
    <button id="logout-menu-button" type="submit" class="nav-link
        btn btn-link text-dark">Logout</button>
</form>
```

11. Remove the <li> elements that contained the <a> and <from> elements that you moved.

12. Add a CSS selector for the **logout-menu-button** id in the *navigation.css* file. Remove all padding from the button to align it with the other menu item.
```
#logout-menu-button {
    padding: 0;
}
```

13. Update the browser and login to see the menu.

14. Test the menu option.

The complete code in the **_LoginPartial** view:

```
@using Microsoft.AspNetCore.Identity
@inject SignInManager<VODUser> SignInManager
@inject UserManager<VODUser> UserManager

<ul class="navbar-nav">
@if (SignInManager.IsSignedIn(User))
{
```

```html
        <li class="nav-item dropdown">
            <a class="nav-link dropdown-toggle" href="#" id="user-drop-down"
              role="button" data-toggle="dropdown" aria-haspopup="true"
              aria-expanded="false">
                @User.Identity.Name <img src="~/images/avatar.png"
                    class="img-circle avatar" height="40" />
            </a>
            <div class="dropdown-menu">
                <a class="dropdown-item" asp-area="Identity"
                  asp-page="/Account/Manage/Index" title="Manage">Manage</a>
                <form class="dropdown-item form-inline"
                  asp-area="Identity" asp-page="/Account/Logout"
                  asp-route-returnUrl="@Url.Action("Index", "Home",
                  new { area = "" })">
                    <button id="logout-menu-button" type="submit"
                      class="nav-link btn btn-link text-dark">Logout
                    </button>
                </form>
            </div>
        </li>
}
else
{
    <li class="nav-item">
        <a class="nav-link text-dark" asp-area="Identity"
          asp-page="/Account/Register">Register</a>
    </li>
    <li class="nav-item">
        <a class="nav-link text-dark" asp-area="Identity"
          asp-page="/Account/Login">Login</a>
    </li>
}
</ul>
```

Summary

In this chapter, you modified the navigation bar and added a drop-down menu, all to make it look more professional and appealing to the user.

Next, you will figure out what Data Transfer Objects are needed to display the data in the *Membership* views.

ASP.NET Core 2.2 MVC, Razor Pages, API, JSON Web Tokens & HttpClient

6. Data Transfer Objects

Introduction
In this chapter, you will begin the creation of the *Membership* views, by figuring out what Data Transfer Objects (DTOs) are needed to transfer the necessary data from the server to the client.

In some solutions, the DTOs are the same as the entities used to create the database. In this solution, you will create DTOs for data transfer only, and entities for database CRUD (Create, Read, Update, Delete) operations. The objects are then transformed from one to the other using AutoMapper that you installed earlier.

Technologies Used in This Chapter
1. **C#** – To create the DTOs.

Overview
Your task is to figure out what DTOs are needed to display the necessary data in the three *Membership* views: **Dashboard**, **Course**, and **Video**.

The DTOs
The best way to figure out what data is needed is to go back and review the use case and look at the mock-view images. Here they are again for easy reference.

ASP.NET Core 2.2 MVC, Razor Pages, API, JSON Web Tokens & HttpClient

Dashboard view

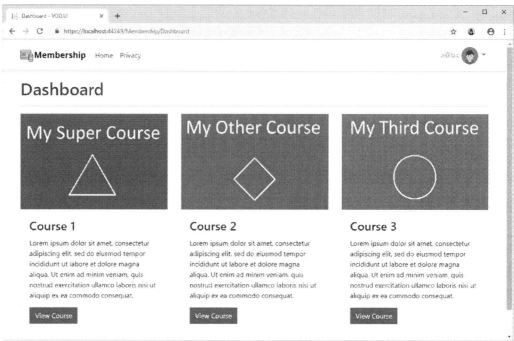

6. Data Transfer Objects

Course View

Video View

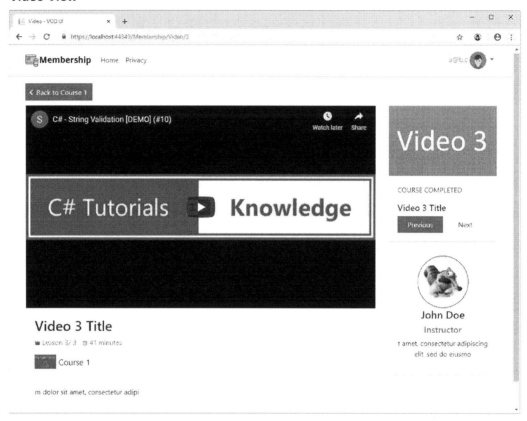

By studying the **Dashboard** view image, you can surmise the data needed for a single course card: course image, title, description, and a button leading to the course view (course id). But if you examine the **Course** view image, you can see that the course also has a marquee image.

How do you translate this into a class? Let's do it together, property by property.

Looking at the **Course** and **Video** view images, you can see that they are more complex than the **Dashboard** view. They both have three distinct areas. The **Course** view has a description area with a marquee image, a list of modules, and an instructor bio. Each module also has lists of videos and downloads. The **Video** view has a video area with a description and video information, an area for navigating to previous and next videos, and an instructor bio.

6. Data Transfer Objects

The first class will be called **CourseDTO**, and have the following properties:

Property name	Type
CourseId	int
CourseTitle	string
CourseDescription	string
MarqueeImageUrl	string
CourseImageUrl	string

The second class is **DownloadDTO**, which has the following properties:

Property name	Type
DownloadUrl	string
DownloadTitle	string

The third class is **VideoDTO**, which has the following properties:

Property name	Type
Id	int
Title	string
Description	string
Duration	string (how long the video is)
Thumbnail	string
Url	string (link to the video)

The fourth class is **InstructorDTO**, which has the following properties:

Property name	Type
InstructorName	string
InstructorDescription	string
InstructorAvatar	string

The fifth class is **ModuleDTO**, which has the following properties:

Property name	Type
Id	int
ModuleTitle	string
Videos	List<VideoDto>
Downloads	List<DownloadDto>

The sixth class is **LessonInfoDTO**, which you will use in the *Coming Up* section of the **Video** view.

Property name	Type
LessonNumber	int
NumberOfLessons	int
PreviousVideoId	int (used for the **Previous** button link)
NextVideoId	int (used for the **Next** button link)
NextVideoTitle	string
NextVideoThumbnail	string (the next video's image)

Adding the DTOs

Now it's time to add all the DTOs to the project. Let's do it together for one of them; then you can add the rest yourself.

1. Open the **Common** project in Visual Studio.
2. Add a new folder named *DTOModels*.
3. Right click on the *DTOModels* folder and a folder named *UI*.
4. Right click on the *DTOModels-UI* folder and select **Add-Class**.
5. Select the **Class** template.
6. Name the class *CourseDTO* and click the **Add** button.
7. Add the properties from the **CourseDTO** list above.
8. Repeat the steps 3-7 for all other DTOs.

9. Open the _ViewImports.cshtml file in the **UI** project and add a **using** statement to the *DTOModels* and the *DTOModels-UI* folders to make the files in those namespaces available from the views.

```
@using VOD.Common.DTOModels
@using VOD.Common.DTOModels.UI
```

The complete code in the **CourseDTO** class:

```
public class CourseDTO
{
    public int CourseId { get; set; }
    public string CourseTitle { get; set; }
    public string CourseDescription { get; set; }
    public string MarqueeImageUrl { get; set; }
    public string CourseImageUrl { get; set; }
}
```

The complete code in the **DownloadDTO** class:

```
public class DownloadDTO
{
    public string DownloadUrl { get; set; }
    public string DownloadTitle { get; set; }
}
```

The complete code in the **VideoDTO** class:

```
public class VideoDTO
{
    public int Id { get; set; }
    public string Title { get; set; }
    public string Description { get; set; }
    public string Duration { get; set; }
    public string Thumbnail { get; set; }
    public string Url { get; set; }
}
```

The complete code in the **InstructorDTO** class:

```
public class InstructorDTO
{
    public string InstructorName { get; set; }
    public string InstructorDescription { get; set; }
    public string InstructorAvatar { get; set; }
}
```

The complete code in the **ModuleDTO** class:

```
public class ModuleDTO
{
    public int Id { get; set; }
    public string ModuleTitle { get; set; }
    public List<VideoDTO> Videos { get; set; }
    public List<DownloadDTO> Downloads { get; set; }
}
```

The complete code in the **LessonInfoDTO** class:

```
public class LessonInfoDTO
{
    public int LessonNumber { get; set; }
    public int NumberOfLessons { get; set; }
    public int PreviousVideoId { get; set; }
    public int NextVideoId { get; set; }
    public string NextVideoTitle { get; set; }
    public string NextVideoThumbnail { get; set; }
}
```

The View Models

That's great – now you know what the individual DTOs contain – but how do you get the information to the views? With the more complex views, there's no easy way to pass multiple DTOs at the same time. You could use Tuples, but that is hard to implement. A better choice is to use a view model, which can contain other objects.

There will be three view models, although you could argue that the first one isn't strictly necessary, because it contains only one property. I beg to differ, however, because it will be easier to update the view with more data if the need should arise.

The first view model is **DashboardViewModel**, which has only one property. The property data type is somewhat complex; it is a list containing a list. The reason for using a list in a list is that you want to display three course cards on each row. An easy way to make sure that is possible is to add lists containing a maximum of three **CourseDTOs**, one list for each row, to the outer list.

Property name	Type
Courses	List<List<CourseDTO>>

The second view model is the **CourseViewModel**, which contains a **CourseDTO**, an **InstructorDTO**, and a list of **ModuleDTOs**.

Property name	Type
Course	CourseDTO
Instructor	InstructorDTO
Modules	IEnumerable<ModuleDTO>

The third view model is the **VideoViewModel**, which contains a **VideoDTO**, an **Instructor-DTO**, a **CourseDTO**, and a **LessonInfoDTO**.

Property name	Type
Video	VideoDTO
Instructor	InstructorDTO
Course	CourseDTO
LessonInfo	LessonInfoDTO

Adding the View Models

Now, it's time to add all the view models to the project. Let's do it together for one of them; then you can add the rest yourself.

1. Open the **UI** project in Visual Studio.
2. Right click on the *Models* folder in the Solution Explorer and select **Add-New Folder**. Name the folder *MembershipViewModels*.
3. Right click on the *MembershipViewModels* folder and select **Add-Class**.

4. Select the **Class** template.
5. Name the class *CourseViewModel* and click the **Add** button.
6. Add the properties from the **CourseViewModel** list above. Don't forget to add a using statement to the **DTOModels** namespace.
7. Repeat steps 3-6 for all the other view models.

The complete **CourseViewModel** class:

```
public class CourseViewModel
{
    public CourseDTO Course { get; set; }
    public InstructorDTO Instructor { get; set; }
    public IEnumerable<ModuleDTO> Modules { get; set; }
}
```

The complete **DashboardViewModel** class:

```
public class DashboardViewModel
{
    public List<List<CourseDTO>> Courses { get; set; }
}
```

The complete **VideoViewModel** class:

```
public class VideoViewModel
{
    public VideoDTO Video { get; set; }
    public InstructorDTO Instructor { get; set; }
    public CourseDTO Course { get; set; }
    public LessonInfoDTO LessonInfo { get; set; }
}
```

Summary

In this chapter, you figured out the Data Transfer Objects (DTOs) needed to display the data in the views. You also figured out how to transport multiple DTOs to the view with one model, a view model.

Next, you will learn how the data will be stored in a data source using entity classes.

7. Entity Classes

Introduction
In this chapter, you will add the entity classes needed to store data in the database. In the next chapter, you will create the tables corresponding to the entity classes you add in this chapter.

Now that you have defined the DTOs, you can figure out what the data objects, the entities, should contain. There will not always be a 1-1 match between a DTO and an entity; that's where an object mapper comes into the picture. In a later chapter, you will use AutoMapper to convert an entity to a DTO.

Technologies Used in This Chapter
1. **C#** – Creating entity classes.
2. **Attributes** – To define behaviors of entity properties.

Overview
Your task is to use your knowledge about the DTOs to create a set of entity classes that will make up the data sources. Remember that an entity doesn't have to contain all properties of a DTO and that sometimes it will contain more properties.

The Entities
Let's go back and review the DTOs one at a time and decide which of their properties belong in the entities. Some of the entity properties need restrictions, like maximum length, required, and if it's a primary key in the table.

The Video Entity
Properties of the **VideoDTO**: Id, Title, Description, Duration, Thumbnail, and Url.

The **Video** entity needs the same properties that the DTO has, but it could use a few more. The **Video** entity needs a **ModuleId** navigation property, as well as a property for the actual module to know to what module it belongs. You will also add navigation properties for the **courseId** and the course. Navigation properties can be used to avoid complex LINQ joins when loaded with data.

A video can only belong to one module in this scenario. If you want a video available in multiple modules, you need to implement a many-to-many relationship entity between the **Video** and **Module** entities. In this application, it is enough that a video only can belong to one module and that a module can have multiple videos associated with it.

You could also add a **CourseId** navigation property, to avoid lengthy joins.

Properties in the **Video** entity class:

Property	Type	Attribute/Comment
Id	int	Key (primary key in Entity Framework table)
Title	string	MaxLength(80) and Required
Description	string	MaxLength(1024)
Thumbnail	string	MaxLength(1024)
Url	string	MaxLength(1024)
Duration	int	
ModuleId	int	Navigation property
Module	Module	Navigation property
CourseId	int	Navigation property
Course	Course	Navigation property

The Download Entity

Properties in the **DownloadDTO**: DownloadUrl and DownloadTitle.

Note that the property names don't have to be the same in the DTO and the entity; there can even be different properties altogether. AutoMapper can be configured to map between properties with different names and types. By default, it uses auto-mapping between properties with identical names.

7. Entity Classes

Properties in the **Download** entity class:

Property	Type	Attribute/Comment
Id	int	Key (will make it the primary key)
Title	string	MaxLength(80) and Required
Url	string	MaxLength(1024)
ModuleId	int	Navigation property
Module	Module	Navigation property
CourseId	int	Navigation property
Course	Course	Navigation property

The Instructor Entity

Properties in the **InstructorDTO**: InstructorName, InstructorDescription, and InstructorAvatar.

Apart from the name, description, and avatar properties, the **Instructor** entity needs a unique id property.

Properties in the **Instructor** entity class:

Property	Type	Attribute/Comment
Id	int	Key (will make it the primary key)
Name	string	MaxLength(80) and Required
Description	string	MaxLength(1024)
Thumbnail	string	MaxLength(1024)

The Course Entity

Properties in the **CourseDTO**: CourseId, CourseTitle, CourseDescription, CourseImageUrl, and MarqueeImageUrl.

Apart from the DTO properties, the **Course** entity needs a unique id, an instructor id and a single **Instructor** entity, and a list of **Module** entities.

The single **Instructor** property is the 1 in the 1-many relationship between the **Course** and **Instructor** entities.

The list of **Module** entities is the many in a 1-many relationship between the **Course** entity and the **Module** entities. A course can have many modules, but a module can only belong to one course.

You could change this behavior by implementing another entity that connects the **Course** and the **Module** entities, creating a many-many relationship. Here you'll implement the 1-many relationship.

Property	Type	Attribute/Comment
Id	int	Key (will make it the primary key)
Title	string	MaxLength(80) and Required
Description	string	MaxLength(1024)
ImageUrl	string	MaxLength(255)
MarqueeImageUrl	string	MaxLength(255)
InstructorId	int	Navigation property
Instructor	Instructor	Navigation property
Modules	List<Module>	Navigation property

The Module Entity

Properties in the **ModuleDTO**: Id, ModuleTitle, Videos, and Downloads.

Apart from the DTO properties, the **Module** entity needs a unique id and a navigation property to its **Course** entity.

The single **Course** entity is the 1 in a 1-many relationship between the **Course** entity and the **Module** entity. A module can only belong to one course, but a course can have many modules.

The lists of **Video** and **Download** entities are the many part of the 1-many relationships between them and a **Module** entity; in other words, a collection property in an entity class signifies that many records of that type can be associated with the entity. For instance, an order has a 1-many relationship with its order rows, where one order can have many order rows. A module can have many videos and downloads, and a download and a video can only belong to one module.

7. Entity Classes

Property	Type	Attribute/Comment
Id	int	Key (will make it the primary key)
Title	string	MaxLength(80) and Required
CourseId	int	Navigation property
Course	Course	Navigation property
Videos	List<Video>	Navigation property
Downloads	List<Download>	Navigation property

The UserCourse Entity

The **UserCourse** entity needs a navigation property to the **Course** entity as well as its id. It also needs a navigation property to the **VODUser** entity and its id.

In earlier versions of Entity Framework, a composite primary key – a primary key made up of more than one property – could be defined using attributes in the entity class. In Entity Framework Core, you define them in the **DbContext** class, which you will do in a later chapter.

Property	Type	Attribute/Comment
UserId	string	Key (part of primary key)
User	User	Navigation property
CourseId	int	Key (part of primary key)
Course	Course	Navigation property

Adding the Entity Classes

With the entity properties defined, you can create their classes. Let's implement one together; then you can add the rest yourself.

Depending on the order you implement the entity classes, you might end up with properties that reference entity classes that you must add. For instance, the **Courses** entity has a property called **Instructor**, which is dependent on the **Instructor** class.

ASP.NET Core 2.2 MVC, Razor Pages, API, JSON Web Tokens & HttpClient

1. Open the **VOD.Common** project in the Solution Explorer.
2. Right click on the *Entities* folder and select **Add-Class**.
3. Name the class *Video* and click the **Add** button.
4. Add a public property named **Id** of type **int**.
5. Add the **[Key]** attribute to it, to make it the primary key. You will have to resolve the namespace **System.ComponentModel.DataAnnotations**. Note that the primary key properties in the **UserCourse** class shouldn't have the **[Key]** attribute because they make up a composite key.
   ```
   public class Video
   {
       [Key]
       public int Id { get; set; }
   }
   ```
6. Add another property named **Title** and restrict it to 80 characters. The title should also be required because the video needs a title.
   ```
   [MaxLength(80), Required]
   public string Title { get; set; }
   ```
7. Add a property of type **string** named **Description** and restrict it to 1024 characters.
8. Add a property of type **string** named **Thumbnail** and restrict it to 1024 characters.
9. Add a property of type **string** named **Url** and restrict it to 1024 characters.
10. Add a property of type **int** named **Duration**.
11. Add a property of type **int** named **ModuleId**.
12. Add a property of type **int** named **CourseId**.
13. Add navigation properties for the other entity classes listed above; these properties make it easier to load related data. Note that these properties will have a red squiggly line because these entity classes does not exist yet.
    ```
    public Course Course { get; set; }
    public Module Module { get; set; }
    ```
14. Now, implement the other entity classes according to their descriptions above.

The complete code for the **Video** entity class:

```
public class Video
{
    [Key]
    public int Id { get; set; }
    [MaxLength(80), Required]
    public string Title { get; set; }
    [MaxLength(1024)]
    public string Description { get; set; }
    public int Duration { get; set; }
    [MaxLength(1024)]
    public string Thumbnail { get; set; }
    [MaxLength(1024)]
    public string Url { get; set; }

    // Side-step from 3rd normal form for easier
    // access to a video's course and module
    public int ModuleId { get; set; }
    public int CourseId { get; set; }
    public Course Course { get; set; }
    public Module Module { get; set; }
}
```

The complete code for the **Download** entity class:

```
public class Download
{
    [Key]
    public int Id { get; set; }
    [MaxLength(80), Required]
    public string Title { get; set; }
    [MaxLength(1024)]
    public string Url { get; set; }

    // Side-step from 3rd normal form for easier
    // access to a video's course and module
    public int ModuleId { get; set; }
    public int CourseId { get; set; }
    public Module Module { get; set; }
    public Course Course { get; set; }
}
```

The complete code for the **Instructor** entity class:

```csharp
public class Instructor
{
    [Key]
    public int Id { get; set; }
    [MaxLength(80), Required]
    public string Name { get; set; }
    [MaxLength(1024)]
    public string Description { get; set; }
    [MaxLength(1024)]
    public string Thumbnail { get; set; }
}
```

The complete code for the **Course** entity class:

```csharp
public class Course
{
    [Key]
    public int Id { get; set; }
    [MaxLength(255)]
    public string ImageUrl { get; set; }
    [MaxLength(255)]
    public string MarqueeImageUrl { get; set; }
    [MaxLength(80), Required]
    public string Title { get; set; }
    [MaxLength(1024)]
    public string Description { get; set; }

    public int InstructorId { get; set; }
    public Instructor Instructor { get; set; }
    public List<Module> Modules { get; set; }
}
```

The complete code for the **Module** entity class:

```csharp
public class Module
{
    [Key]
    public int Id { get; set; }
    [MaxLength(80), Required]
    public string Title { get; set; }

    public int CourseId { get; set; }
    public Course Course { get; set; }
```

```
    public List<Video> Videos { get; set; }
    public List<Download> Downloads { get; set; }
}
```

The complete code for the **UserCourse** entity class:

```
public class UserCourse
{
    public string UserId { get; set; }
    public VODUser User { get; set; }
    public int CourseId { get; set; }
    public Course Course { get; set; }
}
```

Summary

In this chapter, you discovered and implemented the entity classes, and their properties and restrictions.

Next, you will create the database tables from the entity classes you just added to the **Common** project.

ASP.NET Core 2.2 MVC, Razor Pages, API, JSON Web Tokens & HttpClient

8. Creating the Database Tables

Introduction
In this chapter, you will create the database tables for storing the video data; you have already created the tables for user data in an earlier chapter. Although you could have several database contexts for interacting with the database, you will continue using the one that you already have created.

You will also seed the new tables in the database with initial data, which makes it easier for you to follow along as you create the various views because then they will have familiar data to display.

When the tables have been created and seeded, you will create a data repository class called **UIReadService** in the next chapter, using an interface named **IUIReadService**. When implemented, you will register it as a service in the **ConfigureServices** method in the **Startup** class, which will prepare the application to use data from the database.

Technologies Used in This Chapter
1. **C#** – Used when seeding the database and creating the repository.
2. **Entity framework** – To create and interact with the new tables from the repository.
3. **LINQ** – To query the database tables.

Overview
Your first objective is to create the tables for storing video-related data in the database and seed them with data. The second objective is to create a data repository that can communicate with the database tables. After implementing these steps, the application can work with data from the database.

Adding the Tables
You need to add the entity classes as **DbSet** properties in the **VODContext** class to tell Entity Framework to create tables for them in the database.

You can then inject the **VODContext** class into the constructor of the **UIReadService** class to perform CRUD (Create, Read, Update, Delete) operations on the tables.

Adding the Entity Classes to the VODContext

1. Open the **VOD.Database** project in the Solution Explorer.
2. Open the **VODContext** class located in the *Contexts* folder.
3. Add all the entity classes as **DbSet** properties to the class.
   ```
   public DbSet<Course> Courses { get; set; }
   public DbSet<Download> Downloads { get; set; }
   public DbSet<Instructor> Instructors { get; set; }
   public DbSet<Module> Modules { get; set; }
   public DbSet<UserCourse> UserCourses { get; set; }
   public DbSet<Video> Videos { get; set; }
   ```
4. Because the **UserCourses** table has a composite key (**UserId** and **CourseId**), you need to specify that in the **OnModelCreating** method in the **VODContext** class. In previous versions of ASP.NET you could do this in the entity class with attributes, but in ASP.NET Core 2.2 you pass it in as a Lambda expression to the **HasKey** method.
   ```
   builder.Entity<UserCourse>().HasKey(uc => new { uc.UserId, uc.CourseId });
   ```
5. To avoid cascading deletes when a parent record is deleted, you can add a delete behavior to the **OnModelCreating** method. A cascading delete will delete all related records to the one being deleted; for instance, if you delete an order, all its order rows will also be deleted.
   ```
   foreach (var relationship in
   builder.Model.GetEntityTypes().SelectMany(e =>
   e.GetForeignKeys()))
   {
       relationship.DeleteBehavior = DeleteBehavior.Restrict;
   }
   ```

The complete code in the **VODContext** class:

```
public class VODContext : IdentityDbContext<User>
{
    public DbSet<Course> Courses { get; set; }
    public DbSet<Download> Downloads { get; set; }
    public DbSet<Instructor> Instructors { get; set; }
    public DbSet<Module> Modules { get; set; }
    public DbSet<UserCourse> UserCourses { get; set; }
    public DbSet<Video> Videos { get; set; }
```

```csharp
    public VODContext(DbContextOptions<VODContext> options) 
    : base(options) { }

    protected override void OnModelCreating(ModelBuilder builder)
    {
        base.OnModelCreating(builder);

        // Composite key
        builder.Entity<UserCourse>().HasKey(uc =>
            new { uc.UserId, uc.CourseId });

        // Restrict cascading deletes
        foreach (var relationship in builder.Model.GetEntityTypes()
            .SelectMany(e => e.GetForeignKeys()))
        {
            relationship.DeleteBehavior = DeleteBehavior.Restrict;
        }
    }
}
```

Creating the Tables

To add the tables to the database, you must create a new migration and update the database.

1. Open the Package Manager Console and select **VOD.Database** in the right drop-down.
2. Execute the following command to create the migration data.
   add-migration CreateEntityTables
3. Execute the following command to make the migration changes in the database.
   update-database
4. Open the SQL Server Object Explorer and make sure that the tables are in the database.

Adding Seed Data

To have some data to work with in the newly created tables, you add seed data to them. You can do that by adding a class called **DbInitializer** to the *Data* folder and add seed data to it.

The seed data is added using a **static** method called **Initialize**, which you will need to add to the class.

If you want to recreate the database every time migrations are applied, you add the following two code lines at the beginning of the **Initialize** method; this could be useful in certain test scenarios where you need a clean database. You will not add them in this exercise because you want to keep the data you add between migrations.

```
context.Database.EnsureDeleted();
context.Database.EnsureCreated();
```

To add data to a table, you create a list of the entity type and add instances to it. Then you add that list to the entity collection (the **DbSet** for that entity), in the **VODContext** class, using the **context** object passed into the **Initialize** method.

Note that the order in which you add the seed data is important because some tables may be related to other tables and need the primary keys from those tables.

1. Add a public class called **DbInitializer** to the *Migrations* folder in the **Database** project.
2. Add a **public static** method called **RecreateDatabase** to the class. It should take the **VODContext** as a parameter. Call this method if you need to recreate the database; this deletes all data in the entire database.
   ```
   public static void RecreateDatabase(VODContext context)
   {
   }
   ```
3. Add calls to the **EnsureDeleted** and **EnsureCreated** methods on the **context** object to delete the database and create a new one.
   ```
   context.Database.EnsureDeleted();
   context.Database.EnsureCreated();
   ```
4. Add a **public static** method called **Initialize** to the class. It should take the **VODContext** as a parameter.
   ```
   public static void Initialize(VODContext context)
   {
   }
   ```

8. Creating the Database Tables

5. To avoid repeating dummy data, you will reuse text from a variable with some Lorem Ipsum text throughout the seeding process. You can generate Lorem Ipsum text at the following URL: http://loripsum.net/.

   ```
   var description = "Lorem ipsum dolor sit amet, consectetur
   adipiscing elit, sed do eiusmod tempor incididunt ut labore et
   dolore magna aliqua. Ut enim ad minim veniam, quis nostrud
   exercitation ullamco laboris nisi ut aliquip ex ea commodo
   consequat.";
   ```

6. Add three variables for email, admin role id, and user id used throughout the **Initialize** method. The email address should be in the **AspNetUsers** table; if not, then register a user with that email address or change the variable value to an email address in the table. The user should be an administrator; if not, open the **AspNetUserRoles** table and add a record using the user id and *1* (or the id you gave the *Admin* role in the **AspNetRoles** table) in the **RoleId** column.

   ```
   var email = "a@b.c";
   var adminRoleId = string.Empty;
   var userId = string.Empty;
   ```

7. Try to fetch the user id from the **AspNetUsers** table using the **Users** entity.

   ```
   if (context.Users.Any(r => r.Email.Equals(email)))
       userId = context.Users.First(r => r.Email.Equals(email)).Id;
   ```

8. Add an if-block that checks if the user id was successfully fetched. All the remaining code should be placed inside this if-block.

   ```
   if (!userId.Equals(string.Empty))
   {
   }
   ```

9. Use the **Instructors** entity to add instructor data to the **Instructors** table in the database if no data has been added.

   ```
   if (!context.Instructors.Any())
   {
       var instructors = new List<Instructor>
       {
           new Instructor {
               Name = "John Doe",
               Description = description.Substring(20, 50),
               Thumbnail = "/images/Ice-Age-Scrat-icon.png"
           },
   ```

```csharp
            new Instructor {
                Name = "Jane Doe",
                Description = description.Substring(30, 40),
                Thumbnail = "/images/Ice-Age-Scrat-icon.png"
            }
        };
        context.Instructors.AddRange(instructors);
        context.SaveChanges();
    }
```

10. Use the **Courses** entity to add course data to the **Courses** table in the database if no data has been added.

```csharp
    if (!context.Courses.Any())
    {
        var instructorId1 = context.Instructors.First().Id;
        var instructorId2 = int.MinValue;
        var instructor = context.Instructors.Skip(1).FirstOrDefault();
        if (instructor != null) instructorId2 = instructor.Id;
        else instructorId2 = instructorId1;

        var courses = new List<Course>
        {
            new Course {
                InstructorId = instructorId1,
                Title = "Course 1",
                Description = description,
                ImageUrl = "/images/course1.jpg",
                MarqueeImageUrl = "/images/laptop.jpg"
            },
            new Course {
                InstructorId = instructorId2,
                Title = "Course 2",
                Description = description,
                ImageUrl = "/images/course2.jpg",
                MarqueeImageUrl = "/images/laptop.jpg"
            },
            new Course {
                InstructorId = instructorId1,
                Title = "Course 3",
                Description = description,
                ImageUrl = "/images/course3.jpg",
                MarqueeImageUrl = "/images/laptop.jpg"
            }
        };
```

8. Creating the Database Tables

```
        context.Courses.AddRange(courses);
        context.SaveChanges();
    }
```

11. Try to fetch the course ids from the newly added courses. These ids will be used in other tables when referencing courses.

```
    var courseId1 = int.MinValue;
    var courseId2 = int.MinValue;
    var courseId3 = int.MinValue;
    if (context.Courses.Any())
    {
        courseId1 = context.Courses.First().Id;

        var course = context.Courses.Skip(1).FirstOrDefault();
        if (course != null) courseId2 = course.Id;

        course = context.Courses.Skip(2).FirstOrDefault();
        if (course != null) courseId3 = course.Id;
    }
```

12. Use the **UserCourses** entity to connect users and courses.

```
    if (!context.UserCourses.Any())
    {
        if (!courseId1.Equals(int.MinValue))
            context.UserCourses.Add(new UserCourse
                { UserId = userId, CourseId = courseId1 });

        if (!courseId2.Equals(int.MinValue))
            context.UserCourses.Add(new UserCourse
                { UserId = userId, CourseId = courseId2 });

        if (!courseId3.Equals(int.MinValue))
            context.UserCourses.Add(new UserCourse
                { UserId = userId, CourseId = courseId3 });

        context.SaveChanges();
    }
```

13. Use the **Modules** entity to add module data to the **Modules** table in the database if no data has been added.

```
    if (!context.Modules.Any())
    {
        var modules = new List<Module>
        {
```

```
            new Module { Course = context.Find<Course>(courseId1),
                Title = "Module 1" },
            new Module { Course = context.Find<Course>(courseId1),
                Title = "Module 2" },
            new Module { Course = context.Find<Course>(courseId2),
                Title = "Module 3" }
        };
        context.Modules.AddRange(modules);
        context.SaveChanges();
    }
```

14. Try to fetch the module ids from the newly added modules. These ids will be used in other tables when referencing modules.

```
    var moduleId1 = int.MinValue;
    var moduleId2 = int.MinValue;
    var moduleId3 = int.MinValue;
    if (context.Modules.Any())
    {
        moduleId1 = context.Modules.First().Id;

        var module = context.Modules.Skip(1).FirstOrDefault();
        if (module != null) moduleId2 = module.Id;
        else moduleId2 = moduleId1;

        module = context.Modules.Skip(2).FirstOrDefault();
        if (module != null) moduleId3 = module.Id;
        else moduleId3 = moduleId1;
    }
```

15. Use the **Videos** entity to add video data to the **Videos** table in the database if no data has been added.

```
    if (!context.Videos.Any())
    {
        var videos = new List<Video>
        {
            new Video { ModuleId = moduleId1, CourseId = courseId1,
                Title = "Video 1 Title",
                Description = description.Substring(1, 35),
                Duration = 50, Thumbnail = "/images/video1.jpg",
                Url = "https://www.youtube.com/watch?v=BJFyzpBcaCY"
            },
            new Video { ModuleId = moduleId1, CourseId = courseId1,
                Title = "Video 2 Title",
                Description = description.Substring(5, 35),
```

```
                    Duration = 45, Thumbnail = "/images/video2.jpg",
                    Url = "https://www.youtube.com/watch?v=BJFyzpBcaCY"
                },
                new Video { ModuleId = moduleId1, CourseId = courseId1,
                    Title = "Video 3 Title",
                    Description = description.Substring(10, 35),
                    Duration = 41, Thumbnail = "/images/video3.jpg",
                    Url = "https://www.youtube.com/watch?v=BJFyzpBcaCY"
                },
                new Video { ModuleId = moduleId3, CourseId = courseId2,
                    Title = "Video 4 Title",
                    Description = description.Substring(15, 35),
                    Duration = 41, Thumbnail = "/images/video4.jpg",
                    Url = "https://www.youtube.com/watch?v=BJFyzpBcaCY"
                },
                new Video { ModuleId = moduleId2, CourseId = courseId1,
                    Title = "Video 5 Title",
                    Description = description.Substring(20, 35),
                    Duration = 42, Thumbnail = "/images/video5.jpg",
                    Url = "https://www.youtube.com/watch?v=BJFyzpBcaCY"
                }
            };
            context.Videos.AddRange(videos);
            context.SaveChanges();
        }
```

16. Use the **Downloads** entity to add download data to the **Downloads** table in the database if no data has been added.

```
if (!context.Downloads.Any())
{
    var downloads = new List<Download>
    {
        new Download{ModuleId = moduleId1, CourseId = courseId1,
            Title = "ADO.NET 1 (PDF)", Url = "https://some-url" },
        new Download{ModuleId = moduleId1, CourseId = courseId1,
            Title = "ADO.NET 2 (PDF)", Url = "https://some-url" },
        new Download{ModuleId = moduleId3, CourseId = courseId2,
            Title = "ADO.NET 1 (PDF)", Url = "https://some-url" }
    };

    context.Downloads.AddRange(downloads);
    context.SaveChanges();
}
```

17. Inject the **VODContext** class into the **Configure** method in the **Startup** class.
    ```
    public void Configure(IApplicationBuilder app, IHostingEnvironment env, VODContext db) { ... }
    ```
18. Add a **using** statement to the **VOD.Database.Migrations** namespace.
    ```
    using VOD.Database.Migrations
    ```
19. Call the **DbInitializer.Initialize** method with the **db** object, above the **app.UseAuthentication** method call, when the application starts to add the seed data.
    ```
    DbInitializer.Initialize(db);
    ```
20. To fill the tables with the seed data, you must start the application (Ctrl+F5).
21. Stop the application and remove or comment out the call to the **DbInitializer.Initialize** method. Call this method only when you seed the database.
22. Open the *SQL Server Object Explorer*.
23. Right click on the entity tables and select **View Data** to verify that they contain seed data.

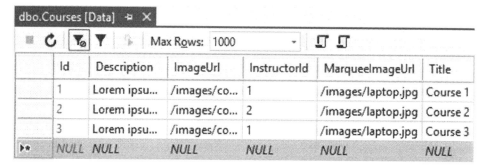

24. If for some reason the data hasn't been added, then recreate the database by calling the **RecreateDatabase** method you added earlier once from the **Configure** method in the **Startup** class. Remember to add a new user with the *a@b.c* email address and assign it the *Admin* role that you must add to the database as you did in an earlier chapter.

8. Creating the Database Tables

The complete code for the **Configure** method in the **Startup** class:

```
public void Configure(IApplicationBuilder app, IHostingEnvironment env,
VODContext db)
{
    if (env.IsDevelopment())
    {
        app.UseDeveloperExceptionPage();
        app.UseDatabaseErrorPage();
    }
    else
    {
        app.UseExceptionHandler("/Home/Error");
        app.UseHsts();
    }

    app.UseHttpsRedirection();
    app.UseStaticFiles();
    app.UseCookiePolicy();

    // Uncomment to recreate the database. ALL DATA WILL BE LOST !
    //DbInitializer.RecreateDatabase(db);

    //Uncomment to seed the database
    DbInitializer.Initialize(db);

    app.UseAuthentication();

    app.UseMvc(routes =>
    {
        routes.MapRoute(
        name: "default",
        template: "{controller=Home}/{action=Index}/{id?}");
    });
}
```

Summary

In this chapter, you created the application-related tables in the database and seeded them with data.

Next, you will create a data repository service that communicates with the database tables and gives the application access to data from the database.

ASP.NET Core 2.2 MVC, Razor Pages, API, JSON Web Tokens & HttpClient

9. The Database Read Service

Introduction
In this chapter, you will create a service called **DbReadService** in the **VOD.Database** project. This service will be used from the **UI** and **Admin** projects to read data from the database.

The service is injected into a second service in the **UI** project called **UIReadService**, using an interface named **IUIReadService**. You will register the **IUIReadService** service in the **ConfigureServices** method in the **Startup** class, which will make the application use the data from the database.

The **Admin** project doesn't have a special read service and will, therefore, use the **DbRead-Service** service directly.

Technologies Used in This Chapter
1. **C#** – Used to create the service.
2. **Entity framework** – The repository interacts with the database through EF.
3. **LINQ** – To query the database tables.

Overview
Your first objective is to create a reusable service that communicates with the database tables from other services that need to read from the database. Your second objective is to create a service that the UI application can use to fetch data from the database using the first service through dependency injection.

Adding the DbReadService Service
You need to add an interface called **IDbReadService** that can be injected into constructors in other services and classes to fetch data from the database. You then need to implement the interface in a class called **DbReadService** that contains the code to access the database.

Implement the methods as generic asynchronous methods that can handle any entity and therefore fetch data from any table in the database.

Adding the Service Interface and Class

1. Open the **VOD.Database** project.
2. Add a new folder to it called *Services*.
3. Right click on the folder and select **Add-New Item**, then select the **Interface** template. Add an interface called **IDbReadService** to the folder.
4. Add the **public** access modifier to the interface to make it accessible from any project.
   ```
   public interface IDbReadService { }
   ```
5. Add a **public** class called **DbReadService** to the *Services* folder.
6. Add the interface to the class.
   ```
   public class DbReadService : IDbReadService
   {
   }
   ```
7. Add a constructor to the class and inject the **VODContext** to get access to the database from the service. Store the object in a class-level variable called **_db**.
   ```
   private VODContext _db;
   public DbReadService(VODContext db)
   {
       _db = db;
   }
   ```
8. Save the files.

The code for the **IDbReadService** interface, so far:

```
public interface IDbReadService { }
```

The code for the **DbReadService** class, so far:

```
public class DbReadService : IDbReadService
{
    private VODContext _db;
    public DbReadService(VODContext db)
    {
        _db = db;
    }
}
```

Fetching All Records in a Table (GetAsync)

The **GetAsync** method will return all records in the specified table asynchronously. Like all the other public methods you will add to this service, this one will be a generic method that can handle any entity. You choose the table to read from by defining the desired entity when calling the method.

Since the method will return all records in the table, no parameters are necessary.

Return the result as an asynchronous task (**Task<List<TEntity>>**), which means that resources are freed up for other tasks while fetching the data.

1. Open the **IDbReadService** interface.
2. Add a method definition for a **GetAsync** method that is defined by the entity type that substitutes the generic **TEntity** type when calling the method. You must limit the **TEntity** type to only classes since an entity only can be created using a class; if you don't do this, a value type such as **int** or **double** can define the method, which would generate an exception. Return the result as a **Task** because the method is asynchronous.
   `Task<List<TEntity>> GetAsync<TEntity>() where TEntity : class;`
3. Add the **GetAsync** method to the **DbReadService** class, either manually or by using the **Quick Actions** light bulb button. If you auto-generate the method with **Quick Actions**, you must remove the **throw** statement. Don't forget to add the **async** keyword to the method to enable asynchronous calls within the method.
4. Use the **Set** method on the **_db** context with the generic **TEntity** type to access the table associated with the defining entity. A **DbSet<TEntity>** can be returned asynchronously by calling the **ToListAsync** method.
   `Return await _db.Set<TEntity>().ToListAsync();`
5. Save all files.

The code for the **IDbReadService** interface, so far:

```
public interface IDbReadService
{
    Task<List<TEntity>> GetAsync<TEntity>() where TEntity : class;
}
```

The complete code for the **GetAsync** method:

```
public async Task<List<TEntity>> GetAsync<TEntity>() where TEntity : class
{
    return await _db.Set<TEntity>().ToListAsync();
}
```

Fetching Records Using a Predicate Function (GetAsync)

This asynchronous **GetAsync** method will return all records in the specified table that fulfill the passed-in Lambda expression wrapped in a **Task**. Like all the other public methods you will add to this service, this one will be a generic method that can handle any entity. You choose the table to read from by defining the desired entity when calling the method.

Because the method will return a subset of the records in the table, a Lambda expression must be passed-in to the method. The lambda expression is defined by an **Expression< Func<TEntity, bool>>** expression, which means that the expression must return either **true** or **false**.

Return the result as an asynchronous task (**Task<List<TEntity>>**), which means that resources are freed up for other tasks while fetching the data.

1. Open the **IDbReadService** interface.
2. Add a method definition for a **GetAsync<TEntity>** method that is defined by the entity type that substitutes the generic **TEntity** type when calling the method. You must limit the **TEntity** type to only classes since an entity only can be created using a class; if you don't do this, a value type such as **int** or **double** can define the method, which would generate an exception. Return the result as a **Task** because the method is asynchronous.
   ```
   Task<List<TEntity>> GetAsync<TEntity>(Expression<Func<TEntity, bool>> expression) where TEntity : class;
   ```
3. Add the **GetAsync** method to the **DbReadService** class, either manually or by using the **Quick Actions** light bulb button. If you auto-generate the method with **Quick Actions**, you must remove the **throw** statement. Don't forget to add the **async** keyword to the method to enable asynchronous calls within the method.
4. This **GetAsync** method returns a **Task<List<TEntity>>** that the passed-in predicate limits the records.
   ```
   return await _db.Set<TEntity>().Where(expression).ToListAsync();
   ```

5. Save all files.

The code for the **IDbReadService** interface, so far:

```
public interface IDbReadService
{
    Task<List<TEntity>> GetAsync<TEntity>() where TEntity : class;
    Task<List<TEntity>> GetAsync<TEntity>(Expression<Func<TEntity,
        bool>> expression) where TEntity : class;
}
```

The complete code for the **GetAsync** method:

```
public async Task<List<TEntity>> GetAsync<TEntity>(
Expression<Func<TEntity, bool>> expression) where TEntity : class
{
    return await _db.Set<TEntity>().Where(expression).ToListAsync();
}
```

Fetching a Single Record Using a Predicate Function (SingleAsync)

The asynchronous **SingleAsync** method will return one record from the specified table that fulfills the passed-in Lambda expression. Like all the other public methods you will add to this service, this one will be a generic asynchronous method that can handle any entity. You choose the table to read from by defining the desired entity when calling the method.

Because the method will return one record from the table, a Lambda expression will be passed-in to the method. The lambda expression is defined by an **Expression<Func< TEntity, bool>>** expression, which means that the expression must return either **true** or **false**.

The Lambda expression limits the result, which is returned asynchronously by calling the **SingleOrDefaultAsync** Linq method.

Return the result as a **Task<TEntity>** or **null**.

1. Open the **IDbReadService** interface.
2. Add a method definition for a **SingleAsync<TEntity>** method that is defined by the entity type that substitutes the generic **TEntity** type when calling the method. You must limit the **TEntity** type to only classes since an entity only can be created using a class; if you don't do this, a value type such as **int** or **double** define the method, which would generate an exception. Return the result as a **Task** because the method is asynchronous.
   ```
   Task<TEntity> SingleAsync<TEntity>(Expression<Func<TEntity, bool>> 
   expression) where TEntity : class;
   ```
3. Add the **SingleAsync** method to the **DbReadService** class, either manually or by using the **Quick Actions** light bulb button. If you auto-generate the method with **Quick Actions**, you must remove the **throw** statement. Don't forget to add the **async** keyword to the method to enable asynchronous calls within the method.
4. You can call the **SingleOrDefaultAsync** Linq method with the expression to return the data asynchronously.
   ```
   return await _db.Set<TEntity>().Where(expression)
       .SingleOrDefaultAsync();
   ```
5. Save all files.

The code for the **IDbReadService** interface, so far:

```
public interface IDbReadService
{
    Task<List<TEntity>> GetAsync<TEntity>() where TEntity : class;
    Task<List<TEntity>> GetAsync<TEntity>(Expression<Func<TEntity, 
        bool>> expression) where TEntity : class;
    Task<TEntity> SingleAsync<TEntity>(Expression<Func<TEntity, bool>> 
        expression) where TEntity : class;
}
```

The complete code for the **SingleAsync** method:

```
public async Task<TEntity> SingleAsync<TEntity>(Expression<Func<TEntity, 
bool>> expression) where TEntity : class
{
    return await _db.Set<TEntity>().SingleOrDefaultAsync(expression);
}
```

Finding Out if an Item Exists (AnyAsync)

The asynchronous **AnyAsync** method will return **true** if a record is found using the specified table in the passed-in Lambda expression. Like all the other public methods you will add to this service, this one will be a generic asynchronous method that can handle any entity. You choose the table to read from by defining the desired entity for the method when calling it.

A Lambda expression that returns **true** if the record is in the table will be passed-in to the method. The Lambda is defined by an **Expression<Func<TEntity, bool>>** expression, which means that it must return either **true** or **false**.

The Lambda expression determines the result that is returned asynchronously by calling the **AnyAsync** Linq method on the entity.

Return the result as a **Task<bool>**.

1. Open the **IDbReadService** interface.
2. Add a method definition for an **AnyAsync<TEntity>** method that is defined by the entity type that substitutes the generic **TEntity** type when calling the method. You must limit the **TEntity** type to only classes since an entity only can be created using a class; if you don't do this, a value type such as **int** or **double** can define the method, which would generate an exception. Return the result as a **Task** because the method is asynchronous.
   ```
   Task<bool> AnyAsync<TEntity>(Expression<Func<TEntity, bool>> expression) where TEntity : class;
   ```
3. Add the **AnyAsync** method to the **DbReadService** class, either manually or by using the **Quick Actions** light bulb button. If you auto-generate the method with **Quick Actions**, you must remove the **throw** statement. Don't forget to add the **async** keyword to the method to enable asynchronous calls within the method.
4. You can call the **AnyAsync** Linq method with the predicate and return the data asynchronously by calling the **AnyAsync** Linq function located in the **System.Linq.Expressions** namespace.
   ```
   return await _db.Set<TEntity>().AnyAsync(expression);
   ```
5. Save all files.

The code for the **IDbReadService** interface, so far:

```
public interface IDbReadService
{
    Task<List<TEntity>> GetAsync<TEntity>() where TEntity : class;
    Task<List<TEntity>> GetAsync<TEntity>(Expression<Func<TEntity,
        bool>> expression) where TEntity : class;
    Task<TEntity> SingleAsync<TEntity>(Expression<Func<TEntity, bool>>
        expression) where TEntity : class;
    Task<bool> AnyAsync<TEntity>(Expression<Func<TEntity, bool>>
        expression) where TEntity : class;
}
```

The complete code for the **AnyAsync** method:

```
public async Task<bool> AnyAsync<TEntity>(Expression<Func<TEntity,
bool>> expression) where TEntity : class
{
    return await _db.Set<TEntity>().AnyAsync(expression);
}
```

Including an Entity's Navigation Properties (Include)

Fetching data for an entity's navigation properties for related entities is not done by default. To enable loading data for navigation properties, you will create two versions of a method named **Include** that use reflection to find all navigation properties in the method's generic entity.

To find the navigation properties, you will use the **Model** object on the **VODContext** context (**_db**). The **Model** object has a method called **FindEntityType** that returns the type of the generic **TEntity** data type. On that result, you then can call the **GetNavigations** method to fetch the navigation properties. You can then call the **Select** method to fetch the names of the returned navigation properties.

When you have the names, you can iterate over them and call the **Include** Linq method on the result from the **_db.Set<TEntity>** method and pass in each property name.

The second **Include** method you create will take two generics (**TEntity1**, **TEntity2**) and call the first **Include** method for each of the two generics; the second method isn't strictly necessary since you can call the first **Include** method twice.

9. The Database Read Service

1. Open the **IDbReadService** interface.
2. Add a method definition for an **Include<TEntity>** method that is defined by the entity type that substitutes the generic **TEntity** type when calling the method. You must limit the **TEntity** type to only classes since an entity only can be created using a class; if you don't do this, a value type such as **int** or **double** can define the method, which would generate an exception.
   `void Include<TEntity>() where TEntity : class;`
3. Add the **Include** method to the **DbReadService** class, either manually or by using the **Quick Actions** light bulb button. If you auto-generate the method with **Quick Actions**, you must remove the **throw** statement. Don't forget to add the **async** keyword to the method to enable asynchronous calls within the method.
4. Fetch the names of the navigation properties inside the **TEntity** class by calling the **FindEntityType**, **GetNavigations** and **Select** methods.
   ```
   var propertyNames =
   _db.Model.FindEntityType(typeof(TEntity)).GetNavigations().Select(
   e => e.Name);
   ```
5. Iterate over the property names you fetched and call the **Include** Linq method on the **_db.Set<TEntity>** method to add data to the navigation properties.
   ```
   foreach (var name in propertyNames)
       _db.Set<TEntity>().Include(name).Load();
   ```
6. Open the **IDbReadService** interface and add the definition for the second **Include** method that will take two generic types. You define the generic types as a comma-separated list inside the brackets.
   `void Include<TEntity1, TEntity2>() where TEntity1 : class where TEntity2 : class;`
7. Add the **Include** method to the **DbReadService** class.
8. Call the first Include method with the two generic types.
   ```
   Include<TEntity1>();
   Include<TEntity2>();
   ```
9. Save all files.

ASP.NET Core 2.2 MVC, Razor Pages, API, JSON Web Tokens & HttpClient

The complete code for the **IDbReadService** interface:

```
public interface IDbReadService
{
    Task<List<TEntity>> GetAsync<TEntity>() where TEntity : class;
    Task<List<TEntity>> GetAsync<TEntity>(Expression<Func<TEntity,
        bool>> expression) where TEntity : class;
    Task<TEntity> SingleAsync<TEntity>(Expression<Func<TEntity, bool>>
        expression) where TEntity : class;
    Task<bool> AnyAsync<TEntity>(Expression<Func<TEntity, bool>>
        expression) where TEntity : class
    void Include<TEntity>() where TEntity : class;
    void Include<TEntity1, TEntity2>() where TEntity1 : class where
        TEntity2 : class;
}
```

The complete code for the **Include** method:

```
public void Include<TEntity>() where TEntity : class
{
    var propertyNames = _db.Model
        .FindEntityType(typeof(TEntity))
        .GetNavigations()
        .Select(e => e.Name);

    foreach (var name in propertyNames)
        _db.Set<TEntity>().Include(name).Load();
}

public void Include<TEntity1, TEntity2>() where TEntity1 : class where
TEntity2 : class
{
    Include<TEntity1>();
    Include<TEntity2>();
}
```

Converting an Entity Collection to a List of SelectList Items (ToSelectList)

This generic **ToSelectList** extension method will return a collection of **SelectList** items from the list of entities (records) passed into the method. **SelectList** items fill drop-down controls with data in Razor Pages or MVC views.

The **ToSelectList** method has two **string** parameters and an extension parameter prefixed with the **this** keyword. The **valueField** parameter holds the name of the value property (usually an id) that is stored in the background. The **textField** property holds the name of the description property; its value is displayed in the drop-down. Each selectable item in the drop-down uses both properties.

This generic method can convert a list of any entity. You choose the table to read from by defining the desired entity for the list when calling the method.

The extension parameter defined with the **this** keyword, named **items**, is passed into an instance of the **SelectList** class, which the method returns.

```
return new SelectList(items, valueField, textField);
```

1. Open the **Common** project and create a folder named *Extensions*.
2. Add a class named **ListExtensions** and make it **public** and **static**.
3. Add a **public static** method named **ToSelectList** with an extension parameter named **items** of type **List<TEntity>** decorated with the **this** keyword; this parameter defines what type that can call the extension method. The method should have two additional parameters: **valueField** of type **string** and **textField** of type **string**. Restrict the generic **TEntity** type to classes; an entity can only be created using a class.
    ```
    public static SelectList ToSelectList<TEntity>(this List<TEntity>
    items, string valueField, string textField) where TEntity : class
    {
    }
    ```
4. Return an instance of the **SelectList** class where you pass in the **items** parameter converted to a list using the **ToList** method, the **valueField** parameter, and **textField** parameter to its constructor.
    ```
    return new SelectList(items, valueField, textField);
    ```
5. Save all files.

The complete code for the **ListExtensions** class:

```
public static class ListExtensions
{
    public static SelectList ToSelectList<TEntity>(
        this List<TEntity> items, string valueField,
        string textField) where TEntity : class
    {
        return new SelectList(items, valueField, textField);
    }
}
```

Adding the Service and Testing the Read Methods

To test the read methods, you need to register the **DbReadService** with the **ConfigureServices** method in the **Startup** class. Then, you need to inject the service into a constructor in the **HomeController** class.

1. Open the **Startup** class and locate the **ConfigureServices** method.
2. Use the **AddScoped** method on the **service** object to register the **IDbReadService** interface at the end of the **ConfigureServices** method.
   `services.AddScoped<IDbReadService, DbReadService>();`
3. Open the **HomeController** class and inject the **IDbReadService** interface to receive an instance of the **DbReadService** class when a user requests one of its views.
   private IDbReadService _db;

   ```
   public HomeController(SignInManager<VODUser> signInMgr,
   IDbReadService db)
   {
       _signInManager = signInMgr;
       _db = db;
   }
   ```
4. Change the return type of the **Index** action to **Task<IActionResult>** and add the **async** keyword to enable asynchronous calls.
5. Call the **_db.SingleAsync** method for the **Download** entity at the top of the **Index** action and specify an existing id for the object from the **Downloads** table. Store the result in a variable called **result1**.
   `var result1 = await _db.SingleAsync<Download>(d => d.Id.Equals(3));`
6. Place a breakpoint on the if-statement in the **Index** action and start the application with debugging (F5). Inspect the **result1** variable; it should contain

the data for the chosen download record but not for its navigation properties (**Module** and **Course**).

7. To load the navigation properties, you need to add a call to one of the **Include** methods you created for the **Download** entity. Add the method call above the call to the **SingleAsync** method.
   ```
   _db.Include<Download>();
   ```

8. Start the application with debugging (F5). Inspect the **result1** variable's navigation properties (**Module** and **Course**) and verify that they have data. Note however that the **Instructor** and **Video** navigation properties in the **Module** and **Course** properties don't have any data.

9. To add data to the **Module** and **Course** navigation properties, add **Include** calls for those entities as well. You can include two entities by calling the second **Include** method you created and pass in the desired entities.
   ```
   _db.Include<Module, Course>();
   ```

10. To test the **GetAsync** methods you created, call one without parameter and one with a Lambda expression on the **_db** service. Store the result in variables named **result2** and **result3**.
    ```
    var result2 = await _db.GetAsync<Download>(); // Fetch all
    // Fetch all that matches the Lambda expression
    var result3 = await _db.GetAsync<Download>(d =>
        d.ModuleId.Equals(1));
    ```

11. To test the **AnyAsync** method to find out if a record exists that matches the Lambda expression, store the result in a variable named **result4**.
    ```
    var result4 = await _db.AnyAsync<Download>(d =>
        d.ModuleId.Equals(1)); // True if a record is found
    ```

12. Stop the application. Comment out or remove the calls to the **Include**, **SingleAsync**, **GetAsync** and **AnyAsync** methods as well as the injection code in the **HomeController**'s constructor and the **_db** variable in the class.

Summary

In this chapter, you created a service for reading data from the database. This service will be used from the **Admin** and **UI** projects to fetch data through other services.

Next, you will add a repository service designed for calls from the **UI** project to the database.

ASP.NET Core 2.2 MVC, Razor Pages, API, JSON Web Tokens & HttpClient

10. The UI Data Service

Introduction
In this chapter, you will create a new data repository class called **UIReadService** using an interface named **IUIReadService** that you register as a service in the **ConfigureServices** method in the **Startup** class. Later, you will inject this service into a new controller named **MembershipController**, which will make the application use data from the database.

Technologies Used in This Chapter
1. **C#** – To create the repository.
2. **LINQ/Lambda** – To query the database tables.

Overview
Now, you will implement an Interface named **IUIReadService** in a class called **UIReadService** to create a service that can communicate with the database tables through the **IDbReadService** that you created in the previous chapter. To make sure that service's methods return correct data, you will call them from a controller.

Adding the IUIReadService Interface
First, you will add the **IUIReadService** interface, and then implement it in the **UIReadService** class.

1. Right click on the **Dependencies** node in the **VOD.UI** project in the Solution Explorer and select **Add-Add Reference** and make sure that the **VOD.Database** and **VOD.Common** projects are selected and click the **OK** button.
2. Open the **VOD.Database** project.
3. Right click on the *Services* folder and select **Add-New Item**.
4. Select the **Interface** template.
5. Name it *IUIReadService* and click the **Add** button. Add the **public** access modifier to the interface, to make it accessible from all projects that reference the **VOD.Database** project.
6. Add an asynchronous method description for the **GetCourses** method. It should return an **IEnumerable** of **Course** entities as a task. Resolve any missing **using** statements.

```
Task<IEnumerable<Course>> GetCourses(string userId);
```

7. Add an asynchronous method description for the **GetCourse** method. It should return an instance of the **Course** entity. Resolve any missing **using** statements.
   ```
   Task<Course> GetCourse(string userId, int courseId);
   ```

8. Add an asynchronous method description for the **GetVideo** method. It should return an instance of the **Video** entity. Resolve any missing **using** statements.
   ```
   Task<Video> GetVideo(string userId, int videoId);
   ```

9. Add an asynchronous method description for the **GetVideos** class. It should return an **IEnumerable** of the **Video** entity and take a **userId (string)** and a **moduleId (int)** as parameters. The module id should be assigned the default value for the **int** data type. Resolve any missing **using** statements.
   ```
   Task<IEnumerable<Video>> GetVideos(string userId, int moduleId = default(int));
   ```

10. Save the files.

The complete code for the **IUIReadService** interface:

```
public interface IUIReadService
{
    Task<IEnumerable<Course>> GetCourses(string userId);
    Task<Course> GetCourse(string userId, int courseId);
    Task<Video> GetVideo(string userId, int videoId);
    Task<IEnumerable<Video>> GetVideos(string userId,
        int moduleId = default(int));
}
```

Adding the UIReadService Class

1. Add a **public** class called **UIReadService** to the *Services* folder in the **VOD.Database** project.
2. Add a constructor and inject the **IDbReadService**. Store the injected object in a **private** read-only class-level variable called **_db**; this will give access to the database through the service in the class.
   ```
   public class UIReadService
   {
       private readonly IDbReadService _db;
   ```

```
        public UIReadService(IDbReadService db)
        {
            _db = db;
        }
    }
```

3. Implement the **IUIReadService** interface in the class; this will add the methods that you need to implement. To add all the methods, you can point to the red squiggly line, click the light bulb button, and select **Implement Interface**.
   ```
   public class UIReadService : IUIReadService
   {
       ...
   }
   ```
4. Add the **async** keyword to the methods to prepare them for asynchronous calls.
5. Open the **Startup** class.
6. Copy the previous service declaration in **ConfigureServices** method and replace **IDbReadService** and **DbReadService** with **IUIReadService** and **UIReadService** in one of the service declarations.
   ```
   services.AddScoped<IDbReadService, DbReadService>();
   services.AddScoped<IUIReadService, UIReadService>();
   ```

The code for the **UIReadService** class:

```
public class UIReadService : IUIReadService
{
    #region Properties
    private readonly IDbReadService _db;
    #endregion

    #region Constructor
    public UIReadService(IDbReadService db)
    {
        _db = db;
    }
    #endregion

    #region Methods
    Public async Task<IEnumerable<Course>> GetCourses(string userId)
    {
        throw new NotImplementedException();
    }
```

```
    Public async Task<Course> GetCourse(string userId, int courseId)
    {
        throw new NotImplementedException();
    }

    Public async Task<Video> GetVideo(string userId, int videoId)
    {
        throw new NotImplementedException();
    }

    Public async Task<IEnumerable<Video>> GetVideos(string userId, 
    int moduleId = default(int))
    {
        throw new NotImplementedException();
    }
    #endregion
}
```

Injecting the IUIReadService into the HomeController's Constructor

You inject the **IUIReadService** as a parameter named **db** into the **HomeController's** constructor to be able to test the methods in the service before implementing the UI. You can use the **db** parameter inside the constructor to call the methods in the service.

1. Open the **HomeController** class.
2. Inject the **IUIReadService** into the constructor as a parameter named **db** and store the instance in a variable named **_db** in the class.
3. Change the **Index** action to an asynchronous method.

The complete code for the **constructor** method:

```
private readonly IUIReadService _db;
public HomeController(SignInManager<VODUser> signInMgr, IUIReadService db)
{
    _signInManager = signInMgr;
    _db = db;
}

public async Task<IActionResult> Index() { }
```

Implementing the GetCourses Method

This method will return all courses associated with a user.

1. Remove the **throw** statement from the **GetCourses** method in the **UIReadService** class.
2. Call the **Include** method on the **_db** service to include data for the navigation properties in the **UserCourse** class.
   `_db.Include<UserCourse>();`
3. Use the **_db** service variable to fetch all courses for a specific user.
   a. Call the **GetAsync** method on the **_db** service for the **UserCourses** entity to fetch all the course id and user id combinations from the database for the logged-in user.
   `var userCourses = await _db.GetAsync<UserCourse>(uc => uc.UserId.Equals(userId));`
   b. Return the **Course** entities included with the **UserCourse** entities by calling the **Select** LINQ method on the fetched records.
   `return userCourses.Select(c => c.Course);`
4. Call the **GetCourses** method on the **_db** object above the if-statement in the **Index** action in the **HomeController** to fetch all courses related to a specific user. Copy the user id from the user you used to seed the database and pass it into the method. Store the result in a variable named **courses**.
   `var courses = (await _db.GetCourses("88f17367-d202-4383-a54e-ec15e86e532e")).ToList();`
5. Place a breakpoint on the if-statement in the **Index** action.
6. Run the application and verify that the **courses** variable contains the courses.
7. Stop the application.

The complete code for the **GetCourses** method:

```
public async Task<IEnumerable<Course>> GetCourses(string userId)
{
    _db.Include<UserCourse>();
    var userCourses = await _db.GetAsync<UserCourse>(uc =>
        uc.UserId.Equals(userId));
    return userCourses.Select(c => c.Course);
}
```

Implementing the GetCourse Method

This method will fetch one course from the database.

1. Remove the **throw** statement from the **GetCourse** method in the **UIReadService** class.
2. Because the **Course** object has navigation properties to **Instructor** and **Module** entities, you want to load them as well. You can achieve this by calling the **Include** method on the **_db** service.
   `_db.Include<Course, Module>();`
3. Try to fetch data for the **UserCourse** entity matching the **userId** and **courseId** parameters in the **GetCourse** method. Call the **SingleAsync** method on the **_db** service with the **UserCourse** entity and the ids and store the result in a variable called **userCourse**. If the result is **null**, then the user doesn't have access to the desired course.
   `var userCourse = await _db.SingleAsync<UserCourse>(c => c.UserId.Equals(userId) && c.CourseId.Equals(courseId));`
4. Return the default value (**null**) for the **Course** entity if the user doesn't have access to the course.
   `if (userCourse == null) return default;`
5. Return the course from the method.
   `return userCourse.Course;`
8. Call the **GetCourse** method on the **_db** object in the Index action in the **HomeController** to fetch the desired course for a specific user. Copy the user id from the user you used to seed the database and pass it into the method along with the course id for the desired course. Store the result in a variable named **course**.
   `var course = db.GetCourse("88f17367-d202-4383-a54e-ec15e86e532e", 1);`
6. Run the application and verify that the course and its navigation properties are available in the **course** variable.
7. Stop the application.

The complete code for the **GetCourse** method:

```
public async Task<Course> GetCourse(string userId, int courseId)
{
    _db.Include<Course, Module>();
    var userCourse = await _db.SingleAsync<UserCourse>(c =>
        c.UserId.Equals(userId) && c.CourseId.Equals(courseId));
    if (userCourse == null) return default;
    return userCourse.Course;
}
```

Implementing the GetVideo Method

This method will fetch one video from the database.

1. Remove the **throw** statement from the **GetVideo** method in the **UIReadService** class.
2. The view model that will use the data from this method needs associated data as well. You, therefore, should include the **Course** entity, which in turn will make sure that the **Module** and **Instructor** entities are loaded.
   ```
   _db.Include<Course>();
   ```
3. Fetch the video matching the video id in the **videoId** parameter passed into the **GetVideo** method by calling the **SingleAsync** method on the **_db** service variable.
   ```
   var video = await _db.SingleAsync<Video>(v =>
       v.Id.Equals(videoId));
   ```
4. Check that a video is returned and return the default value (**null**) for the **Video** entity.
   ```
   if (video == null) return default;
   ```
5. Check that the user can view the video belonging to the course specified by the **CourseId** property of the video object. Return the default value for the **Video** entity if the user doesn't have access.
   ```
   var userCourse = await _db.SingleAsync<UserCourse>(c =>
       c.UserId.Equals(userId) &&
       c.CourseId.Equals(video.CourseId));

   if (userCourse == null) return default;
   ```
6. Return the video in the **video** variable.
   ```
   return video;
   ```

7. Call the **GetVideo** method on the **_db** object from the Index action in the HomeController to fetch the desired video for a specific user. Copy the user id from the user you used to seed the database and pass it into the method along with the video id for the desired video. Store the result in a variable named **video**.
   ```
   var video = await _db.GetVideo("88f17367-d202-4383-a54e-
   ec15e86e532e", 1);
   ```
8. Run the application and verify that the video is displayed in the **video** variable.
9. Stop the application.

The complete code for the **GetVideo** method:

```
public async Task<Video> GetVideo(string userId, int videoId)
{
    _db.Include<Course>();
    var video = await _db.SingleAsync<Video>(v => v.Id.Equals(videoId));
    if (video == null) return default;

    var userCourse = await _db.SingleAsync<UserCourse>(c =>
        c.UserId.Equals(userId) && c.CourseId.Equals(video.CourseId));
    if (userCourse == null) return default;

    return video;
}
```

Implementing the GetVideos Method

This method will fetch all videos associated with the logged in user.

1. Remove the **throw** statement from the **GetVideos** method in the **UIReadService** class.
2. Include the video objects when fetching the data for the **Module** entity.
   ```
   _db.Include<Video>();
   ```
3. Fetch the module matching the module id in the **moduleId** parameter passed into the **GetVideos** method by calling the **SingleAsync** method for the **Module** entity on the **_db** service variable.
   ```
   var module = await _db.SingleAsync<Module>(m =>
       m.Id.Equals(moduleId));
   ```

10. The UI Data Service

4. Check that a module was returned and return the default value for a **List<Video>** if it is **null**.
   ```
   if (module == null) return default(List<Video>);
   ```

5. Check that the user can view the video belonging to the course specified by the **CourseId** property in the **module** object. Return the default value for a list of **Video** entities if the user doesn't have access.
   ```
   var userCourse = await _db.SingleAsync<UserCourse>(uc =>
       uc.UserId.Equals(userId) &&
       uc.CourseId.Equals(module.CourseId));

   if (userCourse == null) return default(List<Video>);
   ```

6. Return the videos in the **module** variable's **Videos** navigation property.
   ```
   return module.Videos;
   ```

7. Call the **GetVideos** method on the **db** object to fetch the desired videos related to a specific user and module. Copy the user id from the user you used to seed the database and pass it into the method along with the module id for the. Store the result in a variable named **videos**.
   ```
   var videos = (await _db.GetVideos("88f17367-d202-4383-a54e-ec15e86e532e", 1)).ToList();
   ```

8. Run the application and verify that the videos are displayed in the **video** variable.
9. Stop the application.

The complete code for the **GetVideos** method:

```
public async Task<IEnumerable<Video>> GetVideos(string userId, int moduleId = 0) {
   _db.Include<Video>();

   var module = await _db.SingleAsync<Module>(m =>
      m.Id.Equals(moduleId));
   if (module == null) return default(List<Video>);

   var userCourse = await _db.SingleAsync<UserCourse>(uc =>
      uc.UserId.Equals(userId) &&
      uc.CourseId.Equals(module.Course.Id));
   if (userCourse == null) return default(List<Video>);

   return module.Videos;
}
```

Removing the Injected Service From the HomeController

Earlier, you injected the **IUIReadService** as a parameter named **db** into the **HomeController's** constructor. Now that the service is completed and tested remove the injected service from the constructor.

You will inject the **IUIReadService** into another controller that you will add in an upcoming chapter.

1. Open the **HomeController** class.
2. Remove the injected **IUIReadService** parameter from the constructor.
3. Remove the **_db** service property from the class.
4. Remove all the code that called methods in the **_db** service object.
5. Remove the **async** and **Task** keywords from the **Index** action.

Summary

In this chapter, you created a service that communicates with the database tables through the **IDbReadService** service in the **Database** project to use live data from the database in the application.

Next, you will start building a user interface.

11. The Membership Controller and AutoMapper

Introduction

In this chapter, you will create a new **Membership** controller and add its three actions: **Dashboard**, **Course**, and **Video**. For now, they won't be serving up any views. You will use them to implement the mapping between entity objects and DTO objects with Auto-Mapper, and to fetch the data for each action from the **UIReadService** you implemented in the previous chapter.

Inject AutoMapper and **IUIReadService** into the **Membership** controller's constructor. Also, inject two other objects into the constructor with dependency Injection; the first is the **UserManager**, which is used to get the user id from the logged in user, and the second is the **IHttpContextAccessor**, which contains information about the logged in user.

Using AutoMapper removes tedious and boring work, code that you otherwise would have to implement manually to convert one object to another, with the risk of writing erroneous conversion code.

Technologies Used in This Chapter

1. **C#** – Creating controller actions, view models, and mapping objects.
2. **AutoMapper** – To map entity objects to DTO objects.

Overview

You will begin by adding the **Membership** controller and its action methods. Then you will use dependency injection to inject the previously mentioned objects into the controller's constructor and save them in private class-level variables.

Then you will set up AutoMapper's configuration in the *Startup.cs* file. With that setup complete, you can proceed with the actual mappings in the action methods.

ASP.NET Core 2.2 MVC, Razor Pages, API, JSON Web Tokens & HttpClient

Adding the Membership Controller

You want to keep the membership actions separate from the **HomeController**, which handles the login and registration. To achieve this, you create the **MembershipController** class and add actions to it.

Three action methods are needed to serve up the views. The first is the **Dashboard** action, which displays the user's courses. From each course card in the **Dashboard** view, the user can click a button to open the course, using the second action method called **Course**. The **Course** view lists the content for that course. Open in the **Video** view when a user clicks a video item; the **Video** action method generates the view.

Adding the Membership Controller

1. Open the **VOD.UI** project.
2. Right click on the *Controllers* folder in the Solution Explorer and select **Add-Controller**.
3. Select the **MVC Controller – Empty** template and click the **Add** button.
4. Name the controller *MembershipController* and click the **Add** button.
5. Rename the **Index** action **Dashboard** and add the **[HttpGet]** attribute to it.
   ```
   [HttpGet]
   public IActionResult Dashboard()
   {
       return View();
   }
   ```
6. Copy the **Dashboard** action method and the attribute.
7. Paste it in twice and rename the methods **Course** and **Video**. Also, add an **int** parameter called **id** to them.
   ```
   [HttpGet]
   public IActionResult Course(int id)
   {
       return View();
   }

   [HttpGet]
   public IActionResult Video(int id)
   {
       return View();
   }
   ```
8. Add a constructor to the controller.

11. The Membership Controller and AutoMapper

```
public MembershipController() { }
```

9. Inject **IHttpContextAccessor** into the constructor and save the user from it to a variable called **user**. Resolve any missing **using** statements.
    ```
    public MembershipController(IHttpContextAccessor
    httpContextAccessor) {
        var user = httpContextAccessor.HttpContext.User;
    }
    ```

10. Inject the **UserManager** into the constructor and call its **GetUserId** method. Save the user id in a private class-level variable called **_userId**. Resolve any missing **using** statements.
    ```
    private readonly string _userId;
    public MembershipController(IHttpContextAccessor
    httpContextAccessor, UserManager<VODUser> userManager)
    {
        var user = httpContextAccessor.HttpContext.User;
        _userId = userManager.GetUserId(user);
    }
    ```

11. Inject **IMapper** into the constructor to get access to AutoMapper in the controller. Save the instance to a private, read-only, class-level variable called **_mapper**.

12. Inject the **IUIReadService** interface into the constructor and save the instance to a private class-level variable called **_db**.

The complete **MembershipController** class so far:

```
public class MembershipController : Controller
{
    private readonly string _userId;
    private readonly IMapper _mapper;
    private readonly IUIReadService _db;

    public MembershipController(
    IHttpContextAccessor httpContextAccessor,
    UserManager<VODUser> userManager, IMapper mapper, IUIReadService db)
    {
        var user = httpContextAccessor.HttpContext.User;
        _userId = userManager.GetUserId(user);
        _mapper = mapper;
        _db = db;
    }
```

115

```
    [HttpGet]
    public IActionResult Dashboard()
    {
        return View();
    }

    [HttpGet]
    public IActionResult Course(int id)
    {
        return View();
    }

    [HttpGet]
    public IActionResult Video(int id)
    {
        return View();
    }
}
```

Configuring AutoMapper

For AutoMapper to work properly, you must add configuration to the **ConfigureServices** method in the *Startup.cs* file. The configuration tells AutoMapper how to map between objects, in this case between entities and DTOs. Default mapping can be achieved by specifying the class names of the objects to be mapped, without naming specific properties. With default matching, only properties with the same name in both classes will be matched.

A more granular mapping is possible by specifying exactly which properties that match. In this scenario, the property names can be different in the classes.

1. Open the *Startup.cs* file and locate the **ConfigureServices** method.
2. Go to the end of the method and call AutoMapper's **MapperConfiguration** method. Store the result in a variable named **config** and use a parameter named **cfg** to make the entity to DTO mappings.
   `var config = new AutoMapper.MapperConfiguration(cfg => { });`
3. Add a mapping for the **Video** entity and **VideoDTO** classes inside the **config** block. Since the properties of interest are named the same in both classes, no specific configuration is necessary. Resolve any missing namespaces.
   `cfg.CreateMap<Video, VideoDTO>();`

11. The Membership Controller and AutoMapper

4. Add a mapping for the **Download** entity and the **DownloadDTO** classes inside the **cfg** block. Here specific configuration is necessary because the properties are named differently in the two classes.
   ```
   cfg.CreateMap<Download, DownloadDTO>()
       .ForMember(dest => dest.DownloadUrl,
           src => src.MapFrom(s => s.Url))
       .ForMember(dest => dest.DownloadTitle,
           src => src.MapFrom(s => s.Title));
   ```

5. Now do the same for the **Instructor**, **Course**, and **Module** entities and their DTOs. Note that there are no mappings for the **LessonInfoDTO** because we don't need any.

6. Create a variable called **mapper** below the ending curly brace for the configuration block. Assign the result from a call to the **CreateMapper** method on the previously created **config** object to the mapper variable.
   ```
   var mapper = config.CreateMapper();
   ```

7. Add the **mapper** object as a singleton instance to the **services** collection, as you did with the **IUIReadService**.
   ```
   services.AddSingleton(mapper);
   ```

8. Open the **Home** controller and replace the call to the **View** method in the **return** statement with a call to the **RedirectToAction** method and redirect to **Membership** controller's **Dashboard** action when the user is logged in.
   ```
   return RedirectToAction("Dashboard", "Membership");
   ```

9. Place a breakpoint at the return statement in all action methods in the **Membership** controller to make it possible to inspect the data returned from the method calls you will add later.

The complete AutoMapper configuration in the **ConfigurationServices** method:
```
var config = new AutoMapper.MapperConfiguration(cfg =>
{
    cfg.CreateMap<Video, VideoDTO>();

    cfg.CreateMap<Instructor, InstructorDTO>()
        .ForMember(dest => dest.InstructorName,
            src => src.MapFrom(s => s.Name))
        .ForMember(dest => dest.InstructorDescription,
            src => src.MapFrom(s => s.Description))
```

```csharp
            .ForMember(dest => dest.InstructorAvatar,
                src => src.MapFrom(s => s.Thumbnail));

        cfg.CreateMap<Download, DownloadDTO>()
            .ForMember(dest => dest.DownloadUrl,
                src => src.MapFrom(s => s.Url))
            .ForMember(dest => dest.DownloadTitle,
                src => src.MapFrom(s => s.Title));

        cfg.CreateMap<Course, CourseDTO>()
            .ForMember(dest => dest.CourseId, src =>
                src.MapFrom(s => s.Id))
            .ForMember(dest => dest.CourseTitle,
                src => src.MapFrom(s => s.Title))
            .ForMember(dest => dest.CourseDescription,
                src => src.MapFrom(s => s.Description))
            .ForMember(dest => dest.MarqueeImageUrl,
                src => src.MapFrom(s => s.MarqueeImageUrl))
            .ForMember(dest => dest.CourseImageUrl,
                src => src.MapFrom(s => s.ImageUrl));

        cfg.CreateMap<Module, ModuleDTO>()
            .ForMember(dest => dest.ModuleTitle,
                src => src.MapFrom(s => s.Title));
});

var mapper = config.CreateMapper();
services.AddSingleton(mapper);
```

Implementing Action Methods

Now that you have set everything up for object mapping with AutoMapper, it's time to utilize that functionality in the three action methods you added to the **Membership-Controller** class earlier.

The Dashboard Action Method

The **Dashboard** action will serve data to the **Dashboard** view, which you will add in a later chapter. Pass an instance of the **DashboardViewModel** class, which you created in an earlier chapter, to the view.

11. The Membership Controller and AutoMapper

The purpose of the **Dashboard** action method is to fill the **DashboardViewModel** with the appropriate data, using the **_db** database service that you added earlier. The **UIRead-Service** object was injected into the **Membership** constructor through the **IUIReadService** parameter, using dependency injection that you configured in the **ConfigureServices** method in the **Startup** class.

Your next task will be to fill the view model using AutoMapper, mapping data from the **_db** database entities to DTO objects used in views that you will add in coming chapters.

The view will be able to display as many courses as the user has access to, but only three to a row, which means that you will have to divide the list of courses into a list of lists, with three **CourseDTO** objects each; this will make it easy to loop out the cards in the view.

To refresh your memory, this is the view that this action method will be serving up.

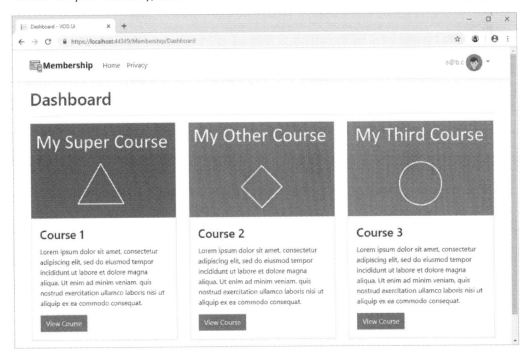

1. Open the **MembershipController** class and locate the **Dashboard** action method.
2. Replace the **IActionResult** return type to **async Task<IActionResult>** for all three actions to enable asynchronous calls.
3. Call the **Map** method on the **_mapper** variable in the **Dashboard** action method to convert the result from a call to the **GetCourses** method on the **_db** variable; don't forget to pass in the logged in user's id, not a hardcoded value. Calling the method fetches all the courses for the user and converts them into **CourseDTO** objects. Store the result in a variable named **courseDtoObjects**.
   ```
   var courseDtoObjects = _mapper.Map<List<CourseDTO>>(
       await _db.GetCourses(_userId));
   ```
4. If you haven't already, place a breakpoint on the **return** statement at the end of the **Dashboard** action method.
5. Run the application with debugging (F5).
6. The execution should halt in the **Dashboard** action method. If not, you can navigate to *http://localhost:xxxxx/Membership/Dashboard* to hit the breakpoint.
7. Inspect the **courseDtoObjects** variable to verify that it contains **CourseDTO** objects with data. If the object is empty, then log in as the user that was used to seed the database; the user information is in the **AspNetUsers** table.

11. The Membership Controller and AutoMapper

```
[HttpGet]
public async Task<IActionResult> Dashbo
{
    var courseDtoObjects = _mapper.Map<

    return View();
}
```

courseDtoObjects | Count = 3
- [0]   {VOD.Common.DTOModels.UI.CourseDTO}
- [1]   {VOD.Common.DTOModels.UI.CourseDTO}
- [2]   {VOD.Common.DTOModels.UI.CourseDTO}
- Raw View

8. Stop the application in Visual Studio.
9. Create an instance of the **DashboardViewModel** and instantiate its **Courses** property below the **courseDtoObjects** variable. Note that the **Courses** property is a list of lists, where each of the inner lists will contain a maximum of three **CourseDTO** objects, to satisfy the view's needs.

   ```
   var dashboardModel = new DashboardViewModel();
   dashboardModel.Courses = new List<List<CourseDTO>>();
   ```

10. Divide the **CourseDTOs** in the **courseDtoObjects** collection into sets of three and add them to new **List<CourseDTO>** instances.

    ```
    var noOfRows = courseDtoObjects.Count <= 3 ? 1 :
        courseDtoObjects.Count / 3;
    for (var i = 0; i < noOfRows; i++) {
        dashboardModel.Courses.Add(courseDtoObjects
            .Skip(i * 3).Take(3).ToList());
    }
    ```

11. Return the **DashboardViewModel** instance in the **View** method.

    ```
    return View(dashboardModel);
    ```

12. Make sure that the breakpoint still is on the **return** statement and start the application with debugging (F5).
13. If you aren't automatically taken to the **Dashboard** action, navigate to *http://localhost:xxxxx/Membership/Dashboard* to hit the breakpoint.

14. Inspect the **dashboardModel** variable and verify that its **Courses** property contains at least one list of **CourseDTO** objects.

```
return View(dashboardModel);
```

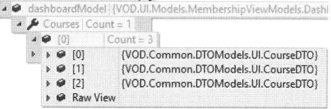

15. Stop the application in Visual Studio and remove the breakpoint.

The complete code for the **Dashboard** action:

```
[HttpGet]
public IActionResult Dashboard()
{
    var courseDtoObjects = _mapper.Map<List<CourseDTO>>(
        await _db.GetCourses(_userId));
    var dashboardModel = new DashboardViewModel();
    dashboardModel.Courses = new List<List<CourseDTO>>();

    var noOfRows = courseDtoObjects.Count <= 3 ? 1 :
        courseDtoObjects.Count / 3;

    for (var i = 0; i < noOfRows; i++)
    {
        dashboardModel.Courses.Add(courseDtoObjects
            .Skip(i * 3).Take(3).ToList());
    }

    return View(dashboardModel);
}
```

The Course Action Method

This action will serve data to the **Course** view, which you will add in a later chapter. Send an instance of the **CourseViewModel** class, which you created in a previous chapter, to the view.

The purpose of the **Course** action method is to fill an instance of the **CourseViewModel** with the appropriate data using the **_db** database service that you added earlier. The

11. The Membership Controller and AutoMapper

UIReadService was injected into the **Membership** constructor through the **IUIReadService** parameter using dependency injection, which you configured in the **ConfigureServices** method in the **Startup** class.

Your next task will be to fill the view model using AutoMapper, to map data from the **_db** entities to DTO objects used in the **Course** view that you will add in an upcoming chapter.

The view will display the selected course and its associated modules. Each module will list the videos and downloadable content associated with it. The instructor bio will also be displayed beside the module list.

To refresh your memory, this is the view that this action method will be serving up.

ASP.NET Core 2.2 MVC, Razor Pages, API, JSON Web Tokens & HttpClient

Modeule 1

Video 1 Title
🕓 50 minutes
orem ipsum dolor sit amet, consecte

Video 2 Title
🕓 45 minutes
ipsum dolor sit amet, consectetur

Video 3 Title
🕓 41 minutes
m dolor sit amet, consectetur adipi

Downloads

⬇ ADO.NET 1 (PDF)
⬇ ADO.NET 2 (PDF)

John Doe
Instructor

t amet, consectetur adipiscing elit, sed do eiusmo

11. The Membership Controller and AutoMapper

1. Open the **MembershipController** class and locate the **Course** action method.
2. Fetch the course matching the id passed into the **Course** action and the logged in user's user id, by calling the **GetCourse** method on the **_db** variable. Store the result in a variable called **course**.
   ```
   var course = await _db.GetCourse(_userId, id);
   ```
3. Call the **Map** method on the **_mapper** variable to convert the course you just fetched into a **CourseDTO** object. Store the result in a variable named **mappedCourseDTOs**.
   ```
   var mappedCourseDTO = _mapper.Map<CourseDTO>(course);
   ```
4. Call the **Map** method on the **_mapper** variable to convert the **Instructor** object in the **course** object into an **InstructorDTO** object. Store the result in a variable named **mappedInstructorDTO**.
   ```
   var mappedInstructorDTO =
   _mapper.Map<InstructorDTO>(course.Instructor);
   ```
5. Call the **Map** method on the **_mapper** variable to convert the **Modules** collection in the **course** object into a **List<ModuleDTO>**. Store the result in a variable named **mappedModuleDTOs**.
   ```
   var mappedModuleDTOs =
   _mapper.Map<List<ModuleDTO>>(course.Modules);
   ```
6. Create an instance of the **CourseViewModel** class named **courseModel**.
7. Assign the three mapped collections: **mappedCourseDTO**, **mappedInstructorDTO**, and **mappedModuleDTOs** to the **courseModel** object's **Course**, **Instructor**, and **Modules** properties.
   ```
   var courseModel = new CourseViewModel
   {
       Course = mappedCourseDTO,
       Instructor = mappedInstructorDTO,
       Modules = mappedModuleDTOs
   };
   ```
8. Return the **courseModel** object with the **View** method.
   ```
   return View(courseModel);
   ```
9. Remove the breakpoint from the **Dashboard** action.
10. Place a breakpoint on the **return** statement at the end of the **Course** action.
11. Run the application with debugging (F5).

12. Ignore the error message displayed in the browser; it is displayed because there is no Dashboard view. Replace Dashboard with *Course/1* in the URI and navigate to *http://localhost:xxxxx/Membership/Course/1* to hit the breakpoint.
13. Inspect the **courseModel** variable to verify that it contains a course, an instructor, and modules with videos and downloads.

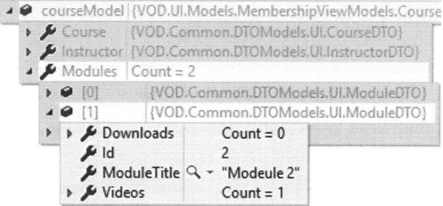

14. Stop the application in Visual Studio and remove the breakpoint.

The complete code for the **Course** action:

```
[HttpGet]
public async Task<IActionResult> Course(int id)
{
    var course = await _db.GetCourse(_userId, id);
    var mappedCourseDTO = _mapper.Map<CourseDTO>(course);
    var mappedInstructorDTO = _mapper.Map<InstructorDTO>(
        course.Instructor);
    var mappedModuleDTOs = _mapper.Map<List<ModuleDTO>>(course.Modules);

    var courseModel = new CourseViewModel
    {
        Course = mappedCourseDTO,
        Instructor = mappedInstructorDTO,
        Modules = mappedModuleDTOs
    };

    return View(courseModel);
}
```

The Video Action Method

In this action, you will create an instance of the **VideoViewModel** class you added earlier. Pass an instance of the model to the **Video** view when you add it in an upcoming chapter.

The model will be filled with appropriate data, using the **_db** database service that you added earlier. The **UIReadService** was injected into the **Membership** controller's constructor through the **IUIReadService** parameter, using dependency injection. You configured the DI in the **ConfigureServices** method in the **Startup** class.

Your next task is to fill the view model using AutoMapper; mapping data from the **_db** database entities to DTO objects used in the **Video** view.

The **Video** view will display the selected video, information about the video, buttons to select the next and previous videos, and an instructor bio.

To refresh your memory, this is the view the **Video** action will display.

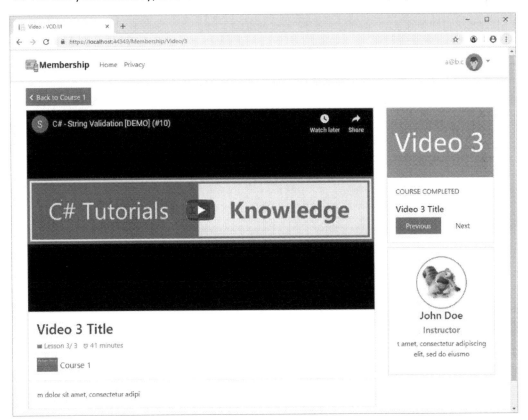

Video 1 Title

🎬 Lesson 1/ 3   ⏰ 50 minutes

 Course 1

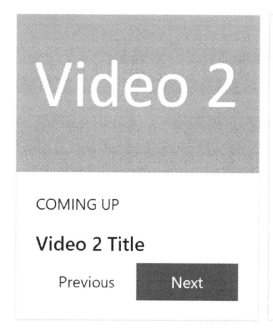

John Doe

Instructor

t amet, consectetur adipiscing elit, sed do eiusmo

1. Open the **MembershipController** class and locate the **Video** action method.
2. Call the **_db.GetVideo** method to fetch the video matching the id passed into the **Video** action, and the logged in user's id. Store the result in a variable called **video**.
   ```
   var video = await _db.GetVideo(_userId, id);
   ```
3. Call the **_db.GetCourse** method to fetch the course matching the course id from the **video** object, and the logged in user's id. Store the result in a variable called **course**.
   ```
   var course = await _db.GetCourse(_userId, video.CourseId);
   ```

11. The Membership Controller and AutoMapper

4. Call the **_mapper.Map** method to convert the **Video** object into a **VideoDTO** object. Store the result in a variable named **videoDTO**.
   ```
   var videoDTO = _mapper.Map<VideoDTO>(video);
   ```

5. Call the **_mapper.Map** method to convert the **course** object into a **CourseDTO** object. Store the result in a variable named **courseDTO**.
   ```
   var courseDTO = _mapper.Map<CourseDTO>(course);
   ```

6. Call the **_mapper.Map** method to convert the **Instructor** object in the **course** object into an **InstructorDTO** object. Store the result in a variable named **instructorDTO**.
   ```
   var instructorDTO = _mapper.Map<InstructorDTO>(
       course.Instructor);
   ```

7. Call the **_db.GetVideos** method to fetch all the videos matching the current module id. You need this data to get the number of videos in the module, and to get the index of the current video. Store the videos in a variable called **videos**.
   ```
   var videos = (await _db.GetVideos(_userId, video.ModuleId))
       .OrderBy(o => o.Id).ToList();
   ```

8. Store the number of videos in a variable called **count**.
   ```
   var count = videos.Count();
   ```

9. Find the index of the current video in the module video list. You will display the index and the video count to the user, in the view. Store the value in a variable called **index**.
   ```
   var index = videos.FindIndex(v => v.Id.Equals(id));
   ```

10. Fetch the id for the previous video in the module by calling the **ElementAtOrDefault** method on the **videos** collection. Store its id in a variable called **previousId**.
    ```
    var previous = videos.ElementAtOrDefault(index - 1);
    var previousId = previous == null ? 0 : previous.Id;
    ```

11. Fetch the id, title, and thumbnail for the next video in the module by calling the **ElementAtOrDefault** method on the **videos** collection. Store the values in variables called **nextId**, **nextTitle**, and **nextThumb**.
    ```
    var next = videos.ElementAtOrDefault(index + 1);
    var nextId = next == null ? 0 : next.Id;
    var nextTitle = next == null ? string.Empty : next.Title;
    var nextThumb = next == null ? string.Empty : next.Thumbnail;
    ```

12. Create an instance of the **VideoViewModel** class named **videoModel**.
    ```
    var videoModel = new VideoViewModel { };
    ```
13. Assign the three mapped collections: **mappedCourseDTO**, **mappedInstructorDTO**, and **mappedVideoDTOs** to the **videoModel** object's **Course**, **Instructor**, and **Video** properties. Create an instance of the **LessonInfoDTO** for the **LessonInfo** property in the **videoModel** object and assign the variable values to its properties. The **LessonInfoDTO** will be used with the previous and next buttons, and to display the index of the current video.
    ```
    var videoModel = new VideoViewModel
    {
        Video = videoDTO,
        Instructor = instructorDTO,
        Course = courseDTO,
        LessonInfo = new LessonInfoDTO
        {
            LessonNumber = index + 1,
            NumberOfLessons = count,
            NextVideoId = nextId,
            PreviousVideoId = previousId,
            NextVideoTitle = nextTitle,
            NextVideoThumbnail = nextThumb
        }
    };
    ```
14. Return the **videoModel** object with the **View** method.
    ```
    return View(videoModel);
    ```
15. Place a breakpoint on the return statement at the end of the **Video** action.
16. Run the application with debugging (F5).
17. Navigate to *http://localhost:xxxxx/Membership/Video/1* to hit the breakpoint.
18. Inspect the **videoModel** object to verify that it contains a video, a course, an instructor, and a lesson info object.

    ```
    return View(videoModel);
    ```
▲ ● videoModel	{VOD.UI.Models.MembershipViewModels.VideoVie|
▶ 🔑 Course	{VOD.Common.DTOModels.UI.CourseDTO}
▶ 🔑 Instructor	{VOD.Common.DTOModels.UI.InstructorDTO}
▶ 🔑 LessonInfo	{VOD.Common.DTOModels.UI.LessonInfoDTO}
▶ 🔑 Video	{VOD.Common.DTOModels.UI.VideoDTO}

19. Stop the application in Visual Studio and remove the breakpoint.

11. The Membership Controller and AutoMapper

The complete code for the **Video** action:

```
[HttpGet]
public async Task<IActionResult> Video(int id)
{
    var video = await _db.GetVideo(_userId, id);
    var course = await _db.GetCourse(_userId, video.CourseId);
    var videoDTO = _mapper.Map<VideoDTO>(video);
    var courseDTO = _mapper.Map<CourseDTO>(course);
    var instructorDTO = _mapper.Map<InstructorDTO>(course.Instructor);

    var videos = (await _db.GetVideos(_userId, video.ModuleId))
        .OrderBy(o => o.Id).ToList();
    var count = videos.Count();
    var index = videos.FindIndex(v => v.Id.Equals(id));

    var previous = videos.ElementAtOrDefault(index - 1);
    var previousId = previous == null ? 0 : previous.Id;

    var next = videos.ElementAtOrDefault(index + 1);
    var nextId = next == null ? 0 : next.Id;
    var nextTitle = next == null ? string.Empty : next.Title;
    var nextThumb = next == null ? string.Empty : next.Thumbnail;

    var videoModel = new VideoViewModel
    {
        Video = videoDTO,
        Instructor = instructorDTO,
        Course = courseDTO,
        LessonInfo = new LessonInfoDTO
        {
            LessonNumber = index + 1,
            NumberOfLessons = count,
            NextVideoId = nextId,
            PreviousVideoId = previousId,
            NextVideoTitle = nextTitle,
            NextVideoThumbnail = nextThumb
        }
    };

    return View(videoModel);
}
```

Summary

In this chapter, you added configuration for entity and DTO classes to AutoMapper in the **Startup** class. You also implemented the **Membership** controller and injected the necessary services into its constructor. Then you implemented the three actions (**Dashboard**, **Course**, and **Video**) that render their corresponding views in coming chapters.

Next, you will implement the **Dashboard** view, and render it from the **Dashboard** action.

12. The Dashboard View

Introduction
In this chapter, the **Dashboard** action in the **Membership** controller will render a view with the same name as the action located in a folder named *Views/Membership*. The **Dashboard** view is the first view the user sees after logging in; it lists all the user's courses.

The courses are displayed three to a row, to make them the optimal size.

Technologies Used in This Chapter
1. **HTML** – To create the view's layout.
2. **CSS** – To style the view.
3. **Razor** – To use C# in the view.

Overview
Your task is to use the view model in the **Dashboard** action to render a view that displays the user's courses in a list. Display each course as a card with the course image, title, description, and a button that opens the **Course** view for that course.

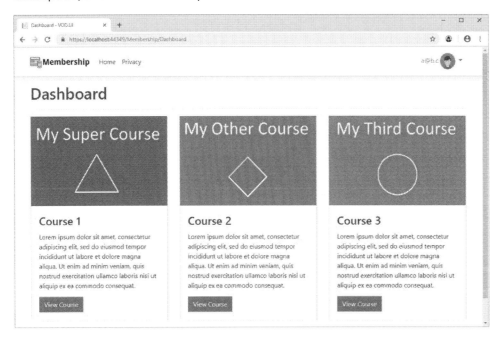

Implementing the Dashboard View

First, you will add the **Dashboard** view to the *Views/Membership* folder. Then you will add HTML to the view, displaying the courses as cards. Iterate over the courses in the view model and render each card with a partial view named **_CourseCardPartial**.

Adding the membership.css Style Sheet

To style the **Dashboard**, **Course**, and **Video** views and their partial views, you need to add a CSS style sheet called *membership.css* to the *wwwroot/css* folder and a link to the file in the **_Layout** view.

1. Right click on the *wwwroot/css* folder and select **Add-New Item**.
2. Select the **Style Sheet** template and name the file *membership.css*.
3. Click the **Add** button to create the file.
4. Open the **_Layout** view and add a link to the file below the other membership stylesheets.
   `<link rel="stylesheet" href="~/css/membership.css" />`
5. Remove the **body** selector in the *membership.css* file.

12. The Dashboard View

6. Add a class selector named **no-border-radius** that sets the radius to **0**. Use this selector on elements that should have a square look (no rounded corners).
   ```
   .no-border-radius {
       border-radius:0;
   }
   ```

7. Add a class selector named **no-left-padding** that sets the left padding to **0**. This selector will be used to remove any undesired left padding on elements.
   ```
   .no-left-padding {
       padding-left: 0;
   }
   ```

8. Add a class selector named **no-right-padding** that sets the right padding to **0**. This selector will be used to remove any undesired right padding on elements.
   ```
   .no-right-padding {
       padding-right: 0;
   }
   ```

9. Add a class selector named **no-top-padding** that sets the top padding to **0**. This selector will be used to remove any undesired top padding on elements.
   ```
   .no-top-padding {
       padding-top: 0;
   }
   ```

10. Add a class selector named **no-bottom-padding** that sets the bottom padding to **0**. This selector will be used to remove any undesired bottom padding on elements.
    ```
    .no-bottom-padding {
        padding-bottom: 0;
    }
    ```

11. Add a class selector named **vertical-align** that sets the vertical align to **middle** to center the content vertically.
    ```
    .vertical-align {
        vertical-align: middle;
    }
    ```

12. Add a class selector named **small-bottom-margin** that adds a 10px bottom margin to the element.
    ```
    .small-bottom-margin{
        margin-bottom:10px;
    }
    ```

13. Add a class selector named **small-top-margin** that adds a 10px top margin to the element.
    ```
    .small-top-margin{
        margin-top:10px;
    }
    ```
14. Add a class selector named **small-left-margin** that adds a 10px left margin to the element.
    ```
    .small-left-margin{
        margin-left:10px;
    }
    ```
15. Add a class selector named **no-margin** that removes all margins from the element.
    ```
    .no-margin{
        margin:0;
    }
    ```
16. Add a class selector named **text-small** that scales down the text.
    ```
    .text-small {
        font-size:small;
    }
    ```
17. Add a class selector named **text-large** that scales up the text.
    ```
    .text-large {
        font-size:larger;
    }
    ```
18. Add a class selector named **no-text-decoration** that removes any decoration from the element, such as underlining on anchor tags.
    ```
    .no-text-decoration {
        text-decoration:none;
    }
    ```
19. Add a class selector named **overflow-hidden** that forces the content to fit into its container.
    ```
    .overflow-hidden{
        overflow:hidden;
    }
    ```
20. Save the files.

12. The Dashboard View

Adding the Dashboard View

The **Dashboard** view must reside in a folder named *Membership* located inside the *Views* folder. Convention states that a view must have the same name as the action displaying it, and it must be placed in a folder with the same name as the controller, inside the *Views* folder.

1. Open the **Membership** controller.
2. Right click on, or in, the **Dashboard** action and select **Add View** in the context menu.
3. You can keep the preselected values and click the **Add** button; this will add the necessary *Membership* folder to the *Views* folder and scaffold the **Dashboard** view.

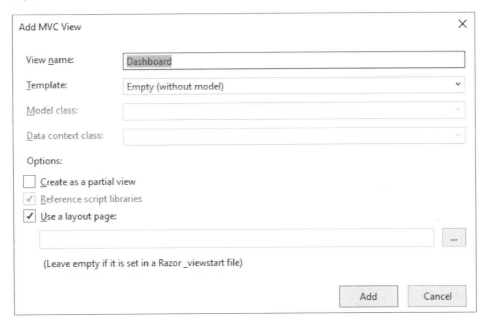

4. Open the *Views* folder and verify that the *Membership* folder and **Dashboard** view exists.
5. Visual Studio can get confused when a view is scaffolded, and display errors that aren't real. Close the view and open it again to get rid of those errors.

6. Open the **_ViewImports** view and add a **using** statement for the **VOD.UI.Models.MembershipViewModels** namespace, to get access to the **DashboardViewModel** class.
   ```
   @using VOD.UI.Models.MembershipViewModels
   ```

7. Add an **@model** directive for the **DashboardViewModel** class at the beginning of the view.
   ```
   @model DashboardViewModel
   ```

8. Open the **HomeController** class and locate the **Index** action.

9. Since we won't be using cookies, you can comment out the **UseCookiePolicy** method in the **Configure** method in the **Startup** class; it activates the cookie middleware in the HTTP request pipeline.
   ```
   //app.UseCookiePolicy();
   ```

10. Also comment out the cookie configuration in the **ConfigureServices** method in the **Startup** class that displays the cookie message in the browser.
    ```
    //services.Configure<CookiePolicyOptions>(options =>
    //{
    //    options.CheckConsentNeeded = context => true;
    //    options.MinimumSameSitePolicy = SameSiteMode.None;
    //});
    ```

11. Start the application without debugging (Ctrl+F5) and log in if necessary. The text *Dashboard* should be displayed in the browser if the **Dashboard** view was rendered correctly.

The markup in the **Dashboard** view:

```
@model DashboardViewModel

@{
    ViewData["Title"] = "Dashboard";
}

<h1>Dashboard</h1>
```

Iterate Over the Courses in the Dashboard View

To display the courses three to a row, you must add two **foreach** loops to the view. The outer loop iterates over the **Courses** collection (the parent collection) to create the rows, and the inner loop iterates over the (three) courses on each row.

12. The Dashboard View

For now, the view will only display a view title and the course titles; later the courses will be displayed as cards.

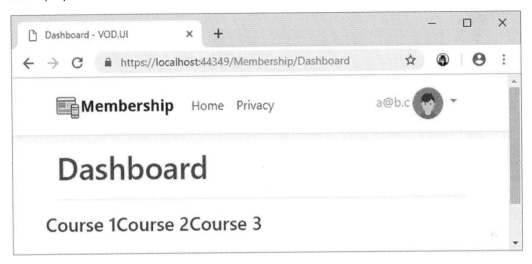

1. Add a horizontal line below the <h1> element.
   ```
   <hr>
   ```
2. Add a **foreach** loop, below the <hr> element, that iterates over the **Course** collection in the view model. This loop represents the rows containing the course cards, where each row should have at most three courses.
   ```
   @foreach (var dashboardRow in Model.Courses) { }
   ```
3. Add a <div> inside the loop and decorate it with the **row** Bootstrap class. The **row** class will style the <div> as a new row in the browser.
   ```
   <div class="row">
   </div>
   ```
4. Add a **foreach** loop inside the <div> that iterates over the (three) courses on that row. For now, add an <h4> element displaying the course title.
   ```
   @foreach (var course in dashboardRow)
   {
       <h4>@course.CourseTitle</h4>
   }
   ```
5. Switch to the browser and refresh the **Dashboard** view (*/membership/dashboard*). Display the course titles below the view's title.

ASP.NET Core 2.2 MVC, Razor Pages, API, JSON Web Tokens & HttpClient

The markup in the **Dashboard** view, so far:

```
@model DashboardViewModel

@{
    ViewData["Title"] = "Dashboard";
}

<h1>Dashboard</h1>
<hr>
@foreach (var dashboardRow in Model.Courses)
{
    <div class="row">
        @foreach (var course in dashboardRow)
        {
            <h4>@course.CourseTitle</h4>
        }
    </div>
}
```

Creating the _CourseCardPartial Partial View

Instead of cluttering the **Dashboard** view with the course card markup, you will create and render a partial view called **_CourseCardPartial** for each course. A Bootstrap **card** will be used to display the course information.

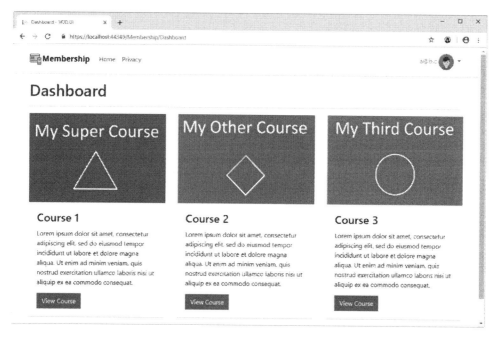

12. The Dashboard View

1. Right click on the *Views/Membership* folder and select **Add-View**.
2. Name the view **_CourseCardPartial** and check the **Create as a partial view** checkbox before clicking the **Add** button.

3. Delete all code in the view.
4. Open the **_ViewImports** view and add a **using** statement for the **VOD.Common.DTOModels.UI** namespace if you haven't already added it. Save the file and close it.
   ```
   @using VOD.Common.DTOModels.UI
   ```
5. Add an **@model** directive for the **CourseDTO** class to the partial view.
   ```
   @model CourseDTO
   ```
6. Add a <div> element and decorate it with the **col-sm-4** Bootstrap class, to give it 1/3 of the row space. The **col-sm-** classes should add up to 12 for each row, and since three courses are added to each row, that is fulfilled.
   ```
   <div class="col-sm-4">
   </div>
   ```
7. Add a <div> inside the previous <div> and decorate it with the Bootstrap **card** class to style it as a card, the outer most container for the course information.

Also, add the **no-border-radius** CSS class from the *membership.css* file to give it square corners.
```
<div class="card no-border-radius">
</div>
```

8. Add an <img> element to the previous <div> and decorate it with a Bootstrap class called **card-img-top** and the **no-border-radius** CSS class to give it square corners. The class will be used when styling the image. Add the **CourseImageUrl** property in the view model as the image source.
```
<img class="card-img-top no-border-radius"
src="@Model.CourseImageUrl">
```

9. Add a <div> element below the image and decorate it with the **card-body** Bootstrap class. This is the area where the video information is displayed.
```
<div class="card-body">
</div>
```

10. Add an <h3> element in the previous <div> and decorate it with a Bootstrap class named **card-title**. Add the **CourseTitle** property in the view model to it.
```
<h3 class="card-title">@Model.CourseTitle</h3>
```

11. Add a <p> element for the **CourseDescription** view model property below the <h3> element. Add the Bootstrap class **card-text** to the element.
```
<p class="card-text">@Model.CourseDescription</p>
```

12. Add an <a> element below the description and style it as a blue button with the **btn btn-primary** Bootstrap classes. Also, add the **no-border-radius** CSS class to give it square corners. Use the **CourseId** view model property in the **href** URL to determine which course will be fetched by the **Course** action and displayed by the **Course** view. Add the text *View Course* to the button.
```
<a class="btn btn-primary no-border-radius"
href="~/Membership/Course/@Model.CourseId">View Course</a>
```

13. Open the **Dashboard** view.
14. Replace the <h4> element with the <partial> Tag Helper, or with a call to the older **PartialAsync** method, that will render the **_CourseCardPartial** partial view for each course.
```
@foreach (var course in dashboardRow)
{
    <partial name="_CourseCardPartial" model="@course" />
```

12. The Dashboard View

```
        @*@await Html.PartialAsync("_CourseCardPartial", course)*@
    }
```

15. Save all files and refresh the **Dashboard** view in the browser.
16. Stop the application in Visual Studio.

The complete markup for the **_CourseCardPartial** partial view:

```
@model CourseDTO
<div class="col-sm-4">
    <div class="card no-border-radius">
        <img class="card-img-top no-border-radius"
            src="@Model.CourseImageUrl">
        <div class="card-body">
            <h3 class="card-title">@Model.CourseTitle</h3>
            <p class="card-text">@Model.CourseDescription</p>
            <a class="btn btn-primary no-border-radius"
                href="~/Membership/Course/@Model.CourseId">View Course
            </a>
        </div>
    </div>
</div>
```

Summary

In this chapter, you added the **Dashboard** view and the **_CourseCardPartial** partial view and styled them with Bootstrap and your own CSS.

Next, you will add the **Course** view and the **_ModuleVideosPartial**, **_ModuleDownloadsPartial**, and **_InstructorBioPartial** partial views that are part of the **Course** view. Then you will style them with CSS and Bootstrap.

ASP.NET Core 2.2 MVC, Razor Pages, API, JSON Web Tokens & HttpClient

13. The Course View

Introduction

In this chapter, you will add the **Course** view and three partial views called **_Module-VideosPartial**, **_ModuleDownloadsPartial**, and **_InstructorBioPartial** that are part of the **Course** view. As you add view and partial view content, you style it with CSS and Bootstrap. The **Course** view is displayed when the user clicks one of the **Dashboard** view's course card buttons. The view contains information about the selected course and has module lists containing all the videos belonging to that course. Display the instructor's bio beside the module lists. You will also add a button at the top of the view that takes the user back to the **Dashboard** view.

Technologies Used in This Chapter

1. **HTML** – To create the view's layout.
2. **CSS** – To style the view.
3. **Razor** – To use C# in the view.

Overview

Your task is to use the view model in the **Course** action and render a view that displays a marquee, course image, title, and description as a separate row below the **Back to Dashboard** button at the top of the view. Below that row, a second row divided into two columns should be displayed. Add rows in the left column for each module in the course and list the videos for each module. Display the instructor's bio in the right column.

ASP.NET Core 2.2 MVC, Razor Pages, API, JSON Web Tokens & HttpClient

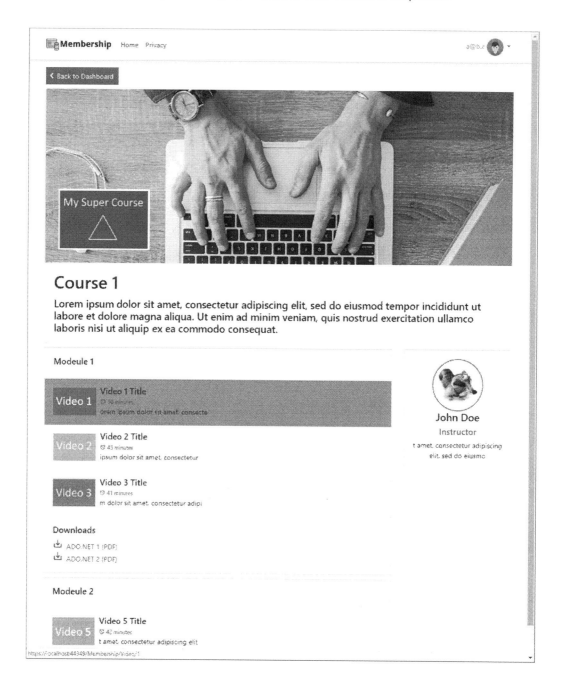

13. The Course View

Adding the Course View

First, you will add the **Course** view to the *Views/Membership* folder.

Then, you will add a button that navigates to the **Dashboard** view, a marquee image, course information, an instructor bio, and modules with videos and downloads. You will create three partial views, one called **_InstructorBioPartial** for the instructor bio, one called **_ModuleVideosPartial** for the videos, and one called **_ModuleDownloadsPartial** for downloads. Style the three areas with Bootstrap and CSS.

1. Open the **Membership** controller.
2. Right click on the **Course** action and select **Add-View**.
3. Make sure that the **Create as partial view** checkbox is unchecked.
4. Click the **Add** button to create the view.

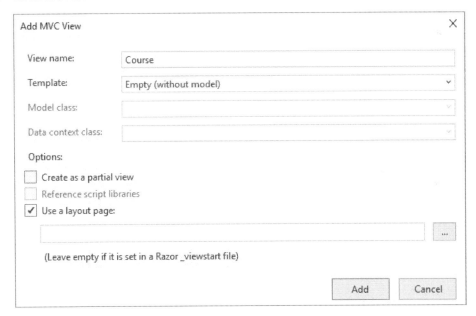

5. Close the **Course** view and open it again to get rid of any errors.
6. Add an **@model** directive for the **CourseViewModel** class at the beginning of the view.
   `@model CourseViewModel`
7. Save all the files.

8. Start the application without debugging (Ctrl+F5) and navigate to *Membership/Dashboard*. Open a course by clicking on one of the cards or navigate to the *Membership/Course/1* URL. The **Course** view displays the text *Course* in the browser.

The markup in the **Course** view, so far:

```
@model CourseViewModel

@{
    ViewData["Title"] = "Course";
}

<h1>Course</h1>
```

Adding the Back to Dashboard Button

Now, you will add the button that takes the user back to the **Dashboard** view. Place the button inside a <div> decorated with two CSS classes named **row** and **small-bottom-margin**.

Place the button on a separate row that takes up the entire page width. Add the **row** and **col-sm-12** Bootstrap classes to two nested <div> elements to add the row and the column.

1. Open the **Course** view.
2. Remove the <h1> heading.
3. Add a row with a <div> element and decorate it with the **row** Bootstrap class. Also, add a CSS class called **small-bottom-margin** from the *membership.css* file that adds a small margin below the button that you will add.
   ```
   <div class="row small-bottom-margin">
   </div>
   ```
4. Add the column with a <div> element, place it inside the previous <div>, and decorate it with the **col-sm-12** Bootstrap class to make it as wide as possible.
   ```
   <div class="col-sm-12">
   </div>
   ```
5. Add a blue button using an <a> element, place it inside the previous <div>, and decorate it with the **btn** and **btn-primary** Bootstrap classes, and the **no-border-radius** and **no-left-padding** CSS classes that you added earlier to the

13. The Course View

membership.css file. Add **Dashboard** to an **asp-action** attribute to specify which **Membership** controller action to target.

```
<a class="btn btn-primary no-border-radius no-left-padding"
asp-action="Dashboard"></a>
```

6. Add a <i> element inside the <a> element and decorate it with the **material-icons** class and the icon name *keyboard_arrow_left* inside the tag to add a caret (<) icon. Also, add the **vertical-align** and **no-left-margin** classes to center the chevron vertically and remove the left margin.

    ```
    <i class="material-icons vertical-align no-left-margin">
    keyboard_arrow_left</i>
    ```

7. Add a <span> with the text *Back to Dashboard* after the <i> tag in the <a> element. If you place the <i> and <span> side-by-side on the same row without a space, the button text will get closer to the icon. Add the **vertical-align** class to center the chevron vertically.

    ```
    <span class="vertical-align">Back to Dashboard</span>
    ```

8. Save the view and refresh it in the browser. A blue button with the text < *Back to Dashboard* should be visible at the top of the view.
9. Click the button to navigate to the **Dashboard** view.
10. Click the button in one of the cards in the **Dashboard** view to get back to the **Course** view.

The markup in the **Course** view, so far:

```
@model CourseViewModel

@{
    ViewData["Title"] = "Course";
}

<div class="row small-bottom-margin">
    <div class="col-sm-12">
        <a class="btn btn-primary no-border-radius no-left-padding"
          asp-action="Dashboard">
            <i class="material-icons vertical-align no-left-margin">
                keyboard_arrow_left</i>
            <span class="vertical-align">Back to Dashboard</span>
        </a>
    </div>
</div>
```

Adding the Course Information to the View

Now, you will add markup for the course information card and style it with Bootstrap and CSS.

Place the card on a separate row that takes up the entire page width. Add the Bootstrap **row** and **col-sm-12** classes to two nested <div> elements; this will create a row and a column. Use the **card** and **card-body** Bootstrap classes to style the card <div> elements.

Use a <div> to display the marquee image as a background image inside the card.

Add the course title as an <h1> element and the course description as an <h4> element inside the **card-body** <div>.

1. Open the **Course** view.
2. Add three nested <div> elements below the previous **row** <div>. Decorate the first <div> with the Bootstrap **row** class, the second with the **col-sm-12** class, and the third with the **card** class and the **no-border-radius** class to give the container square corners.

```
<div class="row">
    <div class="col-sm-12">
        <div class="card no-border-radius">
        </div>
    </div>
</div>
```

13. The Course View

3. Add a `<div>` inside the **card** `<div>` and decorate it with a CSS class called **marquee**. Add the **background-image** style to it and use the **Course.MarqueeImageUrl** property to get the course's marquee image. Call the **url** method to ensure a correctly formatted URL.

   ```
   <div class="marquee" style="background-image:
       url('@Model.Course.MarqueeImageUrl');">
   </div>
   ```

4. Add an `<img>` element for the **Course.CourseImageUrl** property inside the **marquee** `<div>`.

   ```
   <div class="marquee" style="background-image:
       url('@Model.Course.MarqueeImageUrl');">
       <img src="@Model.Course.CourseImageUrl">
   </div>
   ```

5. Add a `<div>` below the **marquee** `<div>` inside the **card** `<div>`. Decorate it with the **card-body** Bootstrap class. This is the area where the course title and description are displayed.

   ```
   <div class="card-body">
   </div>
   ```

6. Add an `<h1>` element for the **Course.CourseTitle** property inside the **card-body** `<div>` and decorate it with the **card-title** Bootstrap class.

7. And an `<h4>` element for the **Course.CourseDescription** property inside the **card-body** `<div>` and decorate it with the **card-text** Bootstrap class.

8. Save all files and switch to the browser and refresh the view.

The markup for the course information row in the **Course** view:

```
<div class="row">
    <div class="col-sm-12">
        <div class="card no-border-radius">
            <div class="marquee" style="background-image:url(
                '@Model.Course.MarqueeImageUrl');">
                <img src="@Model.Course.CourseImageUrl">
            </div>
            <div class="card-body">
                <h1 class="card-title">@Model.Course.CourseTitle</h1>
                <h4 class="card-text">
                    @Model.Course.CourseDescription
                </h4>
            </div>
```

```
        </div>
    </div>
</div>
```

Styling the Course Information Section

Now, you will style the course information card with Bootstrap and CSS. Save the CSS file after adding each selector and refresh the browser to see the changes. You might have to clear the browser history for the CSS to take effect.

Open the *membership.css* file and style the cover image by making its width automatic and the height 140px. Use absolute positioning to place the image at the bottom of the marquee. Add a 30px margin to move the image away from the marquee borders. Add a 4px solid white border around the image and give it a subtle border radius of 2px.

```css
.card .marquee img {
    width: auto;
    height: 140px;
    position: absolute;
    bottom: 0;
    margin: 30px;
    border: 4px solid #FFF;
    border-radius: 2px;
}
```

Now, style the marquee. Make it cover the entire width of its container, give it a height of 400px, and hide any overflow. The marquee position must be relative for the course image to be positioned correctly. Make the background image cover the entire available space.

```css
.card .marquee {
    width: 100%;
    height: 400px;
    overflow: hidden;
    background-size: cover;
    /* Relative positioning of the marquee is needed for the cover
       image's absolute position */
    position: relative;
}
```

Adding Columns for the Modules and the Instructor Bio

Before you can add the modules and the instructor bio, you need to create a new row divided into two columns, below the previous closing **row** </div>. Add the **row, col-sm-9**, and **col-sm-3** Bootstrap classes to nested <div> elements, to create the row and columns.

1. Open the **Course** view and add a <div> element decorated with the **row** Bootstrap class below the previous closing **row** </div> containing the marquee.
   ```
   <div class="row"></div>
   ```

2. Add two <div> elements inside the **row** <div>. Decorate the first <div> with the **col-sm-9** Bootstrap class, and the second with the **col-sm-3** class. This will make the first column take up ¾ of the row width and the second column ¼ of the row width.
   ```
   <div class="col-md-9">
       @*Add modules here*@
   </div>
   <div class="col-md-3">
       @*Add instructor bio here*@
   </div>
   ```

The markup for the new row and columns in the **Course** view:

```
<div class="row">
    <div class="col-sm-9">@*Add modules here*@</div>
    <div class="col-sm-3">@*Add instructor bio here*@</div>
</div>
```

Adding the Modules

Add the modules that the videos and downloads are associated with to display them. The modules should be displayed below the marquee and take up ¾ of the row width. Use Razor to add a **foreach** loop that iterates over the **Modules** collection in the view model and adds a Bootstrap **card** for each module. Display the **ModuleTitle** for each module in the **card-body** section.

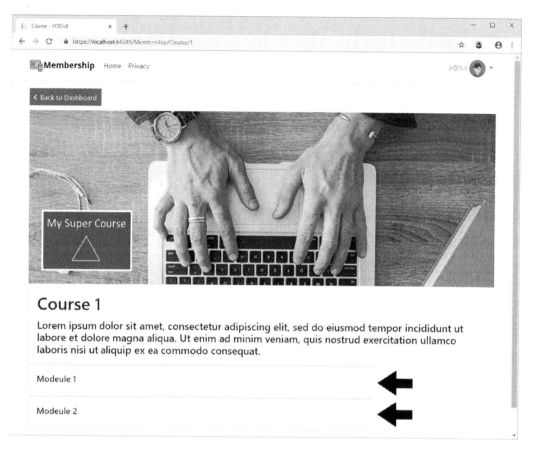

1. Open the **Course** view.
2. Locate the <div> decorated with the **col-sm-9** Bootstrap class and add a **foreach** loop, which iterates over the view model's **Modules** collection.
   ```
   @foreach (var module in Model.Modules)
   {
   }
   ```
3. Add a <div> decorated with the Bootstrap **card** class inside the loop to create a module container for each module in the collection; it will be the parent container for the card's intrinsic elements. Then, add the **small-top-margin** class from the *membership.css* file to add a top margin to all modules, which will add vertical space between them, and the **no-border-radius** class to give the modules square corners.
   ```
   <div class="card small-top-margin no-border-radius"></div>
   ```

4. Add a <div> inside the **card** <div> and decorate it with the **card-body** Bootstrap class. Add an <h5> element containing the **ModuleTitle** property.
   ```
   <div class="card-body">
       <h5>@module.ModuleTitle</h5>
   </div>
   ```
5. Add a horizontal rule below the previous <div> and add the CSS class **no-margin** to remove any margin that is applied to the <hr> element by default.
   ```
   <hr class="no-margin">
   ```
6. Save the files and refresh the browser. The module titles for the course you selected should be listed below the marquee.

The markup for the module cards:
```
<div class="col-sm-9">
    @foreach (var module in Model.Modules)
    {
        <div class="card small-top-margin no-border-radius">
            <div class="card-body">
                <h5>@module.ModuleTitle</h5>
            </div>
            <hr class="no-margin">
        </div>
    }
</div>
```

Adding the Videos

To display the video items for the modules, you will create a partial view called **_Module-VideosPartial** that will be rendered for each video. Pass in the **Video** collection from the current module in the **Course** view's **foreach** loop, to the partial view.

ASP.NET Core 2.2 MVC, Razor Pages, API, JSON Web Tokens & HttpClient

Modeule 1

Video 1 Title
30 minutes
orem ipsum dolor sit amet, consecte

Video 2 Title
45 minutes
ipsum dolor sit amet, consectetur

Video 3 Title
41 minutes
m dolor sit amet, consectetur adipi

Modeule 2

Video 5 Title
42 minutes
t amet, consectetur adipiscing elit

Use the Bootstrap **media** classes to display the video information in a uniform way.

1. Add a partial view called **_ModuleVideosPartial** to the *Views/Membership* folder and delete all its code.
2. Open the **Course** view.
3. Add an if-block below the previously added <hr> element in the **Course** view that checks that the current module's **Videos** collection isn't **null** or empty. Pass in the **Video** collection from the current module to the <partial> Tag Helper that renders the partial view and displays the videos.
   ```
   @if (module.Videos != null && module.Videos.Count > 0)
   {
       <partial name="_ModuleVideosPartial" model="@module.Videos" />
   }
   ```
4. Open the **_ModuleVideosPartial** view.
5. Add an **@model** directive to an **IEnumerable<VideoDTO>**.
   ```
   @model IEnumerable<VideoDTO>
   ```

13. The Course View

6. Add a **foreach** loop that iterates over the view model.
   ```
   @foreach (var video in Model)
   {
   }
   ```

7. Add a <div> element decorated with the **card-body** Bootstrap class and a CSS class called **module-video**, inside the loop. The CSS class will be used for styling later. The <div> will be a container for a single video.
   ```
   <div class="card-body module-video">
   </div>
   ```

8. Add an <a> element with an **href** attribute, inside the previously added <div>, that opens a specific video in the **Video** view that you will add later. Use the current video's **Id** property to target the correct video in the **href**. Add the current video's **Title** property to the <a> element. Add the **no-text-decoration** CSS class to remove any decorations, such as underlines, from the element.
   ```
   <a href="~/Membership/Video/@video.Id" class="no-text-decoration">
       @video.Title
   </a>
   ```

9. Save all files and refresh the **Course** view in the browser. Each module should now have its videos listed as links. The links will not work because you haven't added the **Video** view yet.

10. Replace the **Title** property with a <div> decorated with the **media** Bootstrap class. This will format the content in a specific way, displaying an image to the left and a block of information to the right.
    ```
    <div class="media">
    </div>
    ```

11. Add the left (image) area to the **media** <div> by adding a <div> decorated with the **media-left** Bootstrap class. Add an additional Bootstrap class called **hidden-xs**, which will hide this <div> if the site is viewed on a smartphone or a small handheld device. You typically don't want to send large images to smartphones because they tend to take a long time to load. Add the **overflow-hidden** CSS class to force the content to fit the <div>.
    ```
    <div class="media-left hidden-xs overflow-hidden">
    </div>
    ```

12. Add the video thumbnail to the previous <div> and use the image URL in the current video's **Thumbnail** property for the <img> element's **src** property. Set the image width to 100.
    ```
    <img src="@video.Thumbnail" width="100">
    ```
13. Add a <div> decorated with the **media-body** Bootstrap class below the **media-left** <div>. This will be the (right) video information area.
    ```
    <div class="media-body">
    </div>
    ```
14. Add an <h5> element for the video title inside the **media-body** <div>. Add the view model's **Title** property to the element. Add the **no-margin** CSS class to remove any margins from the heading.
    ```
    <h5 class="no-margin">@video.Title</h5>
    ```
15. Add a <p> element decorated with the **no-margin** and **text-muted** below the title. The latter class will display the video's duration and icon with a muted font. Add an <i> element with an alarm icon; use the **material-icons** class and add the text *alarm* inside the <i> element. Add the duration from the current video's **Duration** property followed by the text *minutes* inside a <span> element after the <i> element. Add the **vertical-align** and **text-small** CSS classes to both the <i> and <span> elements.
    ```
    <p class="text-muted no-margin">
        <i class="material-icons vertical-align text-small">alarm</i>
        <span class="vertical-align text-small">
          @video.Duration minutes</span>
    </p>
    ```
16. Add the video description in a <p> element below the duration; use the current video's **Description** property. Add the **no-margin** CSS class to the element.
    ```
    <p class="no-margin">@video.Description</p>
    ```
17. When you refresh the **Course** view in the browser, you'll see that the video items need some additional styling, which you will do next.

Next, you will style the partial view.

The complete markup for the **_ModuleVideosPartial** view:

```
@model IEnumerable<VideoDTO>

@foreach (var video in Model)
{
    <div class="card-body module-video">
        <a href="~/Membership/Video/@video.Id"
          class="no-text-decoration">
            <div class="media">
                <div class="media-left hidden-xs overflow-hidden">
                    <img src="@video.Thumbnail" width="100">
                </div>
                <div class="media-body small-left-margin text-dark">
                    <h5 class="no-margin">@video.Title</h5>
                    <p class="text-muted no-margin">
                        <i class="material-icons vertical-align
                           text-small">alarm</i>
                        <span class="vertical-align text-small">
                        @video.Duration minutes</span>
                    </p>
                    <p class="no-margin">@video.Description</p>
                </div>
            </div>
        </a>
    </div>
}
```

Styling the _ModuleVideosPartial View
Use the *membership.css* file when styling the **_ModuleVideosPartial** view.

Change the background color to blue when hovering over a video item.

```
.module-video:hover {
    background-color: #5ab3ff;
}
```

Remove any text decoration from the link when hovering over a video item.

```
.module-video a:hover {
    text-decoration: none;
}
```

ASP.NET Core 2.2 MVC, Razor Pages, API, JSON Web Tokens & HttpClient

Add 5px space between the image and the text.

```
.module-video .media-body {
    margin-left: 5px;
}
```

Push the title up 5px to align it with the top of the thumbnail image.

```
.module-video h5 {
    margin-top: -5px;
}
```

Adding the Downloads

To display the downloads in each module, you will create a partial view called **_Module-DownloadsPartial** and render it for each download link. Pass in the **Downloads** collection from the current module in the **Course** view's **foreach** loop, to the partial view.

Use the Bootstrap **card** classes to display the download information uniformly.

13. The Course View

1. Add a partial view called **_ModuleDownloadsPartial** to the *Views/Membership* folder and remove all code in it.
2. Open the **Course** view.
3. Add an if-block, checking that the current module's **Downloads** collection isn't **null** or empty, below the *videos* if-block.
   ```
   @if (module.Downloads != null && module.Downloads.Count > 0)
   {
   }
   ```
4. Add a horizontal line inside the if-block for the **Downloads** collection and decorate it with a CSS class called **no-margin** that will be used later to remove the element's margin.
   ```
   <hr class="no-margin">
   ```
5. Add a <div> decorated with the **card-body** Bootstrap class below the <hr> element inside the if-block. Add the **no-bottom-padding** CSS class to it to remove any padding at the bottom of the element.
   ```
   <div class="card-body no-bottom-padding"></div>
   ```
6. Add an <h5> element with the text *Downloads* inside the previous <div>.
   ```
   <h5>Downloads</h5>
   ```
7. Add a <div> decorated with the **card-body** Bootstrap class below the previous <div> element inside the if-block. Add the **no-top-padding** CSS class to it to remove any top padding to the element.
   ```
   <div class="card-body no-top-padding"></div>
   ```
8. Render the partial view inside the previous <div> element. Pass in the **Downloads** collection from the current module to the <partial> Tag Helper, which renders the **_ModuleDownloadsPartial** and displays the download links.
   ```
   <partial name="_ModuleDownloadsPartial" model="@module.Downloads" />
   ```
9. Open the **_ModuleDownloadsPartial** view.
10. Add an **@model** directive to an **IEnumerable<DownloadDTO>**.
    ```
    @model IEnumerable<DownloadDTO>
    ```
11. Add an unordered list (<ul>) below the **@model** directive.
12. Add a **foreach** loop that iterates over the view model inside the <ul> element.
    ```
    @foreach (var download in Model)
    {
    }
    ```

13. Add a list item (<li>) inside the loop.
14. Add an <a> element inside the <li> element that uses the current download's **DownloadUrl** property in its **href** attribute, and opens the content in a separate browser tab. The <a> element should display a download icon and the text from the current download's **DownloadTitle** property.

    ```
    <li>
        <a href="@download.DownloadUrl" target="_blank">
            <i class="material-icons">save_alt</i>
            <span> @download.DownloadTitle</span>
        </a>
    </li>
    ```

15. Save the files and refresh the **Course** view in the browser. A section with download links should be displayed in the module lists, where downloadable content is available.

Next, you will style the partial view.

The complete markup for the **_ModuleDownloadsPartial** view:

```
@model IEnumerable<DownloadDTO>

<ul>
    @foreach (var download in Model)
    {
        <li>
            <a href="@download.DownloadUrl" target="_blank">
                <i class="material-icons">save_alt</i>
                <span> @download.DownloadTitle</span>
            </a>
        </li>
    }
</ul>
```

The markup for rendering the **_ModuleDownloadsPartial** view in the **Course** view:

```
@if (module.Downloads != null && module.Downloads.Count > 0)
{
    <hr class="no-margin">
    <div class="card-body no-bottom-padding">
        <h5>Downloads</h5>
    </div>
```

```
    <div class="card-body no-top-padding">
      <partial name="_ModuleDownloadsPartial" model="@module.Downloads" />
    </div>
}
```

The complete code for the modules, videos, and downloads in the **Course** view:

```
<div class="col-md-9">
    @*Add modules here*@
    @foreach (var module in Model.Modules)
    {
        <div class="card small-top-margin no-border-radius">
            <div class="card-body">
                <h5>@module.ModuleTitle</h5>
            </div>
            <hr class="no-margin">
            @if (module.Videos != null && module.Videos.Count > 0)
            {
                <partial name="_ModuleVideosPartial"
                 model="@module.Videos" />
            }

            @if (module.Downloads != null && module.Downloads.Count > 0)
            {
                <hr class="no-margin">
                <div class="card-body no-bottom-padding">
                    <h5>Downloads</h5>
                </div>
                <div class="card-body no-top-padding">
                    <partial name="_ModuleDownloadsPartial"
                     model="@module.Downloads" />
                </div>
            }
        </div>
    }
</div>
```

Styling the _ModuleDownloadsPartial View

Open the *membership.css* style sheet and add a selector for <ul> elements in the <div> decorated with the **card-body** class. Remove all bullet styles, margins, and padding.

```
.card-body ul {
    list-style-type: none;
    margin: 0;
    padding: 0;
}
```

Adding the Instructor Bio

Create a partial view called **_InstructorBioPartial** that displays the instructor bio to the right of the module lists in the **Course** view. Add the <partial> Tag Helper inside the <div> decorated with the **col-sm-3** Bootstrap class in the **Course** View. Pass in the **Instructor** object from the view model to the Tag Helper.

1. Add a partial view called **_InstructorBioPartial** to the *Views/Membership* folder.
2. Open the **Course** view.
3. Add an if-block inside the <div> decorated with the **col-sm-3** Bootstrap class. Check that the **Instructor** object in the view model isn't **null** and pass in the **Instructor** object to the <partial> Tag Helper that will render the partial view.
   ```
   @if (Model.Instructor != null)
   {
       <partial name="_InstructorBioPartial"
           model="@Model.Instructor" />
   }
   ```
4. Open the **_InstructorBioPartial** partial view.
5. Add an **@model** directive to the **InstructorDTO** class.
   ```
   @model InstructorDTO
   ```

13. The Course View

6. Add a `<div>` decorated with the **card** Bootstrap class and a CSS class called **instructor-bio**. It will be the parent selector for this card. Also, add the **no-border-radius** class to give the card square corners.
   ```
   <div class="instructor-bio card no-border-radius"></div>
   ```

7. Add a `<div>` decorated with the **card-body** Bootstrap class inside the **card** `<div>`.
   ```
   <div class="card-body"></div>
   ```

8. Add an `<img>` element inside the **card-body** `<div>` for the **InstructorThumbnail** property in the view model. Decorate the `<div>` with the **rounded-circle** Bootstrap class and a CSS class called **avatar**, which will be used when styling the instructor's thumbnail.
   ```
   <img src="@Model.InstructorAvatar" class="avatar rounded-circle">
   ```

9. Add an `<h4>` element for the **InstructorName** property in the view model inside the **card-body** `<div>`.
   ```
   <h4>@Model.InstructorName</h4>
   ```

10. Add an `<h5>` element with the text *Instructor* inside the **card-body** `<div>`. Decorate it with the **text-primary** Bootstrap class to make the text blue.
    ```
    <h5 class="text-primary">Instructor</h5>
    ```

11. Add a `<p>` element for the view model's **InstructorDescription** property inside the **card-body** `<div>`.
    ```
    <p>@Model.InstructorDescription</p>
    ```

12. Save the files and refresh the browser to save the changes.

The complete code for the **_InstructorBioPartial** partial view:

```
@model InstructorDTO

<div class="instructor-bio card no-border-radius">
    <div class="card-body">
        <img src="@Model.InstructorAvatar" class="avatar
          rounded-circle">
        <h4>@Model.InstructorName</h4>
        <h5 class="text-primary">Instructor</h5>
        <p>@Model.InstructorDescription</p>
    </div>
</div>
```

Styling the _InstructorBioPartial Partial View

Open the *membership.css* file to style the instructor bio section of the **Course** view.

Center the text in the **instructor-bio** container and add a 10px top margin.

```
.instructor-bio {
    text-align: center;
    margin-top: 10px;
}
```

Style the avatar to have a blue circle with 8px padding around it and make the image diameter 120px. Create the circle with the **rounded-circle** Bootstrap class, which styles the border of an element.

```
.instructor-bio .rounded-circle {
    border: 2px solid #2d91fb;
    padding: 8px;
    height: 120px;
    width: 120px;
}
```

Summary

In this chapter, you created the **Course** view and its three partial views: **_ModuleVideosPartial**, **_ModuleDownloadsPartial**, and **_InstructorBioPartial**. You also used Bootstrap to create rows and columns in a responsive design and styled the views with Bootstrap and CSS.

Next, you will create the **Video** view that displays the video.

14. The Video View

Introduction

In this chapter, you will create the **Video** view and two partial views called **_VideoComingUpPartial** and **_VideoPlayerPartial**. You will also reuse the already created **_InstructorBioPartial** partial view. The content will be styled with CSS and Bootstrap as you add it. The **Video** view is displayed when the user clicks one of the video links in the **Course** view, and it contains a button that takes the user back to the **Course** view, a video player, information about the selected video, buttons to select the next and previous video, and the instructor's bio.

Technologies Used in This Chapter

1. **HTML** – To create the view's layout.
2. **CSS** – To style the view.
3. **Razor** – To use C# in the view.

Overview

Your task is to use the view model in the **Video** action and render a view that displays a course-image, video duration, title, and description as a separate column, on a new row, below the *Back to Course* button at the top of the view. Add a second column to the right of the video player column. The upper part should contain the **_VideoComingUpPartial** partial view, and the lower part the **_InstructorBioPartial** partial view.

Here, the <video> element shows the video, but you can use any HTML5 video player you like that can play YouTube videos.

ASP.NET Core 2.2 MVC, Razor Pages, API, JSON Web Tokens & HttpClient

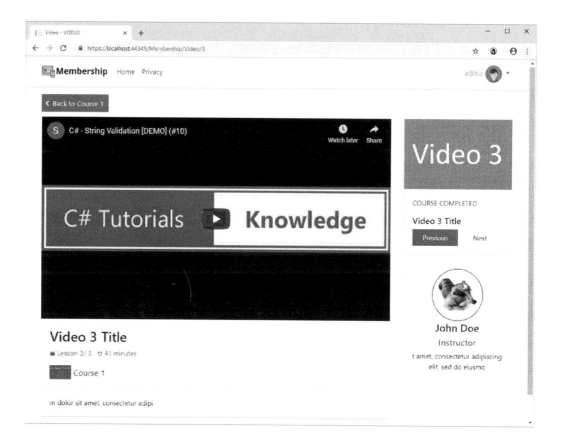

Video 1 Title

📖 Lesson 1/ 3   ⏱ 50 minutes

 Course 1

14. The Video View

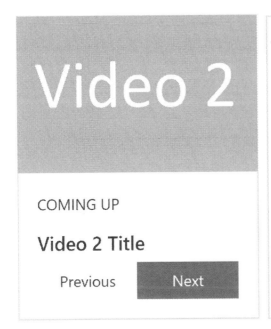

Adding the Video View

First, you will add the **Video** view to the *Views/Membership* folder.

Then, you will add a button that navigates to the **Course** view. Place the video player below the button, along with information about the video. To the right of the video player, in a separate column, the *Coming Up* section, with the **Previous** and **Next** buttons, will be displayed. Display the instructor's bio below that section. You will create two partial views for the video player and the *Coming Up* section called **_VideoPlayerPartial** and **_VideoComingUpPartial**. Reuse the **_InstructorBioPartial** partial view to display the instructor's bio. Style the three areas with Bootstrap and CSS.

1. Open the **Membership** controller.
2. Right click on the **Video** action and select **Add-View**.
3. Make sure that the **Create as partial view** checkbox is unchecked.
4. Click the **Add** button to create the view.

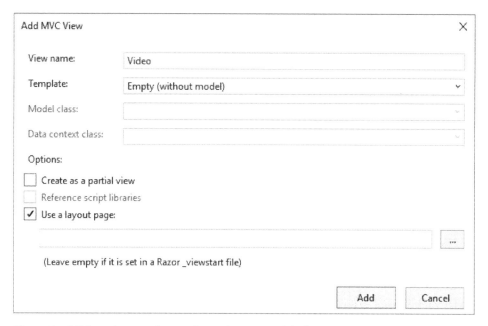

5. Close the **Video** view and open it again to get rid of any errors.
6. Add an **@model** directive for the **VideoViewModel** class at the beginning of the view.

   `@model VideoViewModel`

7. Save all the files.
8. Start the application without debugging (Ctrl+F5). Click on one of the courses in the **Dashboard** view and then on one of the video links in the **Course** view. Display the text *Video* in the browser if the **Video** view renders correctly.

The markup in the **Video** view, so far:

```
@model VideoViewModel

@{
    ViewData["Title"] = "Video";
}

<h1>Video</h1>
```

14. The Video View

Adding the Back to Course Button

Now, add a button that takes the user back to the video's **Course** view.

1. Open the **Course** view and copy the first <div>, which contains the *Back to Dashboard* button. Switch back to the **Video** view and replace the <h1> heading with it.

   ```
   <div class="row small-bottom-margin">
       <div class="col-sm-12">
           <a class="btn btn-primary no-border-radius no-left-padding"
             asp-action="Dashboard">
               <i class="material-icons vertical-align no-left-margin">
                   keyboard_arrow_left</i>
               <span class="vertical-align">Back to Dashboard</span>
           </a>
       </div>
   </div>
   ```

2. Change the name of the action to **Course** in the **asp-action** attribute; this will make the <a> element call the **Course** action in the **Membership** controller.

3. To send the video's course id to the action method, you need to add an **asp-route-id** parameter and assign it the course id from the model.

   ```
   <a class="btn btn-primary no-border-radius no-left-padding"
     asp-action="Course" asp-route-id="@Model.Course.CourseId">
   ```

4. Replace the text Dashboard in the <span> with the course title from the model's **Course.CourseTitle** property.

   ```
   <span class="vertical-align">
     Back to @Model.Course.CourseTitle</span>
   ```

5. Start the application without debugging (Ctrl+F5). Click on a course button in the **Dashboard** view, and then on a video link in the **Course** view.

6. The browser should display a blue button with the text *Back to xxx* at the top of the page. Click the button to get back to the **Course** View.

7. Click on a video link to get back to the **Video** view.

The complete code for the **Back to Course** button:

```
@model VideoViewModel

@{
    ViewData["Title"] = "Video";
}
```

```
<div class="row small-bottom-margin">
    <div class="col-sm-12">
        <a class="btn btn-primary no-border-radius no-left-padding"
          asp-action="Course" asp-route-id="@Model.Course.CourseId">
            <i class="material-icons vertical-align no-left-margin">
                keyboard_arrow_left</i>
            <span class="vertical-align">Back to
                @Model.Course.CourseTitle</span>
        </a>
    </div>
</div>
```

Adding Row and Columns for the Video View Content

Now, you will use Bootstrap classes to add a row and columns that will hold the **Video** view's content.

1. Open the **Video** view.
2. Add a `<div>` element decorated with the **row** class below the previous **row** `<div>`. Add two nested `<div>` elements decorated with the **col-sm-9** and **col-sm-3** classes respectively.
   ```
   <div class="row">
       <div class="col-sm-9">
           @*Place the video player here*@
       </div>

       <div class="col-sm-3">
           @*Place the Coming Up and Instructor Bio sections here*@
       </div>
   </div>
   ```
3. Save the file.

14. The Video View

Adding the _VideoPlayerPartial Partial View

The **_VideoPlayerPartial** partial view will display the card containing the <iframe> video player and its information.

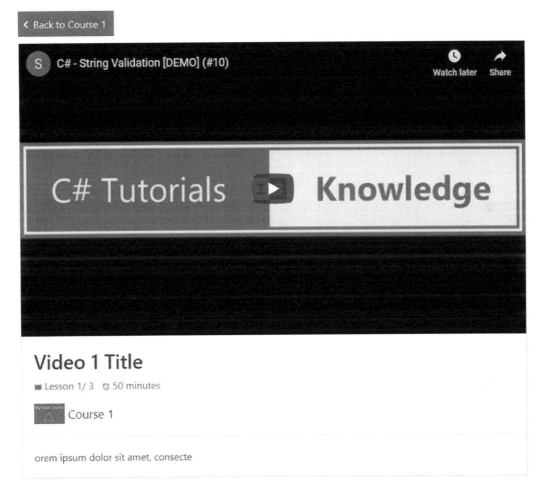

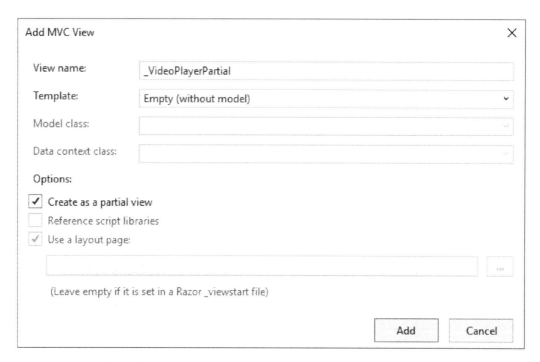

1. Open the **Video** view and render a partial view named **_VideoPlayerPartial** inside the <div> decorated with the **col-sm-9** Bootstrap class. Only render the partial view if the **Model**, **Video**, **LessonInfo**, and **Course** objects contain data.
   ```
   @if (Model != null && Model.Video != null &&
        Model.LessonInfo != null && Model.Course != null)
   {
       <partial name="_VideoPlayerPartial" model="@Model" />
   }
   ```
2. Add a partial view called **_VideoPlayerPartial** to the *Views/membership* folder.
3. Delete all code in the view and save it.
4. Close and open the view to get rid of any errors.
5. Add an **@model** directive to the **VideoViewModel** class. The view needs this view model to display all the information; the data is stored in several objects in the model.
   ```
   @model VideoViewModel
   ```
6. Add a <div> decorated with the **card** Bootstrap class below the **@model** directive. Add the **no-border-radius** class to give it square corners.
   ```
   <div class="card no-border-radius"></div>
   ```

7. Add an if-block inside the **card** <div> that checks that the **Video.Url** property in the view model isn't **null**.
   ```
   @if (Model.Video.Url != null)
   {
   }
   ```
8. Add a <div> element decorated with a class named **video-player** inside the if-block. This element will act as a container for the <iframe> so that the video can be viewed in 16:9 in full width.
   ```
   <div class="video-player"></div>
   ```
9. Add an <iframe> inside the previous <div> and assign the model's video URL to its **src** attribute. You can copy an embed link from YouTube as a starting point and replace the current Url for the videos in the database in case they don't work. Make sure that you remove the settings for width and height. You will style the <iframe> and its container in the *membership.css* file later.
   ```
   <iframe src="@Model.Video.Url" frameborder="0"
   allow="accelerometer; autoplay; encrypted-media; gyroscope;
   picture-in-picture" allowfullscreen></iframe>
   ```
10. Add a <div> decorated with the **card-body** Bootstrap class below the if-block.
    ```
    <div class="card-body">
    </div>
    ```
11. Add an <h2> element for the **Video.Title** property from the view model inside the previous <div>.
    ```
    <h2>@Model.Video.Title</h2>
    ```
12. Add a <p> element for the lesson information; decorate it with the **text-muted** CSS class to make the text a muted light gray. Add a video icon, display the video's position and the number of videos in the module, a watch icon, and the video length followed by the text *minutes*. Use the **LessonInfo.LessonNumber** and **LessonInfo.NumberOfLessons** properties to display the video's position and the number of videos. Use the **Video.Duration** property to display how long the video is. Add the previously defined **vertical-align** and **text-small** classes to align and change size of the icons.

```
<p class="text-muted">
    <i class="material-icons vertical-align text-small">movie</i>
    Lesson @Model.LessonInfo.LessonNumber/
    @Model.LessonInfo.NumberOfLessons  
    <i class="material-icons vertical-align text-small">alarm</i>
    @Model.Video.Duration minutes
</p>
```

13. Add a <div> decorated with a class named **video-course** below the <p> element; this class will be used as a selector to style its content. This is the container for the video thumbnail and the video title.
    ```
    <div class="video-course">
    </div>
    ```

14. Add an <img> element inside the previous <div>. Assign the value form the **Course.CourseImageUrl** property to the **src** attribute.
    ```
    <img src="@Model.Course.CourseImageUrl">
    ```

15. Add a <span> element decorated with the **vertical-align** and **text-large** CSS classes below the <img> element. Add the **Course.CourseTitle** property from the view model to the <span>.
    ```
    <span class="vertical-align text-large">
    @Model.Course.CourseTitle</span>
    ```

16. Add a horizontal line below the **card-body** <div> and remove its margins.
    ```
    <hr class="no-margin">
    ```

17. Add a <div> decorated with the **card-body** Bootstrap class below the <hr> element. Add the **Video.Description** property from the view model to it.
    ```
    <div class="card-body">
        @Model.Video.Description
    </div>
    ```

18. Save all the files and navigate to a video in the browser. You should see the video information and the video loaded in the player.

Next, you will style the **_VideoPlayerPartial** partial view.

The complete code for the **_VideoPlayerPartial** partial view:

```
@model VideoViewModel
<div class="card no-border-radius">
    @if (Model.Video.Url != null)
    {
        <div class="video-player">
            <iframe src="@Model.Video.Url" frameborder="0"
                allow="accelerometer; autoplay; encrypted-media;
                gyroscope; picture-in-picture" allowfullscreen></iframe>
        </div>
    }
    <div class="card-body">
        <h2>@Model.Video.Title</h2>
        <p class="text-muted">
            <i class="material-icons vertical-align text-small">movie</i>
            Lesson @Model.LessonInfo.LessonNumber/
            @Model.LessonInfo.NumberOfLessons  
            <i class="material-icons vertical-align text-small">alarm</i>
            @Model.Video.Duration minutes
        </p>
        <div class="video-course">
            <img src="@Model.Course.CourseImageUrl">
            <span class="vertical-align text-large">
                @Model.Course.CourseTitle</span>
        </div>
    </div>
    <hr class="no-margin">
    <div class="card-body">
        @Model.Video.Description
    </div>
</div>
```

Styling the _VideoPlayerPartial Partial View

Open the *membership.css* file to style the **Video** view and its partial views.

Let's start by styling the video player and its container. Add a selector named **video-player** to style the container; give it relative positioning and 56.25% top padding. These settings are essential to scale the <iframe> to 16:9 full width; the settings need to be set with the **!important** keyword to override the default settings for the video player.

```
.video-player {
    position: relative !important;
    padding-top: 56.25% !important;
}
```

Next, let's style the size and position of the <iframe> itself. It must be positioned absolutely to place it at the top left corner of its container. Assign 100% width and height to make the player cover the entire width and height of its container.

```
.video-player iframe {
    position: absolute;
    top: 0;
    left: 0;
    width: 100%;
    height: 100%;
}
```

Change the width of the course thumbnail to 50px.

```
.video-course img {
    width: 50px;
}
```

Adding Properties to the LessonInfoDTO Class

There is one piece of information that you need to add to the **LessonInfoDTO** and the **Membership** controller. To avoid displaying an empty image container when the user navigates to the last video using the **Next** button in the *Coming Up* section, the current video's thumbnail should be displayed. You, therefore, must include the current video's thumbnail and title in the **LessonInfoDTO** class and add that data to the view model in the **Video** action of the **Membership** controller.

1. Open the **LessonInfoDTO** class in the **Common project**.
2. Add two **string** properties called **CurrentVideoTitle** and **CurrentVideoThumbnail**.
   ```
   public string CurrentVideoTitle { get; set; }
   public string CurrentVideoThumbnail { get; set; }
   ```
3. Open the **Membership** controller and locate the **Video** action.
4. Assign the thumbnail and title from the video object's **Thumbnail** and **Title** properties to the properties you just added to the **LessonInfoDTO** class.
   ```
   CurrentVideoTitle = video.Title,
   CurrentVideoThumbnail = video.Thumbnail
   ```
5. The first module should have at least three videos so that you can use the **Previous** and **Next** buttons properly when you test the *Coming Up* section of the **Video** view.

The complete **LessonInfoDTO** class:

```
public class LessonInfoDTO
{
    public int LessonNumber { get; set; }
    public int NumberOfLessons { get; set; }
    public int PreviousVideoId { get; set; }
    public int NextVideoId { get; set; }
    public string NextVideoTitle { get; set; }
    public string NextVideoThumbnail { get; set; }
    public string CurrentVideoTitle { get; set; }
    public string CurrentVideoThumbnail { get; set; }
}
```

The complete **LessonInfoDTO** object in the **Video** action:

```
LessonInfo = new LessonInfoDTO
{
    LessonNumber = index + 1,
    NumberOfLessons = count,
    NextVideoId = nextId,
    PreviousVideoId = previousId,
    NextVideoTitle = nextTitle,
    NextVideoThumbnail = nextThumb,
    CurrentVideoTitle = video.Title,
    CurrentVideoThumbnail = video.Thumbnail
}
```

Adding the _VideoComingUpPartial Partial View

This partial view will display the card containing the thumbnail of the next video, its title, and the **Previous** and **Next** buttons. The **Previous** button should be disabled when information about the first video is displayed. The **Next** button should be disabled when information about the last video is displayed. The *Coming Up* card should not be displayed if there are no videos.

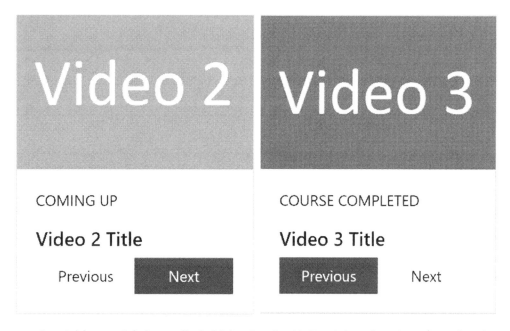

1. Add a partial view called **_VideoComingUpPartial** to the *Views/membership* folder.
2. Delete all code in the view and save it.
3. Close and open the view to get rid of any errors.
4. Add an **@model** directive to the **LessonInfoDTO** class.
   `@model LessonInfoDTO`
5. Add an if-block that checks that one of the **PreviousVideoId** or **NextVideoId** properties has a value greater than 0. If both are 0 then there are no other videos in the module, and the *Coming Up* section shouldn't be displayed. All markup and razor code in this view should be placed inside this if-block.
   ```
   @if (Model.PreviousVideoId > 0 || Model.NextVideoId > 0)
   {
   }
   ```
6. Add a <div> element decorated with the **card** Bootstrap class inside the if-block. Add a CSS class called **coming-up** to the <div> element; it will be the parent selector for this partial view. Also add the **no-border-radius** class to give the container square corners. All markup and razor code in this view should be placed inside this <div>.
   `<div class="card coming-up no-border-radius"></div>`

7. Display a thumbnail for the current video, in the card, if the **NextVideoId** property is 0. Otherwise, display the thumbnail for the next video. Use the **CurrentVideoThumbnail** and **NextVideoThumbnail** properties from the view model to display the correct image.
```
@if (Model.NextVideoId == 0)
{
    <img src="@Model.CurrentVideoThumbnail"
        class="img-responsive">
}
else
{
    <img src="@Model.NextVideoThumbnail" class="img-responsive">
}
```

8. Add a <div> decorated with the **card-body** Bootstrap class below the previous if/else-blocks. This is the container for the *Coming Up* information.
```
<div class="card-body">
</div>
```

9. Add a <p> element with the text *COURSE COMPLETED* and an <h5> element for the **CurrentVideoTitle** property from the view model in the **card-body** <div> if the **NextVideoId** property is 0. Otherwise, add a <p> element with the text *COMING UP* and an <h5> element for the **NextVideoTitle** property.
```
@if (Model.NextVideoId == 0)
{
    <p>COURSE COMPLETED</p>
    <h5>@Model.CurrentVideoTitle</h5>
}
else
{
    <p>COMING UP</p>
    <h5>@Model.NextVideoTitle</h5>
}
```

10. Add a <div> element for the **Previous** and **Next** buttons below the previous if/else-block inside the **card-body** <div>. Decorate it with the **btn-group** Bootstrap class and add the **role** attribute set to **group**.
```
<div class="btn-group" role="group">
</div>
```

11. Add an if-block checking if the **PreviousVideoId** property in the view model is 0 inside the <div> element decorated with the **btn-group** Bootstrap class; if it is, then disable the **Previous** button. Use the **PreviousVideoId** in the <a> element's **href** attribute to target the correct video.

```
@if (Model.PreviousVideoId == 0)
{
    <a class="btn" disabled>Previous</a>
}
else
{
    <a class="btn btn-default"
        href="~/Membership/Video/@Model.PreviousVideoId">
        Previous
    </a>
}
```

12. Add an if-block checking if the **NextVideoId** property in the view model is 0 below the previous if/else-block inside the **btn-group** <div>; if it is, then disable the **Next** button. Use the **NextVideoId** in the <a> element's **href** attribute to target the correct video.

```
@if (Model.NextVideoId == 0)
{
    <a class="btn" disabled>Next</a>
}
else
{
    <a class="btn btn-default"
        href="~/Membership/Video/@Model.NextVideoId">Next</a>
}
```

13. Open the **Video** view.
14. Render the **_VideoComingUpPartial** partial view inside the <div> decorated with the **col-sm-3** Bootstrap class. Pass in the **LessonInfo** object from the view model to the partial view. Surround the <partial> Tag Helper if-block that checks that the view model and the **LessonInfo** object are not **null**.

```
<div class="col-sm-3">
    @if (Model != null && Model.LessonInfo != null) {
        <partial name="_VideoComingUpPartial"
            model="@Model.LessonInfo" />
    }
</div>
```

15. Save all the files and navigate to a video in the browser. You should see the *Coming Up* section beside the video.

Next, you will style the **_VideoComingUpPartial** partial view.

The complete code for the **_VideoComingUpPartial** partial view:

```
@model LessonInfoDTO

@if (Model.PreviousVideoId > 0 || Model.NextVideoId > 0)
{
    <div class="card coming-up no-border-radius">
        @if (Model.NextVideoId == 0)
        {
            <img src="@Model.CurrentVideoThumbnail"
                class="img-responsive">
        }
        else
        {
            <img src="@Model.NextVideoThumbnail" class="img-responsive">
        }

        <div class="card-body">
            @if (Model.NextVideoId == 0)
            {
                <p>COURSE COMPLETED</p>
                <h5>@Model.CurrentVideoTitle</h5>
            }
            else
            {
                <p>COMING UP</p>
                <h5>@Model.NextVideoTitle</h5>
            }

            <div class="btn-group" role="group">
                @if (Model.PreviousVideoId == 0)
                {
                    <a class="btn" disabled>Previous</a>
                }
                else
                {
                    <a class="btn btn-primary" href="~/Membership/Video/
                        @Model.PreviousVideoId">Previous</a>
                }
```

```
                @if (Model.NextVideoId == 0)
                {
                    <a class="btn" disabled>Next</a>
                }
                else
                {
                    <a class="btn btn-primary" href="~/Membership/Video/
                        @Model.NextVideoId">Next</a>
                }
            </div>
        </div>
    </div>
}
```

Styling the _VideoComingUpPartial Partial View

Open the *membership.css* style sheet and make the button group as wide as possible. You might have to clear the browser cache for the styling to be visible.

```
.coming-up .btn-group { width: 100%; }
```

Make each of the buttons take up 50% of the button group's width and remove their rounded corners.

```
.coming-up .btn-group .btn {
    width: 50%;
    border-radius:0;
}
```

Change the mouse pointer to show that the button is disabled when the **disabled** attribute is applied, and the mouse pointer is hovering over the button.

```
.coming-up .btn-group [disabled]:hover {
    cursor: not-allowed;
}
```

Scale the thumbnail for the next video to fit the container.

```
.coming-up img {
    width: 100%;
    height: auto;
}
```

Adding the _InstructorBioPartial Partial View

The last section you will add to the **Video** view is the **_InstructorBioPartial** partial view that displays information about the instructor.

1. Open the **Video** view.
2. Add a <partial> Tag Helper for the **_InstructorBioPartial** partial view below the previous if-block inside the <div> decorated with the **col-sm-3** Bootstrap class. Pass in the **instructor** object from the view model to the partial view. Surround the method call with an if-block that checks that the view model and the **Instructor** object are not **null**.

   ```
   @if (Model != null && Model.Instructor != null)
   {
       <partial name="_InstructorBioPartial"
        model="@Model.Instructor" />
   }
   ```

3. Save the file and refresh the **Video** view in the browser. The **_InstructorBioPartial** partial view should be displayed below the **_VideoComingUpPartial** partial view.

The complete code for the **Video** view:

```razor
@model VideoViewModel

@{
    ViewData["Title"] = "Video";
}

<div class="row small-bottom-margin">
    <div class="col-sm-12">
        <a class="btn btn-primary no-border-radius no-left-padding"
           asp-action="Course" asp-route-id="@Model.Course.CourseId">
            <i class="material-icons vertical-align no-left-margin">
                keyboard_arrow_left</i>
            <span class="vertical-align">Back to
                @Model.Course.CourseTitle</span>
        </a>
    </div>
</div>

<div class="row">
    <div class="col-sm-9">
        @*Place the video player here*@
        @if (Model != null && Model.Video != null &&
        Model.LessonInfo != null && Model.Course != null)
        {
            <partial name="_VideoPlayerPartial" model="@Model" />
        }
    </div>

    <div class="col-sm-3">
        @*Place the Coming Up and Instructor Bio sections here*@
        @if (Model != null && Model.LessonInfo != null)
        {
            <partial name="_VideoComingUpPartial"
                model="@Model.LessonInfo" />
        }

        @if (Model != null && Model.Instructor != null)
        {
            <partial name="_InstructorBioPartial"
                model="@Model.Instructor" />
        }
    </div>
</div>
```

Summary

In this chapter, you added the **Video** view and its partial views.

In the next part of the book, you will begin building the administrator UI with Razor Pages.

ASP.NET Core 2.2 MVC, Razor Pages, API, JSON Web Tokens & HttpClient

Part 2:
Razor Pages
How to Build the Administrator Website

15. Adding the Admin Project

Overview

In this chapter, you will add a **Web Application** project called **VOD.Admin** to the solution. The application will be used by administrators to add, remove, update, and view data that can be accessed by the regular users from the **VOD.UI** project. The application will share the same database context and data read service that you added earlier to the **VOD.Database** project.

You will be using the **Web Application** project template when creating the **Admin** project; this is a new template that wasn't available in ASP.NET Core 1.1. It makes it possible to create a lightweight application using Razor Pages instead of creating a full-fledged MVC application with models, views, and controllers.

A good candidate for this type of application is a small company web page that contains a few pages of data with a navigation menu and maybe a few forms that the visitor can fill out.

Even though you are working with Razor Pages (and not views), they are still part of the same MVC framework, which means that you don't need to learn a whole new framework to create Razor Pages if you already know MVC.

Although it's possible to contain all code, C#, Razor syntax, and HTML in the same file, this is not the recommended practice. Instead, you create two files, one *.cshtml.cs* code-behind C# file and one *.cshtml* file for HTML and Razor syntax. The Solution Explorer displays the two files as one node inside the *Pages* folder.

The Razor Page looks and behaves much like a regular view; the difference is that it has a code-behind file that sort of acts as the page's model and controller in one.

One easy way to determine if a *.cshtml* file is a page (and not a view) is to look for the **@page** directive, which should be present in all Razor Pages.

Just like views, the Razor Pages have a **_Layout** view for shared HTML and imported JavaScripts and CSS style sheets. They also have a **_ViewImports** view with **using**-statements, namespaces, and Tag Helpers that are available in all pages.

ASP.NET Core 2.2 MVC, Razor Pages, API, JSON Web Tokens & HttpClient

Technologies Used in This Chapter

- **ASP.NET Core Web Application** – The project template used to create the MVC Razor Page application.

Creating the Admin Solution

To make the implementation go a little bit smoother, you will use the **Web Application** template instead of an **Empty Template**. The benefit is that much of the plumbing already has been added to the project, so that you can be up-and-running quickly, doing the fun stuff – coding.

The template will install the basic Razor Pages plumbing and an **Account** folder for the account Razor Pages that handles logging in and out from the **Admin** application. In previous versions of ASP.NET Core, MVC controllers implemented the account functionality; from ASP.NET Core 2.2 both MVC and Razor Page applications use the account Razor Pages; the project template hides the pages by default, but they can be scaffolded if needed.

Because the project template adds a lot of files that the **Admin** application doesn't use, you will delete them before beginning the implementation. Most of the files handle database migrations, which you already have added to the **VOD.Common** project.

1. Open the **VideoOnDemand** solution in Visual Studio 2019.
2. Right click on the **VideoOnDemand** solution node in the Solution Explorer and select **File-New Project** in the menu.
3. Type **Web** in the search field and select **ASP.NET Core Web Application** in the template list (see image below).
4. Click the **Next** button.
5. Name the project *VOD.Admin* in the **Name** field.
6. Click the **Create** button.
7. Select **.NET Core** and **ASP.NET Core 2.2** in the drop-downs.
8. Select **Web Application** in the template list.
9. Click the **Change Authentication** link and select **Individual User Accounts** in the pop-up dialog; this will make it possible for visitors to register and log in with your site using an email and a password (see image below).
    a. Select the **Individual User Accounts** radio button.
    b. Select **Store user account in-app** in the drop-down.

15. Adding the Admin Project

   c. Click the **OK** button in the pop-up dialog.
10. Click the **Create** button in the wizard dialog.
11. Open *appsettings.json* and add the following connection string; you can copy it from the *appsettings.json* file in **UI** project. Add the string as a single line of code.
    ```
    "ConnectionStrings": {
        "DefaultConnection": "Server=(localdb)\\mssqllocaldb;
            Database=VOD;Trusted_Connection=True;
            MultipleActiveResultSets=true"
    }
    ```
12. Add a reference to the **Common** and **Database** projects by right clicking on the **Dependencies** node and selecting **Add-Reference**.
13. Delete the *Data* folder and all its content. This folder contains database-related files that already exist in the **Common project**.
14. Open the **_Layout** view and add a link to the Material Icons library; you can find the icons here: https://material.io/tools/icons/?style=baseline.
    ```
    <link rel="stylesheet"
    href="https://fonts.googleapis.com/icon?family=Material+Icons">
    ```
15. Open the **_ViewImports** view and replace the **VOD.Admin.Data using** statement with **VOD.Common.Entities**.
16. Build the project and fix the errors. Remove any faulty **using** statements and replace **ApplicationDbContext** with **VODContext** in the **ConfigureServices** method in the **Startup** class.
17. In the **_Layout** view, comment out or delete the <partial> element that displays the cookie consent partial view.
    ```
    @*<partial name="_CookieConsentPartial" />*@
    ```
18. In the **Startup** class, replace the **IdentityUser** with **VODUser** and add a call to the **AddRoles** service after the call to the **AddDefaultIdentity** method in the **ConfigureServices** method to enable role-based security.
    ```
    services.AddDefaultIdentity<VODUser>()
        .AddRoles<IdentityRole>()
        .AddDefaultUI(UIFramework.Bootstrap4)
        .AddEntityFrameworkStores<VODContext>();
    ```
19. Expand the **Areas** folder and right click on the **Identity** folder, then Select **Add-New Scaffolded Item**.

20. Select **Identity** in the dialog's left menu and select the **Identity** template in the middle of the dialog, then click the **Add** button.
21. Check the **Account\Login** and **Account\Register** checkboxes, and **VODContext** in the **Data context class** drop-down.
22. Click the **Add** button; this should create a new folder called **Account** in the **Areas-Identity-Pages** folder. The folder should contain the **Login** and **Register** Razor Pages. If an error occurs saying that no object reference is available, then close Visual Studio, open the solution, and try again.
23. Open the **Startup** class and locate the **ConfigureServices** method.
24. Change the default **IdentityUser** class defined for the **AddDefaultIdentity** service method to the **VODUser** class in the **Common** project. You need to resolve the **VOD.Common.Entities** namespace.
25. Open the **_LoginPartial** view and replace all occurrences of the **IdentityUser** class with the **VODUser** class from the **Common** project.
26. Comment out the code for cookie policy options in the **ConfigureServices** method.
    ```
    //services.Configure<CookiePolicyOptions>(options =>
    //{
    //    options.CheckConsentNeeded = context => true;
    //    options.MinimumSameSitePolicy = SameSiteMode.None;
    //});
    ```
27. Comment out the call to the **UseCookiePolicy** method in the **Configure** method.
    ```
    //app.UseCookiePolicy();
    ```
28. Save all files. Right click on the **Admin** project in the Solution Explorer and select **Set as StartUp Project** and then press F5 on the keyboard to run the application. Log in as one of the users you have previously added, and then log out.

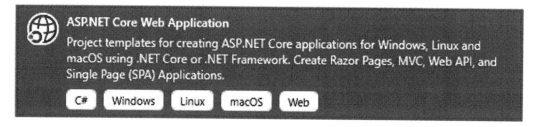

15. Adding the Admin Project

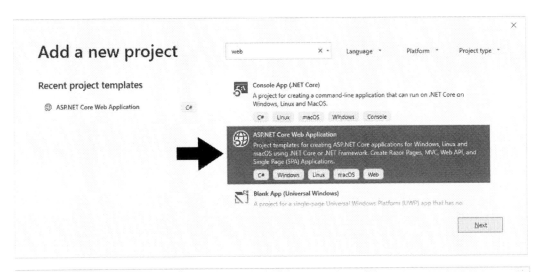

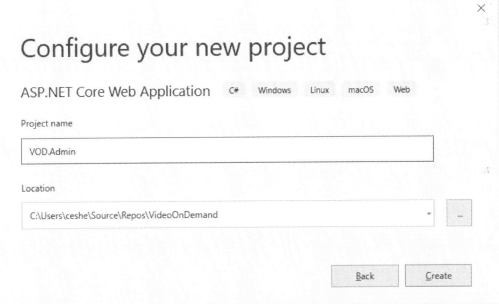

ASP.NET Core 2.2 MVC, Razor Pages, API, JSON Web Tokens & HttpClient

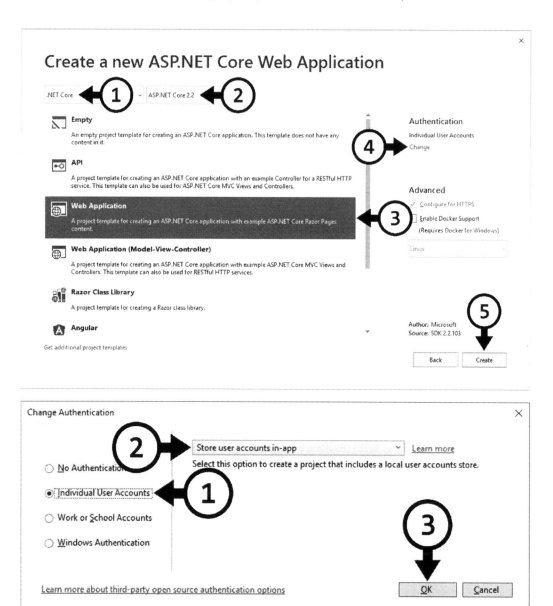

15. Adding the Admin Project

The complete code in the **ConfigureServices** method:

```
public void ConfigureServices(IServiceCollection services)
{
    //services.Configure<CookiePolicyOptions>(options =>
    //{
    //    options.CheckConsentNeeded = context => true;
    //    options.MinimumSameSitePolicy = SameSiteMode.None;
    //});

    services.AddDbContext<VODContext>(options =>
        options.UseSqlServer(
            Configuration.GetConnectionString("DefaultConnection")));

    services.AddDefaultIdentity<VODUser>()
        .AddRoles<IdentityRole>()
        .AddDefaultUI(UIFramework.Bootstrap4)
        .AddEntityFrameworkStores<VODContext>();

    services.AddMvc().SetCompatibilityVersion(
        CompatibilityVersion.Version_2_2);
}
```

The complete code in the **Configure** method:

```
public void Configure(IApplicationBuilder app, IHostingEnvironment env)
{
    if (env.IsDevelopment())
    {
        app.UseDeveloperExceptionPage();
        app.UseDatabaseErrorPage();
    }
    else
    {
        app.UseExceptionHandler("/Error");
        app.UseHsts();
    }

    app.UseHttpsRedirection();
    app.UseStaticFiles();
    //app.UseCookiePolicy();
    app.UseAuthentication();
    app.UseMvc();
}
```

ASP.NET Core 2.2 MVC, Razor Pages, API, JSON Web Tokens & HttpClient

Summary

In this chapter, you created the **VOD.Admin** project that will enable administrators to create, update, delete, add, and view data that will be available to regular users visiting the **VOD.UI** website.

Next, you will start building a user interface for administrators by adding a dashboard and an **Admin** menu that the visitor uses when navigating to the Razor Pages that will manipulate the data in the database.

16. The Administrator Dashboard

Introduction

In this chapter, you will create an **Admin** dashboard with links to all **Index** Razor Pages associated with the entities you have added. Since you know that a folder for pages should have the same name as its corresponding entity, you can add all the dashboard items before creating the actual folders and pages.

You will create the dashboard using two partial views, one for the dashboard called **_DashboardPartial** and one for its items (cards) called **_CardPartial**. Render the dashboard's partial view in the main **Index** page located in the *Pages* folder and restrict it to logged in users. Render the partial views with the <partial> Tag Helper.

You will also remove the **Policy** link and change the text to *Dashboard* for the **Home** link. Then you will move the menu into a partial view named **_MenuPartial** and render it from the **_Layout** view and restrict it to logged in users that belong to the **Admin** role.

Technologies Used in This Chapter

1. **C# and Razor** – To add authorization checks in the **_DashboardPartial** view.
2. **HTML** – To create the dashboard and its items.

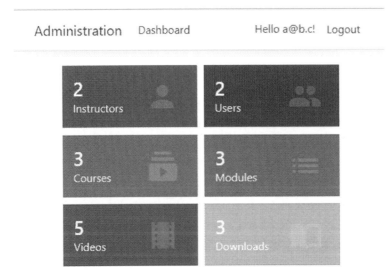

ASP.NET Core 2.2 MVC, Razor Pages, API, JSON Web Tokens & HttpClient

Modifying the Navigation Menu

The first thing you will modify is the menu in the navigation bar. By default, it has two links: **Home** and **Privacy**, which are unnecessary in the administrator application. You will change the **Home** link to **Dashboard** and remove **Privacy** link.

Then you will create a partial view named **_MenuPartial** to which you will move the remaining menu and then reference it from the **_Layout** partial view with the <partial> Tag Helper.

1. Open the **_Layout** partial view in the **Admin** project's **Pages-Shared** folder.
2. Delete the <li> elements that contain the **Privacy** <a> element.
3. Change the text to *Dashboard* for the **Home** <li> element.
4. Right click on the *Pages-Shared* folder and select **Add-New Item**.
5. Add a **Razor View** named **_MenuPartial** and remove all code in it. You use this template because a C# code-behind file is unnecessary. Delete all code in the new Razor view.
6. Open the **_Layout** partial view and cut out the <ul> element containing the **Dashboard** <li> element and paste it into the **_MenuPartial** partial view.
   ```
   <ul class="navbar-nav flex-grow-1">
       <li class="nav-item">
           <a class="nav-link text-dark" asp-area=""
             asp-page="/Index">Dashboard</a>
       </li>
   </ul>
   ```
7. Open the **_Layout** view and use the <Partial> element to render the **_MenuPartial** view below <Partial> element that renders the **_LoginPartial** view.
   ```
   <partial name="_MenuPartial" />
   ```
8. Run the application. Log out if you are logged in. The navigation menu should now only have the **Dashboard**, **Register**, and **Login** links.
9. Now, you will modify the menu to be displayed only when logged in.
10. You need to inject the **SignInManager** for the current user at the top of the **_MenuPartial** view to be able to check if the user is logged in.
    ```
    @inject SignInManager<VODUser> SignInManager
    ```
11. Surround the <ul> element with an if-block that uses the **SignInManager's IsSignedIn** method to check that the user is logged in. Also, call the **IsInRole** method on the **User** entity to check that the user belongs to the **Admin** role.
    ```
    @if (SignInManager.IsSignedIn(User) && User.IsInRole("Admin")) { }
    ```

12. Save all files.
13. Switch to the browser and refresh. The **Dashboard** link should disappear.
14. Open the **AspNetRoles** table in the database and make sure that it contains a record for the **Admin** role. Remember the id in the **Id** column for the **Admin** role.
15. Open the **AspNetUsers** table in the database and copy the value in the **Id** column for the user you will use to login.
16. Open the **AspNetUserRoles** table in the database and make sure that the user id for the user you will log in with is in this table and has the admin role id.
17. Log in as the user you assigned the administrator privileges to. The **Dashboard** link should reappear.
18. Go back to the **_Layout** view in Visual Studio.
19. Change the text *VOD.Admin* in the **navbar-brand** <a> element to *Administration*.
20. Save the file.
21. Switch to the browser and refresh. The brand to the far left in the navigation menu should now show *Administration*.

The complete code for the **_MenuPartial** view:

```
@inject SignInManager<VODUser> SignInManager

@if (SignInManager.IsSignedIn(User) && User.IsInRole("Admin"))
{
    <ul class="navbar-nav flex-grow-1">
        <li class="nav-item">
            <a class="nav-link text-dark" asp-area=""
              asp-page="/Index">Dashboard</a>
        </li>
    </ul>
}
```

Creating the Dashboard

In this section, you will create a dashboard in the main **Index** page in the **Admin** project. This dashboard will act as a menu that displays statistics about the tables.

The first step is to add a method to the **DbReadService** in the **Database** project that returns the necessary statistics for the dashboard from the database.

The second step is to create a partial view called **_CardPartial** that will be used to render the dashboard items (cards).

The third step is to modify the **Index** view and its code-behind file to receive data from the database through the **DbReadService**.

Adding the Count Method to the DbReadService

To be able to display the number of records stored in the entity tables in the database on the cards, you will add a method called **Count** to the **DbReadService** class in the **Database** project. Instead of adding a model class with properties for the record count in each table and returning an object of that class from the method, you will make the method return a tuple containing the values.

Use the **Count** method on the entities in the method to return their number of records.

1. Open the **IDbReadService** interface in the **Database** project.
2. Add a method definition that returns an integer for each entity count. Use camel casing to name the tuple parameters the same as the entities. The **Count** method you add should not take any in-parameters.
   ```
   (int courses, int downloads, int instructors, int modules, int videos, int users) Count();
   ```
3. Open the **DbReadService** class and add the **Count** method.
4. Return the number of records in each entity and assign the values to the appropriate tuple parameter. Use the **Count** method on each entity in the **_db** context object to fetch the number of records.
   ```
   return (
       courses: _db.Courses.Count(),
       downloads: _db.Downloads.Count(),
       instructors: _db.Instructors.Count(),
       modules: _db.Modules.Count(),
       videos: _db.Videos.Count(),
       users: _db.Users.Count());
   ```
5. Open the **Startup** class in the **Admin** project.
6. Add the **IDbReadService** service to the **ConfigureServices** method.
   ```
   services.AddScoped<IDbReadService, DbReadService>();
   ```
7. Save all files.

16. The Administrator Dashboard

The complete code in the **IDbReadService** interface:

```
public interface IDbReadService
{
    Task<List<TEntity>> GetAsync<TEntity>() where TEntity : class;
    Task<List<TEntity>> GetAsync<TEntity>(Expression<Func<TEntity,
        bool>> expression) where TEntity : class;
    Task<TEntity> SingleAsync<TEntity>(Expression<Func<TEntity, bool>>
        expression) where TEntity : class;
    Task<bool> AnyAsync<TEntity>(Expression<Func<TEntity, bool>>
        expression) where TEntity : class;

    void Include<TEntity>() where TEntity : class;
    void Include<TEntity1, TEntity2>() where TEntity1 : class
        where TEntity2 : class;

    (int courses, int downloads, int instructors, int modules,
      int videos, int users) Count();
}
```

The complete code in the **Count** method:

```
public (int courses, int downloads, int instructors, int modules, int
videos, int users) Count()
{
    return (
        courses: _db.Courses.Count(),
        downloads: _db.Downloads.Count(),
        instructors: _db.Instructors.Count(),
        modules: _db.Modules.Count(),
        videos: _db.Videos.Count(),
        users: _db.Users.Count());
}
```

Adding the CardViewModel Class

The **_CardPartial** partial view will take a view model that contains the number of records, the background color of the card, the name of the Material Icon to display on the card, a description, and the URL to navigate to.

Implement the view model with a class called **CardViewModel** in a folder called *Models*.

1. Add a folder to the **Admin** project called *Models*.
2. Add a **public** class called **CardViewModel** in the *Models* folder.

3. Add properties for the previously mentioned data named: **Count (int)**, **Description (string)**, **Icon (string)**, **Url (string)**, **BackgroundColor (string)**.
4. Save the file.

The complete code for the **CardViewModel** class:

```
public class CardViewModel
{
    public int Count { get; set; }
    public string Description { get; set; }
    public string Icon { get; set; }
    public string Url { get; set; }
    public string BackgroundColor { get; set; }
}
```

Adding the _CardPartial Partial View

To keep the code in the **Index** Razor Page as clean as possible, you will create a partial view called **_CardPartial** that will be rendered using the <partial> Tag Helper.

The partial view will use the **CardViewModel** as a model to render the data from the database.

1. Right click on the *Pages* folder and select **Add-New Item**.
2. Add a **Razor View** named **_CardPartial** and remove all code in it.
3. Open the **_ViewImports** file and add a using statement to the **VOD.Admin.Models** namespace and save the file.
4. Use the **@model** directive to add the **CardViewModel** class as a model to the view.
   ```
   @model CardViewModel
   ```
5. Because the dashboard cards should act as links to the other **Index** views, you will add the card markup as <a> elements to the **_CardPartial** view. Use the model's **Url** property in the **href** attribute, add a CSS class called **card**, and use the **BackgroundColor** property to style the card's background color.
   ```
   <a href="@Model.Url" class="card" style="background-color: @Model.BackgroundColor"></a>
   ```
6. Add a <div> element decorated with a CSS class called **card-content** that can be used for styling elements inside the <a> element.

16. The Administrator Dashboard

7. Add a <div> element decorated with a class called **card-data** that can be used for styling elements inside the previously added <div> element.
8. Add an <h3> element for the model's **Count** property inside the previously added <div> element.
9. Add a <p> element for the model's **Description** property below the <h3> element.
10. Add a <span> element below the innermost <div> element for the icon; use the model's **Icon** property to define which icon to display.
    ```
    <span class="material-icons card-icon">@Model.Icon.ToLower()
    </span>
    ```
11. Save the view.

The complete code for the **_CardPartial** view:

```
@model CardViewModel

<a href="@Model.Url" class="card" style="background-color:
@Model.BackgroundColor">
    <div class="card-content">
        <div class="card-data">
            <h3>@Model.Count</h3>
            <p>@Model.Description</p>
        </div>
        <span class="material-icons card-icon">@Model.Icon.ToLower()
        </span>
    </div>
</a>
```

Calling the Count Method From the Index Razor Page

Before adding the **_CardPartial** view to the **Index** Razor Page, the data need to be fetched from the database and added to a property in the main **Index** Razor Page's code-behind file. Use the **Count** method you added to the **DbReadService** in the **Database** project to fetch the data and create instances from the **CardViewModel** and assign the fetched data to them. Also, assign values for the other properties as well.

1. Open the C# file for the **Index** Razor Page in the *Pages* folder.
2. Add a tuple variable called **Cards** to the class. It should contain parameters of the **CardViewModel** class for each value returned from the **Count** method in the **DbReadService** class.

```
        public (CardViewModel Instructors, CardViewModel Users,
                CardViewModel Courses, CardViewModel Modules,
                CardViewModel Videos, CardViewModel Downloads) Cards;
```

3. Use DI to inject the **IDbReadService** interface from the **Database** project into the **IndexModel** constructor and name it **db**. Store the service instance in a private variable named **_db** on class-level; this will give access to the database throughout the file.
   ```
   private readonly IDbReadService _db;
   public IndexModel(IDbReadService db)
   {
       _db = db;
   }
   ```

4. Call the **Count** method on the injected instance of the **DbReadService** class in the **OnGet** method.
   ```
   var (courses, downloads, instructors, modules, videos, users) =
       _db.Count();
   ```

5. Add instances of the **CardViewModel** class to the **Cards** tuple for the cards (see below for complete code).
   ```
   Cards = (
       instructors: new CardViewModel {
           BackgroundColor = "#9c27b0",
           Count = Instructors, Description = "Instructors",
           Icon = "person", Url = "./Instructors/Index" },
       ...
   );
   ```

6. Save all files.

The complete code for the **Index.cshtml.cs** file:

```
public class IndexModel : PageModel
{
    private readonly IDbReadService _db;

    public (CardViewModel Instructors, CardViewModel Users,
            CardViewModel Courses, CardViewModel Modules,
            CardViewModel Videos, CardViewModel Downloads) Cards;

    public IndexModel(IDbReadService db)
    {
        _db = db;
    }
```

16. The Administrator Dashboard

```csharp
public void OnGet()
{
    var (courses, downloads, instructors, modules, videos) =
        _db.Count();

    Cards = (
        Instructors: new CardViewModel
        {
            BackgroundColor = "#9c27b0",
            Count = instructors,
            Description = "Instructors",
            Icon = "person",
            Url = "./Instructors/Index"
        },
        Users: new CardViewModel
        {
            BackgroundColor = "#414141",
            Count = users,
            Description = "Users",
            Icon = "people",
            Url = "./Users/Index"
        },
        Courses: new CardViewModel
        {
            BackgroundColor = "#009688",
            Count = courses,
            Description = "Courses",
            Icon = "subscriptions",
            Url = "./Courses/Index"
        },
        Modules: new CardViewModel
        {
            BackgroundColor = "#f44336",
            Count = modules,
            Description = "Modules",
            Icon = "list",
            Url = "./Modules/Index"
        },
        Videos: new CardViewModel
        {
            BackgroundColor = "#3f51b5",
            Count = videos,
            Description = "Videos",
```

```
                Icon = "theaters",
                Url = "./Videos/Index"
            },
            Downloads: new CardViewModel
            {
                BackgroundColor = "#ffcc00",
                Count = downloads,
                Description = "Downloads",
                Icon = "import_contacts",
                Url = "./Downloads/Index"
            }
        );
    }
}
```

Styling the _CardPartial View

To style the **_CardPartial** view – the dashboard cards – you first must render the view once in the **Index** Razor Page located in the *Pages* folder so that you can see it in the browser. Then you can use CSS to style the view by adding selectors to a new CSS file called *dashboard.css* that you will add to the *wwwroot/css* folder.

1. Open the **Index** Razor Page located in the *Pages* folder.
2. Remove all HTML from the page but leave all Razor code and change the title to *Dashboard*.
   ```
   @page
   @model IndexModel
   @{
       ViewData["Title"] = "Dashboard";
   }
   ```
3. Use the <partial> element and the Instructors instance in the **Cards** model property to render the **_CardPartial** view once.
   `<partial name="_CardPartial" for="Cards.Instructors" />`
4. Add a new style sheet called *dashboard.css* to the *wwwroot/css* folder.
5. Remove the **body** selector.
6. Open the **_Layout** view and drag in a link to the CSS file below the *site.css* link.
   `<link rel="stylesheet" href="~/css/dashboard.css" />`
7. Save all files and open the *dashboard.css* file.
8. Run the application and see what the card looks like un-styled.

16. The Administrator Dashboard

The code for the **Index** Razor Page, so far:

```
@page
@model IndexModel
@{
    ViewData["Title"] = "Dashboard";
}

<partial name="_CardPartial" for="Cards.Instructors" />
```

I suggest that you refresh the browser after each change you make to the *dashboard.css* file.

Add a selector for the **card** class. Add a margin of 3.3rem; rem is relative to the font size of the root element. Float the card to the left and set its width to 24% of its container and its minimal width to 200px. Make the text color white and remove any text decoration from the links (the underlining). Remove the border-radius to give the cards square corners.

```
a.card {
    margin: .33rem;
    float: left;
    width: 24%;
    min-width: 200px;
    color: #fff;
    text-decoration: none;
    border-radius: 0px;
}
```

Next, add a hover effect to the card by adding the **:hover** selector to a new **card** selector. Dial down the opacity to 80%; this makes it look like the color changes when the mouse pointer is hovering over the card.

```
a.card:hover {
    opacity: .8;
}
```

Add 15px padding between the card's border and its content.

```
a .card-content {
    padding: 15px;
}
```

Remove the top and bottom margin for the <h3> element and the bottom margin for the <p> element.

```
a .card-data h3 {
    margin-top: 0;
    margin-bottom: 0;
}

a .card-data p {
    margin-bottom: 0;
}
```

Style the icon with absolute positioning inside its container. Place the icon 25px from the right side and 30% from the top. Change the font size to 35px and its opacity to 0.2.

```
a .card-icon {
    position: absolute;
    right: 25px;
    top: 22%;
    font-size: 50px;
    opacity: .2;
}
```

Modifying the Index Razor Page

Now it's time to put it all together to create the dashboard in the **Index** view. You will use Bootstrap row, column, and offset classes to create the two-card wide list of clickable items. You will add different Bootstrap classes for varying browser sizes, making the dashboard look nice on different devices.

You will also restrict access to the dashboard to logged in users belonging to the **Admin** role.

1. Add a <br /> element above the <partial> element in the **Index** page.
2. Add a <div> element below the <br /> element and decorate it with the **row** Bootstrap class to create a new row.
   `<div class="row"></div>`
3. Add another <div> inside the previous <div> and decorate it with column and offset Bootstrap classes for small and medium device sizes.
   `<div class="offset-sm-2 col-sm-8 offset-md-4 col-md-6"></div>`
4. Move the <partial> element inside the column <div> and copy it.
5. Paste in the copied code and change the model from **Instructors** to **Users**.
   ```
   <partial name="_CardPartial" for="Cards.Instructors" />
   <partial name="_CardPartial" for="Cards.Users" />
   ```
6. Run the application. Two cards should be displayed, one for instructors and one for users. Clicking on them will display an error page because you must add the necessary **Index** Razor Pages first.
7. Copy the <div> element decorated with the row class and all its content. Paste it in two more times so that you end up with three rows below one another.
8. Change the model parameter for the cards to reflect the remaining pages: **Courses**, **Modules**, **Videos**, and **Downloads**.
9. Run the application. All six entity cards should be displayed.
10. Use the **@inject** directive in the **Index** Razor Page to Inject the **SignInManager** for the **User** entity below the **using** statements; this will give access to the **IsSignedIn** method in the **SignInManager** that checks if a user is logged in.
    `@inject SignInManager<VODUser> SignInManager`
11. Add an if-block around the HTML below the <br /> element. Call the **IsSignedIn** method and pass in the **User** entity to it and check that the user belongs to the **Admin** role by calling the **IsInRole** method on the **User** entity.
    `@if (SignInManager.IsSignedIn(User) && User.IsInRole("Admin")) { }`

12. Run the application and log out; the dashboard shouldn't be visible. Log in as a regular user; the dashboard shouldn't be visible.
13. Log in as an **Admin** user for the dashboard to be visible.

The complete code for the **Index** Razor Page:

```
@page
@inject SignInManager<VODUser> SignInManager
@model IndexModel
@{ ViewData["Title"] = "Dashboard"; }
<br />
@if (SignInManager.IsSignedIn(User) && User.IsInRole("Admin"))
{
    <div class="row">
        <div class="offset-sm-2 col-sm-8 offset-md-4 col-md-6">
            <partial name="_CardPartial" for="Cards.Instructors" />
            <partial name="_CardPartial" for="Cards.Users" />
        </div>
    </div>

    <div class="row">
        <div class="offset-sm-2 col-sm-8 offset-md-4 col-md-6">
            <partial name="_CardPartial" for="Cards.Courses" />
            <partial name="_CardPartial" for="Cards.Modules" />
        </div>
    </div>

    <div class="row">
        <div class="offset-sm-2 col-sm-8 offset-md-4 col-md-6">
            <partial name="_CardPartial" for="Cards.Videos" />
            <partial name="_CardPartial" for="Cards.Downloads" />
        </div>
    </div>
}
```

Summary

In this chapter, you added a dashboard for administrators. The cards (items) displayed in the dashboard were added as links to enable navigation to the other **Index** Razor Pages you will add in upcoming chapters.

In the next chapter, you will add a menu with the same links as the dashboard cards.

17. The Admin Menu

Introduction

In this chapter, you will create an **Admin** menu with links to all **Index** Razor Pages associated with the entities in the **Common** project. Since you know that a Razor Page folder will have the same name as its corresponding entity, you can add the menu items before adding the pages.

You will create the menu in a partial view called **_AdminMenuPartial** that is rendered in the **_Layout** view, using the <partial> Tag Helper.

Technologies Used in This Chapter

1. **C#** – To add authorization checks in the **_AdminMenuPartial** partial view.
2. **HTML** – To create the drop-down menu and its items

Overview

Your task is to create a menu for all the **Index** Razor Pages, in a partial view named **_AdminMenuPartial**, and then render it from the **_Layout** view.

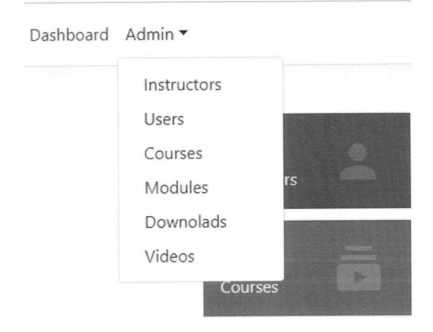

Adding the _AdminMenuPartial Partial View

Create a partial view called **_AdminMenuPartial** in the *Pages-Shared* folder. Add an <ul> element styled with the **nav navbar-nav** Bootstrap classes, to make it look nice in the navigation bar. Add an <li> element styled with the **drop-down** Bootstrap class to make it a drop-down button. Add an <a> element with the text *Admin* and a caret symbol, to the <li> element. Add a <ul> element styled with the **drop-down-menu** Bootstrap class that contains all the menu items as <li> elements. Use the **asp-page** Tag Helper to target the appropriate Razor Page.

1. Right click on the *Pages-Shared* folder and select **Add-New Item**.
2. Add a **Razor View** named **_AdminMenuPartial** and delete all code in it.

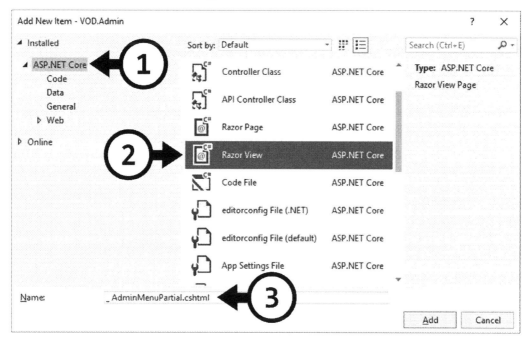

3. Use the **@inject** directive to inject the **SignInManager** for the **VODUser** entity. This will give access to the **IsSignedIn** method in the **SignInManager** that checks if a user is logged in.
   `@inject SignInManager<VODUser> SignInManager`
4. Add an if-block that checks if the user is signed in and belongs to the **Admin** role.
   `@if (SignInManager.IsSignedIn(User) && User.IsInRole("Admin")) { }`

17. The Admin Menu

5. You can find the markup for the menu on Bootstrap's website (version 4.3). Add an <li> element inside the if-block and decorate it with the **dropdown** and **nav-item** Bootstrap class. This will be the container for the button that opens the menu and the menu itself.
   ```
   <li class="nav-item dropdown">
   </li>
   ```

6. Add an <a> element that will act as the link in the navigation bar.
   ```
   <a class="nav-link dropdown-toggle" data-toggle="dropdown" href="#" role="button" aria-haspopup="true" aria-expanded="false">Admin</a>
   ```

7. Create the drop-down menu section of the menu by adding a <ul> element decorated with the **drop-down-menu** Bootstrap class, below the <a> element.
   ```
   <ul class="dropdown-menu">
   </ul>
   ```

8. Add an <a> element for each of the **Index** Razor Pages that you create. You can figure out all the folder names by looking at the entity class names; a folder should have the same name as the entity property in the **VODContext** class in the **Database** project. The URL path in the **href** attribute on the <a> element should contain the page folder followed by */Index*. Also, add a suitable description in the <a> element.
   ```
   <a class="dropdown-item" href="/Instructors/Index">Instructor</a>
   ```

9. Open the **_ManuPartial** view and use the <partial> element to render the **_AdminMenuPartial** partial view. Place the <partial> element below the <li> element for the **Dashboard** link.
   ```
   <partial name="_AdminMenuPartial" />
   ```

10. Save all the files and run the application (F5) and make sure that you are logged in as an administrator. Click the **Admin** menu to open it. Clicking any of the menu items will display an empty page because you haven't added the necessary **Index** Razor Pages yet.

The complete markup in the **_AdminMenuPartial** partial view:

```
@inject SignInManager<User> SignInManager

@if (SignInManager.IsSignedIn(User) && User.IsInRole("Admin"))
{
    <li class="nav-item dropdown">
        <a class="nav-link dropdown-toggle" data-toggle="dropdown"
            href="#" role="button" aria-haspopup="true"
            aria-expanded="false">Admin</a>
        <div class="dropdown-menu">
            <a class="dropdown-item" href="/Instructors/Index">
                Instructors</a>
            <a class="dropdown-item" href="/Users/Index">Users</a>
            <a class="dropdown-item" href="/Courses/Index">Courses</a>
            <a class="dropdown-item" href="/Modules/Index">Modules</a>
            <a class="dropdown-item" href="/Downloads/Index">
                Downloads</a>
            <a class="dropdown-item" href="/Videos/Index">Videos</a>
        </div>
    </li>
}
```

Summary

In this chapter, you added the **Admin** menu and targeted the **Index** Razor Pages that you will add throughout this part of the book.

In the next chapter, you will create a custom Tag Helper that will render the buttons you will add to the Razor Pages.

18. Custom Button Tag Helper

Introduction

In this chapter, you will create a configurable button Tag Helper that will be used instead of links in the Razor Pages. The Tag Helper will inherit from the **AnchorTagHelper** class to reuse the <a> tag's functionality. It will also use new attributes and attribute values to configure the finished HTML elements, such as Bootstrap button style and size and what icon to display, if any. Fetch the button description from the text between the start and end tag. The ids needed for some of the Razor Pages will be assigned using the inherited anchor tag's **asp-route-{value}** attributes.

`<btn asp-page="Delete" asp-route-id="1" icon="close"></btn>`

Example URL: *http://localhost:55962/Videos/Delete?id=1*

A C# class builds the Tag Helper's HTML element with C# code. Then you insert the Tag Helper into the views and pages as an HTML markup-like element.

The class must inherit from the **TagHelper** class, or another class that inherits that class, and implement a method called **Process**, which creates or modifies the HTML element. Tag Helper attributes can be added as properties in the class, or dynamically to a collection, by adding them to the HTML Tag Helper element.

Technologies Used in This Chapter

1. **C#** – to create the Tag Helper.
2. **HTML** – To add the Tag Helper to the Razor Pages.

Overview

Your task is to create a custom Tag Helper called **btn**. You'll inherit the **AnchorTagHelper** class to reuse the anchor tag's functionality, such as attributes. You will add a new **string** property called **Icon** that can be used to specify an icon to be displayed left of the button's description. Here, we use Google's Material Icons library, but you could use any icon library of your choosing.

You should be able to configure the following with the Tag Helper: anything that you can configure for an anchor tag plus an icon to be displayed. Apply the default styles (**btn-sm** and **btn-default**); you can override them by adding other Bootstrap **btn** classes.

Implementing the Btn Tag Helper

Create the **btn** Tag Helper in a class called **BtnTagHelper** in a folder named *Tag Helpers* located directly under the project node. Use the **New Item** dialog's **Tag Helper Class** template.

You can use the **HtmlTargetElement** attribute to limit the scope of the Tag Helper to a specific HTML element type.

```
[HtmlTargetElement("my-tag-helper")]
public class MyTagHelperTagHelper : TagHelper
```

The Tag Helper will produce an <a> element styled as a Bootstrap button.

To make the Tag Helper available in Razor Pages, you need to add an **@addTagHelper** directive that includes all Tag Helpers in the project assembly, to the **_ViewImports** view.

`@addTagHelper *, VOD.Admin`

When you add the Tag Helper to the view, it's very important that you use a closing tag; otherwise, the Tag Helper won't work.

`<btn></btn>`

Creating the Tag Helper

1. Add an **@addTagHelper** directive that includes all Tag Helpers in the project assembly, to the **_ViewImports** view in the *Pages* folder.
   `@addTagHelper *, VOD.Admin`
2. Add a folder named *TagHelpers* to the project.
3. Add a **Tag Helper Class** called **BtnTagHelper** to the folder. Right click on the folder and select **Add-New Item**. Select the **Tag Helper Class** template, name it, and click the **Add** button.

18. Custom Button Tag Helper

4. Inherit from the **AnchorTagHelper** class instead of the default **TagHelper** class to inherit the anchor tag's functionality; this saves you the trouble of implementing it in your class.
   ```
   [HtmlTargetElement("tag-name")]
   public class PageButtonTagHelper : AnchorTagHelper
   {
       public override void Process(TagHelperContext context,
       TagHelperOutput output) { }
   }
   ```

5. Add a constructor that gets the **IHtmlGenerator** service injected and add it to the base class; this is a must because the **AnchorTagHelper** class demands such a constructor.
   ```
   public BtnTagHelper(IHtmlGenerator generator) : base(generator)
   {
   }
   ```

6. Change the **HtmlTargetElement** attribute to **btn**; this will be the Tag Helper's "element" name; you use <btn></btn> to add the Tag Helper to the Razor page, and when rendered, it will turn into an anchor tag. It's not a real HTML element, but it looks like one, to blend in with the HTML markup. It will, however, generate a real HTML anchor tag element when rendered.
   ```
   [HtmlTargetElement("btn")]
   ```

7. Because the **AnchorTagHelper** class doesn't have an **Icon** property to specify an icon, you need to add it to the class.
   a. **Icon (string)**: The name of the icon from Google's Material Icons to display on the button. Don't add this attribute to the HTML element if you want a button without an icon. It should have an empty string as a default value. You can find icon names here: https://material.io/tools/icons/?style=baseline.
      ```
      public string Icon { get; set; } = string.Empty;
      ```

8. Add constants for the different button styles that should be available and the icon provider.
   ```
   const string btnPrimary = "btn-primary";
   const string btnDanger = "btn-danger";
   const string btnDefault = "btn-default";
   const string btnInfo = "btn-info";
   ```

```
const string btnSucess = "btn-success";
const string btnWarning = "btn-warning";
// Google's Material Icons provider name
const string iconProvider = "material-icons";
```

9. Add if-statements that determine if exceptions should be thrown in the **Process** method.
   ```
   if (context == null)
       throw new ArgumentNullException(nameof(context));
   if (output == null)
       throw new ArgumentNullException(nameof(output));
   ```

10. Change the output element to an anchor tag (<a>) below the second if-statement.
    ```
    output.TagName = "a";
    ```

11. Call the **Process** method in the base class that builds the output anchor element at the end of the method.
    ```
    base.Process(context, output);
    ```

12. Add a <btn> Tag Helper to the **Index** page on the *Pages* folder. Remember that from ASP.NET Core 2.2 the **asp-page** attribute will result in an empty **href** output element if the referenced page doesn't exist. To test the Tag Helper, you can reference the **Error** page in the *Pages* folder to get a non-empty **href** value.
    ```
    <btn asp-page="Error">Error</btn>
    ```

13. Start the application (Ctrl+F5) and hover over the link to ensure that the **href** contains the specified page. Open the developer tools window (F12) to see that the <btn> Tag Helper rendered as an anchor tag.
    ```
    <a href="/Error">Error</a>
    ```

14. Stop the application if you started it with debugging (F5).

The code for the **btn** Tag Helper, so far:

```
[HtmlTargetElement("btn")]
public class BtnTagHelper : AnchorTagHelper
{
    #region Properties
    public string Icon { get; set; } = string.Empty;
    #endregion
```

18. Custom Button Tag Helper

```
#region Constants
const string btnPrimary = "btn-primary";
const string btnDanger = "btn-danger";
const string btnDefault = "btn-default";
const string btnInfo = "btn-info";
const string btnSucess = "btn-success";
const string btnWarning = "btn-warning";
// Google's Material Icons provider name
const string iconProvider = "material-icons";
#endregion

#region This constructor is needed for AnchorTagHelper inheritance
public BtnTagHelper(IHtmlGenerator generator) : base(generator)
{
}
#endregion

public override void Process(TagHelperContext context,
TagHelperOutput output)
{
    if (context == null)
        throw new  ArgumentNullException(nameof(context));
    if (output == null)
        throw new ArgumentNullException(nameof(output));

    // Changes <btn> tag to <a> tag when rendered
    output.TagName = "a";

    base.Process(context, output);
}
}
```

Turn the Anchor Tag into a Bootstrap Button

Now, you will turn the anchor tag into a Bootstrap button by adding **btn-** classes depending on the page the button is referencing. You will read the value in the **asp-page** attribute and add Bootstrap CSS classes to the **class** attribute. Add the code directly above the **base.Process** method call.

1. Begin by fetching the **asp-page** attribute if it exists. You will use its value to determine which Bootstrap button type should be applied using the previously added constants.
   ```
   var aspPageAttribute = context.AllAttributes.SingleOrDefault(p =>
   p.Name.ToLower().Equals("asp-page"));
   ```

2. Now, fetch the **class** attribute if it exists. You will append the Bootstrap classes to its current value.
   ```
   var classAttribute = context.AllAttributes.SingleOrDefault(p =>
   p.Name.ToLower().Equals("class"));
   ```

3. Add a **string** variable called **buttonStyle** and add the value from the **btnDefault** constant to it. This variable will be assigned a value based on the value of the **asp-page** value.
   ```
   var buttonStyle = btnDefault;
   ```

4. Add an if-block that checks if the **asp-page** attribute exists.
   ```
   if (aspPageAttribute != null) {}
   ```

5. Fetch the value of the **asp-page** attribute inside the if-block.
   ```
   var pageValue = aspPageAttribute.Value.ToString().ToLower();
   ```

6. Assign the Bootstrap button type to the **buttonType** variable you added earlier based on the page value inside the if-block. The error value is only added to test the button and can be removed when the <btn> Tag Helper is complete.
   ```
   buttonStyle =
       pageValue.Equals("create") ? btnPrimary :
       pageValue.Equals("delete") ? btnDanger :
       pageValue.Equals("edit") ? btnSucess :
       pageValue.Equals("index") ? btnPrimary :
       pageValue.Equals("details") ? btnInfo :
       pageValue.Equals("/index") ? btnWarning :
       pageValue.Equals("error") ? btnDanger :
       btnDefault;
   ```

7. Below the if-block, use the **buttonStyle** variable when adding Bootstrap classes to a variable called **bootstrapClasses**.
   ```
   var bootstrapClasses = $"btn-sm {buttonStyle}";
   ```

8. Add an if-else-block that checks if the **class** attribute exists.
   ```
   if (classAttribute != null) {}
   else {}
   ```

9. Inside the if-block, fetch the value from the **class** attribute and store it in a variable called **css**.
   ```
   var css = classAttribute.Value.ToString();
   ```

10. Below the **css** variable, add another if-block that checks that the **class** attribute doesn't already contain Bootstrap button style classes; if it does, then skip the code in the if-block.
    ```
    if (!css.ToLower().Contains("btn-")) {}
    ```

11. Inside the previous if-block, remove the **class** attribute from the element and rebuild the **class** attribute and its content with the added Bootstrap classes.
    ```
    output.Attributes.Remove(classAttribute);
    classAttribute = new TagHelperAttribute(
        "class", $"{css} {bootstrapClasses}");
    output.Attributes.Add(classAttribute);
    ```

12. Inside the else-block, you add the **class** attribute to the element directly because it doesn't have that attribute.
    ```
    output.Attributes.Add("class", bootstrapClasses);
    ```

13. Run the application (F5) and make sure that the element is rendered as a red button with the text *Error*.

14. Stop the application.

The code in the **Process** method, so far:

```
public override void Process(TagHelperContext context, TagHelperOutput output)
{
    if (context == null)
        throw new ArgumentNullException(nameof(context));
    if (output == null)
        throw new ArgumentNullException(nameof(output));

    // Change <btn> tag to <a> tag
    output.TagName = "a";

    #region Bootstrap Button
    // Fetch page and class attribute to see if they exist
    var aspPageAttribute = context.AllAttributes.SingleOrDefault(
        p => p.Name.ToLower().Equals("asp-page"));
```

```csharp
        var classAttribute = context.AllAttributes.SingleOrDefault(
            p => p.Name.ToLower().Equals("class"));

        var buttonStyle = btnDefault;

        if (aspPageAttribute != null)
        {
            var pageValue = aspPageAttribute.Value.ToString().ToLower();
            buttonStyle =
                pageValue.Equals("create") ? btnPrimary :
                pageValue.Equals("delete") ? btnDanger :
                pageValue.Equals("edit") ? btnSucess :
                pageValue.Equals("index") ? btnPrimary :
                pageValue.Equals("details") ? btnInfo :
                pageValue.Equals("/index") ? btnWarning :
                pageValue.Equals("error") ? btnDanger :
                btnDefault;
        }

        var bootstrapClasses = $"btn-sm {buttonStyle}";

        if (classAttribute != null)
        {
            var css = classAttribute.Value.ToString();
            if (!css.ToLower().Contains("btn-"))
            {
                output.Attributes.Remove(classAttribute);
                classAttribute = new TagHelperAttribute("class",
                    $"{css} {bootstrapClasses}");
                output.Attributes.Add(classAttribute);
            }
        }
        else
        {
            output.Attributes.Add("class", bootstrapClasses);
        }
        #endregion

        base.Process(context, output);
    }
```

18. Custom Button Tag Helper

Adding an Icon and Styling the Button

Now, you will add an icon from Google's Material Icons to the element's description using the **Icon** property you added earlier that holds the name of the icon.

1. Above the **base.Process** method call, add an if-block that checks that the **Icon** property has a value; an icon can only be added if the property has a valid icon name.
   ```
   if (!Icon.Equals(string.Empty)) {}
   ```

2. Inside the if-block, fetch the already existing content between the start and end tags, if any, and store it in a variable called **content**. If there is content, then add a space ( ) before the content.
   ```
   var childContext = output.GetChildContentAsync().Result;
   var content = childContext.GetContent().Trim();
   if (content.Length > 0) content = $" {content}";
   ```

3. Add an <i> element in the if-block with the icon information from the **iconProvider** constant and the **Icon** property before the content stored in the **content** variable displayed in a <span> element to make it easier to style.
   ```
   output.Content.SetHtmlContent($"<i class='{iconProvider}' style='display: inline-flex; vertical-align: top; line-height: inherit;font-size: medium;'>{Icon}</i> <span style='font-size: medium;'>{content}</span>");
   ```

4. Add an icon to the <btn> Tag Helper.
   ```
   <btn asp-page="Error" icon="create">Error</btn>
   ```

5. Run the application and make sure that the icon is displayed in front of the text inside the button.
6. Stop the application.

7. To style the button, you need to fetch the **style** attribute from the Tag Helper below the if-block and assign values to it or add it if it's missing. Store the style in a variable named **style** and the existing value in a variable named **styleValue**.
   ```
   var style = context.AllAttributes.SingleOrDefault(s =>
       s.Name.ToLower().Equals("style"));

   var styleValue = style == null ? "" : style.Value;
   ```

8. Create a **TagHelperAttribute** instance and add the style attribute and its values to it. Display the anchor tag as part of the flex content on the row where it is displayed, remove the border radius to give it square corners, and remove the text decoration (underlining).
   ```
   var newStyle = new TagHelperAttribute("style",
       $"{styleValue} display:inline-flex;border-radius:0px;
       text-decoration: none;");
   ```

9. Append the new styling if the **style** attribute exists, otherwise add it.
   ```
   if (style != null) output.Attributes.Remove(style);
   output.Attributes.Add(newStyle);
   ```

10. Add another <btn> Tag Helper without any text below the previous one.
    ```
    <btn asp-page="Error" icon="create"></btn>
    ```

11. Run the application. One of the buttons should display an icon and text, the other one only an icon. Also, make sure that the buttons have square corners and that no underlining is visible when hovering over the button. Remove the two <btn> Tag Helpers from the **Index** view when you stop the application.

The code for adding the icon in the **Process** method:

```
if (!Icon.Equals(string.Empty))
{
    var childContext = output.GetChildContentAsync().Result;
    var content = childContext.GetContent().Trim();
    if (content.Length > 0) content = $" {content}";

    output.Content.SetHtmlContent($"<i class='{iconProvider}'
        style='display: inline-flex; vertical-align: top;
        line-height: inherit;font-size: medium;'>{Icon}</i>");
```

```
            <span style='font-size: medium;'>{content}</span>");
}
```

The code for styling the button in the **Process** method:

```
// Fetch style attribute if it exists
var style = context.AllAttributes.SingleOrDefault(s =>
    s.Name.ToLower().Equals("style"));
var styleValue = style == null ? "" : style.Value;
var newStyle = new TagHelperAttribute("style", $"{styleValue}
    display:inline-flex;border-radius:0px;text-decoration: none;");
if (style != null) output.Attributes.Remove(style);
output.Attributes.Add(newStyle);
```

The complete code for the **btn** Tag Helper:

```
[HtmlTargetElement("btn")]
public class BtnTagHelper : AnchorTagHelper
{
    #region Properties
    public string Icon { get; set; } = string.Empty;
    #endregion

    #region Constants
    const string btnPrimary = "btn-primary";
    const string btnDanger = "btn-danger";
    const string btnDefault = "btn-default";
    const string btnInfo = "btn-info";
    const string btnSucess = "btn-success";
    const string btnWarning = "btn-warning";
    // Google's Material Icons provider name
    const string iconProvider = "material-icons";
    #endregion

    #region This constructor is needed for AnchorTagHelper inheritance
    public BtnTagHelper(IHtmlGenerator generator) : base(generator)
    {
    }
    #endregion

    public override void Process(TagHelperContext context,
    TagHelperOutput output)
    {
        if (context == null)
            throw new ArgumentNullException(nameof(context));
```

```csharp
            if (output == null)
                throw new ArgumentNullException(nameof(output));

            // Changes <btn> tag to <a> tag when rendered
            output.TagName = "a";

            #region Bootstrap Button
            // Fetch page and class attribute to see if they exist
            var aspPageAttribute =
                context.AllAttributes.SingleOrDefault(p =>
                p.Name.ToLower().Equals("asp-page"));
            var classAttribute = context.AllAttributes.SingleOrDefault(p =>
                p.Name.ToLower().Equals("class"));
            var buttonStyle = btnDefault;
            if (aspPageAttribute != null)
            {
                var pageValue = aspPageAttribute.Value.ToString().ToLower();
                buttonStyle =
                    pageValue.Equals("create") ? btnPrimary :
                    pageValue.Equals("delete") ? btnDanger :
                    pageValue.Equals("edit") ? btnSucess :
                    pageValue.Equals("index") ? btnPrimary :
                    pageValue.Equals("details") ? btnInfo :
                    pageValue.Equals("/index") ? btnWarning :
                    pageValue.Equals("error") ? btnDanger :
                    btnDefault;
            }

            var bootstrapClasses = $"btn-sm {buttonStyle}";

            if (classAttribute != null)
            {
                var css = classAttribute.Value.ToString();
                if (!css.ToLower().Contains("btn-"))
                {
                    output.Attributes.Remove(classAttribute);
                    classAttribute = new TagHelperAttribute(
                        "class", $"{css} {bootstrapClasses}");
                    output.Attributes.Add(classAttribute);
                }
            }
            else { output.Attributes.Add("class", bootstrapClasses); }
            #endregion
```

18. Custom Button Tag Helper

```
            #region Icon
            if (!Icon.Equals(string.Empty))
            {
                var childContext = output.GetChildContentAsync().Result;
                var content = childContext.GetContent().Trim();
                if (content.Length > 0) content = $" {content}";

                output.Content.SetHtmlContent($"<i class='{iconProvider}'
                    style='display: inline-flex; vertical-align: top;
                    line-height: inherit;font-size: medium;'>{Icon}</i>
                    <span style='font-size: medium;'>{content}</span>");
            }
            #endregion

            #region Style Attribute
            // Fetch style attribute if it exists
            var style = context.AllAttributes.SingleOrDefault(s =>
                s.Name.ToLower().Equals("style"));
            var styleValue = style == null ? "" : style.Value;
            var newStyle = new TagHelperAttribute("style", $"{styleValue}
                display:inline-flex;border-radius:0px;text-decoration:
                none;");
            if (style != null) output.Attributes.Remove(style);
            output.Attributes.Add(newStyle);
            #endregion

            base.Process(context, output);
        }
    }
}
```

Summary

In this chapter, you implemented a custom button Tag Helper and tested it in a Razor Page. You learned a dynamic way to find out what attributes have been added and read their values.

The purpose of the Tag Helper you created is to replace links with Bootstrap-styled buttons. You can, however, use Tag Helpers for so much more.

In the upcoming chapters, you will use the button Tag Helper to add buttons to the various Razor Pages you will create for the **Admin** UI.

In the next chapter, you will add a new service for writing data to the database.

ASP.NET Core 2.2 MVC, Razor Pages, API, JSON Web Tokens & HttpClient

19. The Database Write Service

Introduction
In this chapter, you will create a service called **DbWriteService** in the **VOD. Database** project. This service will be used from the **Admin** project to write data to the database.

The **Admin** project doesn't have an existing service for writing data and will, therefore, use the **DbWriteService** service you will create in the **Database** project directly.

Technologies Used in This Chapter
1. **C#** – To create the service.
2. **Entity framework** – To interact with the tables in the database.
3. **LINQ** – To query the database tables.

Overview
Your objective is to create a data service that adds, updates, and deletes data in the database tables.

Adding the DbWriteService Service
You need to add an interface called **IDbWriteService** that can be used from other projects with dependency injection to add and modify data in the database. You then need to implement the interface in a class called **DbWriteService** that contains the code to access the database.

Implement the methods as generic methods that can handle any entity and therefore add or modify data in any table in the database.

Adding the Service Interface and Class
1. Open the **VOD.Database** project.
2. Open the *Services* folder.
3. Add a public interface called **IDbWriteService** to the folder. Right click on the folder, select **Add-New Item**, and select the **Interface** template.
4. Add the **public** access modifier to the interface to make it accessible from any project.
   `public interface IDbWriteService`

5. Add a **public** class called **DbWriteService** to the *Services* folder.
6. Add the interface to the class.
   ```
   public class DbWriteService : IDbWriteService
   {
   }
   ```
7. Add a constructor to the class and inject the **VODContext** to get access to the database from the service. Store the object in a class-level variable called **_db**.
   ```
   private readonly VODContext _db;
   public DbWriteService(VODContext db)
   {
       _db = db;
   }
   ```
8. Open the **Startup** class in the **Admin** project.
9. Add the **IDbWriteService** service to the **ConfigureServices** method.
   ```
   services.AddScoped<IDbWriteService, DbWriteService>();
   ```
8. Save the files.

The code for the **IDbWriteService** interface, so far:

```
public interface IDbWriteService { }
```

The code for the **DbWriteService** class, so far:

```
public class DbWriteService : IDbWriteService
{
    #region Properties
    private readonly VODContext _db;
    #endregion

    #region Constructor
    public DbWriteService(VODContext db)
    {
        _db = db;
    }
    #endregion
}
```

The SaveChangesAsync Method

The **SaveChangesAsync** method will persist all changes made by the **Add**, **Delete**, and **Update** methods to the database. Before calling this method, all changes are only in-memory; this is the only asynchronous method in the interface and class since you want to be able to make many changes and persist them together; therefore, asynchronous calls are unnecessary because no long-running tasks are involved.

The method should return a Boolean value specifying if the database call was successful.

1. Open the **IDbWriteService** interface.
2. Add a method definition for the parameterless asynchronous **SaveChangesAsync** method that will persist the changes to the database.
   `Task<bool> SaveChangesAsync();`
3. Add the **SaveChangesAsync** method to the **DbWriteService** class, either manually or by using the **Quick Actions** light bulb button. If you auto-generate the method with **Quick Actions**, you must remove the **throw** statement. Don't forget to make it asynchronous by adding the **async** keyword to the method definition.
4. Add a try/catch-block where the catch-block returns **false**, to show the calling method that the data couldn't be persisted to the table.
5. Call the **SaveChangesAsync** method inside the try-block. The method should return **true** or **false** depending on if persisting the changes to the table succeeded or failed.
   `return await _db.SaveChangesAsync() >= 0;`
6. Save all files.

The complete code for the **SaveChangesAsync** method:

```
public async Task<bool> SaveChangesAsync()
{
    try
    {
        return await _db.SaveChangesAsync() >= 0;
    }
    catch
    {
        return false;
    }
}
```

The code for the **IDbWriteService** interface, so far:

```
public interface IDbWriteService
{
    Task<bool> SaveChangesAsync();
}
```

The Add Method

The **Add** method will add a new entity in-memory that Entity Framework tracks for changes. You must call the **SaveChangesAsync** method to persist the entity to the database.

Because the method adds a new generic entity, it must be passed in as a parameter with the same type as the **Add** method's defining entity.

Since the underlying data in the database hasn't changed, there's no point in returning a value from the method; you only re-throw any exception that occurs.

Avoid calling the **AddAsync** method on the context, unless it's a special value generator (see a comment from Microsoft's website below). Instead, call the **Add** method on the context, which makes Entity Framework begin tracking the entity in-memory.

```
// This method is async only to allow special value generators
```

The **Add** context method will incur overhead since persisting the entity to the database requires calling the **SaveChangesAsync** method; that call should be asynchronous since it is a long-running task that could benefit from using the thread pool, freeing up resources.

```
public void Add<TEntity>(TEntity item) where TEntity : class
{
}
```

1. Open the **IDbWriteService** interface.
2. Add a generic method definition for an **Add** method that is defined by the entity type that substitutes the generic **TEntity** type when calling the method. You must limit the **TEntity** type to only classes since an entity only can be created using a class; if you don't do this, a value type such as **int** or **double** can define the method, which will generate an exception. The method should not return anything (**void**).
   ```
   void Add<TEntity>(TEntity item) where TEntity : class;
   ```

19. The Database Write Service

3. Add the **Add** method to the **DbWriteService** class, either manually or by using the **Quick Actions** light bulb button. If you auto-generate the method with **Quick Actions**, you must remove the **throw** statement.
4. Add a try/catch-block where the catch-block throws the exception to the calling method.
5. Call the **Add** method on the **_db** context inside the try-block and pass in the item to add from the method's **item** parameter; you don't have to specify the generic **TEntity** type to access the table associated with the defining entity; the **item** infers it.
   `_db.Add(item);`
6. Save all files.

The code for the **IDbWriteService** interface, so far:

```
public interface IDbWriteService
{
    Task<bool> SaveChangesAsync();
    void Add<TEntity>(TEntity item) where TEntity : class;
}
```

The complete code for the **Add** method:

```
void Add<TEntity>(TEntity item) where TEntity : class;
{
    try
    {
        _db.Add(item);
    }
    catch
    {
        throw;
    }
}
```

The Delete Method

The **Delete** method will remove an entity that Entity Framework tracks in-memory. The entity remains in the database until calling the **SaveChangesAsync** method.

Since the method removes a generic entity, it must be passed in as a parameter with the same type as the **Delete** method's defining entity.

Because there are no changes to the underlying database, there's no point in returning a value from the method; you only re-throw any exception that occurs.

The **Remove** context method will incur overhead because persisting the changes to the database requires calling the **SaveChangesAsync** method; that call should be asynchronous since it is a long-running task that could benefit from using the thread pool, freeing up resources.

```
public void Delete<TEntity>(TEntity item) where TEntity : class { }
```

1. Open the **IDbWriteService** interface.
2. Add a method definition for the **Delete** method that is defined by the entity type that substitutes the generic **TEntity** type when calling the method. You must limit the **TEntity** type to only classes since an entity only can be created using a class; if you don't do this, a value type such as **int** or **double** can define the method, which will generate an exception. The method should not return any value (**void**).
   ```
   void Delete<TEntity>(TEntity item) where TEntity : class;
   ```
3. Add the **Delete** method to the **DbWriteService** class, either manually or by using the **Quick Actions** light bulb button. If you auto-generate the method with **Quick Actions**, you must remove the **throw** statement.
4. Add a try/catch-block where the catch re-throws any exception.
5. Call the **Remove** method on the **Set<TEntity>** method on the **_db** context with the item to remove, inside the try-block.
   ```
   _db.Set<TEntity>().Remove(item);
   ```
6. Save all files.

The complete code for the **Delete** method:

```
public void Delete<TEntity>(TEntity item) where TEntity : class
{
    try
    {
        _db.Set<TEntity>().Remove(item);
    }
    catch
    {
        throw;
    }
}
```

19. The Database Write Service

The code for the **IDbWriteService** interface, so far:

```
public interface IDbWriteService
{
    Task<bool> SaveChangesAsync();
    void Add<TEntity>(TEntity item) where TEntity : class;
    void Delete<TEntity>(TEntity item) where TEntity : class;
}
```

The Update Method

The **Update** method will update a record in the specified table. Like all the other public methods you have added to this service, this one will be a generic asynchronous method that can handle any entity. You choose the table to update data in by defining the desired entity for the method call.

The **Update** method will update an entity that Entity Framework tracks in-memory. The entity will not update in the database before calling the **SaveChangesAsync** method.

Since the method updates a generic entity, it must be passed in as a parameter with the same type as the **Update** method's defining entity.

Because the underlying data in the database is unmodified, there's no point in returning a value from the method; you only re-throw any exception that occurs.

The **Update** context method will incur overhead since the underlying data in the database is unmodified until calling the **SaveChangesAsync** method; that call should be asynchronous since it is a long-running task that could benefit from using the thread pool, freeing up resources.

```
public void Update<TEntity>(TEntity item) where TEntity : class { }
```

1. Open the **IDbWriteService** interface.
2. Copy the **Delete** method definition and paste it in. Rename the passed-in method **Update**.
   ```
   void Update<TEntity>(TEntity item) where TEntity : class;
   ```
3. Open the **DbWriteService** class and copy the **Delete** method and paste it in.
4. Rename the method to **Update**.
5. Change the **Remove** method call to call the **Update** method.
   ```
   _db.Set<TEntity>().Update(item);
   ```

6. Above the **Update** method, check if the entity is being tracked by Entity Framework.
   ```
   var entity = _db.Find<TEntity>(item.GetType().GetProperty("Id")
       .GetValue(item));
   ```

7. Detach the entity if it is being tracked above the **Update** method; you do this to be able to update the entity in the **item** parameter.
   ```
   if (entity != null) _db.Entry(entity).State =
       Microsoft.EntityFrameworkCore.EntityState.Detached;
   ```

8. Save all files.

The code for the **IDbWriteService** interface, so far:

```
public interface IDbWriteService
{
    Task<bool> SaveChangesAsync();
    void Add<TEntity>(TEntity item) where TEntity : class;
    void Delete<TEntity>(TEntity item) where TEntity : class;
    void Update<TEntity>(TEntity item) where TEntity : class;
}
```

The complete code for the **Update** method:

```
void Update<TEntity>(TEntity item) where TEntity : class
{
    try
    {
        var entity = _db.Find<TEntity>(item.GetType().GetProperty("Id")
            .GetValue(item));

        if (entity != null) _db.Entry(entity).State =
            Microsoft.EntityFrameworkCore.EntityState.Detached;

        _db.Set<TEntity>().Update(item);
    }
    catch
    {
        throw;
    }
}
```

Summary

In this chapter, you created a service for writing data to the database. This service will be used from the **Admin** project to manipulate data.

Next, you will add a user service that will be used from the **Admin** project to manage users in the **AspNetUsers** table and their roles in the **AspNetUserRoles** table.

ASP.NET Core 2.2 MVC, Razor Pages, API, JSON Web Tokens & HttpClient

20. The User Service

Introduction
In this chapter, you will create a service called **UserService** in the **Database** project. The service will be used to manage users in the **AspNetUsers** table and their roles in the **AspNetUserRoles** table.

Technologies Used in This Chapter
1. **C#** – To create the service.
2. **Entity framework** – To interact with the tables in the database.
3. **LINQ** – To query the database tables.

Overview
Your objective is to create a data service that adds, updates, and deletes data in the **AspNetUsers** and **AspNetUserRoles** database tables.

Adding the UserService Service
You need to add an interface called **IUserService** in the *Services* folder in the **Database** project. Implement the interface in a class named **UserService** that accesses the database through its methods.

The methods will not be implemented as generic methods since they only will be used with the **AspNetUsers** and **AspNetUserRoles** database tables.

The UserDTO Class
This class will transport the data fetched from the database to the **User** CRUD Razor Pages. It will contain three properties: the first is **Id (string)** representing the user id. Decorate it with the **[Required]** and **[Display]** attributes; the first attribute will require a value to be accepted, and the second will change the label text to *User Id*. The second property is **Email (string)**. Decorate it with the **[Required]** and **[EmailAddress]** attributes; the first attribute will require an email address to be accepted, and the second will perform checks on the entered data to ensure that it is a valid email address. The third property is **IsAdmin (bool)**, which will have the same attributes as the **Id** property. It will display as a checkbox on the page; the value specifies whether the user is in the **Admin** role.

ASP.NET Core 2.2 MVC, Razor Pages, API, JSON Web Tokens & HttpClient

Adding the ButtonDTO Class

Use this class as the model for a partial view that you will add later; use its properties with the <btn> Tag Helper to add a course id, module id, and entity/user id to the buttons. The ids will form parameters for the button Uris.

1. Add a new folder named *Admin* to the *DTOModels* folder in the **Common** project.
2. Add a **public** class named **ButtonDTO** to the *DTOModels-Admin* folder in the **Common** project; this will be the model class for the next partial view.
3. Add three public **int** properties named **Id**, **CourseId**, and **ModuleId**, and a **string** property named **UserId**. They will hold the ids for the buttons in the partial view.
4. To make it easier to handle the **string UserId** and the **int Id** properties that will be added to the same attribute when used (never at the same time), add another **string** property named **ItemId** that returns either the value from the **Id** property converted to a **string** or the **UserId**.
   `public string ItemId { get { return Id > 0 ? Id.ToString() : UserId; } }`
5. Add four constructors; the first with three **int** parameters for the course id, module id, and id; the second with two **int** parameters for the course id and id; the third with one **int** parameter for the id; the fourth with one **string** parameter for the user id.
6. Save the class.

The complete code for the **ButtonDTO** class:

```
public class ButtonDTO
{
    #region Properties
    public int CourseId { get; set; }
    public int ModuleId { get; set; }
    public int Id { get; set; }
    public string UserId { get; set; }
    public string ItemId {
        get { return Id > 0 ? Id.ToString() : UserId; }
    }
    #endregion
```

```
    #region Constructors
    public ButtonDTO(int courseId, int moduleId, int id)
    {
        CourseId = courseId;
        ModuleId = moduleId;
        Id = id;
    }

    public ButtonDTO(int courseId, int id)
    {
        CourseId = courseId;
        Id = id;
    }

    public ButtonDTO(int id)
    {
        Id = id;
    }

    public ButtonDTO(string userId)
    {
        UserId = userId;
    }
    #endregion
}
```

Adding the UserDTO Class

1. Add a **public** class called **UserDTO** to the *DTOModels* folder in the **Common** project.
2. Add a **public** property named **Id** (**string**).
3. Add the **[Required]** and **[Display]** attributes. The **[Display]** attribute should change the text to *User id*.
   ```
   [Required]
   [Display(Name = "User Id")]
   public string Id { get; set; }
   ```
4. Add a **public** property named **Email** (**string**).
5. Add the **[Required]** and **[EmailAddress]** attributes.
6. Add a **public** property named **IsAdmin** (**bool**).
7. Add the **[Required]** and **[Display]** attributes. The **[Display]** attribute should change the text to *Is Admin*.

8. Add a property for the **ButtonDTO** class and pass in the value from the **Id** property to the class's constructor; this will add the ids to the **Edit** and **Delete** buttons in the **_TableRowButtonsPartial** partial view that you will add later.
9. Save the class.

The complete code for the **UserDTO** class:

```
public class UserDTO
{
    [Required]
    [Display(Name = "User Id")]
    public string Id { get; set; }
    [Required]
    [EmailAddress]
    public string Email { get; set; }
    [Required]
    [Display(Name = "Is Admin")]
    public bool IsAdmin { get; set; }

    public ButtonDTO ButtonDTO { get { return new ButtonDTO(Id); } }
}
```

Adding the Service Interface and Class

1. Open the **VOD.Database** project.
2. Add a **public** interface called **IUserService** to the *Services* folder. Right click on the folder, select **Add-New Item**, and select the **Interface** template.
3. Add the **public** access modifier to the interface to make it accessible from any project.
   public interface IUserService
4. Add a **public** class called **UserService** to the *Services* folder.
5. Add the interface to the class.
   ```
   public class UserService : IUserService
   {
   }
   ```
6. Add a constructor to the class and inject the **VODContext** to get access to the database from the service. Store the object in a class-level variable called **_db**. Also, inject the **UserManager** that adds a new user and store it in a read-only variable named **_userManager**.
   private readonly VODContext _db;

```
        private readonly UserManager<VODUser> _userManager;
        public UserService(VODContext db, UserManager<VODUser>
        userManager)
        {
            _db = db;
            _userManager = userManager;
        }
```

7. Open the **Startup** class and add the **UserService** service to the **ConfigureServices** method.
   ```
   services.AddScoped<IUserService, UserService>();
   ```

8. Save the files.

The code for the **IUserService** interface, so far:

```
public interface IUserService { }
```

The code for the **UserService** class, so far:

```
public class UserService : IUserService
{
    private readonly VODContext _db;
    private readonly UserManager<VODUser> _userManager;

    public UserService(VODContext db, UserManager<VODUser> userManager)
    {
        _db = db;
        _userManager = userManager;
    }
}
```

The GetUsersAsync Method

The asynchronous **GetUsersAsync** method will fetch all users in the **AspNetUsers** table ordered by email address and return them as an **IEnumerable<UserDTO>** collection. The collection is then used to display the users in the **Index** Razor Page.

```
Task<IEnumerable<UserDTO>> GetUsersAsync();
```

1. Open the **IUserService** interface.
2. Add a method definition for the **GetUsersAsync** method that returns an **IEnumerable<UserDTO>** collection.
   ```
   Task<IEnumerable<UserDTO>> GetUsersAsync();
   ```

3. Open the **UserService** class.
4. Add a **using** statement to the **System.Linq** namespace to gain access to the **orderby** LINQ keyword to be able to sort the records by email.
5. Add a **using** statement to the **Microsoft.EntityFrameworkCore** namespace to gain access to the **ToListAsync** method.
6. Add the **GetUsersAsync** method to the **UserService** class, either manually or by using the **Quick Actions** light bulb button. If you auto-generate the method with **Quick Actions**, you must remove the **throw** statement. Don't forget to add the **async** keyword to enable asynchronous method calls.
7. Return all users converted into **UserDTO** objects ordered by the user's email addresses. Use the **Any** LINQ method on the **AspNetUserRoles** table to figure out if the user is an administrator.

```
return await _db.Users
    .OrderBy(u => u.Email)
    .Select(user => new UserDTO
    {
        Id = user.Id,
        Email = user.Email,
        IsAdmin = _db.UserRoles.Any(ur =>
            ur.UserId.Equals(user.Id) &&
            ur.RoleId.Equals(1.ToString()))
    }
).ToListAsync();
```

8. Save all files.

The code for the **IUserService** interface, so far:

```
public interface IUserService
{
    Task<IEnumerable<UserDTO>> GetUsersAsync();
}
```

The complete code for the **GetUsersAsync** method:

```
public async Task<IEnumerable<UserDTO>> GetUsersAsync()
{
    return await _db.Users
        .OrderBy(u => u.Email)
        .Select(user => new UserDTO
        {
            Id = user.Id,
```

```
                Email = user.Email,
                IsAdmin = _db.UserRoles.Any(ur =>
                    ur.UserId.Equals(user.Id) &&
                    ur.RoleId.Equals(1.ToString()))
            }
        ).ToListAsync();
}
```

The GetUserAsync Method

The asynchronous **GetUserAsync** method will fetch one user in the **AspNetUsers** table and return it as a **UserDTO** object; the object is then used when displaying the user in the **Create, Edit**, and **Delete** Razor Pages. The method should use a **userId (string)** parameter when fetching the desired user from the database.

```
Task<UserDTO> GetUserAsync(string userId);
```

1. Open the **IUserService** interface.
2. Add a method definition for the **GetUserAsync** method that returns a **UserDTO** object. The method should have a **userId (string)** parameter.
   ```
   Task<UserDTO> GetUserAsync(string userId);
   ```
3. Add the **GetUserAsync** method to the **UserService** class, either manually or by using the **Quick Actions** light bulb button. If you auto-generate the method with **Quick Actions**, you must remove the **throw** statement. Don't forget to add the **async** keyword to enable asynchronous method calls.
4. Return the user matching the passed-in user id converted into a **UserDTO** object. Use the **Any** LINQ method on the **AspNetUserRoles** table to figure out if the user is an administrator. **FirstOrDefaultAsync** requires a **using** statement to the **Microsoft.EntityFrameworkCore;** namespace.
   ```
   return await (_db.Users
       .Select(user => new UserDTO
       {
           Id = user.Id,
           Email = user.Email,
           IsAdmin = _db.UserRoles.Any(ur =>
               ur.UserId.Equals(user.Id) &&
               ur.RoleId.Equals(1.ToString()))
       })
   ).FirstOrDefaultAsync(u => u.Id.Equals(userId));
   ```
5. Save all files.

The code for the **IUserService** interface, so far:

```
public interface IUserService
{
    Task<IEnumerable<UserDTO>> GetUsersAsync();
    Task<UserDTO> GetUserAsync(string userId);
}
```

The complete code for the **GetUserAsync** method:

```
public async Task<UserDTO> GetUserAsync(string userId)
{
    return await (_db.Users
        .Select(user => new UserDTO
        {
            Id = user.Id,
            Email = user.Email,
            IsAdmin = _db.UserRoles.Any(ur =>
                ur.UserId.Equals(user.Id) &&
                ur.RoleId.Equals(1.ToString()))
        })
    ).FirstOrDefaultAsync(u => u.Id.Equals(userId));
}
```

The GetUserByEmailAsync Method

The asynchronous **GetUserByEmailAsync** method will fetch one user in the **AspNetUsers** table and return it as a **UserDTO** object. The method should use an **email (string)** parameter when fetching the desired user from the database.

```
Task<UserDTO> GetUserAsync(string email);
```

1. Open the **IUserService** interface.
2. Add a method definition for the **GetUserByEmailAsync** method that returns a **UserDTO** object. The method should have an **email (string)** parameter.
   ```
   Task<UserDTO> GetUserByEmailAsync(string email);
   ```
3. Add the **GetUserByEmailAsync** method to the **UserService** class, either manually or by using the **Quick Actions** light bulb button. If you auto-generate the method with **Quick Actions**, you must remove the **throw** statement. Don't forget to add the **async** keyword to enable asynchronous method calls.
4. Return the user matching the passed-in email converted into a **UserDTO** object. Use the **Any** LINQ method on the **AspNetUserRoles** table to figure out if the user

20. The User Service

is an administrator. **FirstOrDefaultAsync** requires a **using** statement to the **Microsoft.EntityFrameworkCore;** namespace.

```
return await (_db.Users
    .Select(user => new UserDTO
    {
        Id = user.Id,
        Email = user.Email,
        IsAdmin = _db.UserRoles.Any(ur =>
            ur.UserId.Equals(user.Id) &&
            ur.RoleId.Equals(1.ToString()))
    })
).FirstOrDefaultAsync(u => u.Email.Equals(email));
```

5. Save all files.

The code for the **IUserService** interface, so far:

```
public interface IUserService
{
    Task<IEnumerable<UserDTO>> GetUsersAsync();
    Task<UserDTO> GetUserAsync(string userId);
    Task<UserDTO> GetUserByEmailAsync(string email);
}
```

The complete code for the **GetUserAsync** method:

```
public async Task<UserDTO> GetUserByEmailAsync(string email)
{
    return await (_db.Users
        .Select(user => new UserDTO
        {
            Id = user.Id,
            Email = user.Email,
            IsAdmin = _db.UserRoles.Any(ur =>
                ur.UserId.Equals(user.Id) &&
                ur.RoleId.Equals(1.ToString()))
        })
    ).FirstOrDefaultAsync(u => u.Email.Equals(email));
}
```

The RegisterUserDTO Class

Use the **RegisterUserDTO** class in the **Create** Razor Page for the **AspNetUsers** table. The class should contain tree **string** properties called **Email, Password**, and **ConfirmPassword**. Decorate the properties with attributes that help with client-side validation.

Decorate the **Email** and **Password** properties with the **[Required]** attribute.

Also, decorate the **Email** property with the **[EmailAddress]** attribute.

Also, format the text displayed for the **Password** property as a password with dots and give it a maximum length of 100 characters.

Format the displayed text for the value in the **ConfirmPassword** property as a password with dots and compare it with the value in the **Password** property with the **[Compare]** attribute.

1. Add a **public** class called **RegisterUserDTO** to the *DTOModels* folder in the **Common** project.
2. Add an **Email (string)** property decorated with **[Required]** and **[EmailAddress]** attributes.
   ```
   [Required]
   [EmailAddress]
   public string Email { get; set; }
   ```
3. Add a **Password (string)** property decorated with **[Required], [StringLength]**, and **[DataType]** attributes.
   ```
   [Required]
   [StringLength(100, ErrorMessage = "The {0} must be at least {2}
       and at max {1} characters long.", MinimumLength = 6)]
   [DataType(DataType.Password)]
   public string Password { get; set; }
   ```
4. Add a **ConfirmPassword (string)** property decorated with **[Display], [Compare]**, and **[DataType]** attributes.
   ```
   [DataType(DataType.Password)]
   [Display(Name = "Confirm password")]
   [Compare("Password", ErrorMessage =
       "The password and confirmation password do not match.")]
   public string ConfirmPassword { get; set; }
   ```
5. Save all files.

The complete code for the **RegisterUserDTO** class:

```
public class RegisterUserDTO
{
    [Required]
    [EmailAddress]
    public string Email { get; set; }

    [Required]
    [StringLength(100, ErrorMessage = "The {0} must be at least {2}
        and at max {1} characters long.", MinimumLength = 6)]
    [DataType(DataType.Password)]
    public string Password { get; set; }

    [DataType(DataType.Password)]
    [Display(Name = "Confirm password")]
    [Compare("Password", ErrorMessage =
        "The password and confirmation password do not match.")]
    public string ConfirmPassword { get; set; }
}
```

The LoginUserDTO Class

Use the **LoginUserDTO** class when logging in through the API application you will add in an upcoming chapter. The class should contain three **string** properties called **Email**, **Password**, and **PasswordHash**. Add the class to the *DTOModels* folder in the **Common** project.

The complete code for the **LoginUserDTO** class:

```
public class LoginUserDTO
{
    public string Email { get; set; }
    public string Password { get; set; }
    public string PasswordHash { get; set; }
}
```

The AddUserAsync Method

The **AddUser** method will add a new user in the **AspNetUsers** table asynchronously and return an **IdentityResult** object returned from the **CreateAsync** method call on the **UserManager** object. The method should take a **RegisterUserDTO** instance as a parameter named **user**.

```
Task<IdentityResult> AddUser(RegisterUserDTO user);
```

1. Open the **IUserService** interface.
2. Add a method definition for the **AddUserAsync** method that returns **Task<IdentityResult>** and have a **RegisterUserDTO** parameter.
   ```
   Task<IdentityResult> AddUserAsync(RegisterUserDTO user);
   ```
3. Add the **AddUserAsync** method to the **UserService** class, either manually or by using the **Quick Actions** light bulb button. If you auto-generate the method with **Quick Actions**, you must remove the **throw** statement. Don't forget to add the **async** keyword to enable asynchronous method calls.
4. Create an instance of the **VODUser** class and assign the email from the passed-in user object to the newly created **VODUser** instance. Also, assign **true** to the **EmailConfirmed** property to signal receiving an email confirmation. Although not strictly necessary in this scenario, it could be vital if you choose to implement email verification later.
   ```
   var dbUser = new VODUser { UserName = user.Email, Email = user.Email, EmailConfirmed = true };
   ```
5. Call the **CreateAsync** method on the **_userManager** instance to try to add the new user. Store the returned result in a variable called **result**. You must call the method with the **await** keyword since it is an asynchronous method.
   ```
   var result = await _userManager.CreateAsync(dbUser, user.Password);
   ```
6. Return the result in the **result** variable from the method.
   ```
   return result;
   ```
7. Save all files.

The code for the **IUserService** interface, so far:

```
public interface IUserService
{
    Task<IEnumerable<UserDTO>> GetUsersAsync();
    Task<UserDTO> GetUserAsync(string userId);
    Task<UserDTO> GetUserByEmailAsync(string email);
    Task<IdentityResult> AddUserAsync(RegisterUserDTO user);
}
```

The complete code for the **AddUserAsync** method:

```
public async Task<IdentityResult> AddUserAsync(RegisterUserDTO user)
{
    var dbUser = new VODUser
    {
        UserName = user.Email,
        Email = user.Email,
        EmailConfirmed = true
    };
    var result = await _userManager.CreateAsync(dbUser, user.Password);
    return result;
}
```

The UpdateUserAsync Method

The **UpdateUserAsync** method will update a user in the **AspNetUsers** table asynchronously and return a **bool** value based on the result from the value returned from the **SaveChangesAsync** method call on the **_db** context object. The method should take a **UserDTO** instance as a parameter named **user**.

```
Task<bool> UpdateUserAsync(UserDTO user);
```

The first thing the method should do is to fetch the user from the **AspNetUsers** table matching the value of the **Id** property in the passed-in object. Store the user in a variable called **dbUser**.

Then, the **dbUser** needs to be checked to make sure that it isn't **null** and that the email in the passed-in object isn't an empty string. You could add more checks to see that the email is a valid email address, but I leave that as an extra exercise for you to solve on your own.

Then you assign the email address from the passed-in user to the **dbUser** fetched from the database to update it.

Next, you need to find out if the user in the database — matching the passed-in user id in the **user** object — is an administrator. You do that by calling the **IsInRoleAsync** method on the **UserManager** instance; save the result in a variable named **isAdmin**. To avoid misspelling the name of the *Admin* role, you should add it to a variable named **admin** above the **IsInRoleAsync** call and use the variable in the call.

If the value in the **isAdmin** variable is **true** and the value in the **IsAdmin** property in the **user** object is **false**, then the admin role checkbox is unchecked in the UI; remove the role from the **AspNetUserRoles** table by calling the **RemoveFromRoleAsync** method on the **UserManager** instance.

If the value in the **IsAdmin** property in the **user** parameter is **true** and the value in the **isAdmin** variable is **false**, then the admin role checkbox is checked in the UI; add the role to the **AspNetUserRoles** table by awaiting a call to the **AddToRoleAsync** method on the **UserManager** instance.

Then **await** the result from the **SaveChangesAsync** method and return **true** if the data was persisted to the database, otherwise return **false**.

1. Open the **IUserService** interface.
2. Add a method definition for the **UpdateUserAsync** method that returns a **bool** value and has a **UserDTO** parameter called **user**.
   ```
   Task<bool> UpdateUserAsync(UserDTO user);
   ```
3. Add the **UpdateUserAsync** method to the **UserService** class, either manually or by using the **Quick Actions** light bulb button. If you auto-generate the method with **Quick Actions**, you must remove the **throw** statement. Don't forget to add the **async** keyword to enable asynchronous method calls.
4. Fetch the user matching the user id from the passed-in **user** parameter and store the user in a variable called **dbUser**. **FirstOrDefaultAsync** requires a using statement to the **Microsoft.EntityFrameworkCore;** namespace.
   ```
   var dbUser = await _db.Users.FirstOrDefaultAsync(u =>
       u.Id.Equals(user.Id));
   ```
5. Return **false** if the **dbUser** is **null** (the user doesn't exist) or the email address in the passed-in **user** parameter is an empty string.
   ```
   if (dbUser == null) return false;
   if (string.IsNullOrEmpty(user.Email)) return false;
   ```
6. Assign the email address from the passed-in **user** parameter to the fetched user in the **dbUser** variable to update its email address.
   ```
   dbUser.Email = user.Email;
   ```
7. Query the **AspNetUserRoles** table with the **IsInRoleAsync** method on the **_userManager** object.
   ```
   var admin = "Admin";
   var isAdmin = await _userManager.IsInRoleAsync(dbUser, admin);
   ```

20. The User Service

8. Add an if/else if-block that removes the **Admin** role if the admin checkbox is unchecked in the UI or adds the role if the checkbox is checked.
    ```
    if(isAdmin && !user.IsAdmin)
        await _userManager.RemoveFromRoleAsync(dbUser, admin);
    else if (!isAdmin && user.IsAdmin)
        await _userManager.AddToRoleAsync(dbUser, admin);
    ```

9. Call the **SaveChangesAsync** method to persist the changes in the database and **await** the result. If EF persisted the data, return **true**; otherwise, return **false**.
    ```
    var result = await _db.SaveChangesAsync();
    return result >= 0;
    ```

10. Save all files.

The code for the **IUserService** interface, so far:

```
public interface IUserService
{
    Task<IEnumerable<UserDTO>> GetUsersAsync();
    Task<UserDTO> GetUserAsync(string userId);
    Task<UserDTO> GetUserByEmailAsync(string email);
    Task<IdentityResult> AddUserAsync(RegisterUserDTO user);
    Task<bool> UpdateUserAsync(UserDTO user);
}
```

The complete code for the **UpdateUserAsync** method:

```
public async Task<bool> UpdateUserAsync(UserDTO user)
{
    var dbUser = await _db.Users.FirstOrDefaultAsync(u =>
        u.Id.Equals(user.Id));
    if (dbUser == null) return false;
    if (string.IsNullOrEmpty(user.Email)) return false;

    dbUser.Email = user.Email;
    #region Admin Role
    var admin = "Admin";
    var isAdmin = await _userManager.IsInRoleAsync(dbUser, admin);

    if(isAdmin && !user.IsAdmin)
        await _userManager.RemoveFromRoleAsync(dbUser, admin);
    else if (!isAdmin && user.IsAdmin)
        await _userManager.AddToRoleAsync(dbUser, admin);
    #endregion
```

```
        var result = await _db.SaveChangesAsync();
        return result >= 0;
}
```

The DeleteUserAsync Method

Let's implement the **DeleteUserAsync** method using only the **UserManager**; the method will remove a user from the **AspNetUsers** table asynchronously and return a **bool** value based on the result returned from the **DeleteAsync** method call on the **_userManager** instance. The method should take a **string** parameter named **userId** representing the user to remove.

```
Task<bool> DeleteUserAsync(string userId);
```

The first thing the method should do is to fetch the user from the **AspNetUsers** table matching the value of the **userId** parameter. Store the user in a variable called **dbUser**.

Then check that the **dbUser** isn't **null** to make sure that the user exists and return **false** if it doesn't exist.

Next, you remove the roles associated with the user id in the **AspNetUserRoles** table. Fetch the roles by calling the **GetRolesAsync** method and remove them from the user by calling the **RemoveFromRolesAsync** method on the **_userManager** instance.

Then, you remove the user from the **AspNetUsers** table by calling the **DeleteAsync** method on the **_userManager** instance.

Return the result from the **DeleteAsync** method to signal if the user was removed or not.

1. Open the **IUserService** interface.
2. Add a method definition for the **DeleteUserAsync** method that returns a **bool** value and has a **string** parameter called **userId**.
   ```
   Task<bool> DeleteUserAsync(string userId);
   ```
3. Add the **DeleteUserAsync** method to the **UserService** class, either manually or by using the **Quick Actions** light bulb button. If you auto-generate the method with **Quick Actions**, you must remove the **throw** statement. Don't forget to add the **async** keyword to enable asynchronous method calls.
4. Add a try/catch-block where the catch-block returns **false**.
5. Fetch the user matching the user id from the passed-in **userId** parameter in the try-block.

```
var dbUser = await _userManager.FindByIdAsync(userId);
```

6. Return **false** if the **dbUser** is **null** (the user doesn't exist).
   ```
   if (dbUser == null) return false;
   ```

7. Fetch the roles associated with the user id and remove them from the **AspNetUserRoles** table.
   ```
   var userRoles = await _userManager.GetRolesAsync(dbUser);
   var roleRemoved = _userManager.RemoveFromRolesAsync(dbUser,
       userRoles);
   ```

8. Remove the user from the **AspNetUsers** table.
   ```
   var deleted = await _userManager.DeleteAsync(dbUser);
   ```

9. Return the result from the **DeleteAsync** method to signal if the user was removed or not.
   ```
   return deleted.Succeeded;
   ```

10. Save all files.

The complete code for the **IUserService** interface:

```
public interface IUserService {
    Task<IEnumerable<UserDTO>> GetUsersAsync();
    Task<UserDTO> GetUserAsync(string userId);
    Task<UserDTO> GetUserByEmailAsync(string email);
    Task<IdentityResult> AddUserAsync(RegisterUserDTO user);
    Task<bool> UpdateUserAsync(UserDTO user);
    Task<bool> DeleteUserAsync(string userId);
}
```

The complete code for the **DeleteUserAsync** method:

```
public async Task<bool> DeleteUserAsync(string userId)
{
    Try
    {
        // Fetch user
        var dbUser = await _userManager.FindByIdAsync(userId);
        if (dbUser == null) return false;

        // Remove roles from user
        var userRoles = await _userManager.GetRolesAsync(dbUser);
        var roleRemoved = await _userManager
            .RemoveFromRolesAsync(dbUser, userRoles);
```

```
            // Remove the user
            var deleted = await _userManager.DeleteAsync(dbUser);
            return deleted.Succeeded;
        }
        catch
        {
            return false;
        }
    }
}
```

The Truncate and IsNullOrEmptyOrWhiteSpace Extension Methods

To avoid displaying long descriptions, you will create an extension method that truncates a string to the desired number of characters. Later, you will use this method in **Index** Razor Pages. To make it easier to check if a string or an array of strings contains values, you will add two methods named **IsNullOrEmptyOrWhiteSpace** that checks for empty strings and **null** values.

1. Open the folder named *Extensions* to the **Common** project.
2. Add a **public** class named **StringExtensions** to the *Extensions* folder in the **Common** project and add the **static** keyword to the class; this is required when creating extension methods since you don't want to create an instance of the class to use them.
3. Add a **static** method named **Truncate** that returns a string and operates on strings and has a parameter for the desired number of characters from the string.
   ```
   public static string Truncate(this string value, int length) { }
   ```
4. Return an empty string if the incoming string is **null** or empty.
   ```
   if (string.IsNullOrEmpty(value)) return string.Empty;
   ```
5. Return the string as is if it is shorter or of equal length to the value in the **length** parameter.
   ```
   if (value.Length <= length) return value;
   ```
6. Truncate the string and add three ellipses at the end to indicate that it is part of a longer text.
   ```
   return $"{value.Substring(0, length)} ...";
   ```

20. The User Service

Let's add the **IsNullOrEmptyOrWhiteSpace** method that checks if a string is empty, **null**, or contains only whitespace.

1. Add another method named **IsNullOrEmptyOrWhiteSpace** that returns a Boolean and operates on a **string**.
   ```
   return string.IsNullOrEmpty(value) ||
          string.IsNullOrWhiteSpace(value);
   ```

Let's add the **IsNullOrEmptyOrWhiteSpace** method that checks if a string array contains an empty, null, or whitespace value.

2. Add another method named **IsNullOrEmptyOrWhiteSpace** that returns a Boolean and operates on a **string** array.
3. Iterate through the values in the array and check if the string is empty, **null**, or whitespace. Return **true** if such a value is found, otherwise return **false**.
   ```
   foreach (var val in values)
       if (string.IsNullOrEmpty(val) || string.IsNullOrWhiteSpace(val))
           return true;

   return false;
   ```

The complete code in the **StringExtensions** class:

```
public static class StringExtensions
{
    #region String Checking
    public static bool IsNullOrEmptyOrWhiteSpace(this string[] values)
    {
        foreach (var val in values)
            if (string.IsNullOrEmpty(val) ||
                string.IsNullOrWhiteSpace(val))
                return true;

        return false;
    }

    public static bool IsNullOrEmptyOrWhiteSpace(this string value)
    {
        return string.IsNullOrEmpty(value) ||
               string.IsNullOrWhiteSpace(value);
    }
    #endregion
```

```
    #region String Manipulation
    public static string Truncate(this string value, int length)
    {
        if (string.IsNullOrEmpty(value)) return string.Empty;
        if (value.Length <= length) return value;

        return $"{value.Substring(0, length)} ...";
    }
    #endregion
}
```

The GetUserAsync Method

The asynchronous **GetUserAsync** method will fetch one user in the **AspNetUsers** table and return it as a **VODUser** object. The method should have a **loginUser** parameter of type **LoginUserDTO** and a **bool** parameter named **includeClaims** that determines if loading the user's claims into the **VODUser** object's **Claims** collection should be done.

```
Task<VODUser> GetUserAsync(LoginUserDTO loginUser);
```

1. Open the **IUserService** interface.
2. Add a method definition for the **GetUserAsync** method that returns a **VODUser** object. The method should have a **loginUser** parameter of type **LoginUserDTO** and a **bool** parameter named **includeClaims** that will be used in a later chapter to determine if the user's claims should be loaded; assign **false** as its default value.
   ```
   Task<VODUser> GetUserAsync(LoginUserDTO loginUser , bool includeClaims = false);
   ```
3. Add the **GetUserAsync** method to the **UserService** class, either manually or by using the **Quick Actions** light bulb button. If you auto-generate the method with **Quick Actions**, you must remove the **throw** statement. Don't forget to add the **async** keyword to enable asynchronous method calls.
4. Add a try/catch-block that throws the exception to the calling method in the catch-block.
5. Fetch the user by calling the **FindByEmailAsync** method on the **_userManager** object.
   ```
   var user = await _userManager.FindByEmailAsync(loginUser.Email);
   ```

6. Return **null** if the user wasn't found and the **user** variable is **null**.
   ```
   if (user == null) return null;
   ```
7. Return **null** if the **Password** and **PasswordHash** properties in the **loginUser** object are empty; the user must have either a **Password** from a login/register scenario or a **PasswordHash** from an already logged-in user.
   ```
   if(loginUser.Password.IsNullOrEmptyOrWhiteSpace() &&
       loginUser.PasswordHash.IsNullOrEmptyOrWhiteSpace()) return null;
   ```
8. Use the **Password** property if it contains a value, otherwise use the value in the **passwordHash** property. Return **null** if either password isn't equal to the password hash stored in the **AspNetUser** table for the user.
   ```
   if (loginUser.Password.Length > 0)
   {
       var password = _userManager.PasswordHasher
           .VerifyHashedPassword(user, user.PasswordHash,
               loginUser.Password);

       if (password == PasswordVerificationResult.Failed)
           return null;
   }
   else
   {
       if (!user.PasswordHash.Equals(loginUser.PasswordHash))
           return null;
   }
   ```
9. Add the claims to the **VODUser's Claims** collection if the **includeClaims** parameter is **true**.
   ```
   if (includeClaims) user.Claims =
       await _userManager.GetClaimsAsync(user);
   ```
10. Return the user.
    ```
    return user;
    ```
11. Save all files.

The code for the **IUserService** interface, so far:

```
public interface IUserService
{
    Task<IEnumerable<UserDTO>> GetUsersAsync();
    Task<UserDTO> GetUserAsync(string userId);
    Task<UserDTO> GetUserByEmailAsync(string email);
    Task<IdentityResult> AddUserAsync(RegisterUserDTO user);
```

```
    Task<bool> UpdateUserAsync(UserDTO user);
    Task<bool> DeleteUserAsync(string userId);
    Task<VODUser> GetUserAsync(LoginUserDTO loginUser,
        bool includeClaims = false)
}
```

The complete code for the **GetUserAsync** method:

```
public async Task<VODUser> GetUserAsync(LoginUserDTO loginUser, bool includeClaims = false)
{
    try
    {
        var user = await _userManager.FindByEmailAsync(loginUser.Email);
        if (user == null) return null;
        if (loginUser.Password.IsNullOrEmptyOrWhiteSpace() &&
            loginUser.PasswordHash.IsNullOrEmptyOrWhiteSpace())
            return null;

        if (loginUser.Password.Length > 0)
        {
            var password = _userManager.PasswordHasher
                .VerifyHashedPassword(user, user.PasswordHash,
                    loginUser.Password);

            if (password == PasswordVerificationResult.Failed)
                return null;
        }
        else
        {
            if (!user.PasswordHash.Equals(loginUser.PasswordHash))
                return null;
        }

        if (includeClaims) user.Claims =
            await _userManager.GetClaimsAsync(user);

        return user;
    }
    catch
    {
        throw;
    }
}
```

Summary

In this chapter, you created a service for handling users and their roles in the **AspNetUsers** and **AspNetUserRoles** database tables. This service will be used from the **Admin** project to handle user data and assign administrator privileges to users.

Next, you will begin adding the Razor Pages that make up the administrator UI.

ASP.NET Core 2.2 MVC, Razor Pages, API, JSON Web Tokens & HttpClient

21. The User Razor Pages

In this chapter, you will create the **User** Razor Pages, which are used to perform CRUD operations against the **AspNetUsers** and the **AspNetUserRoles** tables in the database. These Razor Pages are a bit different, in that they use a page model instead of an entity class. The **AspNetUsers** table handles users, and the **AspNetUserRoles** assigns roles to registered users.

You will use the **ViewData** container to send data to the pages that display it in drop-downs; this prevents the item indices to display as numbers in text boxes.

Technologies Used in This Chapter

1. **C#** – To write code in Razor Page code-behind methods.
2. **HTML** – To add content to the Razor Pages.
3. **Entity framework** – To perform CRUD operations.

Overview

In this chapter, you will create the **User** Razor Pages; this enables the administrator to display, add, update, and delete data in the **AspNetUsers** and the **AspNetUserRoles** tables.

In this scenario where the entity classes don't link the two database tables, you use a view model class called **UserDTO** to pass the data from the code-behind to the page with either a property of type **UserDTO** or **IEnumerable<UserDTO>** declared directly in the code-behind. Remember that the code-behind doubles as a model and controller.

All the **PageModel** classes in the Razor Page code-behinds need access to the **IUserService** service in the **Admin** project to fetch and modify data in the **AspNetUsers** and **AspNetUserRoles** tables in the database. The easiest way to achieve this is to add a constructor to the class and use DI to inject the service into the class.

The code-behind file belonging to a Razor Page can be accessed by expanding the Razor Page node and opening the nested *.cshtml.cs* file.

Each Razor Page comes with a predefined **@page** directive signifying that it is a Razor Page and not an MVC view. It also has an **@model** directive defined that is linked directly to the code-behind class; through this model, you can access the public properties that you add to the class from the HTML in the page using Razor syntax.

The code-behind class comes with an empty **OnGet** method that can be used to fetch data for the Razor Page, much like an **HttpGet** action method in a controller.

You can also add an asynchronous **OnPostAsync** method that can be used to handle posts from the client to the server; for instance, a form that is submitted. This method is like the **HttpPost** action method in a controller.

As you can see, the code-behind class works kind of like a combined controller and model. You can use controllers, if needed, to handle requests that don't require a Razor Page, such as logging in and out a user.

The [TempData] Attribute

The **[TempData]** attribute is relatively new to ASP.NET Core and can be used with properties in controllers and Razor Pages to store data until reading it. It is particularly useful for redirection when one request writes the data, and another reads it. **Keep** and **Peek** methods can be used to examine the data without deletion.

The **[TempData]** attribute can be shared between Razor Pages because it works on top of session state. You will take advantage of this when sending a message from one Razor Page to another, and display it using the <alert> Tag Helper that you will implement in the next chapter.

You will prepare for the Tag Helper by adding a **[TempData]** property called **Alert** (**string**) to the code-behind class for the Razor Pages you create. This property will hold the message assigned in one of the **Create**, **Edit**, or **Delete** Razor Pages and display it in the Tag Helper that you will add to the **Index** Razor Page. By adding the property to several code-behind classes, the message can be changed as needed because the session state only creates one backing property.

The Users/Index Razor Page

The **Index** Razor Page in the *Users* folder can be viewed as a dashboard for users, listing them in a table with data about the users and buttons to edit and delete each user. It also has a **Create New** button above the HTML table for creating a new user in the **AspNetUsers** database table.

There will be five Razor Pages in the *Users* folder when you have added them all: **Index**, **Create**, **Edit**, **Details**, and **Delete**.

21. The User Razor Pages

Inject the **IUserService** service into the **IndexModel** class's constructor in the Razor Page and stored it in a private field called **_userService** to be able to add, read, and modify user data.

Altering the IndexModel Class

The first thing you want to do is to restrict the usage to administrators only with the **[Authorize]** attribute.

Then you need to inject the **IUserService** into the constructor that you will add to the class. Store the service instance in a private class-level variable called **_userService**.

Then fetch all users with the **GetUsersAsync** method on the **_userService** object in the **OnGet** method and store them in an **IEnumerable<UserDTO>** collection called **Users**; this collection will be part of the model passed to the HTML Razor Page.

Add a **string** property called **Alert** and decorate it with the **[TempData]** attribute. This property will get its value from the other Razor Pages when a successful result has been achieved, such as adding a new user.

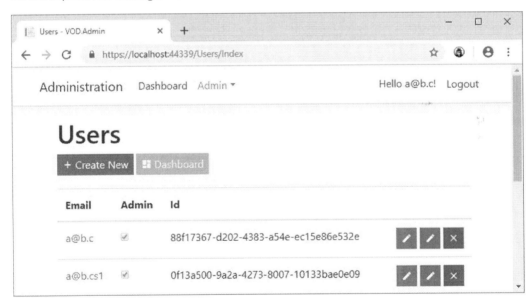

1. Open the **_Layout** view and change the container <div> to be fluid; making the content resize when the browser size changes.
   ```
   <div class="container-fluid">
   ```

2. Add configuration for the **IUserService** in the **Startup** class.
   ```
   services.AddScoped<IUserService, UserService>();
   ```
3. Create a folder named *Users* in the *Pages* folder.
4. Add a Razor Page to the *Users* folder, using the template with the same name, and name it **Index**.
5. Expand the **Index** node in the Solution Explorer and open the *Index.cshtml.cs* file.
6. Add the **[Authorize]** attribute to the class and specify that the **Admin** role is needed to access the page from the browser.
   ```
   [Authorize(Roles = "Admin")]
   public class IndexModel : PageModel
   ```
7. Inject **IUserService** into a constructor and save the injected object in a class-level variable called **_userService**. The variable will give you access to the service from any method in the class.
   ```
   private readonly IUserService _userService;
   public IndexModel(IUserService userService)
   {
       _userService = userService;
   }
   ```
8. Add a **public** class-level **IEnumerable<UserDTO>** collection variable called **Users**.
   ```
   public IEnumerable<UserDTO> Users = new List<UserDTO>();
   ```
9. Add the **async** and **Task** keyword to the **OnGet** action method to enable asynchronous calls within. Rename the method **OnGetAsync**. Call the asynchronous **GetUsersAsync** method on the **_userServices** service inside the **OnGetAsync** method and store the result in the **Users** property you just added.
   ```
   public async Task OnGetAsync()
   {
       Users = await _userService.GetUsersAsync();
   }
   ```
10. Add a **public string** property named **Alert** to the class and decorate it with the **[TempData]** attribute. This property will get its value from the other Razor Pages when a successful result has been achieved, such as adding a new user.
    ```
    [TempData]
    public string Alert { get; set; }
    ```
11. Save all files.

21. The User Razor Pages

The complete code in the **Index** code-behind file:

```
[Authorize(Roles = "Admin")]
public class IndexModel : PageModel
{
    #region Properties
    private readonly IUserService _userService;
    public IEnumerable<UserDTO> Users = new List<UserDTO>();
    [TempData] public string Alert { get; set; }
    #endregion

    #region Constructor
    public IndexModel(IUserService userService)
    {
        _userService = userService;
    }
    #endregion

    public async Task OnGetAsync()
    {
        Users = await _userService.GetUsersAsync();
    }
}
```

Creating Button Partial Views

To be able to reuse the buttons more efficiently, you will create three partial views. The first, **_PageButtonsPartial**, displays **Create** and **Dashboard** buttons on every **Index** page. The second, **_TableRowButtonsPartial**, displays edit and delete buttons in every table row. The third, **_BackToIndexButtonsPartial**, navigates to the **Index** and **Dashboard** pages.

1. Add a Razor View named **_PageButtonsPartial** to the *Pages-Shared* folder.
2. Delete all code in the view.
3. Add an empty <div> element.
4. Add the **Create** button inside the <div> using the <btn> Tag Helper you created earlier. Assign *Create* to the **asp-page** attribute to target the **Create** Razor Page you will add later, *add* to the **icon** attribute, and *Create New* between the start and end tags.
   `<btn asp-page="Create" icon="add">Create New</btn>`
5. Add another <btn> Tag Helper inside the <div> that targets the **Index** view in the *Pages* folder (not the one in the *Pages/Users* folder) to display the main

269

dashboard. Assign */Index* to the **asp-page** attribute to target the main **Index** Razor Page; add *dashboard* to the **icon** attribute, *text-light* to the **class** attribute to change the default dark gray text color to white, and *Dashboard* between the start and end tags.
```
<btn class="text-light" asp-page="/Index" icon="dashboard">
    Dashboard</btn>
```

6. Add another Razor View named **_TableRowButtonsPartial** to the *Pages-Shared* folder.
7. Add a **using** statement for the **VOD.Common.DTOModels.Admin** namespace to the *_ViewImports.cshtml* file in the **Admin** project to make the **ButtonDTO** class available to the Razor Pages.
8. Activate the changes by saving the file.
9. Delete all code in the view.
10. Add an **@model** directive for the **ButtonDTO** class that will receive the entity ids.
    `@model ButtonDTO`
11. Add the **Delete** and **Edit** buttons for the **Edit** and **Delete** Razor Pages using the <btn> Tag Helper you created earlier. Don't forget to add three **asp-route-** attributes for the course id, module id, and the id or user id; the ids are needed to fetch the correct entity for the Razor Page. Note that the **ItemId** property either can contain the value of the **Id** or the **UserId** property.
```
<btn class="float-right" asp-page="Delete" icon="close"
    asp-route-id="@Model.ItemId"
    asp-route-courseId="@Model.CourseId"
    asp-route-moduleId="@Model.ModuleId"></btn>
<btn class="float-right" style="margin-right:5px;"
    asp-page="Edit" icon="edit" asp-route-id="@Model.ItemId"
    asp-route-courseId="@Model.CourseId"
    asp-route-moduleId="@Model.ModuleId"></btn>
```
12. Add another Razor View named **_BackToIndexButtonsPartial** to the *Pages-Shared* folder.
13. Add the **Back to List (Index)** and **Dashboard** buttons inside an empty <div> using the <btn> Tag Helper you created earlier.
```
<div>
    <btn asp-page="Index" icon="list_alt">Back to List</btn>
    <btn class="text-light" asp-page="/Index"
      icon="dashboard">Dashboard</btn>
</div>
```

14. Save all files.

Altering the Index Razor Page

First, add **using** statements to the **Identity** and **Entities** namespaces and inject the **SignInManager** to be able to check that the user has the correct credentials.

Use the **ViewData** object to add a **Title** property with the text *Users* to it. This value will show on the browser tab.

Add an if-block that checks that the user is signed in and belongs to the **Admin** role. All remaining code should be placed inside the if-block so that only administrators can view it.

`@if (SignInManager.IsSignedIn(User) && User.IsInRole("Admin")) { }`

Add a <div> decorated with the Bootstrap **row** class to create a new row of data on the page. Then add a <div> decorated with the Bootstrap **col-md-8** and **offset-md-2** classes to create a column that has been offset by two columns (pushed in from the left) inside the row.

Add a page title displaying the text *Users* using an <h1> element inside the column <div>.

Use the <partial> Tag Helper to add the **_PageButtonsPartial** Razor View to add the **Create New** and **Dashboard** buttons below the <h1> heading.

`<partial name="_PageButtonsPartial" />`

Add a table with four columns where the first three have the following headings: **Email**, **Admin**, and **Id**. The fourth heading should be empty. Decorate the <table> element with the Bootstrap **table** class. Also, add a table body to the table.

Iterate over the users in the **Model.Users** property – the **Users** property you added to the code-behind file – and display the data in the **Email**, **IsAdmin**, and **Id** properties in the first three columns.

Use the <partial> Tag Helper to add the **_TableRowButtonsPartial** Razor View to add the **Edit** and **Delete** buttons to a new <td> column inside the table. Don't forget to add the **model** attribute containing an instance of the **ButtonDTO** class; the instance's **ItemId** property is needed to fetch the correct user for the Razor Page. Also, add a separate <btn> Tag Helper for the **Details** Razor Page below the previous <partial> Tag Helper; don't forget to pass in the user id through the **asp-route-id** attribute.

```
<td style="min-width:150px;">
    <partial name="_TableRowButtonsPartial" model="@user.ButtonDTO" />
    <btn class="float-right" style="margin-right:5px;"
      asp-page="Details" icon="edit" asp-route-id="@user.Id"></btn>
</td>
```

Add an empty <div> decorated with the **col-md-2** Bootstrap class below the previous column <div> to fill the entire row with columns. A Bootstrap row should have 12 columns. Bootstrap is very forgiving if you forget to add up the columns on a row.

1. Open the *Index.cshtml* HTML Razor page.
2. Remove the **VOD.Admin.Pages.Users** namespace path from the **@model** directive.
3. Add **using** statements to the **Identity** namespace and inject the **SignInManager** to be able to check that the user has the correct credentials.
   `@inject SignInManager<VODUser> SignInManager`
4. Change the **Title** property to store the text *Users*.
   ```
   @{
       ViewData["Title"] = "Users";
   }
   ```
5. Add an if-block that checks that the user is signed in and belongs to the **Admin** role.
   `@if (SignInManager.IsSignedIn(User) && User.IsInRole("Admin")) { }`
6. Add a <div> decorated with the Bootstrap **row** class to create a new row of data on the page. Then add a <div> decorated with the Bootstrap **col-md-8** and **offset-md-2** classes to create a column that has been offset by two columns inside the row. Add a column for the remaining Bootstrap columns below the previous column. All remaining code and HTML will be added to the first column <div>.
   ```
   <div class="row">
       <div class="col-md-8 offset-md-2"></div>
       <div class="col-md-2"></div>
   </div>
   ```

21. The User Razor Pages

7. Move the <h1> element inside the first column <div> and display the value from the Title attribute inside it.
   ```
   <h1>@ViewData["Title"]</h1>
   ```

8. Use the <partial> Tag Helper to add the **_PageButtonsPartial** Razor View to add the **Create New** and **Dashboard** buttons below the <h1> heading.
   ```
   <partial name="_PageButtonsPartial" />
   ```

9. Add a table with four columns where the first three have the following headings: **Email**, **Admin**, and **Id**. The fourth heading should be empty. Decorate the <table> element with the Bootstrap **table** class and add a 20px top margin. Also, add a table body to the table.
   ```
   <table style="margin-top:20px;" class="table">
       <thead>
           <tr>
               <th>Email</th>
               <th>Admin</th>
               <th>Id</th>
               <th></th>
           </tr>
       </thead>
       <tbody>
       </tbody>
   </table>
   ```

10. Iterate over the users in the **Model.Users** property in the <tbody> element and display the data in the **Email**, **IsAdmin**, and **Id** properties in the first three columns. The **DisplayFor** method will add an appropriate HTML element for the property's data type and display the property value in it.
    ```
    <tbody>
        @foreach (var user in Model.Users)
        {
            <tr>
                <td>@Html.DisplayFor(modelItem => user.Email)</td>
                <td>@Html.DisplayFor(modelItem => user.IsAdmin)</td>
                <td>@Html.DisplayFor(modelItem => user.Id)</td>
            </tr>
        }
    </tbody>
    ```

11. Use the <partial> Tag Helper to add the **_TableRowButtonsPartial** Razor View to add the **Edit** and **Delete** buttons to a new <td> column inside the table. Don't forget to add the **asp-model** attribute with an instance of the **ButtonDTO** for the

current user in the iteration; the id is needed to fetch the correct user for the Razor Page that is opened. Add a separate <btn> Tag Helper for the **Details** Razor Page below the previous <partial> Tag Helper; don't forget to pass in the user id though the **asp-route-id** attribute.

```
<td style="min-width:150px;">
    <partial name="_TableRowButtonsPartial"
        model="@user.ButtonDTO" />

    <btn class="float-right" style="margin-right:5px;"
        asp-page="Details" icon="edit" asp-route-id="@user.Id">
    </btn>
</td>
```

12. Run the application (Ctrl+F5) and click the **Users** card on the main dashboard or select **Users** in the **Admin** menu. Make sure the Razor Page is displaying the users in a table and that the buttons are present. You must add the corresponding Razor Pages to use the **Create**, **Edit**, and **Delete** buttons.

The complete code in the **Index** Razor Page:

```
@page
@model IndexModel
@inject SignInManager<VODUser> SignInManager
@{
    ViewData["Title"] = "Users";
}

@if (SignInManager.IsSignedIn(User) && User.IsInRole("Admin"))
{
    <div class="row">
        <div class="col-md-8 offset-md-2">
            <h1>@ViewData["Title"]</h1>
            <partial name="_PageButtonsPartial" />

            <table style="margin-top:20px;" class="table">
                <thead>
                    <tr>
                        <th>Email</th>
                        <th>Admin</th>
                        <th>Id</th>
                        <th></th>
                    </tr>
                </thead>
```

```
                    <tbody>
                        @foreach (var user in Model.Users)
                        {
                            <tr>
                                <td>@Html.DisplayFor(modelItem =>
                                    user.Email)</td>
                                <td>@Html.DisplayFor(modelItem =>
                                    user.IsAdmin)</td>
                                <td>@Html.DisplayFor(modelItem =>
                                    user.Id)</td>
                                <td style="min-width:150px;">
                                    <partial name="_TableRowButtonsPartial"
                                     model="@user.ButtonDTO" />

                                    <btn class="float-right"
                                         style="margin-right:5px;"
                                         asp-page="Details" icon="edit"
                                         asp-route-id="@user.Id">
                                    </btn>
                                </td>
                            </tr>
                        }
                    </tbody>
                </table>
            </div>
            <div class="col-md-2">
            </div>
        </div>
}
```

The Users/Create Razor Page

The **Create** Razor Page in the *Users* folder is used to add a new user to the **AspNetUsers** table in the database. It can be reached by clicking the **Create New** button above the table in the **Index** Razor Page, or by navigating to the */Users/Create* URI.

The **IUserService** service must be injected into the **CreateModel** class's constructor in the Razor Page code-behind and stored in a private field called **_userService** to add a new user.

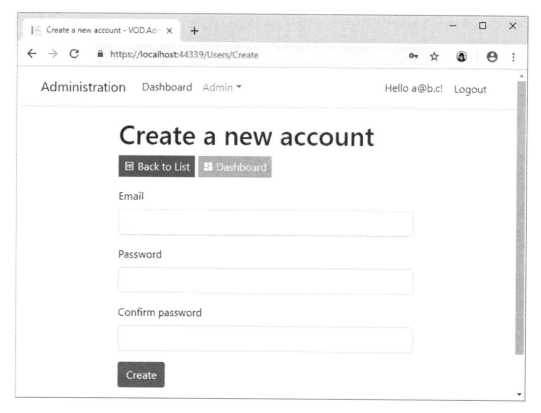

Altering the Razor Page CreateModel Class

The first thing you want to do is to restrict the usage to administrators only with the **[Authorize]** attribute.

Then you need to inject the **UserService** into the constructor that you will add to the class. Store the service instance in a private class-level variable called **_userService** to add the user to the database.

No data is needed to display the **Create** Razor Page, but it needs a **RegisterUserDTO** variable called **Input** that can pass the form data from the UI to the **OnPostAsync** code-behind method; call the **AddUserAsync** method on the **_userService** object to create the user in the database.

Add a **string** property called **Alert** and decorate it with the **[TempData]** attribute. This property will be assigned a message to be displayed in the **Index** Razor Page after the form

21. The User Razor Pages

data has been processed successfully in the **OnPostAsync** method and the action redirects to the **Index** Razor Page.

In the **OnPostAsync** method, you need to check that the model state is valid before performing any other action.

If the asynchronous **AddUserAsync** method returns **true** in the **Succeeded** property of the method's result, then assign a message to the **Alert** property that is used in the **Index** Razor Page and redirect to that page by returning a call to the **RedirectToPage** method.

Iterate over the errors in the **result.Errors** collection and add them to the **ModelState** object with the **AddModelError** method so that the errors can be used in the UI validation when redisplaying the form to the user.

1. Add a Razor Page to the *Pages-Users* folder, using the template with the same name, and name it **Create**.
2. Expand the **Create** node in the Solution Explorer and open the *Create.cshtml.cs* file.
3. Add the **[Authorize]** attribute to the class and specify that the **Admin** role is needed to access the page from the browser.
   ```
   [Authorize(Roles = "Admin")]
   public class CreateModel : PageModel
   ```
4. Inject **IUserService** into a constructor and save the injected object in a class-level variable called **_userService**. The variable will give you access to the service from any method in the class.
   ```
   private readonly IUserService _userService;

   public CreateModel(IUserService userService)
   {
       _userService = userService;
   }
   ```
5. Add a **public** class-level **RegisterUserDTO** variable decorated with the **[BindProperty]** attribute called **Input**. This property will be bound to the form controls in the HTML Razor Page.
   ```
   [BindProperty] public RegisterUserDTO Input { get; set; } =
       new RegisterUserDTO();
   ```

6. Add a **public string** property called **Alert** and decorate it with the **[TempData]** attribute. This property will get its value from the other Razor Pages when a successful result has been achieved, such as adding a new user.
   `[TempData] public string Alert { get; set; }`

7. Leave the **OnGet** method empty and make it asynchronous by adding the **async** and **Task** keywords. Rename the method **OnGetAsync**.
   `Public async Task OnGetAsync() { }`

8. Add a new asynchronous method called **OnPostAsync** that returns **Task<IActionResult>**, which essentially makes it the same as an **HttpPost** MVC action method.
   `public async Task<IActionResult> OnPostAsync() { }`

9. Check that the model state is valid with an if-block in the **OnPostAsync** method.
   `if (ModelState.IsValid) { }`

10. Call the **AddUserAsync** method in the **UserService** service and pass in the **Input** object returned from the form inside the if-block to add the user. Store the returned object in a variable called **result**.
    `var result = await _userService.AddUserAsync(Input);`

11. Add an if-block that checks if the **result.Succeeded** property is **true**, which means that EF successfully added the user to the database.
    `if (result.Succeeded) { }`

12. Assign a success message to the **Alert** property and redirect to the **Index** Razor Page inside the **Succeeded** if-block.
    ```
    Alert = $"Created a new account for {Input.Email}.";
    return RedirectToPage("Index");
    ```

13. Add a **foreach** loop below the **Succeeded** if-block that iterates over any errors in the **result.Errors** collection and adds them to the **ModelState** with the **AddModelError** method for use in UI validation when reposting the form.
    ```
    foreach (var error in result.Errors)
    {
        ModelState.AddModelError(string.Empty, error.Description);
    }
    ```

14. Return the page using the **Page** method below the **ModelState.IsValid** if-block at the end of the method; this will return the **Create** Razor Page displaying any validation errors.
    `return Page();`

15. Save all files.

The complete code in the **Create** code-behind file:

```csharp
[Authorize(Roles = "Admin")]
public class CreateModel : PageModel
{
    #region Properties and Variables
    private readonly IUserService _userService;
    [BindProperty] public RegisterUserDTO Input { get; set; } =
        new RegisterUserDTO();
    [TempData] public string Alert { get; set; }
    #endregion

    #region Constructor
    public CreateModel(IUserService userService)
    {
        _userService = userService;
    }
    #endregion

    #region Actions
    public async Task OnGetAsync()
    {
    }

    public async Task<IActionResult> OnPostAsync()
    {
        if (ModelState.IsValid)
        {
            var result = await _userService.AddUserAsync(Input);

            if (result.Succeeded)
            {
                // Message sent back to the Index Razor Page.
                Alert = $"Created a new account for {Input.Email}.";

                return RedirectToPage("Index");
            }

            foreach (var error in result.Errors)
            {
                ModelState.AddModelError(string.Empty,
                    error.Description);
            }
```

```
        }

        // Something failed, redisplay the form.
        return Page();
    }
    #endregion
}
```

Altering the Create Razor Page

First, add **using** statements to the **Identity** namespace and inject the **SignInManager** to be able to check that the user has the correct credentials.

Use the **ViewData** object to add a **Title** property with the text *Create a new account* to it. This value shows on the browser tab.

Add an if-block that checks that the user is signed in and belongs to the **Admin** role. All remaining code should be placed inside the if-block so that only administrators can view it.

```
@if (SignInManager.IsSignedIn(User) && User.IsInRole("Admin")) { }
```

Add a <div> decorated with the Bootstrap **row** class to create a new row of data on the page. Then add a <div> decorated with the Bootstrap **col-md-8** and **offset-md-2** classes to create a column that has been offset by four columns (pushed in from the left) inside the row.

Add a page title displaying the text in the **ViewData** object's **Title** property using an <h1> element inside the column <div>.

Use the <partial> Tag Helper to add the **_BackToIndexButtonsPartial** partial Razor View that contain the **Back to List** and **Dashboard** buttons. Add the <partial> Tag Helper below the <h1> heading.

```
<partial name="_BackToIndexButtonsPartial" />
```

Add an empty <p></p> element to create some distance between the buttons and the form.

Add a form that validates on all errors using the <form> element and a <div> element with the **asp-validation-summary** Tag Helper.

```
<form method="post">
    <div asp-validation-summary="All" class="text-danger"></div>
</form>
```

Add a <div> decorated with the **form-group** class below the previous <div> inside the <form> element. Add a <label> element with its **asp-for** attribute assigned a value from the **Input.Email** model property, inside the previous <div> element.

```
<label asp-for="Input.Email"></label>
```

Add an <input> element with its **asp-for** attribute assigned a value from the **Input.Email** model property below the <label> element. Decorate the <input> element with the **form-control** class to denote that the element belongs to a form and gives it nice styling.

```
<input asp-for="Input.Email" class="form-control" />
```

Add a <span> element with its **asp-validation-for** attribute assigned a value from the **Input.Email** model property, below the <input> element. Decorate the <span> element with the **text-danger** class to make the text red.

```
<span asp-validation-for="Input.Email" class="text-danger"></span>
```

Copy the **form-group** decorated <div> you just finished and paste it in twice. Modify the pasted in code to target the **Password** and **ConfirmPassword** model properties.

Add a **submit** button above the closing </form> element and decorate it with the **btn** and **btn-success** Bootstrap classes to make it a styled green button.

Load the **_ValidationScriptsPartial** partial view inside a **@section** block named **Scripts** below the if-block to load the necessary UI validation scripts.

1. Open the *Create.cshtml* HTML Razor page.
2. Remove the **VOD.Admin.Pages.Users** namespace path from the **@model** directive; the **_ViewImports** file already defines it.
3. Inject the **SignInManager** to be able to check that the user has the correct credentials.
   ```
   @inject SignInManager<VODUser> SignInManager
   ```

4. Add a **Title** property with the text *Create a new account* to the **ViewData** object.
   ```
   @{
       ViewData["Title"] = "Create a new account";
   }
   ```
5. Display the text in the **Title** property inside the <h1> element.
   ```
   <h1>@ViewData["Title"]</h1>
   ```
6. Add an if-block that checks that the user is signed in and belongs to the **Admin** role below the <h1> element.
   ```
   @if (SignInManager.IsSignedIn(User) && User.IsInRole("Admin")) { }
   ```
7. Add a <div> decorated with the Bootstrap **row** class to create a new row of data on the page. Then add a <div> decorated with the Bootstrap **col-md-8** and **offset-md-2** classes to create a column that has been offset by two columns inside the row.
   ```
   <div class="row">
       <div class="col-md-8 offset-md-2"></div>
   </div>
   ```
8. Move the <h1> heading inside the column <div>.
9. Use the <partial> Tag Helper to add the **_BackToIndexButtonsPartial** partial Razor View that contains the **Back to List** and **Dashboard** buttons. Add the <partial> Tag Helper below the <h1> heading.
   ```
   <partial name="_BackToIndexButtonsPartial" />
   ```
10. Add an empty <p></p> element to create some distance between the buttons and the form.
    ```
    <p></p>
    ```
11. Add a form that validates on all errors using the <form> element and a <div> element with the **asp-validation-summary** Tag Helper. Decorate the <div> element with the **text-danger** Bootstrap class to give the text a red color.
    ```
    <form method="post">
        <div asp-validation-summary="All" class="text-danger"></div>
    </form>
    ```
12. Add a <div> decorated with the **form-group** class below the previous <div> inside the <form> element.
    a. Add a <label> element with its **asp-for** attribute assigned a value from the **Input.Email** model property, inside the previous <div> element.

21. The User Razor Pages

b. Add an <input> element with its **asp-for** attribute assigned a value from the **Input.Email** model property below the <label> element.
c. Add a <span> element with its **asp-validation-for** attribute assigned a value from the **Input.Email** model property below the <input> element. Decorate the <span> element with the **text-danger** class to give the text red color.

```
<div class="form-group">
    <label asp-for="Input.Email"></label>
    <input asp-for="Input.Email" class="form-control" />
    <span asp-validation-for="Input.Email"
        class="text-danger"></span>
</div>
```

13. Copy the **form-group** decorated <div> you just finished and paste it in twice. Modify the pasted in code to target the **Password** and **ConfirmPassword** model properties.
14. Add a submit button above the closing </form> element and decorate it with the **btn** and **btn-success** Bootstrap classes to make it a styled green button.
```
<button type="submit" class="btn btn-success">Create</button>
```
15. Load the **_ValidationScriptsPartial** partial view inside a **@section** block named **Scripts** below the if-block, to load the necessary UI validation scripts.
```
@section Scripts {
    @await Html.PartialAsync("_ValidationScriptsPartial")
}
```
16. Run the application (Ctrl+F5) and click the **Users** card on the main dashboard or select **Users** in the **Admin** menu. Make sure the Razor Page is displaying the users in a table and that the buttons are present. Click the **Create New** button to open the **Create** Razor Page. Try to add a new user and check that it is in the **AspNetUsers** table in the database. Also, try the **Back to List** and **Dashboard** buttons to navigate to the *Users/Index* and *Pages/Index* Razor Pages respectively.

The complete code in the **Create** HTML Razor Page:

```
@page
@inject SignInManager<VODUser> SignInManager

@model CreateModel
@{ ViewData["Title"] = "Create a new account"; }
```

```
@if (SignInManager.IsSignedIn(User) && User.IsInRole("Admin"))
{
    <div class="row">
        <div class="col-md-4 offset-md-4">
            <h2>@ViewData["Title"]</h2>

            <partial name="_BackToIndexButtonsPartial" />
            <p></p>

            <form method="post">
                <div asp-validation-summary="All"
                 class="text-danger"></div>

                <div class="form-group">
                    <label asp-for="Input.Email"></label>
                    <input asp-for="Input.Email" class="form-control" />
                    <span asp-validation-for="Input.Email"
                     class="text-danger"></span>
                </div>
                <div class="form-group">
                    <label asp-for="Input.Password"></label>
                    <input asp-for="Input.Password"
                     class="form-control" />
                    <span asp-validation-for="Input.Password"
                     class="text-danger"></span>
                </div>
                <div class="form-group">
                    <label asp-for="Input.ConfirmPassword"></label>
                    <input asp-for="Input.ConfirmPassword"
                     class="form-control" />
                    <span asp-validation-for="Input.ConfirmPassword"
                     class="text-danger"></span>
                </div>
                <button type="submit" class="btn btn-success">Create
                </button>
            </form>
        </div>
    </div>
}

@section Scripts {
    @await Html.PartialAsync("_ValidationScriptsPartial") }
```

The Users/Edit Razor Page

Because the **Edit** Razor Page is almost identical to the **Create** Razor Page, you will copy the **Create** page and make changes to it.

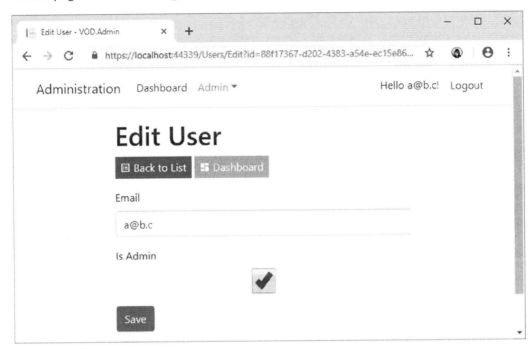

Altering the Razor Page EditModel class

1. Copy the **Create** Razor Page and its code-behind file in the *Users* folder, paste them into the same folder, and change their names to **Edit**.
2. Open the *Edit.cshtml.cs* file.
3. Change the class name and constructor to **EditModel**.
4. Change the data type for the **Input** property to **UserDTO**.
   `public UserDTO Input { get; set; } = new UserDTO();`
5. Locate the **OnGet** method and make it asynchronous. Rename the method **OnGetAsync**. Add a **string** property called **id**; the property name must match the last part of the **asp-route-*id*** attribute name on the **Edit** button.
   `public async Task OnGetAsync(string id)`
6. In the **OnGetAsync** method, assign an empty string to the **Alert** property to clear any residual message.
   `Alert = string.Empty;`

7. Call the **GetUserAsync** method in the **_userService** service instance and assign the fetched user to the **Input** property. The **Input** property is part of the model sent to the **Edit** page and is bound to the form controls.

    ```
    public async void OnGet(string id)
    {
        Alert = string.Empty;
        Input = await _userService.GetUserAsync(id);
    }
    ```

8. Replace the call to the **AddUserAsync** method with a call to the **UpdateUserAsync** method in the **OnPostAsync** method.

    ```
    var result = await _userService.UpdateUserAsync(Input);
    ```

9. Because the result from the **UpdateUserAsync** is a Boolean value, you must remove the **IsSucceeded** property that doesn't exist.

10. Change the text assigned to the **Alert** to:

    ```
    if (result)
    {
        Alert = $"User {Input.Email} was updated.";
        return RedirectToPage("Index");
    }
    ```

11. Remove the **foreach** loop and its contents.

The complete code for the **EditModel** class:

```
[Authorize(Roles = "Admin")]
public class EditModel : PageModel
{
    private readonly IUserService _userService;

    [BindProperty]
    public UserDTO Input { get; set; } = new UserDTO();

    [TempData]
    public string Alert { get; set; }

    public EditModel(IUserService userService)
    {
        _userService = userService;
    }
}
```

```csharp
public async Task OnGetAsync(string id)
{
    Alert = string.Empty;
    Input = _userService.GetUserAsync(id);
}

public async Task<IActionResult> OnPostAsync()
{
    if (ModelState.IsValid)
    {
        var result = await _userService.UpdateUserAsync(Input);

        if (result)
        {
            Alert = $"User {Input.Email} was updated.";
            return RedirectToPage("Index");
        }
    }

    return Page();
}
}
```

Altering the Edit Razor Page

1. Open the *Edit.cshtml* file.
2. Change the name of the model class to **EditModel**. You might have to close the Razor Page and open it again after changing the model class.
3. Change the **ViewData** object's **Title** property to *Edit User*.
4. Add a hidden <input> element for the **Input.Id** property above the first **form-group** decorated <div>.
   ```html
   <input type="hidden" asp-for="Input.Id" />
   ```
5. Change the second **form-group**'s intrinsic elements to target the **Input.IsAdmin** property.
   ```html
   <div class="form-group">
       <label asp-for="Input.IsAdmin"></label>
       <input asp-for="Input.IsAdmin" class="form-control" />
       <span asp-validation-for="Input.IsAdmin"
         class="text-danger"></span>
   </div>
   ```
6. Remove the third **form-group** and all its content.

7. Change the text on the **submit** button to *Save*.
8. Start the application and edit one of the users.

The complete code in the **Edit** Razor Page:

```
@page
@inject SignInManager<User> SignInManager
@model EditModel
@{ ViewData["Title"] = "Edit User"; }

@if (SignInManager.IsSignedIn(User) && User.IsInRole("Admin"))
{
    <div class="row">
        <div class="col-md-8 offset-md-2">
            <h1>@ViewData["Title"]</h1>

            <partial name="_BackToIndexButtonsPartial" />
            <p></p>

            <form method="post">
                <div asp-validation-summary="All"
                    class="text-danger"></div>

                <input type="hidden" asp-for="Input.Id" />

                <div class="form-group">
                    <label asp-for="Input.Email"></label>
                    <input asp-for="Input.Email" class="form-control" />
                    <span asp-validation-for="Input.Email"
                      class="text-danger"></span>
                </div>
                <div class="form-group">
                    <label asp-for="Input.IsAdmin"></label>
                    <input asp-for="Input.IsAdmin"
                     class="form-control" />
                    <span asp-validation-for="Input.IsAdmin"
                     class="text-danger"></span>
                </div>
                <button type="submit" class="btn btn-success">
                    Save</button>
            </form>
        </div>
    </div>
}
```

```
@section Scripts {
    @await Html.PartialAsync("_ValidationScriptsPartial")
}
```

The Users/Delete Razor Page

This Razor Page will display information about the user and a button to delete the user. You will copy the **Edit** page and alter it.

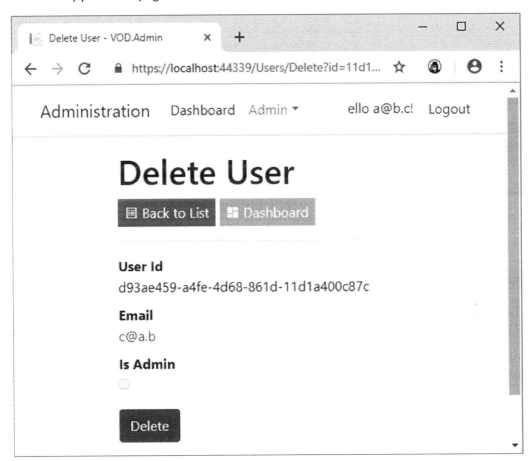

Altering the DeleteModel Class

1. Copy the **Edit** Razor Page and its code-behind file in the *Users* folder, paste them into the same folder, and change their names to **Delete**.
2. Open the *Delete.cshtml.cs* file.
3. Change the class and constructor name to **DeleteModel**.

4. Replace the call to the **UpdateUserAsync** method with a call to the **DeleteUserAsync** method in the **OnPostAsync** method. Pass in the **Id** property value of the **Input** object to the **DeleteUserAsync** method to specify which user to delete.
   ```
   var result = await _userService.DeleteUserAsync(Input.Id);
   ```

5. Change the text assigned to the **Alert** to:
   ```
   Alert = $"User {Input.Email} was deleted.";
   ```

The complete code for the **DeleteModel** class:

```
public class DeleteModel : PageModel
{
    #region Properties and Variables
    private readonly IUserService _userService;

    [BindProperty]
    public UserDTO Input { get; set; } = new UserDTO();

    [TempData]
    public string Alert { get; set; }
    #endregion

    #region Constructor
    public DeleteModel(IUserService userService)
    {
        _userService = userService;
    }
    #endregion

    #region Actions
    Public async Task OnGetAsync(string userId)
    {
        Alert = string.Empty;
        Input = await _userService.GetUserAsync(id);
    }

    public async Task<IActionResult> OnPostAsync()
    {
        if (ModelState.IsValid)
        {
            var result = await _userService.DeleteUserAsync(Input.Id);
```

```
            if (result)
            {
                Alert = $"User {Input.Email} was deleted.";
                return RedirectToPage("Index");
            }
        }

        return Page();
    }
    #endregion
}
```

Altering the Delete Razor Page
1. Open the *Delete.cshtml* file.
2. Change the name of the model class to **DeleteModel**.
3. Change the **ViewData** object's **Title** property to *Delete User*.
4. Replace the <p></p> paragraph element with a horizontal rule.
   ```
   <hr />
   ```
5. Add a data list (not a table) below the horizontal rule above the <form> element. Add <dt> and <dd> elements for the **Id**, **Email**, and **IsAdmin** properties in the **Input** object. The <dt> element contains the label and the <dd> element contains the data. The **DisplayNameFor** method fetches the name of the property or the name in the **[Display]** attribute. The **DisplayFor** method fetches the value stored in the property.
   ```
   <dl class="dl-horizontal">
       <dt>@Html.DisplayNameFor(model => model.Input.Id)</dt>
       <dd>@Html.DisplayFor(model => model.Input.Id)</dd>
       <dt>@Html.DisplayNameFor(model => model.Input.Email)</dt>
       <dd>@Html.DisplayFor(model => model.Input.Email)</dd>
       <dt>@Html.DisplayNameFor(model => model.Input.IsAdmin)</dt>
       <dd>@Html.DisplayFor(model => model.Input.IsAdmin)</dd>
   </dl>
   ```
6. Remove all the **form-group** decorated <div> elements and their contents. The controls are no longer needed, since no data is altered with the form.
7. Add hidden <input> elements for the **Input.Email** and **Input.IsAdmin** properties below the existing hidden <input> element.
   ```
   <input type="hidden" asp-for="Input.Id" />
   <input type="hidden" asp-for="Input.Email" />
   <input type="hidden" asp-for="Input.IsAdmin" />
   ```

8. Change the text to *Delete* and the Bootstrap button style to **btn-danger** on the **submit** button.
   ```
   <button type="submit" class="btn btn-danger">Delete</button>
   ```
9. Save all files.
10. Try to delete a user that you have added.

The complete code in the **Delete** Razor Page:

```
@page
@model DeleteModel
@inject SignInManager<VODUser> SignInManager
@{ ViewData["Title"] = "Delete User"; }

@if (SignInManager.IsSignedIn(User) && User.IsInRole("Admin"))
{
    <div class="row">
        <div class="col-md-6 offset-md-3">
            <h1>@ViewData["Title"]</h1>

            <partial name="_BackToIndexButtonsPartial" />
            <hr />

            <dl class="dl-horizontal">
                <dt>@Html.DisplayNameFor(model => model.Input.Id)</dt>
                <dd>@Html.DisplayFor(model => model.Input.Id)</dd>
                <dt>@Html.DisplayNameFor(model => model.Input.Email)</dt>
                <dd>@Html.DisplayFor(model => model.Input.Email)</dd>
                <dt>@Html.DisplayNameFor(model => model.Input.IsAdmin)</dt>
                <dd>@Html.DisplayFor(model => model.Input.IsAdmin)</dd>
            </dl>

            <form method="post">
                <div asp-validation-summary="All"
                    class="text-danger"></div>
                <input type="hidden" asp-for="Input.Id" />
                <input type="hidden" asp-for="Input.Email" />
                <input type="hidden" asp-for="Input.IsAdmin" />

                <button type="submit" class="btn btn-danger">Delete</button>
            </form>
        </div>
    </div>
}

@section Scripts { @await Html.PartialAsync("_ValidationScriptsPartial") }
```

The Users/Details Razor Page

The **Details** Razor Page in the *Users* folder grants the user access to courses. The page can be reached by clicking the **Details** button for the desired user on the **Index** Razor Page, or by navigating to the */Users/Details* URI.

To enroll a user in a course, you select a course in the drop-down and click the **Add** button, and to revoke access to a course, you click the **Remove** button for the course. Inject the **IDbReadService** and **IDbWriteService** services into the **DetailsModel** class's constructor in the **Details** Razor Page code-behind to handle these two scenarios.

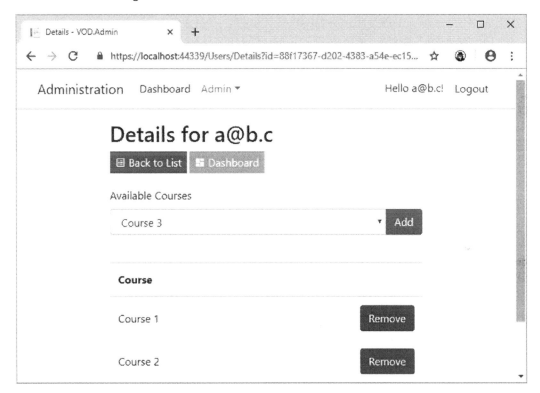

Adding the Details Razor Page
1. Right-click on the *Users* folder and select **Add-Razor Page**.
2. Select the **Razor Page** template and click the **Add** button.
3. Enter the name *Details* into the **Razor Page name** field and click the **Add** button.

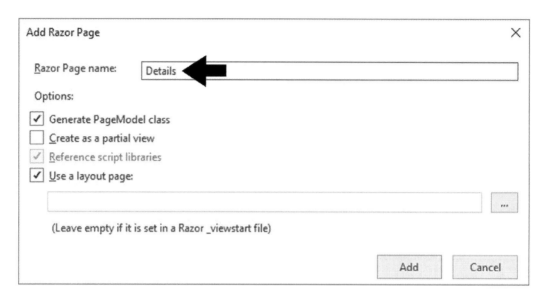

Altering the Razor Page DetailsModel Class

The first thing you want to do is to restrict the usage to administrators only with the **[Authorize]** attribute.

Then you need to inject the **IDbReadService** and **IDbWriteService** services into the constructor that you will add to the class. Store the service instances in private class-level variables called **_dbRead** and **_dbWrite**.

Add a public **IEnumerable<Course>** collection property named **Courses** and instantiate it to an empty list to avoid **null** reference errors; this collection will hold the user's available courses.

Add a public **SelectList** property named **Courses**; this collection will hold the courses available to the user. It needs to be a **SelectList** because the drop-down needs the data in that format.

Add a public **int** property named **CourseId** and decorate it with the **BindPropertry** attribute so that it can be bound to the value selected in the drop-down. Also, decorate it with the **Display** attribute and assign the text *Available Courses* to its **Name** property. The **Display** attribute will change the text in the label describing the drop-down.

Add a public **UserDTO** property named **Customer** that will hold the necessary user data to display on the page.

Add a try/catch block to the **OnPostAsync** method that you will add. In the try-block, save the user id and course id combination by creating an instance of the **UserCourse** entity. Below the catch-block, reload the collections before rendering the page.

1. Expand the **Details** node in the Solution Explorer and open the *Details.cshtml.cs* file.
2. Add the **[Authorize]** attribute to the class and specify that the **Admin** role is needed to access the page from the browser.
   ```
   [Authorize(Roles = "Admin")]
   public class DetailsModel : PageModel
   ```
3. Inject **IDbReadService** and **IDbWriteService** services into a constructor and save the injected objects in class-level variables called **_dbRead** and **_dbWrite**. The variables will give you access to the services from any method in the class.
   ```
   private readonly IDbReadService _dbRead;
   private readonly IDbWriteService _dbWrite;
   public DetailsModel(IDbReadService dbReadService, IDbWriteService dbWriteService)
   {
       _dbRead = dbReadService;
       _dbWrite = dbWriteService;
   }
   ```
4. Add an **IEnumerable<Course>** collection named **Courses** as a **public** property and instantiate it to an empty list to avoid **null** reference errors; this collection will hold the courses that the user/customer has access to.
   ```
   public IEnumerable<Course> Courses { get; set; } = new List<Course>();
   ```
5. Add a public **SelectList** property named **Courses**; this collection will hold the courses that the user/customer can enroll in. It needs to be a **SelectList** because the drop-down needs the data in that format.
   ```
   public SelectList AvailableCourses { get; set; }
   ```
6. Add a public **int** property named **CourseId** and decorate it with the **BindPropertry** attribute so that it can be bound to the value selected in the drop-down. Also, decorate it with the **Display** attribute and assign the text *Available Courses* to its **Name** property. The **Display** attribute will change the text in the label describing the drop-down.
   ```
   [BindProperty, Display(Name = "Available Courses")] public int CourseId { get; set; }
   ```

7. Add a public **UserDTO** property named **Customer** that will hold the necessary user data displaying on the page.
   ```
   public UserDTO Customer { get; set; }
   ```

8. Because both the **OnGetAsync** and the two **OnPostAsync** methods use the data in the collection and **SelectList**, it's best to create a private asynchronous method named **FillViewData** and call it where needed. The method should return **Task** and have a **string** parameter named **userId**.
   ```
   private async Task FillViewData(string userId) { }
   ```

9. Inside the **FillViewData** method, fetch the user with the value in the **userId** parameter. Store the user in a variable named **user** and use its data to create an instance of the **UserDTO** class that you store in the **Customer** property you added earlier.
   ```
   var user = await _dbRead.SingleAsync<VODUser>(u =>
       u.Id.Equals(userId));
   Customer = new UserDTO { Id = user.Id, Email = user.Email };
   ```

10. Inside the **FillViewData** method, fetch the user's courses and their ids. The easiest way is to call the **GetAsync** method on the **_dbRead** service and include the data for the navigation properties of the **UserCourse** objects.
    ```
    _dbRead.Include<UserCourse>();
    var userCourses = await _dbRead.GetAsync<UserCourse>(uc =>
        uc.UserId.Equals(userId));
    var usersCourseIds = userCourses.Select(c => c.CourseId).ToList();
    ```

11. Select the **Course** objects from the **userCourses IQueryable** by calling the **ToList** method on the **Select** method. Store the objects in the **Courses** collection you added earlier.
    ```
    Courses = userCourses.Select(c => c.Course).ToList();
    ```

12. Use the course ids stored in the **usedCourseIds** variable to exclude courses that the user already is enrolled in when creating the **SelectList** of available courses. Store the available courses in the **AvailableCourses** property you added earlier. You need to call the **ToSelectList** extension method you created earlier to convert the course collection into a **SelectList**.
    ```
    var availableCourses = await _dbRead.GetAsync<Course>(uc =>
        !usersCourseIds.Contains(uc.Id));
    AvailableCourses = availableCourses.ToSelectList("Id", "Title");
    ```

21. The User Razor Pages

13. Add a **string** parameter named **id** to the **OnGetAsync** method and call the **FillViewData** method with the id.
    ```
    public async Task OnGetAsync(string id)
    {
        await FillViewData(id);
    }
    ```

14. Add a new asynchronous method called **OnPostAddAsync** and call it when the **Add** button is clicked to enroll a customer in a course. The method should have a **string** parameter named **userId** and return a **Task<IActionResult>**, which essentially makes it the same as an **HttpPost** MVC action method.
    ```
    public async Task<IActionResult> OnPostAddAsync(string userId) { }
    ```

15. Add a try/catch-block and add a new instance of the **UserCourse** class and assign its values from the **userId** parameter and the **CourseId** property you added earlier that gets its value from the drop-down selection. Don't forget to call the **SaveChangesAsync** method to persist the changes to the database.
    ```
    try
    {
        _dbWrite.Add(new UserCourse { CourseId = CourseId,
            UserId = userId });
        var succeeded = await _dbWrite.SaveChangesAsync();
    }
    catch
    {
    }
    ```

16. Call the **FillViewData** method with the value from the **userId** parameter below the catch-block to load the course and user data. Then render the page by calling the **Page** method.
    ```
    await FillViewData(userId);
    return Page();
    ```

17. Add a new asynchronous method called **OnPostRemoveAsync** and call it when the **Remove** button for a course is clicked to revoke access to the course. The method should have a **string** parameter named **userId** and an **int** parameter named **courseId**, and return a **Task<IActionResult>**, which essentially makes it the same as an **HttpPost** MVC action method.
    ```
    public async Task<IActionResult> OnPostRemoveAsync(int courseId,
        string userId) { }
    ```

18. Add a try/catch-block and make sure that the user-course combination exists by fetching the record from the database before removing it; you can check for a **null** value to determine if the record exists. Call the **Delete** method on the **_dbWrite** service with the **UserCourse** instance you fetched. Don't forget to call the **SaveChangesAsync** method to persist the changes in the database.

```
try
{
    var userCourse = await _dbRead.SingleAsync<UserCourse>(uc =>
        uc.UserId.Equals(userId) &&
        uc .CourseId.Equals(courseId));

    if (userCourse != null)
    {
        _dbWrite.Delete(userCourse);
        await _dbWrite.SaveChangesAsync();
    }
}
catch
{
}
```

19. Call the **FillViewData** method with the value from the **userId** parameter below the catch-block to load the course and user data. Then render the page by calling the **Page** method.

```
await FillViewData(userId);
return Page();
```

The complete code in the **Details** code-behind file:

```
public class DetailsModel : PageModel
{
    #region Properties and Variables
    private readonly IDbReadService _dbRead;
    private readonly IDbWriteService _dbWrite;
    public IEnumerable<Course> Courses { get; set; } =
        new List<Course>();
    public SelectList AvailableCourses { get; set; }

    [BindProperty, Display(Name = "Available Courses")]
    public int CourseId { get; set; }

    public UserDTO Customer { get; set; }
    #endregion
```

```csharp
#region Constructor
public DetailsModel(IDbReadService dbReadService,
IDbWriteService dbWriteService)
{
    _dbRead = dbReadService;
    _dbWrite = dbWriteService;
}
#endregion

private async Task FillViewData(string userId)
{
    // Fetch the user/customer
    var user = await _dbRead.SingleAsync<VODUser>(u =>
        u.Id.Equals(userId));
    Customer = new UserDTO { Id = user.Id, Email = user.Email };

    // Fetch the user's courses and course ids
    _dbRead.Include<UserCourse>();
    var userCourses = await _dbRead.GetAsync<UserCourse>(uc =>
        uc.UserId.Equals(userId));
    var usersCourseIds = userCourses.Select(c =>
        c.CourseId).ToList();
    Courses = userCourses.Select(c => c.Course).ToList();

    // Fetch courses that the user doesn't already have access to
    var availableCourses = await _dbRead.GetAsync<Course>(uc =>
        !usersCourseIds.Contains(uc.Id));
    AvailableCourses = availableCourses.ToSelectList("Id", "Title");
}

public async Task OnGetASync(string id)
{
    await FillViewData(id);
}

public async Task<IActionResult> OnPostAddAsync(string userId)
{
    try
    {
        _dbWrite.Add(new UserCourse { CourseId = CourseId,
            UserId = userId });
        var succeeded = await _dbWrite.SaveChangesAsync();
    }
    catch { }
```

```
            await FillViewData(userId);
            return Page();
        }

        public async Task<IActionResult> OnPostRemoveAsync(int courseId,
        string userId)
        {
            try
            {
                var userCourse = await _dbRead.SingleAsync<UserCourse>(uc =>
                    uc.UserId.Equals(userId) &&
                    uc.CourseId.Equals(courseId));

                if (userCourse != null)
                {
                    _dbWrite.Delete(userCourse);
                    await _dbWrite.SaveChangesAsync();
                }
            }
            catch
            {
            }

            await FillViewData(userId);
            return Page();
        }
    }
}
```

Altering the Details Razor Page

First, add **using** statements to the **Identity** namespace and inject the **SignInManager** to be able to check that the user has the correct credentials.

Use the **ViewData** object to add a **Title** property with the text *Details* to it. This value will be displayed on the browser tab and in the page header.

Add an if-block that checks that the user is signed in and belongs to the **Admin** role. All remaining code should be placed inside the if-block so that only administrators can view it.

```
@if (SignInManager.IsSignedIn(User) && User.IsInRole("Admin")) { }
```

Add a <div> decorated with the Bootstrap **row** class to create a new row of data on the page. Then add a <div> decorated with the Bootstrap **col-md-8** and **offset-md-2** classes to create a column that has been offset by two columns (pushed in from the left) inside the row.

Add a page title displaying the text in the **ViewData** object's **Title** property and the user's email using an <h1> element inside the column <div>.

Use the <partial> Tag Helper to add the **_BackToIndexButtonsPartial** partial Razor View that contains the **Back to List** and **Dashboard** buttons. Add the <partial> Tag Helper below the <h1> heading.

```
<partial name="_BackToIndexButtonsPartial" />
```

Add an if-block that checks if there are any courses that the user can enroll in; if there aren't, then the drop-down and **Add** button shouldn't be rendered.

Add a form inside the if-block that posts to the **OnPostAddAsync** method when clicking the **Add** button. The **asp-page-handler** attribute on the submit button determines which method to call when more than one post method is available. The value should not contain **OnPost** or **Async**, only the unique part of the name; in this case **Add**.

```
<form method="post" style="margin:20px 0px;">
    ...
    <button type="submit" asp-page-handler="Add" class="btn
        btn-success">Add</button>
    ...
</form>
```

The form should contain a <select> list (drop-down) with the available courses from the **AvailableCourses SelectList**, and a **submit** button with the text **Add**. You also need to add a hidden field for the user id so that it gets posted back to the server. You can place a <div> decorated with the **input-group** Bootstrap class around the drop-down and the button, and a <div> decorated with the **input-group-append** Bootstrap class around the button to make them appear as one control.

Add a new row <div> with a column <div> decorated with the **col-md-8 offset-md-2** Bootstrap classes. Add a table with two columns where the first displays the title *Courses*.

Display all the courses that the customer is enrolled in with a **Remove** button for each inside the <tbody>. The **asp-page-handler** attribute on the **Remove** submit button should contain the value *Remove*.

1. Open the *Details.cshtml* HTML Razor page.
2. Remove the **VOD.Admin.Pages.Users** namespace path from the **@model** directive; the **_ViewImports** file already defines it.
3. Inject the **SignInManager** to be able to check that the user has the correct credentials.
   `@inject` `SignInManager<VODUser> SignInManager`
4. Add an if-block that checks that the user is signed in and belongs to the **Admin** role below the <h1> element.
   `@if (SignInManager.IsSignedIn(User) && User.IsInRole("Admin")) { }`
5. Add a <div> decorated with the Bootstrap **row** class to create a new row of data on the page. Then add a <div> decorated with the Bootstrap **col-md-8** and **offset-md-2** classes to create a column that has been offset by two columns inside the row.
   ```
   <div class="row">
       <div class="col-md-8 offset-md-2">
       </div>
   </div>
   ```
6. Move the <h1> heading inside the column <div> and change it to an <h2> heading.
7. Display the text in the **Title** property and the user's email inside the <h2> element.
   `<h2>@ViewData["Title"] for @Model.Customer.Email</h2>`
8. Use the <partial> Tag Helper to add the **_BackToIndexButtonsPartial** partial Razor View that contains the **Back to List** and **Dashboard** buttons. Add the <partial> Tag Helper below the <h2> heading.
   `<partial name="_BackToIndexButtonsPartial" />`
9. Add a form decorated with the **method** attribute set to *post* inside an if-block that checks that there are courses available that the customer can enroll in. The finished form will post to the **OnPostAddAsync** method when the **Add** submit button is clicked.
   ```
   @if (Model.AvailableCourses.Count() > 0) {
       <form method="post" style="margin:20px 0px;"></form>
   }
   ```

10. Add a hidden field for the user id inside the form.
    `<input type="hidden" asp-for="Customer.Id" name="userId" />`
11. Add a `<div>` decorated with the **form-group** class below the `<input>` holding the hidden user id.
    a. Add a `<label>` element with its **asp-for** attribute, assigned a value from the **CourseId** model property, inside the **form-group** `<div>` element.
    b. Add a `<div>` element decorated with the **input-group** Bootstrap class below the label.
    c. Add a `<select>` element below the label with its **asp-for** attribute assigned a value from the **CourseId** model property and its **asp-items** assigned values from the **AvailableCourses** model property.
    `<select asp-for="CourseId" class="form-control" asp-items="@Model.AvailableCourses"></select>`
    d. Add a `<div>` element decorated with the **input-group-append** Bootstrap class below the label.
    e. Add a submit button with its **asp-page-handler** attribute set to *Add* to target the **OnPostAddAsync** method.
    `<button type="submit" asp-page-handler="Add" class="btn btn-success">Add</button>`
12. Add a `<div>` decorated with the Bootstrap **row** class below the previous row to create a new row of data on the page. Then add a `<div>` decorated with the Bootstrap **col-md-8** and **offset-md-2** classes to create a column that has been offset by two columns inside the row.
    ```
    <div class="row">
        <div class="col-md-8 offset-md-2">
        </div>
    </div>
    ```
13. Add a table with two columns inside the column `<div>` and add the text *Course* as the first column title and leave the second column title empty.
14. Add a foreach loop that iterates over the user's courses in the **Courses** property and displays them in rows inside the `<tbody>` element.
    ```
    <tbody>
        @foreach (var course in Model.Courses)
        {
        }
    </tbody>
    ```

15. Align the text vertically in the first column and display the course title in it.
    ```
    <td style="vertical-align:middle">@Html.DisplayFor(modelItem =>
    course.Title)</td>
    ```
16. Make the second column 110px wide to accommodate the **Remove** button. Add a form that posts to the **OnPostRemoveAsync** method in the column element. The form needs hidden fields for the course id and user id.
    ```
    <td style="width:110px;">
        <form method="post">
            <input type="hidden" asp-for="Customer.Id" name="userId" />
            <input type="hidden" asp-for="@course.Id" name="courseId" />
            <button type="submit" asp-page-handler="Remove"
                class="btn btn-danger float-right">Remove</button>
        </form>
    </td>
    ```

The complete code in the **Details** HTML Razor Page:

```
@page
@model DetailsModel
@inject SignInManager<VODUser> SignInManager

@{ ViewData["Title"] = "Details"; }

@if (SignInManager.IsSignedIn(User) && User.IsInRole("Admin"))
{
    <div class="row">
        <div class="col-md-8 offset-md-2">
            <h2>@ViewData["Title"] for @Model.Customer.Email</h2>
            <partial name="_BackToIndexButtonsPartial" />
            @if (Model.AvailableCourses.Count() > 0)
            {
                <form method="post" style="margin:20px 0px;">
                    <input type="hidden" asp-for="Customer.Id"
                        name="userId" />

                    <div class="form-group">
                        <label asp-for="CourseId"
                            class="control-label"></label>
                        <div class=" input-group">
                            <select asp-for="CourseId"
                                class="form-control"
                                asp-items="@Model.AvailableCourses">
                            </select>
```

```html
                            <div class="input-group-append">
                                <button type="submit"
                                    asp-page-handler="Add"
                                    class="btn btn-success">Add
                                </button>
                            </div>
                        </div>
                    </div>
                </form>
            }
        </div>
        <div class="col-md-2">
        </div>
    </div>

    <div class="row">
        <div class="col-md-8 offset-md-2">
            <table style="margin-top:20px;" class="table">
                <thead>
                    <tr>
                        <th>Course</th>
                        <th></th>
                    </tr>
                </thead>
                <tbody>
                    @foreach (var course in Model.Courses)
                    {
                        <tr>
                            <td style="vertical-align:middle">
                                @Html.DisplayFor(modelItem =>
                                    course.Title)</td>
                            <td style="width:110px;">
                                <form method="post">
                                    <input type="hidden"
                                        asp-for="Customer.Id"
                                        name="userId" />
                                    <input type="hidden"
                                        asp-for="@course.Id"
                                        name="courseId" />
                                    <button type="submit"
                                        asp-page-handler="Remove"
                                        class="btn btn-danger
                                            float-right">Remove
                                    </button>
```

```
                            </form>
                        </td>
                    </tr>
                }
                </tbody>
            </table>

        </div>
        <div class="col-md-2">
        </div>
    </div>
}
```

Summary

In this chapter, you used the **UserService** service for handling users and user roles in the **AspNetUsers** and **AspNetUserRoles** database tables from the Razor Pages you added to the *Users* folder. The pages you added perform CRUD operations on the previously mentioned tables.

You also added a **Details** Razor Page that enables users to enroll and leave courses. The page uses the **DbReadService** and **DbWriteService** services to persist the data to the database.

Next, you will create a new Tag Helper that displays the text from the **Alert** property you added to the code-behind of the Razor Pages.

22. The Alert Tag Helper

Introduction

In this chapter, you will create a Tag Helper that displays a success message sent from another page when data has been successfully added, updated, or deleted. The Tag Helper will use attributes and attribute values to configure the finished HTML elements, such as the message and the message type.

The **Alert** property you added earlier to the Razor Pages will be used to store the message that is assigned in the **OnPostAsync** method when the data has been modified. You can see an example of the **alert** message under the heading in the image below. The message element is a <div> decorated with the Bootstrap **alert** classes.

The **[TempData]** attribute is relatively new to ASP.NET Core and can be used with properties in controllers and Razor Pages to store read-once data. It is particularly useful for redirection when the data is stored by one request and read by a subsequent request. **Keep** and **Peek** methods can be used to examine the data without deletion.

Because the **[TempData]** attribute builds on top of session state, different Razor Pages can share it. You will use this to send a message from one Razor Page to another and display it using the <alert> Tag Helper that you will implement in this chapter.

You can add the <alert> Tag Helper with or without the **alert-type** attribute; the **alert-type** attribute uses the default *success* alert type if left out. You can assign *primary, secondary, success, danger, warning, info, light,* or *dark* to the **alert-type** attribute.

```
<alert alert-type="success">@Model.Alert</alert>
```

```
<alert>@Model.Alert</alert>
```

Technologies Used in This Chapter

1. **C#** – To create the Tag Helper.
2. **HTML** – To add the Tag Helper to the Razor Pages.

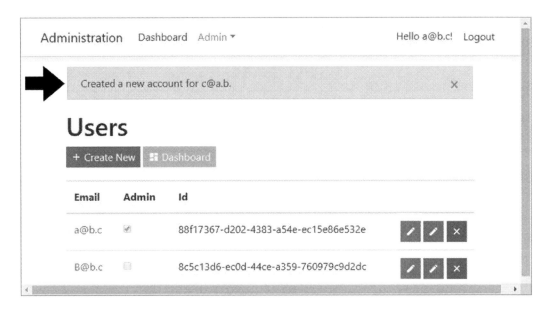

Adding the Alert Tag Helper Class

1. Add a Razor **Tag Helper Class** called **AlertTagHelper** to the *Tag Helpers* folder.
   ```
   [HtmlTargetElement("tag-name")]
   public class AlertTagHelper : TagHelper
   {
       public override void Process(TagHelperContext context,
       TagHelperOutput output) { }
   }
   ```

2. Change the **HtmlTargetElement** attribute to **alert**; this will be the Tag Helper's "element" name. It's not a real HTML element, but it looks like one, to blend in with the HTML markup. It will, however, generate a real HTML element when rendered.
   ```
   [HtmlTargetElement("alert")]
   ```

3. Add a **string** property called **AlertType** to the class and assign *success* to it. This property will be a Tag Helper attribute that will set the background color on the <alert> element.
   ```
   // Possible Bootstrap classes: primary, secondary, success,
   // danger, warning, info, light, dark.
   public string AlertType { get; set; } = "success";
   ```

4. In the **Process** method, throw an **ArgumentNullException** if either of the **context** or **output** method parameters are **null**. Don't render the Tag Helper if either of them is **null**.
   ```
   if (context == null)
       throw new ArgumentNullException(nameof(context));
   if (output == null)
       throw new ArgumentNullException(nameof(output));
   ```
5. Fetch already existing content between the start and end tags.
   ```
   var content = output.GetChildContentAsync().Result.GetContent();
   ```
6. Return without rendering the <div> if no content is available between the start and end tags. No alerts should be displayed without content.
   ```
   if (content.Trim().Equals(string.Empty)) return;
   ```
7. Add a variable named **close** that contains the HTML markup for the button and icon that closes the alert when clicked.
   ```
   var close = $"<button type='button' class='close' " +
               $"data-dismiss='alert' aria-label='Close'>" +
               $"<span aria-hidden='true'>&times;</span></button>";
   ```
8. Add a variable named **html** that will hold the HTML markup that will be displayed in the **alert** <div> element.
   ```
   var html = $"{content}{close}";
   ```
9. Create the <div> element with all classes and attributes, and the HTML content that you created earlier.
   ```
   output.TagName = "div";
   output.Attributes.Add("class",
       $"alert alert-{AlertType} alert-dismissible fade show");
   output.Attributes.Add("role", "alert");
   output.Attributes.Add("style",
       "border-radius: 0px; margin-bottom: 0;");
   output.Content.SetHtmlContent(html);
   output.Content.AppendHtml("</div>");
   ```
10. Call the **base** class's **Process** method with the two method parameters to create the alert <div>.
    ```
    base.Process(context, output);
    ```
11. Save the file.
12. Open the **Index** Razor Page in the *Users* folder.

13. Add an <alert> element inside row and column <div> elements above the already existing <div> decorated with the **row** class. Add the **@Model.Alert** property between the start and end tag and assign one of the following values to the **alert-type** attribute: *primary, secondary, success, danger, warning, info, light*, or *dark* (you can skip this attribute if you want the default *success* type). You can use HTML markup inside the start and end tag.
    ```
    <div class="row">
        <div class="col-md-8 offset-md-2" style="padding-left:0;
        padding-right:0;">
            <alert alert-type="success">@Model.Alert</alert>
        </div>
    </div>
    ```
14. Open the **Index** Razor Page in the *Pages* folder.
15. Add an <alert> element inside row and column <div> elements above the already existing <div> decorated with the **row** class. Assign *danger* to the **alert-type** attribute to give it a red background.
    ```
    <div class="row">
        <div class="col-md-8 offset-md-2" style="padding-left:0;
        padding-right:0;">
            <alert alert-type="danger">@Model.Alert</alert>
        </div>
    </div>
    ```
16. Save all files and start the application.
17. Open the *Users/Index* page and add a new user. A success message should be displayed with the Tag Helper when redirecting to the **Index** page.
18. Edit the user you just added. A success message should be displayed with the Tag Helper when redirecting to the **Index** page.
19. Delete the user you added. A success message should be displayed with the Tag Helper when removing the user and redirecting to the **Index** page.

The complete code for the **AlertTagHelper** class:

```
[HtmlTargetElement("alert")]
public class AlertTagHelper : TagHelper
{
    #region Properties
    // Possible Bootstrap classes: primary, secondary,
    // success, danger, warning, info, light, dark.
    public string AlertType { get; set; } = "success";
```

```
        #endregion

        public override void Process(TagHelperContext context,
        TagHelperOutput output)
        {
            if (context == null)
                throw new ArgumentNullException(nameof(context));
            if (output == null)
                throw new ArgumentNullException(nameof(output));

            // Fetch existing content between the start and end tags
            var content = output.GetChildContentAsync()
                                .Result
                                .GetContent();

            // Don't render the <alert> Tag Helper
            if (content.Trim().Equals(string.Empty)) return;

            // Create the close button inside the alert
            var close = $"<button type='button' class='close' " +
                        $"data-dismiss='alert' aria-label='Close'>" +
                        $"<span aria-hidden='true'>&times;</span></button>";

            var html = $"{content}{close}";

            // Create the <div> and add necessary attributes and HTML
            output.TagName = "div";
            output.Attributes.Add("class",
                $"alert alert-{AlertType} alert-dismissible fade show");
            output.Attributes.Add("role", "alert");
            output.Attributes.Add("style",
                "border-radius: 0;margin-bottom: 0;");
            output.Content.SetHtmlContent(html);
            output.Content.AppendHtml("</div>");

            // Create the alert <div> element
            base.Process(context, output);
        }
    }
}
```

The complete markup to add the Tag Helper to the **Index** Razor Page:

```
<div class="row">
    <div class="col-md-10 offset-md-1"
        style="padding-left:0;padding-right:0;">
```

```
            <alert alert-type="success">@Model.Alert</alert>
        </div>
        <div class="col-md-1">
        </div>
</div>
```

Summary

In this chapter, you created an **Alert** Tag Helper that displays the text from content between its start and end tags. You also used the **Alert** property you added to the code-behind of the Razor Pages to style the alert background.

Next, you will create a new service that communicates with the **DbReadService** and **DbWriteService** services to read and modify data in the database. By doing this, you only must inject one service into the constructors of the Razor Pages.

23. The AdminEFService

Overview

In this chapter, you will create a new service that will communicate with the **DbReadService** and **DbWriteService** services to read and modify data in the database. By doing this, you only must inject one service into the constructors of the Razor Pages you will add in the next chapter. It also minimizes the code you must add to the **OnGetAsync** and **OnPostAsync** actions. Because the **API** project uses the same method definitions, you will create an interface named **IAdminSerivce** that declares them.

The **IAdminSerivce** interface will declare asynchronous generic CRUD methods named **GetAsync**, **SingleAsync**, **AnyAsync**, **CreateAsync**, **UpdateAsync**, and **DeleteAsync**. The methods will take one or two generic types named **TSource** and **TDestination** that determines which entity and DTO are affected by the call. The **TSource** type defies the entity in the database, and **TDestination** is the DTO type to return from the method.

The **AdminEFService** class implements the **IAdminSerivce** interface, and its methods call methods in the **DbReadService** and **DbWriteService** services to perform CRUD operations in the database, and AutoMapper is used to convert the entity data into a DTO and vice versa.

DTOs will transfer data between the services and the Admin UI. You will create one DTO class for each entity; larger systems that need more granularity or better data optimization use several DTOs for each entity to transfer different data based on the scenario.

Technologies Used in This Chapter
1. **C#** – To write code in the Razor Pages code-behind methods.
2. **AutoMapper** – To convert between types.
3. **Entity framework** – Performs CRUD operations in the database.

The IAdminService Interface
1. Create a folder named *Services* in the **Common** project.
2. Add a **public** interface named **IAdminService** to the folder.
3. Add a method definition for a method named **GetAsync** that returns a list of a generic type named **TDestination** as a **Task**. The method should define two

generic types named **TSource** and **TDestination** and have a Boolean parameter named **include** that determines if data for the entity's navigation properties should be loaded. The generic types must be restricted to classes because entity classes must be reference types.
```
Task<List<TDestination>> GetAsync<TSource, TDestination>(bool
include = false) where TSource : class where TDestination : class;
```

4. Copy the previous method definition and add a function expression that uses the **TSource** type and returns a **bool**. By adding an expression, you can use Lambda expressions to build a predicate that can filter the result on property values.
```
Task<List<TDestination>> GetAsync<TSource, TDestination>
(Expression<Func<TSource, bool>> expression, bool include = false)
where TSource : class where TDestination : class;
```

5. Copy the previous method definition and change the return type to a single **TDestination** object and rename the method **SingleAsync**. This method will return a single object or **null** based on the predicate.
```
Task<TDestination> SingleAsync<TSource, TDestination>(
Expression<Func<TSource, bool>> expression, bool include = false)
where TSource : class where TDestination : class;
```

6. Copy the previous method definition and rename it **CreateAsync**, then change the return type to a single **int** value that will contain the id of the created entity. Also, replace the two parameters with a **TSource** parameter named **item**, which is the entity to add.
```
Task<int> CreateAsync<TSource, TDestination>(TSource item) where
TSource : class where TDestination : class;
```

7. Copy the previous method definition and rename it **UpdateAsync**, then change the return type to a single **bool** value that specifies if the CRUD operation succeeded.
```
Task<bool> UpdateAsync<TSource, TDestination>(TSource item) where
TSource : class where TDestination : class;
```

8. Copy the previous method definition and rename it **DeleteAsync**. Also, remove the **TDestination** generic type and replace the **item** parameter with the same expression you used earlier. The **TDestination** type is unnecessary since no data transformation will occur.
```
Task<bool> DeleteAsync<TSource>(Expression<Func<TSource, bool>>
expression) where TSource: class;
```

9. Copy the previous method definition and rename it **AnyAsync**. This method will return **true** if EF can find a matching record in the table represented by the **TEntity** generic type.
   ```
   Task<bool> AnyAsync<TEntity>(Expression<Func<TEntity, bool>> expression) where TEntity : class;
   ```

The complete code in the **IAdminService** interface:

```
public interface IAdminService
{
    #region CRUD Methods
    Task<List<TDestination>> GetAsync<TSource, TDestination>(bool
    include = false) where TSource : class where TDestination : class;

    Task<List<TDestination>> GetAsync<TSource, TDestination>(Expression
    <Func<TSource, bool>> expression, bool include = false)
    where TSource : class where TDestination : class;

    Task<TDestination> SingleAsync<TSource, TDestination>(Expression
    <Func<TSource, bool>> expression, bool include = false)
    where TSource : class where TDestination : class;

    Task<int> CreateAsync<TSource, TDestination>(TSource item)
    where TSource : class where TDestination : class;

    Task<bool> UpdateAsync<TSource, TDestination>(TSource item)
    where TSource : class where TDestination : class;

    Task<bool> DeleteAsync<TSource>(Expression<Func<TSource, bool>>
    expression) where TSource : class;

    Task<bool> AnyAsync<TEntity>(Expression<Func<TEntity, bool>>
    expression) where TEntity : class;
    #endregion
}
```

The AdminEFService Class

The **AdminEFService** class requires AutoMapper because data mapping will be used.

1. Add a **public** class named **AdminEFService** to the *Services* folder in the **Database** project and implement the **IAdminService** interface.
2. Add the **async** keyword to all the methods to enable asynchronous calls in them.

1. Add the **AdminEFService** service to the **ConfigureServices** method in the **Startup** class in the **Admin** project.
   ```
   services.AddScoped<IAdminService, AdminEFService>();
   ```
3. Install the AutoMapper NuGet package to the **VOD.Database** project like you did in the **VOD.UI** project.
4. Add a constructor and inject the **DbReadService**, **DbWriteService**, and **IMapper** services and store their instances in read-only class-level variables named **_dbRead**, **_dbWrite**, and **_mapper**.
   ```
   private readonly IDbReadService _dbRead;
   private readonly IDbWriteService _dbWrite;
   private readonly IMapper _mapper;

   public AdminEFService(IDbReadService dbReadService,
   IDbWriteService dbWrite, IMapper mapper)
   {
       _dbRead = dbReadService;
       _dbWrite = dbWrite;
       _mapper = mapper;
   }
   ```
5. Remove the **throw** statement from the **GetAsync** method that returns a list and has a **bool** parameter. Add an if-statement that checks the **include** parameter and loads the related entities if it is **true**.
   ```
   if (include) _dbRead.Include<TSource>();
   ```
6. Call the **GetAsync** method in the **_dbRead** service below the if-statement to return a list of the entity specified by the **TSource** type.
   ```
   var entities = await _dbRead.GetAsync<TSource>();
   ```
7. Use AutoMapper to convert the list of entities to the DTO specified by the **TDestination** type.
   ```
   return _mapper.Map<List<TDestination>>(entities);
   ```
8. Copy the code from the **GetAsync** method and replace the **throw** statement in the second **GetAsync** method with the copied code. Pass in the predicate parameter to the **GetAsync** method.
   ```
   var entities = await _dbRead.GetAsync(expression);
   ```
9. Copy the code from the previous **GetAsync** method and rename it **SingleAsync**. Replace the **throw** statement with the copied code and the name of the **GetAsync** method to **SingleAsync**.

```
var entity = await _dbRead.SingleAsync(expression);
```

10. Change the AutoMapper conversion to map from the fetched item and the **TDestination** type.
```
return _mapper.Map<TDestination>(entity);
```

11. Copy the code from the **SingleAsync** method and replace the **throw** statement in the **DeleteAsync** method with the copied code.

12. Remove the **include** parameter, the if-statement, and the call to the **Include** method.

13. Call the **_dbWrite.Delete** method below the **_DbRead.SingleAsync** call and pass in the fetched entity.
```
_dbWrite.Delete(entity);
```

14. Return the result from a call to the asynchronous **_dbWrite.SaveChanges** method that removes the entity from the database.
```
return await _dbWrite.SaveChangesAsync();
```

15. Wrap the code inside the **DeleteAsync** method in a try-block and let the catch-block return **false** to denote that an error occurred.

16. Remove the **throw** statement from the **CreateAsync** method and a **try/catch**.

17. Convert the passed-in **TSource** DTO into a **TDestination** entity with AutoMapper inside the **try**-block.
```
var entity = _mapper.Map<TDestination>(item);
```

18. Call the **_dbWrite.Add** method to add the entity to Entity Framework's in-memory entity tracking; this does not persist it to the database.
```
_dbWrite.Add(entity);
```

19. Call the asynchronous **_dbWrite.SaveChanges** method to persist the entity in the database. Store the result in a variable named **succeeded**.
```
var succeeded = await _dbWrite.SaveChangesAsync();
```

20. Return the id from the persisted entity if the **succeeded** variable is **true**, otherwise return **-1** to denote that the EF couldn't persist the entity.
```
        if (succeeded) return (int)entity.GetType().GetProperty("Id")
            .GetValue(entity);
}
Catch { }

return -1;
```

21. Copy the code inside the **CreateAsync** method and replace the **throw** statement in the **UpdateAsync** method with it. Replace the **Add** method call with a call to the **Update** method.
    `_dbWrite.Update(entity);`

22. Remove the if-statement and return the result from the **SaveChangesAsync** method. Return **false** from the **catch**-block.
    ```
        return await _dbWrite.SaveChangesAsync();
    }
    Catch { }

    return false;
    ```

23. Call the **AnyAsync** method on the **DbReadService** service instance inside the **AnyAsync** method and return the result.
    `return await _dbRead.AnyAsync(expression);`

The complete code in the **AdminEFService** class:

```
public class AdminEFService : IAdminService
{
    /** NEEDS: AutoMapper **/

    #region Properties
    private readonly IDbReadService _dbRead;
    private readonly IDbWriteService _dbWrite;
    private readonly IMapper _mapper;
    #endregion

    #region Constructor
    public AdminEFService(IDbReadService dbReadService,
    IDbWriteService dbWrite, IMapper mapper)
    {
        _dbRead = dbReadService;
        _dbWrite = dbWrite;
        _mapper = mapper;
    }
    #endregion
```

```csharp
#region CRUD Methods
public async Task<List<TDestination>> GetAsync<TSource,
TDestination>(bool include = false) where TSource : class
where TDestination : class
{
    if (include) _dbRead.Include<TSource>();
    var entities = await _dbRead.GetAsync<TSource>();
    return _mapper.Map<List<TDestination>>(entities);
}

public async Task<List<TDestination>> GetAsync<TSource,
TDestination>(Expression<Func<TSource, bool>> expression, bool
include = false) where TSource : class where TDestination : class
{
    if (include) _dbRead.Include<TSource>();
    var entities = await _dbRead.GetAsync(expression);
    return _mapper.Map<List<TDestination>>(entities);
}

public async Task<TDestination> SingleAsync<TSource, TDestination>
(Expression<Func<TSource, bool>> expression, bool include = false)
where TSource : class where TDestination : class
{
    if (include) _dbRead.Include<TSource>();
    var entities = await _dbRead.SingleAsync(expression);
    return _mapper.Map<TDestination>(entities);
}

public async Task<bool> DeleteAsync<TSource>(
Expression<Func<TSource, bool>> expression) where TSource : class
{
    try
    {
        var entity = await _dbRead.SingleAsync(expression);
        _dbWrite.Delete(entity);
        return await _dbWrite.SaveChangesAsync();
    }
    catch
    {
        return false;
    }
}
```

```csharp
public async Task<int> CreateAsync<TSource, TDestination>(
TSource item) where TSource : class where TDestination : class
{
    try
    {
        var entity = _mapper.Map<TDestination>(item);
        _dbWrite.Add(entity);
        var succeeded = await _dbWrite.SaveChangesAsync();
        if (succeeded) return (int)entity.GetType()
            .GetProperty("Id").GetValue(entity);
    }
    catch { }

    return -1;
}
public async Task<bool> UpdateAsync<TSource, TDestination>(
TSource item) where TSource : class where TDestination : class
{
    try
    {
        var entity = _mapper.Map<TDestination>(item);
        _dbWrite.Update(entity);
        return await _dbWrite.SaveChangesAsync();
    }
    catch { }

    return false;
}

public async Task<bool> AnyAsync<TEntity>(
Expression<Func<TEntity, bool>> expression) where TEntity : class
{
    return await _dbRead.AnyAsync(expression);
}
#endregion
}
```

The DTO Classes

You generally want to avoid using entity classes for data transfer in all but the simplest applications. Instead, DTO classes are used. One advantage of using DTOs is that you can transform the data, like concatenating the first and the last name into one name property. Another, and potentially larger, advantage is that you can limit the data transferred over the network or Internet.

In this application, you will create one DTO per entity; in larger applications, it is not uncommon to be more granular and create at least one per HTTP verb or type of action.

1. Add the following DTO classes inside the *DTOModels-Admin* folder in the **Common** project.

The Course DTO

You can copy the properties and attributes from the **Course** entity class and paste them into the **CourseDTO** class you create in the *DTOModels-Admin* folder. Remove the **[Key]** attribute and change the datatype from **Instructor** to **string** for the **Instructor** property in the **CourseDTO** class. Also, add a property for the **ButtonDTO** class and pass in the value from the **Id** property to the class's constructor; this will add the course id to the **Edit** and **Delete** buttons in the **_TableRowButtonsPartial** partial view. The **ModuleDTO** is the next DTO you will create.

```
public class CourseDTO
{
    public int Id { get; set; }
    [MaxLength(255)]
    public string ImageUrl { get; set; }
    [MaxLength(255)]
    public string MarqueeImageUrl { get; set; }
    [MaxLength(80), Required]
    public string Title { get; set; }
    [MaxLength(1024)]
    public string Description { get; set; }

    public int InstructorId { get; set; }
    public string Instructor { get; set; }
    public ICollection<ModuleDTO> Modules { get; set; }

    public ButtonDTO ButtonDTO { get { return new ButtonDTO(Id); } }
}
```

The Module DTO

You can copy the properties and attributes from the **Module** entity class and paste them into the **ModuleDTO** class you create in the *DTOModels-Admin* folder. Remove the **[Key]** attribute and change the datatype from **Course** to **string** for the **Course** property in the **ModuleDTO** class. Also, add a property for the **ButtonDTO** class and pass in the values from the **CourseId** and **Id** properties to the class's constructor; this will add the ids to the **Edit** and **Delete** buttons in the **_TableRowButtonsPartial** partial view. Also, add a **string** property named **CourseAndModule** that returns the module title and course name as a formatted string; use this property in drop-downs to display values from more than one property. You will add the **VideoDTO** and **DownloadDTO** DTOs momentarily.

```
public class ModuleDTO
{
    public int Id { get; set; }
    [MaxLength(80), Required]
    public string Title { get; set; }

    public int CourseId { get; set; }
    public string Course { get; set; }
    public ICollection<VideoDTO> Videos { get; set; }
    public ICollection<DownloadDTO> Downloads { get; set; }

    public ButtonDTO ButtonDTO { get { return new ButtonDTO(
        CourseId, Id); } }

    public string CourseAndModule { get {
        return $"{Title} ({Course})"; } }
}
```

The Download DTO

You can copy the properties and attributes from the **Download** entity class and paste them into the **DownloadDTO** class you create in the *DTOModels-Admin* folder. Remove the **[Key]** attribute and change the datatype from **Course** and **Module** to **string** for the **Course** and **Module** properties in the **DownloadDTO** class. Also, add a property for the **ButtonDTO** class and pass in the values from the **CourseId**, **ModuleId**, and **Id** properties to the class's constructor; this will add the ids to the **Edit** and **Delete** buttons in the **_TableRowButtonsPartial** partial view.

```
public class DownloadDTO
{
    public int Id { get; set; }
    [MaxLength(80), Required]
    public string Title { get; set; }
    [MaxLength(1024)]
    public string Url { get; set; }

    // Side-step from 3rd normal form for easier
    // access to a video's course and Module
    public int ModuleId { get; set; }
    public int CourseId { get; set; }
    public string Course { get; set; }
    public string Module { get; set; }

    public ButtonDTO ButtonDTO { get { return new ButtonDTO(
        CourseId, ModuleId, Id); } }
}
```

The Video DTO

You can copy the properties and attributes from the **Video** entity class and paste them into the **VideoDTO** class you create in the *DTOModels-Admin* folder. Remove the **[Key]** attribute and change the datatype from **Course** and **Module** to **string** for the **Course** and **Module** properties in the **VideoDTO** class. Also, add a property for the **ButtonDTO** class and pass in the values from the **CourseId**, **ModuleId**, and **Id** properties to the class's constructor; this will add the ids to the **Edit** and **Delete** buttons in the **_TableRowButtons-Partial** partial view.

```
public class VideoDTO
{
    public int Id { get; set; }
    [MaxLength(80), Required]
    public string Title { get; set; }
    [MaxLength(1024)]
    public string Description { get; set; }
    public int Duration { get; set; }
    [MaxLength(1024)]
    public string Thumbnail { get; set; }
    [MaxLength(1024)]
    public string Url { get; set; }
```

```
        // Side-step from 3rd normal form for easier
        // access to a video's course and Module
        public int ModuleId { get; set; }
        public int CourseId { get; set; }
        public string Course { get; set; }
        public string Module { get; set; }

        public ButtonDTO ButtonDTO { get { return new ButtonDTO(
            CourseId, ModuleId, Id); } }
}
```

The Instructor DTO

You can copy the properties and attributes from the **Instructor** entity class and paste them into the **InstructorDTO** class you create in the *DTOModels-Admin* folder. Remove the **[Key]** attribute in the **InstructorDTO** class. Also, add a property for the **ButtonDTO** class and pass in the value from the **Id** property to the class's constructor; this will add the ids to the **Edit** and **Delete** buttons in the **_TableRowButtonsPartial** partial view.

```
public class InstructorDTO
{
    public int Id { get; set; }
    [MaxLength(80), Required]
    public string Name { get; set; }
    [MaxLength(1024)]
    public string Description { get; set; }
    [MaxLength(1024)]
    public string Thumbnail { get; set; }

    public ButtonDTO ButtonDTO { get { return new ButtonDTO(Id); } }
}
```

AutoMapper Mappings

Adding the AutoMapper service changed with the release version 6.1.0 of the **AutoMapper.Extensions.Microsoft.DependencyInjection** NuGet package. In earlier versions, you called the **AddAutoMapper** method on the **service** object in the **ConfigureServices** method in the **Startup** class; in the 6.1.0 version, you pass in the mapped types to the **AddAutoMapper** method.

Example (6.0.0):
```
services.AddAutoMapper();
```

23. The AdminEFService

Example (6.1.0):
```
services.AddAutoMapper(typeof(Startup), typeof(Instructor),
typeof(Course), typeof(Module), typeof(Video), typeof(Download));
```

1. Add a dependency to the **AutoMapper.Extensions.Microsoft.DependencyInjection** NuGet package to the **Admin** and **Common** projects to install AutoMapper.
2. Add the AutoMapper service to the **ConfigureServices** method in the **Startup** class in the **Admin** project.
   ```
   services.AddAutoMapper(); // Version 6.0.0
   ```
   ```
   services.AddAutoMapper(typeof(Startup), typeof(Instructor),
       typeof(Course), typeof(Module), typeof(Video),
       typeof(Download)); // Version 6.1.0
   ```
3. Add a folder named *AutoMapper* to the **Common** project.
4. Add a class named **MapProfile** that inherits AutoMapper's **Profile** class to the *AutoMapper* folder.
5. Add a constructor to the class.
6. Call the **CreateMap** AutoMapper method to add a mapping between the **Video** entity and the **VideoDTO** class.
   ```
   CreateMap<Video, VideoDTO>()
   ```
7. Call the **ForMemeber** extension method for the string **Module** property of the **VideoDTO** class and add a map from the **Video** entity's **Module.Title** navigation property.
   ```
   .ForMember(d => d.Module, a => a.MapFrom(c => c.Module.Title))
   ```
8. Call the **ForMemeber** extension method for the string **Course** property of the **VideoDTO** class and add a map from the **Video** entity's **Course.Title** navigation property.
   ```
   .ForMember(d => d.Course, a => a.MapFrom(c => c.Course.Title));
   ```
9. Call the **ReverseMap** method to implement mapping from a **VideoDTO** to a **Video** entity.
   ```
   .ReverseMap()
   ```
10. Call the **ForMemeber** extension method to skip mapping the navigation properties when mapping from a **VideoDTO** to a **Video** entity.
    ```
    .ForMember(d => d.Module, a => a.Ignore())
    .ForMember(d => d.Course, a => a.Ignore());
    ```

11. Copy the **Video** map and paste it in. Change the entity to **Download** and the DTO to **DownloadDTO**.
12. Copy the **Video** map and paste it in. Change the entity to **Module** and the DTO to **ModuleDTO**.
13. Remove the mapping from **Module** to **Module.Title**.
14. Change the ignore statement from **Module** to **Videos**.
15. Copy the previous ignore statement and change from **Videos** to **Downloads**.
16. Copy the **Module** map and paste it in. Change the entity to **Course** and the DTO to **CourseDTO**.
17. Remove the ignore statement for **Videos**.
18. Change **Title** to **Name**.
    ```
    .ForMember(d => d.Instructor, a => a.MapFrom(c =>
        c.Instructor.Name))
    ```
19. Create a mapping from **Instructor** to **InstructorDTO** and reverse it.
    ```
    CreateMap<Instructor, InstructorDTO>().ReverseMap();
    ```

The complete code in the **MapProfile** class:

```
public class MapProfile : Profile
{
    public MapProfile()
    {
        CreateMap<Instructor, InstructorDTO>().ReverseMap();

        CreateMap<Course, CourseDTO>()
            .ForMember(d => d.Instructor, a => a.MapFrom(c =>
                c.Instructor.Name))
            .ReverseMap()
            .ForMember(d => d.Instructor, a => a.Ignore());

        CreateMap<Module, ModuleDTO>()
            .ForMember(d => d.Course, a => a.MapFrom(c =>
                c.Course.Title))
            .ReverseMap()
            .ForMember(d => d.Course, a => a.Ignore())
            .ForMember(d => d.Downloads, a => a.Ignore())
            .ForMember(d => d.Videos, a => a.Ignore());
```

```
        CreateMap<Video, VideoDTO>()
            .ForMember(d => d.Module, a => a.MapFrom(c =>
                c.Module.Title))
            .ForMember(d => d.Course, a => a.MapFrom(c =>
                c.Course.Title))
            .ReverseMap()
            .ForMember(d => d.Module, a => a.Ignore())
            .ForMember(d => d.Course, a => a.Ignore());

        CreateMap<Download, DownloadDTO>()
            .ForMember(d => d.Module, a => a.MapFrom(c =>
                c.Module.Title))
            .ForMember(d => d.Course, a => a.MapFrom(c =>
                c.Course.Title))
            .ReverseMap()
            .ForMember(d => d.Module, a => a.Ignore())
            .ForMember(d => d.Course, a => a.Ignore());
    }
}
```

Summary

In this chapter, you created DTOs and added AutoMapper configuration mappings between DTOs and entities.

ASP.NET Core 2.2 MVC, Razor Pages, API, JSON Web Tokens & HttpClient

24. The Remaining Razor Pages

Overview

In this chapter, you will create the Razor Pages for the other entities by copying and modifying the Razor Pages in the *Users* folder. In most cases, you only need to make small changes to the HTML and code-behind files. Depending on the purpose of the page, you must add or remove the services injected into the constructor.

Some of the pages have drop-down elements that you must add because the *User* pages don't have any. You add a drop-down to the form by adding a <select> element and assign a collection of **SelectList** items to it; you can create such a list by calling the **ToSelectList** extension method on a **List<TEntity>** collection; the method resides in the **ListExtensions** class you added earlier to the **Common** project. You can send the collection to the page with the **ViewData** object and use the **ViewBag** object to assign it to the <select> element.

```
public void OnGet()
{
    ViewData["Modules"] = (await _dbRead.Get<Module>()).ToSelectList(
        "Id", "Title");
}

<div class="form-group">
    <label asp-for="Input.ModuleId" class="control-label"></label>
    <select asp-for="Input.ModuleId" class="form-control"
        asp-items="ViewBag.Modules"></select>
</div>
```

Technologies Used in This Chapter
1. **C#** – To write code in the Razor Pages code-behind methods.
2. **HTML** – To add content to the Razor Pages.
3. **Entity framework** – To perform CRUD operations.

Example of Typical Razor Pages
The following images show typical CRUD Razor Pages that you will create.

ASP.NET Core 2.2 MVC, Razor Pages, API, JSON Web Tokens & HttpClient

The typical **Index** Razor Page

The typical **Delete** Razor Page

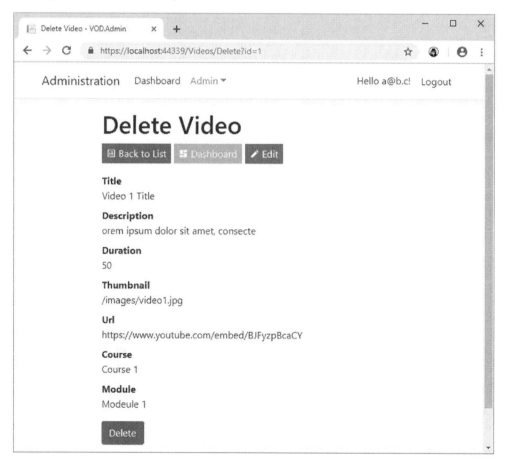

24. The Remaining Razor Pages

The typical **Create** Razor Page

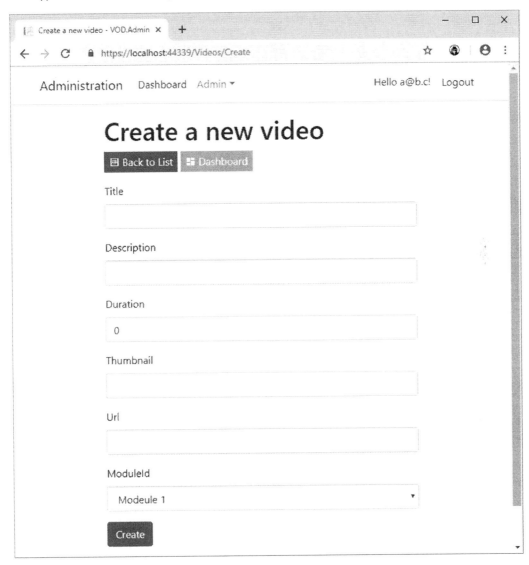

ASP.NET Core 2.2 MVC, Razor Pages, API, JSON Web Tokens & HttpClient

The typical **Edit** Razor Page

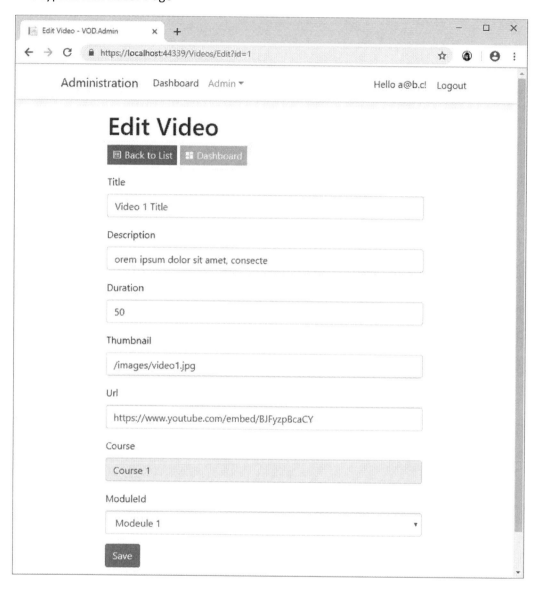

The _DeletePageButtons Partial Razor View

1. Copy the **_BackToIndexButtonsPartial** partial Razor View in the Pages-Shared folder and paste in a copy and rename it **_DeletePageButtons**.
2. Add a **@model** directive for the **ButtonDTO** datatype.
3. Add a new <btn> Tag Helper inside an if-block that checks that the passed in model's **Id** property value is greater than zero. The <btn> Tag Helper should target the **Edit** Razor Page, show the *edit* icon, and have the model's properties as **asp-route-id, asp-route-courseId, asp-route-moduleId** attributes.

```
@if(Model.Id > 0)
{
    <btn asp-page="Edit" icon="edit"
        asp-route-id="@Model.Id"
        asp-route-courseId="@Model.CourseId"
        asp-route-moduleId="@Model.ModuleId">Edit</btn>
}
```

4. Save the view

The complete HTML Markup for the **_DeletePageButtons** partial view:

```
@model ButtonDTO
<div>
    <btn asp-page="Index" icon="list_alt">Back to List</btn>
    <btn class="text-light" asp-page="/Index" icon="dashboard">
        Dashboard</btn>
    @if(Model.Id > 0)
    {
        <btn asp-page="Edit" icon="edit"
            asp-route-id="@Model.Id"
            asp-route-courseId="@Model.CourseId"
            asp-route-moduleId="@Model.ModuleId">Edit</btn>
    }
</div>
```

The Instructors Razor Pages

1. Copy the *Users* folder and all its contents.
2. Paste in the copied folder in the *Pages* folder and rename it *Instructors*.
3. Delete the **Details** view and its *.cs* file.
4. Open the **Index** Razor Page in the *Instructors* folder and copy the row <div> containing the <alert> TagHelper and all its content.

```
<div class="row">
    <div class="col-md-10 offset-md-1"
        style="padding-left:0;padding-right:0;">
        <alert alert-type="danger">@Model.Alert</alert>
    </div>
    <div class="col-md-1">
    </div>
</div>
```

5. Open the **Index** Razor Page in the *Pages* folder and paste in the HTML you copied above the first row inside the if-block.
6. Open the *Index.cshtml.cs* file in the *Instructors* folder and copy the **Alert** property.
   `[TempData] public string Alert { get; set; }`
7. Open the *Index.cshtml.cs* file in the *Pages* folder and paste in the **Alert** property above the constructor.

The IndexModel Class

1. Open the **IndexModel** class in the *Instructors* folder (the *.cshtml.cs* file).
2. Change the namespace to **Instructors**.
   `namespace VOD.Admin.Pages.Instructors`
3. Change the **IEnumerable** collection to store **InstructorDTO** objects and rename it **Items**.
   ```
   public IEnumerable<InstructorDTO> Items =
       new List<InstructorDTO>();
   ```
4. Replace the **IUserService** injection with **IAdminService** and name the backing variable **_db**.
   ```
   private readonly IAdminService _db;
   public IndexModel(IAdminService db)
   {
       _db = db;
   }
   ```
5. Change the return type of the **OnGetAsync** method to **Task<IActionResult>** to make it possible to redirect to other pages; if an error occurs, redirect to the main **Index** page with an error message.
   `public async Task<IActionResult> OnGetAsync()`

24. The Remaining Razor Pages

6. Add a try/catch-block and move the already existing code inside the try-block and call the **Page** method at the end of the try-block to display the Razor Page; this is necessary when using **Task<IActionResult>** as a return type.
7. Inside the catch-block, replace the **throw**-statement with code that assigns an error message to the **Alert** property and redirects to the main **Index** page in the *Pages* folder.
   ```
   Alert = "You do not have access to this page.";
   return RedirectToPage("/Index");
   ```
8. Replace the call to the **GetUserAsync** with a call to the **GetAsync** method in the **IAdminService** and specify the **Instructor** entity as the **TSource** and the **InstructorDTO** as the **TDestination** type. Pass in **true** to the method to load the navigation properties for the **Instructor** entity.
   ```
   Items = await _db.GetAsync<Instructor, InstructorDTO>(true);
   ```
9. Save all files.

The complete code for the **IndexModel** class:

```
[Authorize(Roles = "Admin")]
public class IndexModel : PageModel
{
    #region Properties
    private readonly IAdminService _db;
    public IEnumerable<InstructorDTO> Items = new List<InstructorDTO>();
    [TempData] public string Alert { get; set; }
    #endregion

    #region Constructor
    public IndexModel(IAdminService db)
    {
        _db = db;
    }
    #endregion

    public async Task<IActionResult> OnGetAsync()
    {
        try
        {
            Items = await _db.GetAsync<Instructor, InstructorDTO>(true);
            return Page();
        }
```

```
        catch
        {
            Alert = "You do not have access to this page.";
            return RedirectToPage("/Index");
        }
    }
}
```

The Index Razor Page

1. Open the **Index** Razor Page in the *Instructors* folder (the *.cshtml* file).
2. Change the **ViewData** title to *Instructors*.
3. Replace **col-md-8 offset-md-2** with **col-md-10 offset-md-1** and **col-md-2** with **col-md-1**.
4. Change the headings in the <th> elements to match the property values of the entity (*Name* and *Description*). Add and remove <th> elements as needed.
5. Rename the **user** loop variable **item** and the **Users** collection **Items**.
6. Change the <td> elements to display the values from the properties in the **item** loop variable. Add and remove <td> elements as needed.
7. Remove the <btn> Tag Helper.
8. Save all files.

The complete code for the **Index** Razor Page:

```
@page
@model IndexModel
@inject SignInManager<VODUser> SignInManager

@{
    ViewData["Title"] = "Instructors";
}

@if (SignInManager.IsSignedIn(User) && User.IsInRole("Admin"))
{
    <div class="row">
        <div class="col-md-10 offset-md-1"
             style="padding-left:0;padding-right:0;">
            <alert alert-type="success">@Model.Alert</alert>
        </div>
        <div class="col-md-1">
        </div>
    </div>
```

```html
    <div class="row">
        <div class="col-md-10 offset-md-1">
            <h1>@ViewData["Title"]</h1>

            <partial name="_PageButtonsPartial" />

            <table style="margin-top:20px;" class="table">
                <thead>
                    <tr>
                        <th>Name</th>
                        <th>Description</th>
                        <th></th>
                    </tr>
                </thead>
                <tbody>
                    @foreach (var item in Model.Items)
                    {
                        <tr>
                            <td>@Html.DisplayFor(modelItem =>
                                item.Name)</td>
                            <td>@Html.DisplayFor(modelItem =>
                                item.Description)</td>
                            <td style="min-width:100px;">
                                <partial name="_TableRowButtonsPartial"
                                    model="@item.ButtonDTO" /></td>
                        </tr>
                    }
                </tbody>
            </table>
        </div>
        <div class="col-md-1">
        </div>
    </div>
}
```

The CreateModel Class

1. Open the **CreateModel** class in the *Instructors* folder (the *.cshtml.cs* file).
2. Change the namespace to **Instructors**.
   `namespace VOD.Admin.Pages.Instructors`
3. Change the DTO to **InstructorDTO** for the **Input** property.
   `[BindProperty] public InstructorDTO Input { get; set; } = new InstructorDTO();`

10. Replace the **IUserService** injection to **IAdminService** and name the backing variable **_db**.
    ```
    private readonly IAdminService _db;

    public CreateModel(IAdminService db)
    {
        _db = db;
    }
    ```
11. Replace the call to the **AddUserAsync** with a call to the **CreateAsync** method in the **IAdminService** and specify **InstructorDTO** as the **TSource** and the **Instructor** as the **TDestination** type. Check if the creation was successful and save the result in a variable called **succeeded**. If the method returns a value greater than 0, then the creation was successful since the returned value is the id of the created resource.
    ```
    var succeeded = (await _db.CreateAsync<InstructorDTO,
    Instructor>(Input)) > 0;
    ```
4. Replace the **result.Succeeded** property with the **succeeded** variable.
5. Change the text in the **Alert** property to *Created a new Instructor:* followed by the name of the instructor. Change the **Input.Title** property to **Input.Name**.
    ```
    Alert = $"Created a new Instructor: {Input.Name}.";
    ```
6. Remove the **foreach** loop.
7. Save all files.

The complete code for the **CreateModel** class:

```
[Authorize(Roles = "Admin")]
public class CreateModel : PageModel
{
    #region Properties
    private readonly IAdminService _db;
    [BindProperty] public InstructorDTO Input { get; set; } =
        new InstructorDTO();
    [TempData] public string Alert { get; set; }
    #endregion
```

```csharp
    #region Constructor
    public CreateModel(IAdminService db)
    {
        _db = db;
    }
    #endregion

    #region Actions
    public async Task OnGetAsync()
    {
    }

    public async Task<IActionResult> OnPostAsync()
    {
        if (ModelState.IsValid)
        {
            var succeeded = (await _db.CreateAsync<InstructorDTO,
                Instructor>(Input)) > 0;

            if (succeeded)
            {
                // Message sent back to the Index Razor Page.
                Alert = $"Created a new Instructor: {Input.Name}.";

                return RedirectToPage("Index");
            }
        }

        // Something failed, redisplay the form.
        return Page();
    }
    #endregion
}
```

The Create Razor Page

1. Open the **Create** Razor Page in the *Instructors* folder (the *.cshtml* file).
2. Change the **ViewData** title to *Add Instructor*.
3. Change the content in the **form-group** <div> elements to display the values from the properties in the **Input** variable. Add and remove **form-group** <div> elements as needed.
4. Save all files.

The complete code for the **Create** Razor Page:

```
@page
@model CreateModel
@inject SignInManager<VODUser> SignInManager
@{
    ViewData["Title"] = "Add Instructor";
}

@if (SignInManager.IsSignedIn(User) && User.IsInRole("Admin"))
{
    <div class="row">
        <div class="col-md-8 offset-md-2">
            <h1>@ViewData["Title"]</h1>

            <partial name="_BackToIndexButtonsPartial" />
            <p></p>

            <form method="post">
                <div asp-validation-summary="All"
                     class="text-danger"></div>

                <div class="form-group">
                    <label asp-for="Input.Name"></label>
                    <input asp-for="Input.Name" class="form-control" />
                    <span asp-validation-for="Input.Name"
                          class="text-danger"></span>
                </div>
                <div class="form-group">
                    <label asp-for="Input.Description"></label>
                    <input asp-for="Input.Description"
                           class="form-control" />
                    <span asp-validation-for="Input.Description"
                          class="text-danger"></span>
                </div>
                <div class="form-group">
                    <label asp-for="Input.Thumbnail"></label>
                    <input asp-for="Input.Thumbnail"
                           class="form-control" />
                    <span asp-validation-for="Input.Thumbnail"
                          class="text-danger"></span>
                </div>
```

```
                <button type="submit" class="btn btn-success">Create
                </button>
            </form>
        </div>
    </div>
}

@section Scripts {
    @await Html.PartialAsync("_ValidationScriptsPartial")
}
```

The EditModel Class

1. Open the **EditModel** class in the *Instructors* folder (the *.cshtml.cs* file).
2. Change the namespace to **Instructors**.
   `namespace VOD.Admin.Pages.Instructors`
3. Change the data type to **InstructorDTO** for the **Input** variable.
   `public InstructorDTO Input { get; set; } = new InstructorDTO();`
4. Replace the **IUserService** injection to **IAdminService** and name the backing variable **_db**.
   ```
   private readonly IAdminService _db;
   public EditModel(IAdminService db)
   {
       _db = db;
   }
   ```
5. Change the return type of the **OnGetAsync** method to **Task<IActionResult>** to make it possible to redirect to other pages; if an error occurs, redirect to the main **Index** page with an error message. Change the data type to int for the **id** parameter.
   `public async Task<IActionResult> OnGetAsync(int id)`
6. Add a try/catch-block and move the already existing code inside the try-block and call the **Page** method at the end of the try-block to display the Razor Page; this is necessary when using **Task<IActionResult>** as a return type.
7. Inside the catch-block, replace the **throw**-statement with a redirect to the main **Index** page in the **Pages** folder and pass an error message along with the redirect.
   `return RedirectToPage("/Index", new { alert = "You do not have access to this page." });`

8. Replace the call to the **GetUserAsync** with a call to the **SingleAsync** method in the **IAdminService** and specify **Instructor** as the **TSource** and the **InstructorDTO** as the **TDestination** type. Add a Lambda expression to the method that compares the value in the **id** parameter with the **Id** property of the entities.
   ```
   Input = await _db.SingleAsync<Instructor, InstructorDTO>(s =>
   s.Id.Equals(id));
   ```
9. Rename the **result** variable **succeeded**.
10. Replace the **UpdateUserAsync** method with the **UpdateAsync** method in the **IAdminService** service and specify **InstructorDTO** as the **TSource** and **Instructor** as the **TDestination**.
    ```
    var succeeded = await _db.UpdateAsync<InstructorDTO,
    Instructor>(Input);
    ```
11. Replace the text in the **Alert** property to *Updated Instructor:* followed by the name of the instructor. Change the **Input.Title** property to **Input.Name**.
    ```
    Alert = $"Updated Instructor: {Input.Name}.";
    ```
12. Save all files.

The complete code for the **EditModel** class:

```
[Authorize(Roles = "Admin")]
public class EditModel : PageModel
{
    #region Properties
    private readonly IAdminService _db;
    [BindProperty] public InstructorDTO Input { get; set; } =
        new InstructorDTO();
    [TempData] public string Alert { get; set; }
    #endregion

    #region Constructor
    public EditModel(IAdminService db)
    {
        _db = db;
    }
    #endregion

    #region Actions
    public async Task<IActionResult> OnGetAsync(int id)
    {
```

```csharp
        try
        {
            Input = await _db.SingleAsync<Instructor, InstructorDTO>(
                s => s.Id.Equals(id));
            return Page();
        }
        catch
        {
            return RedirectToPage("/Index", new {
                alert = "You do not have access to this page." });
        }
    }

    public async Task<IActionResult> OnPostAsync()
    {
        if (ModelState.IsValid)
        {
            var succeeded = await _db.UpdateAsync<InstructorDTO,
                Instructor>(Input);

            if (succeeded)
            {
                // Message sent back to the Index Razor Page.
                Alert = $"Updated Instructor: {Input.Name}.";

                return RedirectToPage("Index");
            }
        }

        // Something failed, redisplay the form.
        return Page();
    }
    #endregion
}
```

The Edit Razor Page

1. Open the **Edit** Razor Page in the *Instructors* folder (the *.cshtml* file).
2. Change the **ViewData** title to *Edit Instructor*.
3. Change the content in the **form-group** <div> elements to display the values from the properties in the **Input** variable. Add and remove **form-group** <div> elements as needed.
4. Save all files.

ASP.NET Core 2.2 MVC, Razor Pages, API, JSON Web Tokens & HttpClient

The complete code for the **Edit** Razor Page:

```
@page
@model EditModel
@inject SignInManager<VODUser> SignInManager
@{ ViewData["Title"] = "Edit Instructor"; }

@if (SignInManager.IsSignedIn(User) && User.IsInRole("Admin"))
{
    <div class="row">
        <div class="col-md-8 offset-md-2">
            <h1>@ViewData["Title"]</h1>

            <partial name="_BackToIndexButtonsPartial" />
            <p></p>

            <form method="post">
                <div asp-validation-summary="All"
                    class="text-danger"></div>

                <input type="hidden" asp-for="Input.Id" />

                <div class="form-group">
                    <label asp-for="Input.Name"></label>
                    <input asp-for="Input.Name" class="form-control" />
                    <span asp-validation-for="Input.Name"
                        class="text-danger"></span>
                </div>
                <div class="form-group">
                    <label asp-for="Input.Description"></label>
                    <input asp-for="Input.Description"
                        class="form-control" />
                    <span asp-validation-for="Input.Description"
                        class="text-danger"></span>
                </div>
                <div class="form-group">
                    <label asp-for="Input.Thumbnail"></label>
                    <input asp-for="Input.Thumbnail"
                        class="form-control" />
                    <span asp-validation-for="Input.Thumbnail"
                        class="text-danger"></span>
                </div>
```

```
                    <button type="submit" class="btn btn-success">Save
                    </button>
                </form>
            </div>
        </div>
}

@section Scripts {
    @await Html.PartialAsync("_ValidationScriptsPartial")
}
```

The DeleteModel Class

1. Open the **DeleteModel** class in the *Instructors* folder (the *.cshtml.cs* file).
2. Change the namespace to **Instructors**.
   ```
   namespace VOD.Admin.Pages.Instructors
   ```

3. Change the data type to **InstructorDTO** for the **Input** variable.
   ```
   public InstructorDTO Input { get; set; } = new InstructorDTO();
   ```

4. Replace the **IUserService** injection with **IAdminService** and name the backing variable **_db**.
   ```
   private readonly IAdminService _db;
   public DeleteModel(IAdminService db)
   {
       _db = db;
   }
   ```

5. Change the return type of the **OnGetAsync** method to **Task<IActionResult>** to make it possible to redirect to other pages; if an error occurs, redirect to the main **Index** page with an error message. Change the data type to int for the **id** parameter.
   ```
   public async Task<IActionResult> OnGetAsync(int id)
   ```

6. Add a try/catch-block and move the already existing code inside the try-block and call the **Page** method at the end of the try-block to display the Razor Page; this is necessary when using **Task<IActionResult>** as a return type.

7. Inside the catch-block, replace the **throw**-statement with a redirect to the main **Index** page in the **Pages** folder and pass an error message along with the redirect.
   ```
   return RedirectToPage("/Index", new { alert = "You do not have access to this page." });
   ```

8. Replace the call to the **GetUserAsync** with a call to the **SingleAsync** method in the **IAdminService** and specify **Instructor** as the **TSource** and the **InstructorDTO** as the **TDestination** type. Add a Lambda expression to the method that compares the value in the **id** parameter with the **Id** property of the entities. Copy the method call and paste it in above the **return** statement in the **OnPostAsync** method.
   ```
   Input = await _db.SingleAsync<Instructor, InstructorDTO>(s =>
   s.Id.Equals(id));
   ```
9. Add a variable named **id** above the **ModelState.IsValid** if-block in the **OnPostAsync** action and assign the **Id** from the **Input** object.
   ```
   var id = Input.Id;
   ```
10. Rename the **result** variable **succeeded**.
11. Replace the **DeleteUserAsync** method with the **DeleteAsync** method in the **IAdminService** and specify **Instructor** as the **TSource**. This method doesn't have a **TDestination** since it will return a Boolean value specifying if EF could delete the entity.
    ```
    var succeeded = await _db.DeleteAsync<Instructor>(d =>
    d.Id.Equals(id));
    ```
12. Replace the text in the **Alert** property with *Deleted Instructor:* followed by the name of the instructor. Change the **Input.Title** property to **Input.Name**.
    ```
    Alert = $"Deleted Instructor: {Input.Name}.";
    ```
13. Save all files.

The complete code for the **DeleteModel** class:

```
[Authorize(Roles = "Admin")]
public class DeleteModel : PageModel
{
    #region Properties
    private readonly IAdminService _db;
    [BindProperty] public InstructorDTO Input { get; set; } =
        new InstructorDTO();
    [TempData] public string Alert { get; set; }
    #endregion

    #region Constructor
    public DeleteModel(IAdminService db) { _db = db; }
    #endregion
```

```csharp
#region Actions
public async Task<IActionResult> OnGetAsync(int id)
{
    try
    {
        Input = await _db.SingleAsync<Instructor, InstructorDTO>(
            s => s.Id.Equals(id));
        return Page();
    }
    catch
    {
        return RedirectToPage("/Index", new {
            alert = "You do not have access to this page." });
    }
}

public async Task<IActionResult> OnPostAsync()
{
    var id = Input.Id;

    if (ModelState.IsValid)
    {
        var succeeded = await _db.DeleteAsync<Instructor>(d =>
            d.Id.Equals(id));

        if (succeeded)
        {
            // Message sent back to the Index Razor Page.
            Alert = $"Deleted Instructor: {Input.Name}.";

            return RedirectToPage("Index");
        }
    }

    // Something failed, redisplay the form.
    Input = await _db.SingleAsync<Instructor, InstructorDTO>(s =>
        s.Id.Equals(id));

    return Page();
}
#endregion
}
```

The Delete Razor Page

1. Open the **Delete** Razor Page in the *Instructors* folder (the *.cshtml* file).
2. Change the **ViewData** title to *Delete Instructor*.
3. Replace the **_BackToIndexButtonsPartial** partial with **_DeletePageButtons** and pass in the model's **Input.ButtonDTO** property.
   ```
   <partial name="_DeletePageButtons"
       model="@Model.Input.ButtonDTO" />
   ```
4. Change the contents of the <dd> and <dt> elements to match the properties in the **Input** object.
5. Change the **Input.Email** to **Input.Name** for the second hidden <input> element.
   ```
   <input type="hidden" asp-for="Input.Name" />
   ```
6. Remove the hidden element for **Input.IsAdmin**.
7. Save all files.
8. Start the **Admin** application and try the CRUD operations on the **Instructor** entity. Note the messages displayed on the *Instructor/Index* page.
9. Stop the application in Visual Studio.

The complete code for the **Delete** Razor Page:

```
@page
@model DeleteModel
@inject SignInManager<VODUser> SignInManager
@{
    ViewData["Title"] = "Delete Instructor";
}

@if (SignInManager.IsSignedIn(User) && User.IsInRole("Admin"))
{
    <div class="row">
        <div class="col-md-8 offset-md-2">
            <h1>@ViewData["Title"]</h1>

            <partial name="_DeletePageButtons"
                model="@Model.Input.ButtonDTO" />

            <p></p>

            <dl class="dl-horizontal">
                <dt>@Html.DisplayNameFor(model => model.Input.Name)</dt>
                <dd>@Html.DisplayFor(model => model.Input.Name)</dd>
```

```razor
                <dt>@Html.DisplayNameFor(model =>
                    model.Input.Description)</dt>
                <dd>@Html.DisplayFor(model =>
                    model.Input.Description)</dd>
                <dt>@Html.DisplayNameFor(model =>
                    model.Input.Thumbnail)</dt>
                <dd>@Html.DisplayFor(model =>
                    model.Input.Thumbnail)</dd>
            </dl>

            <form method="post">
                <div asp-validation-summary="All"
                    class="text-danger"></div>

                <input type="hidden" asp-for="Input.Id" />
                <input type="hidden" asp-for="Input.Name" />

                <button type="submit" class="btn btn-danger">Delete
                </button>
            </form>
        </div>
    </div>
}

@section Scripts {
    @await Html.PartialAsync("_ValidationScriptsPartial")
}
```

The Courses Razor Pages

1. Copy the *Instructors* folder and all its contents.
2. Paste in the copied folder in the *Pages* folder and rename it *Courses*.

The IndexModel Class

1. Open the **IndexModel** class in the *Courses* folder (the *.cshtml.cs* file).
2. Change the namespace to **Courses**.
   `namespace VOD.Admin.Pages.Courses`
3. Replace all occurrences of the **Instructor** entity and the **InstructorDTO** with **Course** and **CourseDTO**.
4. Save all files.

The complete code for the **IndexModel** class:

```
[Authorize(Roles = "Admin")]
public class IndexModel : PageModel
{
    #region Properties
    private readonly IAdminService _db;
    public IEnumerable<CourseDTO> Items = new List<CourseDTO>();
    [TempData] public string Alert { get; set; }
    #endregion

    #region Constructor
    public IndexModel(IAdminService db)
    {
        _db = db;
    }
    #endregion

    public async Task<IActionResult> OnGetAsync()
    {
        try
        {
            Items = await _db.GetAsync<Course, CourseDTO>(true);
            return Page();
        }
        catch
        {
            Alert = "You do not have access to this page.";
            return RedirectToPage("/Index");
        }
    }
}
```

The Index Razor Page

1. Open the *_ViewImports.cshtml* file and add the following **using**-statement to gain access to the **Truncate** extension method you added earlier.
   @using VOD.Common.Extensions

2. Open the **Index** Razor Page in the *Courses* folder (the *.cshtml* file).
3. Change the **ViewData** title to *Courses*.
4. Change the headings in the <th> elements to match the property values of the table. Add and remove <th> elements as needed.

24. The Remaining Razor Pages

5. Add a variable named **description** for the truncated description in the **foreach** loop and assign the truncated string from the **item.Description** property.
   `var description = item.Description.Truncate(100);`

6. Change the <td> elements to display the values from the properties in the **item** loop variable. Add and remove <td> elements as needed.

7. Use the **description** variable instead of the **item.Description** property.
   `<td>@Html.DisplayFor(modelItem => description)</td>`

8. Change the width of the button column to 100px; there are only two buttons for each row in this table.

9. Save all files.

The complete code for the **Index** Razor Page:

```
@page
@model IndexModel
@inject SignInManager<VODUser> SignInManager

@{
    ViewData["Title"] = "Courses";
}

@if (SignInManager.IsSignedIn(User) && User.IsInRole("Admin"))
{
    <div class="row">
        <div class="col-md-10 offset-md-1"
            style="padding-left:0;padding-right:0;">
            <alert alert-type="success">@Model.Alert</alert>
        </div>
        <div class="col-md-1">
        </div>
    </div>

    <div class="row">
        <div class="col-md-10 offset-md-1">
            <h1>@ViewData["Title"]</h1>

            <partial name="_PageButtonsPartial" />
```

```html
            <table style="margin-top:20px;" class="table">
                <thead>
                    <tr>
                        <th>Title</th>
                        <th>Instructor</th>
                        <th>Description</th>
                        <th></th>
                    </tr>
                </thead>
                <tbody>
                    @foreach (var item in Model.Items)
                    {
                        var description =
                            item.Description.Truncate(100);
                        <tr>
                            <td>@Html.DisplayFor(modelItem =>
                                item.Title)</td>
                            <td>@Html.DisplayFor(modelItem =>
                                item.Instructor)</td>
                            <td>@Html.DisplayFor(modelItem =>
                                description)</td>
                            <td style="min-width:100px;">
                                <partial name="_TableRowButtonsPartial"
                                    model="@item.ButtonDTO" /></td>
                        </tr>
                    }
                </tbody>
            </table>
        </div>
        <div class="col-md-1">
        </div>
    </div>
}
```

The CreateModel Class

1. Open the **CreateModel** class in the *Courses* folder (the *.cshtml.cs* file).
2. Change the namespace to **Courses**.
   namespace VOD.Admin.Pages.Courses

3. Replace all occurrences of the **Instructor** entity and the **InstructorDTO** with **Course** and **CourseDTO**.
4. Change the return type to **Task<IActionResult>** for the **OnGetAsync** action.

24. The Remaining Razor Pages

5. Add a try/catch block to the **OnGetAsync** action where the try-block returns the page by calling the **Page** method and the catch-block redirect to the **Index** page win an error message.
   ```
   try
   {
       return Page();
   }
   catch
   {
       return RedirectToPage("/Index", new { alert =
           "You do not have access to this page." });
   }
   ```
6. Add a dynamic **Modules** property named **Instructors** and fetch all instructors and convert them into a **SelectList** instance above the **return** statement in the **OnGetAsync** action; add the same code above the **return** statement inside the **OnPostAsync** method.
   ```
   ViewData["Instructors"] = (await _db.GetAsync<Instructor,
   InstructorDTO>()).ToSelectList("Id", "Name");
   ```
7. Change the text in the **Alert** property to *Created a new Course:* followed by the course title.
   ```
   Alert = $"Created a new Course: {Input.Title}.";
   ```
8. Save all files.

The complete code for the **CreateModel** class:

```
[Authorize(Roles = "Admin")]
public class CreateModel : PageModel
{
    #region Properties
    private readonly IAdminService _db;
    [BindProperty] public CourseDTO Input { get; set; } =
        new CourseDTO();
    [TempData] public string Alert { get; set; }
    #endregion

    #region Constructor
    public CreateModel(IAdminService db)
    {
        _db = db;
    }
    #endregion
```

353

```csharp
#region Actions
public async Task<IActionResult> OnGetAsync()
{
    try
    {
        ViewData["Instructors"] = (await _db.GetAsync<Instructor,
            InstructorDTO>()).ToSelectList("Id", "Name");
        return Page();
    }
    catch
    {
        return RedirectToPage("/Index", new {
            alert = "You do not have access to this page." });
    }
}

public async Task<IActionResult> OnPostAsync()
{
    if (ModelState.IsValid)
    {
        var succeeded = (await _db.CreateAsync<CourseDTO,
            Course>(Input)) > 0;

        if (succeeded)
        {
            // Message sent back to the Index Razor Page.
            Alert = $"Created a new Course: {Input.Title}.";

            return RedirectToPage("Index");
        }
    }

    // Something failed, redisplay the form.
    ViewData["Instructors"] = (await _db.GetAsync<Instructor,
        InstructorDTO>()).ToSelectList("Id", "Name");

    return Page();
}
#endregion
}
```

24. The Remaining Razor Pages

The Create Razor Page

1. Open the **Create** Razor Page in the *Courses* folder (the *.cshtml* file).
2. Change the **ViewData** title to *Create Course*.
3. Change the content in the **form-group** <div> elements to display the values from the properties in the **Input** variable. Add and remove **form-group** <div> elements as needed.
4. Use the data in the **ViewData** object to create a drop-down for all instructors.
   ```
   <div class="form-group">
       <label asp-for="Input.Instructor" class="control-label">
       </label>
       <select asp-for="Input.InstructorId" class="form-control"
           asp-items="ViewBag.Instructors"></select>
   </div>
   ```
5. Save all files.

The complete code for the **Create** Razor Page:

```
@page
@model CreateModel
@inject SignInManager<VODUser> SignInManager
@{
    ViewData["Title"] = "Create Course";
}

@if (SignInManager.IsSignedIn(User) && User.IsInRole("Admin"))
{
    <div class="row">
        <div class="col-md-8 offset-md-2">
            <h1>@ViewData["Title"]</h1>

            <partial name="_BackToIndexButtonsPartial" />
            <p></p>

            <form method="post">
                <div asp-validation-summary="All"
                    class="text-danger"></div>

                <div class="form-group">
                    <label asp-for="Input.Title"></label>
                    <input asp-for="Input.Title" class="form-control" />
                    <span asp-validation-for="Input.Title"
                        class="text-danger"></span>
```

```html
                    </div>
                    <div class="form-group">
                        <label asp-for="Input.Description"></label>
                        <input asp-for="Input.Description"
                            class="form-control" />
                        <span asp-validation-for="Input.Description"
                            class="text-danger"></span>
                    </div>
                    <div class="form-group">
                        <label asp-for="Input.ImageUrl"></label>
                        <input asp-for="Input.ImageUrl"
                            class="form-control" />
                        <span asp-validation-for="Input.ImageUrl"
                            class="text-danger"></span>
                    </div>
                    <div class="form-group">
                        <label asp-for="Input.MarqueeImageUrl"></label>
                        <input asp-for="Input.MarqueeImageUrl"
                            class="form-control" />
                        <span asp-validation-for="Input.MarqueeImageUrl"
                            class="text-danger"></span>
                    </div>
                    <div class="form-group">
                        <label asp-for="Input.InstructorId"
                            class="control-label"></label>
                        <select asp-for="Input.InstructorId"
                            class="form-control"
                            asp-items="ViewBag.Instructors"></select>
                    </div>

                    <button type="submit" class="btn btn-success">Create
                    </button>
                </form>
            </div>
        </div>
}

@section Scripts {
    @await Html.PartialAsync("_ValidationScriptsPartial")
}
```

The EditModel Class

1. Open the **EditModel** class in the *Courses* folder (the *.cshtml.cs* file).
2. Change the namespace to **Courses**.
   ```
   namespace VOD.Admin.Pages.Courses
   ```
3. Replace all occurrences of the **Instructor** entity and the **InstructorDTO** with **Course** and **CourseDTO**.
4. Add a dynamic **Modules** property named **Instructors** and fetch all instructors and convert them into a **SelectList** instance below the **Alert** property assignment in the **OnGetAsync** action and above the **return** statement inside the **OnPostAsync** method.
   ```
   ViewData["Instructors"] = (await _db.GetAsync<Instructor,
   InstructorDTO>()).ToSelectList("Id", "Name");
   ```
5. Replace the text in the **Alert** property to *Updated Course:* followed by the course title. Replace the **Name** property with the **Title** property.
   ```
   Alert = $"Updated Course: {Input.Title}.";
   ```
6. Save all files.

The complete code for the **EditModel** class:

```
[Authorize(Roles = "Admin")]
public class EditModel : PageModel
{
    #region Properties
    private readonly IAdminService _db;
    [BindProperty] public CourseDTO Input { get; set; } =
        new CourseDTO();
    [TempData] public string Alert { get; set; }
    #endregion

    #region Constructor
    public EditModel(IAdminService db)
    {
        _db = db;
    }
    #endregion
```

```csharp
#region Actions
public async Task<IActionResult> OnGetAsync(int id)
{
    try
    {
        Alert = string.Empty;
        ViewData["Instructors"] = (await _db.GetAsync<Instructor,
            InstructorDTO>()).ToSelectList("Id", "Name");
        Input = await _db.SingleAsync<Course, CourseDTO>(s =>
            s.Id.Equals(id), true);
        return Page();
    }
    catch
    {
        return RedirectToPage("/Index", new {
            alert = "You do not have access to this page." });
    }
}

public async Task<IActionResult> OnPostAsync()
{
    if (ModelState.IsValid)
    {
        var succeeded = await _db.UpdateAsync<CourseDTO,
            Course>(Input);

        if (succeeded)
        {
            // Message sent back to the Index Razor Page.
            Alert = $"Updated Course: {Input.Title}.";

            return RedirectToPage("Index");
        }
    }

    // Reload the modules when the page is reloaded
    ViewData["Instructors"] = (await _db.GetAsync<Instructor,
        InstructorDTO>()).ToSelectList("Id", "Name");

    // Something failed, redisplay the form.
    return Page();
}
#endregion
}
```

The Edit Razor Page

1. Open the **Edit** Razor Page in the *Courses* folder (the *.cshtml* file).
2. Change the **ViewData** title to *Edit Course*.
3. Change the **form-group** <div> elements' contents to match the properties in the **Input** object.
4. Use the data in the **ViewData** object to create a drop-down for all instructors.
   ```
   <div class="form-group">
       <label asp-for="Input.Instructor" class="control-label">
       </label>
       <select asp-for="Input.InstructorId" class="form-control"
           asp-items="ViewBag.Instructors"></select>
   </div>
   ```
5. Save all files.

The complete code for the **Edit** Razor Page:

```
@page
@model EditModel
@inject SignInManager<VODUser> SignInManager
@{
    ViewData["Title"] = "Edit Course";
}

@if (SignInManager.IsSignedIn(User) && User.IsInRole("Admin"))
{
    <div class="row">
        <div class="col-md-8 offset-md-2">
            <h1>@ViewData["Title"]</h1>

            <partial name="_BackToIndexButtonsPartial" />
            <p></p>

            <form method="post">
                <div asp-validation-summary="All"
                    class="text-danger"></div>

                <input type="hidden" asp-for="Input.Id" />

                <div class="form-group">
                    <label asp-for="Input.Title"></label>
                    <input asp-for="Input.Title" class="form-control" />
                    <span asp-validation-for="Input.Title"
```

```html
                        class="text-danger"></span>
                </div>
                <div class="form-group">
                    <label asp-for="Input.Description"></label>
                    <input asp-for="Input.Description"
                        class="form-control" />
                    <span asp-validation-for="Input.Description"
                        class="text-danger"></span>
                </div>
                <div class="form-group">
                    <label asp-for="Input.ImageUrl"></label>
                    <input asp-for="Input.ImageUrl"
                        class="form-control" />
                    <span asp-validation-for="Input.ImageUrl"
                        class="text-danger"></span>
                </div>
                <div class="form-group">
                    <label asp-for="Input.MarqueeImageUrl"></label>
                    <input asp-for="Input.MarqueeImageUrl"
                        class="form-control" />
                    <span asp-validation-for="Input.MarqueeImageUrl"
                        class="text-danger"></span>
                </div>

                <div class="form-group">
                    <label asp-for="Input.InstructorId"
                        class="control-label"></label>
                    <select asp-for="Input.InstructorId"
                        class="form-control"
                        asp-items="ViewBag.Instructors"></select>
                </div>

                <button type="submit" class="btn btn-success">Save
                </button>
            </form>
        </div>
    </div>
}

@section Scripts {
    @await Html.PartialAsync("_ValidationScriptsPartial")
}
```

The DeleteModel Class

1. Open the **DeleteModel** class in the *Courses* folder (the *.cshtml.cs* file).
2. Change the namespace to **Courses**.
   ```
   namespace VOD.Admin.Pages.Courses
   ```
3. Replace all occurrences of the **Instructor** entity and the **InstructorDTO** with **Course** and **CourseDTO**.
4. Pass in **true** as a second parameter to the **SingleAsync** method inside both the **OnGetAsync** and the **OnPostAsync** methods.
   ```
   Input = await _db.SingleAsync<Course, CourseDTO>(s =>
   s.Id.Equals(id), true);
   ```
5. Change the text in the **Alert** property to *Deleted Course:* followed by the course title.
   ```
   Alert = $"Deleted Course: {Input.Title}.";
   ```
6. Save all files.

The complete code for the **DeleteModel** class:

```
[Authorize(Roles = "Admin")]
public class DeleteModel : PageModel
{
    #region Properties
    private readonly IAdminService _db;
    [BindProperty] public CourseDTO Input { get; set; } =
        new CourseDTO();
    [TempData] public string Alert { get; set; }
    #endregion

    #region Constructor
    public DeleteModel(IAdminService db)
    {
        _db = db;
    }
    #endregion
```

```csharp
#region Actions
public async Task<IActionResult> OnGetAsync(int id)
{
    try
    {
        Alert = string.Empty;
        Input = await _db.SingleAsync<Course, CourseDTO>(s =>
            s.Id.Equals(id), true);
        return Page();
    }
    catch
    {
        return RedirectToPage("/Index", new {
            alert = "You do not have access to this page." });
    }
}

public async Task<IActionResult> OnPostAsync()
{
    var id = Input.Id;
    if (ModelState.IsValid)
    {
        var succeeded = await _db.DeleteAsync<Course>(d =>
            d.Id.Equals(id));

        if (succeeded)
        {
            // Message sent back to the Index Razor Page.
            Alert = $"Deleted Course: {Input.Title}.";

            return RedirectToPage("Index");
        }
    }

    // Something failed, redisplay the form.
    Input = await _db.SingleAsync<Course, CourseDTO>(s =>
        s.Id.Equals(id), true);
    return Page();
}
#endregion
}
```

24. The Remaining Razor Pages

The Delete Razor Page

1. Open the **Delete** Razor Page in the *Courses* folder (the *.cshtml* file).
2. Change the **ViewData** title to *Delete Course*.
3. Add a variable named **description** below the **ViewData** object in the Razor-block at the top of the Razor Page. Truncate the string in the **Input.Description** model property with the **Truncate** extension method you created earlier and assign it to the variable.

   ```
   @{
       ViewData["Title"] = "Delete Course";
       var description = Model.Input.Description.Truncate(100);
   }
   ```

4. Change the contents of the <dd> and <dt> elements to match the properties in the **Input** object.
5. Use the **description** variable instead of the **model.Input.Description** property.

   ```
   <dd>@Html.DisplayFor(model => description)</dd>
   ```

6. Replace the hidden **Name** property with the **Title** property.

   ```
   <input type="hidden" asp-for="Input.Title" />
   ```

7. Save all files.
8. Start the **Admin** application and try the CRUD operations for the **Course** entity. Note the **Alert** messages.
9. Stop the application in Visual Studio.

The complete code for the **Delete** Razor Page:

```
@page
@model DeleteModel
@inject SignInManager<VODUser> SignInManager
@{
    ViewData["Title"] = "Delete Course";
    var description = Model.Input.Description.Truncate(100);
}

@if (SignInManager.IsSignedIn(User) && User.IsInRole("Admin"))
{
    <div class="row">
        <div class="col-md-8 offset-md-2">
            <h1>@ViewData["Title"]</h1>

            <partial name="_DeletePageButtons"
                model="@Model.Input.ButtonDTO" />
```

```
            <p></p>

            <dl class="dl-horizontal">
                <dt>@Html.DisplayNameFor(model =>
                    model.Input.Title)</dt>
                <dd>@Html.DisplayFor(model => model.Input.Title)</dd>
                <dt>@Html.DisplayNameFor(model =>
                    model.Input.Description)</dt>
                <dd>@Html.DisplayFor(model => description)</dd>
                <dt>@Html.DisplayNameFor(model =>
                    model.Input.ImageUrl)</dt>
                <dd>@Html.DisplayFor(model => model.Input.ImageUrl)</dd>
                <dt>@Html.DisplayNameFor(model =>
                    model.Input.MarqueeImageUrl)</dt>
                <dd>@Html.DisplayFor(model =>
                    model.Input.MarqueeImageUrl)</dd>
                <dt>@Html.DisplayNameFor(model =>
                    model.Input.Instructor)</dt>
                <dd>@Html.DisplayFor(model =>
                    model.Input.Instructor)</dd>
            </dl>

            <form method="post">
                <div asp-validation-summary="All"
                    class="text-danger"></div>

                <input type="hidden" asp-for="Input.Id" />
                <input type="hidden" asp-for="Input.Title" />

                <button type="submit" class="btn btn-danger">Delete
                </button>
            </form>
        </div>
    </div>
}

@section Scripts {
    @await Html.PartialAsync("_ValidationScriptsPartial") }
```

The Modules Razor Pages

1. Copy the *Courses* folder and all its contents.
2. Paste in the copied folder in the *Pages* folder and rename it *Modules*.

24. The Remaining Razor Pages

The IndexModel Class

1. Open the **IndexModel** class in the *Modules* folder (the *.cshtml.cs* file).
2. Change the namespace to **Modules**.
   namespace VOD.Admin.Pages.**Modules**
3. Replace all instances of the **Course** entity and the **CourseDTO** with **Module** and **ModuleDTO**.
4. Save all files.

The complete code for the **IndexModel** class:

```
[Authorize(Roles = "Admin")]
public class IndexModel : PageModel
{
    #region Properties
    private readonly IAdminService _db;
    public IEnumerable<ModuleDTO> Items = new List<ModuleDTO>();
    [TempData] public string Alert { get; set; }
    #endregion

    #region Constructor
    public IndexModel(IAdminService db)
    {
        _db = db;
    }
    #endregion

    public async Task<IActionResult> OnGetAsync()
    {
        try
        {
            Items = await _db.GetAsync<Module, ModuleDTO>(true);
            return Page();
        }
        catch
        {
            Alert = "You do not have access to this page.";
            return RedirectToPage("/Index");
        }
    }
}
```

The Index Razor Page

1. Open the **Index** Razor Page in the *Modules* folder (the *.cshtml* file).
2. Change the **ViewData** title to *Modules*.
3. Change the headings in the <th> elements to match the property values of the table. Add and remove <th> elements as needed.
4. Change the <td> elements to display the values from the properties in the **item** loop variable. Add and remove <td> elements as needed.
5. Remove the **description** variable from the loop.
   ```
   var description = item.Description.Truncate(100);
   ```
6. Save all files.

The complete code for the **Index** Razor Page:

```
@page
@model IndexModel
@inject SignInManager<VODUser> SignInManager

@{
    ViewData["Title"] = "Modules";
}

@if (SignInManager.IsSignedIn(User) && User.IsInRole("Admin"))
{
    <div class="row">
        <div class="col-md-10 offset-md-1"
            style="padding-left:0;padding-right:0;">
            <alert alert-type="success">@Model.Alert</alert>
        </div>
        <div class="col-md-1">
        </div>
    </div>

    <div class="row">
        <div class="col-md-10 offset-md-1">
            <h1>@ViewData["Title"]</h1>

            <partial name="_PageButtonsPartial" />
```

```html
            <table style="margin-top:20px;" class="table">
                <thead>
                    <tr>
                        <th>Title</th>
                        <th>Course Title</th>
                        <th></th>
                    </tr>
                </thead>
                <tbody>
                    @foreach (var item in Model.Items)
                    {
                        <tr>
                            <td>@Html.DisplayFor(modelItem =>
                                item.Title)</td>
                            <td>@Html.DisplayFor(modelItem =>
                                item.Course)</td>
                            <td style="min-width:100px;">
                                <partial name="_TableRowButtonsPartial"
                                    model="@item.ButtonDTO" /></td>
                        </tr>
                    }
                </tbody>
            </table>
        </div>
        <div class="col-md-1">
        </div>
    </div>
}
```

The CreateModel Class

1. Open the **CreateModel** class in the *Modules* folder (the *.cshtml.cs* file).
2. Change the namespace to **Modules**.
   ```
   namespace VOD.Admin.Pages.Modules
   ```
3. Replace all instances of the **Course** entity and the **CourseDTO** with **Module** and **ModuleDTO**.
4. Rename the dynamic **Instructors** property **Courses** and change the method's defining types to **Course** and **CourseDTO**, in the **OnGetAsync** and **OnPostAsync** methods.
   ```
   ViewData["Courses"] = (await _db.GetAsync<Course, CourseDTO>())
       .ToSelectList("Id", "Title");
   ```

5. Change the text in the **Alert** property to *Created a new Module:* followed by the course title.
   ```
   Alert = $"Created a new Module: {Input.Title}.";
   ```
6. Save all files.

The complete code for the **CreateModel** class:

```
[Authorize(Roles = "Admin")]
public class CreateModel : PageModel
{
    #region Properties
    private readonly IAdminService _db;
    [BindProperty] public ModuleDTO Input { get; set; } =
        new ModuleDTO();
    [TempData] public string Alert { get; set; }
    #endregion

    #region Constructor
    public CreateModel(IAdminService db)
    {
        _db = db;
    }
    #endregion

    #region Actions
    public async Task<IActionResult> OnGetAsync()
    {
        try
        {
            ViewData["Courses"] = (await _db.GetAsync<Course,
                CourseDTO>()).ToSelectList("Id", "Title");
            return Page();
        }
        catch
        {
            return RedirectToPage("/Index", new {
                alert = "You do not have access to this page." });
        }
    }
```

24. The Remaining Razor Pages

```
    public async Task<IActionResult> OnPostAsync()
    {
        if (ModelState.IsValid)
        {
            var succeeded = (await _db.CreateAsync<ModuleDTO,
                Module>(Input)) > 0;

            if (succeeded)
            {
                // Message sent back to the Index Razor Page.
                Alert = $"Created a new Module: {Input.Title}.";

                return RedirectToPage("Index");
            }
        }

        // Something failed, redisplay the form.
        ViewData["Courses"] = (await _db.GetAsync<Course,
            CourseDTO>()).ToSelectList("Id", "Title");

        return Page();
    }
    #endregion
}
```

The Create Razor Page

1. Open the **Create** Razor Page in the *Modules* folder (the *.cshtml* file).
2. Change the **ViewData** title to *Create Module*.
3. Change the content in the **form-group** <div> elements to display the values from the properties in the **Input** variable. Add and remove **form-group** <div> elements as needed.
4. Replace **Instructor**, **InstructorId**, and **Instructors** with **Course**, **CourseId**, and **Courses** for the drop-down.
5. Save all files.

The complete code for the **Create** Razor Page:

```
@page
@model CreateModel
@inject SignInManager<VODUser> SignInManager
@{ ViewData["Title"] = "Create Module"; }
```

```
@if (SignInManager.IsSignedIn(User) && User.IsInRole("Admin"))
{
    <div class="row">
        <div class="col-md-8 offset-md-2">
            <h1>@ViewData["Title"]</h1>

            <partial name="_BackToIndexButtonsPartial" />
            <p></p>

            <form method="post">
                <div asp-validation-summary="All"
                    class="text-danger"></div>

                <div class="form-group">
                    <label asp-for="Input.Title"></label>
                    <input asp-for="Input.Title" class="form-control" />
                    <span asp-validation-for="Input.Title"
                        class="text-danger"></span>
                </div>

                <div class="form-group">
                    <label asp-for="Input.Course"
                        class="control-label"></label>
                    <select asp-for="Input.CourseId"
                        class="form-control"
                        asp-items="ViewBag.Courses"></select>
                </div>

                <button type="submit" class="btn btn-success">Create
                </button>
            </form>
        </div>
    </div>
}

@section Scripts {
    @await Html.PartialAsync("_ValidationScriptsPartial")
}
```

The EditModel Class

1. Open the **EditModel** class in the *Modules* folder (the *.cshtml.cs* file).
2. Change the namespace to **Modules**.
   namespace VOD.Admin.Pages.Modules
3. Replace all instances of the **Course** entity and the **CourseDTO** with **Module** and **ModuleDTO**.
4. Rename the dynamic **Instructors** property **Courses** and change the method's defining types to **Course** and **CourseDTO**, in the **OnGetAsync** and **OnPostAsync** methods.
   ViewData["Courses"] = (await _db.GetAsync<Course, CourseDTO>())
       .ToSelectList("Id", "Title");
5. Add an **int** parameter named **courseId** to the **OnGetAsync** action.
6. Add a check for the **CourseId** property to the Lambda expression in the **SingleAsync** method call.
   && s.CourseId.Equals(courseId)
7. Replace the text in the **Alert** property to *Updated Module:* followed by the course title.
   Alert = $"Updated Module: {Input.Title}.";
8. Save all files.

The complete code for the **EditModel** class:

```
[Authorize(Roles = "Admin")]
public class EditModel : PageModel
{
    #region Properties
    private readonly IAdminService _db;
    [BindProperty] public ModuleDTO Input { get; set; } = new
        ModuleDTO();
    [TempData] public string Alert { get; set; }
    #endregion

    #region Constructor
    public EditModel(IAdminService db)
    {
        _db = db;
    }
    #endregion
```

```csharp
#region Actions
public async Task<IActionResult> OnGetAsync(int id, int courseId)
{
    try
    {
        ViewData["Courses"] = (await _db.GetAsync<Course,
            CourseDTO>()).ToSelectList("Id", "Title");
        Input = await _db.SingleAsync<Module, ModuleDTO>(s =>
            s.Id.Equals(id) && s.CourseId.Equals(courseId));
        return Page();
    }
    catch
    {
        return RedirectToPage("/Index", new {
            alert = "You do not have access to this page." });
    }
}

public async Task<IActionResult> OnPostAsync()
{
    if (ModelState.IsValid)
    {
        var succeeded = await _db.UpdateAsync<ModuleDTO,
            Module>(Input);

        if (succeeded)
        {
            // Message sent back to the Index Razor Page.
            Alert = $"Updated Module: {Input.Title}.";

            return RedirectToPage("Index");
        }
    }

    // Something failed, redisplay the form.
    // Reload the modules when the page is reloaded
    ViewData["Courses"] = (await _db.GetAsync<Course,
        CourseDTO>()).ToSelectList("Id", "Title");

    return Page();
}
#endregion
}
```

24. The Remaining Razor Pages

The Edit Razor Page

1. Open the **Edit** Razor Page in the *Modules* folder (the *.cshtml* file).
2. Change the **ViewData** title to *Edit Module*.
3. Change the **form-group** <div> elements' contents to match the properties in the **Input** object.
4. Replace **Instructor**, **InstructorId**, and **Instructor** with **Course**, **CourseId**, and **Courses** for the drop-down.
5. Save all files.

The complete code for the **Edit** Razor Page:

```
@page
@model EditModel
@inject SignInManager<VODUser> SignInManager
@{
    ViewData["Title"] = "Edit Module";
}

@if (SignInManager.IsSignedIn(User) && User.IsInRole("Admin"))
{
    <div class="row">
        <div class="col-md-8 offset-md-2">
            <h1>@ViewData["Title"]</h1>

            <partial name="_BackToIndexButtonsPartial" />
            <p></p>

            <form method="post">
                <div asp-validation-summary="All"
                    class="text-danger"></div>

                <input type="hidden" asp-for="Input.Id" />

                <div class="form-group">
                    <label asp-for="Input.Title"></label>
                    <input asp-for="Input.Title" class="form-control" />
                    <span asp-validation-for="Input.Title"
                        class="text-danger"></span>
                </div>
                <div class="form-group">
                    <label asp-for="Input.Course"
                        class="control-label"></label>
```

```
                <select asp-for="Input.CourseId"
                    class="form-control"
                    asp-items="ViewBag.Courses"></select>
            </div>

                <button type="submit" class="btn btn-success">Save
                </button>
            </form>
        </div>
    </div>
}
@section Scripts {
    @await Html.PartialAsync("_ValidationScriptsPartial")
}
```

The DeleteModel Class

1. Open the **DeleteModel** class in the *Modules* folder (the *.cshtml.cs* file).
2. Change the namespace to **Modules**.
   `namespace VOD.Admin.Pages.Modules`

3. Replace all instances of the **Course** entity and the **CourseDTO** with **Module** and **ModuleDTO**.
4. Add an **int** parameter named **courseId** to the **OnGetAsync** action.
5. Add a variable named **courseId** above the **ModelState.IsValid** if-block and assign **CourseId** property values from the **Input** object.
   `int id = Input.Id, courseId = Input.CourseId;`

6. Add a check for the **CourseId** property to the Lambda expression for the **SingleAsync** and **DeleteAsync** methods call.
   `&& s.CourseId.Equals(courseId)`

7. Change the text in the **Alert** property to *Deleted Module:* followed by the module title.
   `Alert = $"Deleted Module: {Input.Title}.";`

8. Save all files.

24. The Remaining Razor Pages

The complete code for the **DeleteModel** class:

```
[Authorize(Roles = "Admin")]
public class DeleteModel : PageModel
{
    #region Properties
    private readonly IAdminService _db;
    [BindProperty] public ModuleDTO Input { get; set; } =
        new ModuleDTO();
    [TempData] public string Alert { get; set; }
    #endregion

    #region Constructor
    public DeleteModel(IAdminService db)
    {
        _db = db;
    }
    #endregion

    #region Actions
    public async Task<IActionResult> OnGetAsync(int id, int courseId)
    {
        try
        {
            Input = await _db.SingleAsync<Module, ModuleDTO>(s =>
                s.Id.Equals(id) && s.CourseId.Equals(courseId), true);
            return Page();
        }
        catch
        {
            return RedirectToPage("/Index", new {
                alert = "You do not have access to this page." });
        }
    }

    public async Task<IActionResult> OnPostAsync()
    {
        int id = Input.Id, courseId = Input.CourseId;
        if (ModelState.IsValid)
        {
            var succeeded = await _db.DeleteAsync<Module>(d =>
                d.Id.Equals(id) && d.CourseId.Equals(courseId));
```

```
            if (succeeded)
            {
                // Message sent back to the Index Razor Page.
                Alert = $"Deleted Module: {Input.Title}.";

                return RedirectToPage("Index");
            }
        }

        // Something failed, redisplay the form.
        Input = await _db.SingleAsync<Module, ModuleDTO>(s =>
            s.Id.Equals(id) && s.CourseId.Equals(courseId), true);
        return Page();
    }
    #endregion
}
```

The Delete Razor Page

1. Open the **Delete** Razor Page in the *Modules* folder (the *.cshtml* file).
2. Change the **ViewData** title to *Delete Module*.
3. Remove the **description** variable.
4. Change the contents of the <dd> and <dt> elements to match the properties in the **Input** object.
5. Add a hidden element for the **CourseId**.
6. Save all files.
7. Start the **Admin** application and try the CRUD operations for the Module entity. Note the **Alert** messages.
8. Stop the application in Visual Studio.

The complete code for the **Delete** Razor Page:

```
@page
@model DeleteModel
@inject SignInManager<VODUser> SignInManager
@{
    ViewData["Title"] = "Delete Module";
}
```

```
@if (SignInManager.IsSignedIn(User) && User.IsInRole("Admin"))
{
    <div class="row">
        <div class="col-md-8 offset-md-2">
            <h1>@ViewData["Title"]</h1>

            <partial name="_DeletePageButtons"
                model="@Model.Input.ButtonDTO" />

            <p></p>

            <dl class="dl-horizontal">
                <dt>@Html.DisplayNameFor(model =>
                    model.Input.Title)</dt>
                <dd>@Html.DisplayFor(model => model.Input.Title)</dd>
                <dt>@Html.DisplayNameFor(model =>
                    model.Input.Course)</dt>
                <dd>@Html.DisplayFor(model => model.Input.Course)</dd>
            </dl>

            <form method="post">
                <div asp-validation-summary="All"
                    class="text-danger"></div>

                <input type="hidden" asp-for="Input.Id" />
                <input type="hidden" asp-for="Input.Title" />
                <input type="hidden" asp-for="Input.CourseId" />

                <button type="submit" class="btn btn-danger">Delete
                </button>
            </form>
        </div>
    </div>
}

@section Scripts {
    @await Html.PartialAsync("_ValidationScriptsPartial")
}
```

The Video Razor Pages

1. Copy the *Courses* folder and all its contents.
2. Paste in the copied folder in the *Pages* folder and rename it *Videos*.

The IndexModel Class

1. Open the **IndexModel** class in the *Videos* folder (the *.cshtml.cs* file).
2. Change the namespace to **Videos**.
   namespace VOD.Admin.Pages.Videos
3. Replace all instances of the **Course** entity and the **CourseDTO** with **Video** and **VideoDTO**.
4. Save all files.

The complete code for the **IndexModel** class:

```
[Authorize(Roles = "Admin")]
public class IndexModel : PageModel
{
    #region Properties
    private readonly IAdminService _db;
    public IEnumerable<VideoDTO> Items = new List<VideoDTO>();
    [TempData] public string Alert { get; set; }
    #endregion

    #region Constructor
    public IndexModel(IAdminService db)
    {
        _db = db;
    }
    #endregion

    public async Task<IActionResult> OnGetAsync()
    {
        try
        {
            Items = await _db.GetAsync<Video, VideoDTO>(true);
            return Page();
        }
        catch
        {
            Alert = "You do not have access to this page.";
            return RedirectToPage("/Index");
        }

    }
}
```

24. The Remaining Razor Pages

The Index Razor Page

1. Open the **Index** Razor Page in the *Videos* folder (the *.cshtml* file).
2. Change the **ViewData** title to *Videos*.
3. Change the <td> elements to display the values from the properties in the **item** loop variable. Add and remove <td> elements as needed.
4. Change the <th> elements to display the correct headings for the <td> elements in the **item** loop.
5. Save all files.

The complete code for the **Index** Razor Page:

```
@page
@model IndexModel
@inject SignInManager<VODUser> SignInManager
@{ ViewData["Title"] = "Videos"; }

@if (SignInManager.IsSignedIn(User) && User.IsInRole("Admin"))
{
    <div class="row">
        <div class="col-md-10 offset-md-1"
            style="padding-left:0;padding-right:0;">
            <alert alert-type="success">@Model.Alert</alert>
        </div>
        <div class="col-md-1"></div>
    </div>

    <div class="row">
        <div class="col-md-10 offset-md-1">
            <h1>@ViewData["Title"]</h1>

            <partial name="_PageButtonsPartial" />

            <table style="margin-top:20px;" class="table">
                <thead>
                    <tr>
                        <th>Title</th>
                        <th>Course</th>
                        <th>Module</th>
                        <th>Description</th>
                        <th></th>
                    </tr>
                </thead>
```

```
            <tbody>
                @foreach (var item in Model.Items)
                {
                    var description =
                        item.Description.Truncate(100);
                    <tr>
                        <td>@Html.DisplayFor(modelItem =>
                            item.Title)</td>
                        <td>@Html.DisplayFor(modelItem =>
                            item.Course)</td>
                        <td>@Html.DisplayFor(modelItem =>
                            item.Module)</td>
                        <td>@Html.DisplayFor(modelItem =>
                            description)</td>
                        <td style="min-width:100px;">
                            <partial name="_TableRowButtonsPartial"
                                model="@item.ButtonDTO" /></td>
                    </tr>
                }
            </tbody>
        </table>
    </div>
    <div class="col-md-1">
    </div>
  </div>
}
```

The CreateModel Class

1. Open the **CreateModel** class in the *Videos* folder (the *.cshtml.cs* file).
2. Change the namespace to **Videos**.
   `namespace VOD.Admin.Pages.Videos`

3. Replace all instances of the **Course** entity and the **CourseDTO** with **Video** and **VideoDTO**.

4. Rename the dynamic **Instructors** variable **Modules** and replace the **Instructor** and **InstructorDTO** with **Module** and **ModuleDTO** in both **OnGetAsync** and **OnPostAsync** methods.
   `ViewData["Modules"] = (await _db.GetAsync<Module,`
   `ModuleDTO>(true)).ToSelectList("Id", "CourseAndModule");`

5. Add a variable named **id** inside the **ModelState.IsValid** if-block and assign the **ModuleId** from the **Input** object. Use the id to fetch the corresponding module.

24. The Remaining Razor Pages

This is necessary in case a different module has been selected in the **Modules** drop-down.

```
var id = Input.ModuleId;

Input.CourseId = (await _db.SingleAsync<Module, ModuleDTO>(s =>
s.Id.Equals(id))).CourseId;
```

6. Replace *Course* with *Video* in the **Alert** message.
7. Save all files.

The complete code for the **CreateModel** class:

```
[Authorize(Roles = "Admin")]
public class CreateModel : PageModel
{
    #region Properties
    private readonly IAdminService _db;
    [BindProperty] public VideoDTO Input { get; set; } = new VideoDTO();
    [TempData] public string Alert { get; set; }
    #endregion

    #region Constructor
    public CreateModel(IAdminService db)
    {
        _db = db;
    }
    #endregion

    #region Actions
    public async Task<IActionResult> OnGetAsync()
    {
        try
        {
            ViewData["Modules"] = (await _db.GetAsync<Module,
                ModuleDTO>(true)).ToSelectList("Id", "CourseAndModule");
            return Page();
        }
        catch
        {
            return RedirectToPage("/Index", new {
                alert = "You do not have access to this page." });
        }
    }
```

```csharp
    public async Task<IActionResult> OnPostAsync()
    {

        if (ModelState.IsValid)
        {
            var id = Input.ModuleId;
            Input.CourseId = (await _db.SingleAsync<Module, ModuleDTO>(
                s => s.Id.Equals(id))).CourseId;
            var succeeded = (await _db.CreateAsync<VideoDTO,
                Video>(Input)) > 0;

            if (succeeded)
            {
                // Message sent back to the Index Razor Page.
                Alert = $"Created a new Video: {Input.Title}.";

                return RedirectToPage("Index");
            }
        }

        // Something failed, redisplay the form.
        ViewData["Modules"] = (await _db.GetAsync<Module,
            ModuleDTO>(true)).ToSelectList("Id", "CourseAndModule");
        return Page();
    }
    #endregion
}
```

The Create Razor Page
1. Open the **Create** Razor Page in the *Videos* folder (the *.cshtml* file).
2. Change the **ViewData** title to *Add Video*.
3. Change the content in the **form-group** <div> elements to display the values from the properties in the **Input** variable. Add and remove **form-group** <div> elements as needed.
4. Replace the **Instructor, InstructorId,** and **Instructors** properties with **Module, ModuleId,** and **Modules** for the drop-down.
   ```html
   <div class="form-group">
       <label asp-for="Input.Module" class="control-label"></label>
       <select asp-for="Input.ModuleId" class="form-control"
           asp-items="ViewBag.Modules"></select>
   </div>
   ```

The complete code for the **Create** Razor Page:

```
@page
@model CreateModel
@inject SignInManager<VODUser> SignInManager
@{
    ViewData["Title"] = "Create a new video";
}

@if (SignInManager.IsSignedIn(User) && User.IsInRole("Admin"))
{
    <div class="row">
        <div class="col-md-8 offset-md-2">
            <h1>@ViewData["Title"]</h1>

            <partial name="_BackToIndexButtonsPartial" />
            <p></p>

            <form method="post">
                <div asp-validation-summary="All"
                    class="text-danger"></div>

                <div class="form-group">
                    <label asp-for="Input.Title"></label>
                    <input asp-for="Input.Title" class="form-control" />
                    <span asp-validation-for="Input.Title"
                        class="text-danger"></span>
                </div>
                <div class="form-group">
                    <label asp-for="Input.Description"></label>
                    <input asp-for="Input.Description"
                        class="form-control" />
                    <span asp-validation-for="Input.Description"
                        class="text-danger"></span>
                </div>
                <div class="form-group">
                    <label asp-for="Input.Duration"></label>
                    <input asp-for="Input.Duration"
                        class="form-control" />
                    <span asp-validation-for="Input.Duration"
                        class="text-danger"></span>
                </div>
                <div class="form-group">
                    <label asp-for="Input.Thumbnail"></label>
```

```html
                    <input asp-for="Input.Thumbnail"
                        class="form-control" />
                    <span asp-validation-for="Input.Thumbnail"
                        class="text-danger"></span>
                </div>
                <div class="form-group">
                    <label asp-for="Input.Url"></label>
                    <input asp-for="Input.Url" class="form-control" />
                    <span asp-validation-for="Input.Url"
                        class="text-danger"></span>
                </div>
                <div class="form-group">
                    <label asp-for="Input.Module"
                        class="control-label"></label>
                    <select asp-for="Input.ModuleId"
                        class="form-control"
                        asp-items="ViewBag.Modules"></select>
                </div>

                <button type="submit" class="btn btn-success">Create
                </button>
            </form>
        </div>
    </div>
}

@section Scripts {
    @await Html.PartialAsync("_ValidationScriptsPartial")
}
```

The EditModel Class

1. Open the **EditModel** class in the *Videos* folder (the *.cshtml.cs* file).
2. Change the namespace to **Videos**.
   `namespace VOD.Admin.Pages.Videos`

3. Replace all instances of the **Course** entity and the **CourseDTO** with **Video** and **VideoDTO**.
4. Rename the dynamic **Instructors** variable **Modules** and replace the **Instructor** and **InstructorDTO** with **Module** and **ModuleDTO** in both **OnGetAsync** and **OnPostAsync** methods.
   `ViewData["Modules"] = (await _db.GetAsync<Module, ModuleDTO>(true)).ToSelectList("Id", "CourseAndModule");`

5. Add two **int** parameters named **moduleId** and **courseId** to the **OnGetAsync** action.
6. Check the module id and course id in the Lambda expression and that the include parameter is **true** in the **SingleAsync** method call in the **OnGetAsync** action.
```
Input = await _db.SingleAsync<Video, VideoDTO>(s =>
    s.Id.Equals(id) && s.ModuleId.Equals(moduleId) &&
    s.CourseId.Equals(courseId), true);
```
7. Add a variable named **id** inside the **ModelState.IsValid** if-block and store the **Input.ModuleId** property value in it.
```
var id = Input.ModuleId;
```
8. Assign the course id from the fetched module to the **Input.CourseId** property above the **UpdateAsync** call in the **OnPostAsync**. This is necessary in case a different module has been selected in the **Modules** drop-down.
```
Input.CourseId = (await _db.SingleAsync<Module, ModuleDTO>(s =>
s.Id.Equals(id))).CourseId;
```
1. Replace the text in the **Alert** property with *Updated Video:* followed by the title of the video.
```
Alert = $"Updated Video: {Input.Title}.";
```
2. Save all files.

The complete code for the **EditModel** class:
```
[Authorize(Roles = "Admin")]
public class EditModel : PageModel
{
    #region Properties
    private readonly IAdminService _db;
    [BindProperty] public VideoDTO Input { get; set; } = new VideoDTO();
    [TempData] public string Alert { get; set; }
    #endregion

    #region Constructor
    public EditModel(IAdminService db)
    {
        _db = db;
    }
    #endregion
```

```csharp
#region Actions
public async Task<IActionResult> OnGetAsync(int id, int courseId,
int moduleId)
{
    try
    {
        ViewData["Modules"] = (await _db.GetAsync<Module,
            ModuleDTO>(true)).ToSelectList("Id", "CourseAndModule");
        Input = await _db.SingleAsync<Video, VideoDTO>(s =>
            s.Id.Equals(id) && s.ModuleId.Equals(moduleId) &&
            s.CourseId.Equals(courseId), true);
        return Page();
    }
    catch
    {
        return RedirectToPage("/Index", new {
            alert = "You do not have access to this page." });
    }
}

public async Task<IActionResult> OnPostAsync()
{
    if (ModelState.IsValid)
    {
        var id = Input.ModuleId;
        Input.CourseId = (await _db.SingleAsync<Module, ModuleDTO>(
            s => s.Id.Equals(id))).CourseId;
        var succeeded = await _db.UpdateAsync<VideoDTO,
            Video>(Input);

        if (succeeded) {
            // Message sent back to the Index Razor Page.
            Alert = $"Updated Video: {Input.Title}.";
            return RedirectToPage("Index");
        }
    }

    ViewData["Modules"] = (await _db.GetAsync<Module,
        ModuleDTO>(true)).ToSelectList("Id", "CourseAndModule");
    // Something failed, redisplay the form.
    return Page();
}
#endregion
}
```

The Edit Razor Page

1. Open the **Edit** Razor Page in the *Videos* folder (the *.cshtml* file).
2. Change the title to *Edit Video*.
3. Change the content in the **form-group** <div> elements to display the values from the properties in the **Input** variable. Add and remove **form-group** <div> elements as needed.
4. Replace the **Instructor**, **InstructorId**, and **Instructors** properties with **Module**, **ModuleId**, and **Modules** for the drop-down.

   ```
   <div class="form-group">
       <label asp-for="Input.Module" class="control-label"></label>
       <select asp-for="Input.ModuleId" class="form-control"
           asp-items="ViewBag.Modules"></select>
   </div>
   ```

5. Save all files.

The complete code for the **Edit** Razor Page:

```
@page
@model EditModel
@inject SignInManager<VODUser> SignInManager
@{
    ViewData["Title"] = "Edit Video";
}

@if (SignInManager.IsSignedIn(User) && User.IsInRole("Admin"))
{
    <div class="row">
        <div class="col-md-8 offset-md-2">
            <h1>@ViewData["Title"]</h1>

            <partial name="_BackToIndexButtonsPartial" />
            <p></p>

            <form method="post">
                <div asp-validation-summary="All"
                    class="text-danger"></div>

                <input type="hidden" asp-for="Input.Id" />

                <div class="form-group">
                    <label asp-for="Input.Title"></label>
                    <input asp-for="Input.Title" class="form-control" />
```

```html
            <span asp-validation-for="Input.Title"
                class="text-danger"></span>
        </div>
        <div class="form-group">
            <label asp-for="Input.Description"></label>
            <input asp-for="Input.Description"
                class="form-control" />
            <span asp-validation-for="Input.Description"
                class="text-danger"></span>
        </div>
        <div class="form-group">
            <label asp-for="Input.Duration"></label>
            <input asp-for="Input.Duration"
                class="form-control" />
            <span asp-validation-for="Input.Duration"
                class="text-danger"></span>
        </div>
        <div class="form-group">
            <label asp-for="Input.Thumbnail"></label>
            <input asp-for="Input.Thumbnail"
                class="form-control" />
            <span asp-validation-for="Input.Thumbnail"
                class="text-danger"></span>
        </div>
        <div class="form-group">
            <label asp-for="Input.Url"></label>
            <input asp-for="Input.Url" class="form-control" />
            <span asp-validation-for="Input.Url"
                class="text-danger"></span>
        </div>
        <div class="form-group">
            <label asp-for="Input.Course"
                class="control-label"></label>
            <input asp-for="Input.Course" readonly
                class="form-control" />
        </div>
        <div class="form-group">
            <label asp-for="Input.Module"
                class="control-label"></label>
            <select asp-for="Input.ModuleId"
                class="form-control"
                asp-items="ViewBag.Modules"></select>
        </div>
```

24. The Remaining Razor Pages

```
                <button type="submit" class="btn btn-success">Save
                </button>
            </form>
        </div>
    </div>
}

@section Scripts {
    @await Html.PartialAsync("_ValidationScriptsPartial")
}
```

The DeleteModel Class

1. Open the **DeleteModel** class in the *Videos* folder (the *.cshtml.cs* file).
2. Change the namespace to **Videos**.
   `namespace VOD.Admin.Pages.Videos`
3. Replace all instances of the **Course** entity and the **CourseDTO** with **Video** and **VideoDTO**.
4. Add **int** parameters named **courseId** and **moduleId** to the **OnGetAsync** action.
5. Add checks for the **ModuleId** and **CourseId** properties to the Lambda expression in the **SingleAsync** and **DeleteAsync** methods.
   `&& s.ModuleId.Equals(moduleId) && s.CourseId.Equals(courseId)`
6. Add variables named **id**, **moduleId** and **courseId** at the top of the **OnPostAsync** action and assign the respective property values from the **Input** object.
7. Replace the text in the **Alert** property to *Deleted Video:* followed by the title of the video.
   `Alert = $"Deleted Video: {Input.Title}.";`
8. Save all files.

The complete code for the **DeleteModel** class:

```
[Authorize(Roles = "Admin")]
public class DeleteModel : PageModel
{
    #region Properties
    private readonly IAdminService _db;
    [BindProperty] public VideoDTO Input { get; set; } = new VideoDTO();
    [TempData] public string Alert { get; set; }
    #endregion
```

```csharp
#region Constructor
public DeleteModel(IAdminService db)
{
    _db = db;
}
#endregion

#region Actions
public async Task<IActionResult> OnGet(int id, int courseId, 
int moduleId)
{
    try
    {
        Input = await _db.SingleAsync<Video, VideoDTO>(s =>
            s.Id.Equals(id) && s.ModuleId.Equals(moduleId) &&
            s.CourseId.Equals(courseId), true);
        return Page();
    }
    catch
    {
        return RedirectToPage("/Index", new {
            alert = "You do not have access to this page." });
    }
}

public async Task<IActionResult> OnPostAsync()
{
    int id = Input.Id, moduleId = Input.ModuleId,
        courseId = Input.CourseId;

    if (ModelState.IsValid)
    {
        var succeeded = await _db.DeleteAsync<Video>(s =>
            s.Id.Equals(id) && s.ModuleId.Equals(moduleId) &&
            s.CourseId.Equals(courseId));

        if (succeeded)
        {
            // Message sent back to the Index Razor Page.
            Alert = $"Deleted Video: {Input.Title}.";

            return RedirectToPage("Index");
        }
    }
```

```
        // Something failed, redisplay the form.
        Input = await _db.SingleAsync<Video, VideoDTO>(s =>
            s.Id.Equals(id) && s.ModuleId.Equals(moduleId) &&
            s.CourseId.Equals(courseId), true);

        return Page();
    }
    #endregion
}
```

The Delete Razor Page

1. Open the **Delete** Razor Page in the *Videos* folder (the *.cshtml* file).
2. Change the **ViewData** title to *Delete Video*.
3. Add a data list using <dl>, <dt>, and <dd> elements for the properties in the **Input** object above the <form> element.
4. Add a hidden <input> elements for the **Input.CourseId** and **Input.ModuleId** property values below the existing hidden <input> element.
   ```
   <input type="hidden" asp-for="Input.Id" />
   <input type="hidden" asp-for="Input.Title" />
   <input type="hidden" asp-for="Input.CourseId" />
   <input type="hidden" asp-for="Input.ModuleId" />
   ```
5. Save all files.
6. Start the Admin application and try the CRUD operations for the **Video** entity. Note the **Alert** messages.
7. Stop the application in Visual Studio.

The complete code for the **Delete** Razor Page:

```
@page
@model DeleteModel
@inject SignInManager<VODUser> SignInManager
@{ ViewData["Title"] = "Delete Video"; }

@if (SignInManager.IsSignedIn(User) && User.IsInRole("Admin"))
{
    <div class="row">
        <div class="col-md-8 offset-md-2">
            <h1>@ViewData["Title"]</h1>
```

```html
            <partial name="_DeletePageButtons"
                model="@Model.Input.ButtonDTO" />

            <p></p>
            <dl class="dl-horizontal">
                <dt>@Html.DisplayNameFor(model =>
                    model.Input.Title)</dt>
                <dd>@Html.DisplayFor(model => model.Input.Title)</dd>
                <dt>@Html.DisplayNameFor(model =>
                    model.Input.Description)</dt>
                <dd>@Html.DisplayFor(model =>
                    model.Input.Description)</dd>
                <dt>@Html.DisplayNameFor(model =>
                    model.Input.Duration)</dt>
                <dd>@Html.DisplayFor(model => model.Input.Duration)</dd>
                <dt>@Html.DisplayNameFor(model =>
                    model.Input.Thumbnail)</dt>
                <dd>@Html.DisplayFor(model =>
                    model.Input.Thumbnail)</dd>
                <dt>@Html.DisplayNameFor(model => model.Input.Url)</dt>
                <dd>@Html.DisplayFor(model => model.Input.Url)</dd>
                <dt>@Html.DisplayNameFor(model =>
                    model.Input.Course)</dt>
                <dd>@Html.DisplayFor(model => model.Input.Course)</dd>
                <dt>@Html.DisplayNameFor(model =>
                    model.Input.Module)</dt>
                <dd>@Html.DisplayFor(model => model.Input.Module)</dd>
            </dl>

            <form method="post">
                <div asp-validation-summary="All"
                    class="text-danger"></div>

                <input type="hidden" asp-for="Input.Id" />
                <input type="hidden" asp-for="Input.Title" />
                <input type="hidden" asp-for="Input.CourseId" />
                <input type="hidden" asp-for="Input.ModuleId" />

                <button type="submit" class="btn btn-danger">Delete
                </button>
            </form>
        </div>
    </div>
}
```

```
@section Scripts {
    @await Html.PartialAsync("_ValidationScriptsPartial")
}
```

The Downloads Razor Pages

1. Copy the *Videos* folder and all its contents.
2. Paste in the copied folder in the *Pages* folder and rename it *Downloads*.

The IndexModel Class

1. Open the **IndexModel** class in the *Downloads* folder (the *.cshtml.cs* file).
2. Change the namespace to **Downloads**.
   namespace VOD.Admin.Pages.Downloads
3. Replace all occurrences of the **Video** entity and the **VideoDTO** with **Download** and **DownloadDTO**.
4. Save all files.

The complete code for the **IndexModel** class:

```
[Authorize(Roles = "Admin")]
public class IndexModel : PageModel
{
    #region Properties
    private readonly IAdminService _db;
    public IEnumerable<DownloadDTO> Items = new List<DownloadDTO>();
    [TempData] public string Alert { get; set; }
    #endregion

    #region Constructor
    public IndexModel(IAdminService db)
    {
        _db = db;
    }
    #endregion
```

```
        public async Task<IActionResult> OnGetAsync()
        {
            try
            {
                Items = await _db.GetAsync<Download, DownloadDTO>(true);
                return Page();
            }
            catch
            {
                Alert = "You do not have access to this page.";
                return RedirectToPage("/Index");
            }
        }
    }
}
```

The Index Razor Page

1. Open the **Index** Razor Page in the *Downloads* folder (the *.cshtml* file).
2. Change the **ViewData** title to *Downloads*.
3. Change the headings in the <th> elements to match the property values of the entity. Add and remove <th> elements as needed.
   <th>Title</th>
   <th>Course</th>
   <th>Module</th>
   <th></th>
4. Remove the **description** variable and its corresponding <td> element in the **foreach** loop.
5. Change the <td> elements to display the values from the properties in the **item** loop variable. Add and remove <td> elements as needed.
6. Save all files.

The complete code for the **Index** Razor Page:

```
@page
@model IndexModel
@inject SignInManager<VODUser> SignInManager

@{ ViewData["Title"] = "Downloads"; }

@if (SignInManager.IsSignedIn(User) && User.IsInRole("Admin"))
{
```

```html
    <div class="row">
        <div class="col-md-10 offset-md-1"
            style="padding-left:0;padding-right:0;">
            <alert alert-type="success">@Model.Alert</alert>
        </div>
        <div class="col-md-1"></div>
    </div>

    <div class="row">
        <div class="col-md-10 offset-md-1">
            <h1>@ViewData["Title"]</h1>

            <partial name="_PageButtonsPartial" />

            <table style="margin-top:20px;" class="table">
                <thead>
                    <tr>
                        <th>Title</th>
                        <th>Course</th>
                        <th>Module</th>
                        <th></th>
                    </tr>
                </thead>
                <tbody>
                    @foreach (var item in Model.Items)
                    {
                    <tr>
                        <td>@Html.DisplayFor(modelItem =>
                            item.Title)</td>
                        <td>@Html.DisplayFor(modelItem =>
                            item.Course)</td>
                        <td>@Html.DisplayFor(modelItem =>
                            item.Module)</td>
                        <td style="min-width:100px;">
                            <partial name="_TableRowButtonsPartial"
                                model="@item.ButtonDTO" /></td>
                    </tr>
                    }
                </tbody>
            </table>
        </div>
        <div class="col-md-1"></div>
    </div>
}
```

The CreateModel Class

1. Open the **CreateModel** class in the *Downloads* folder (the *.cshtml.cs* file).
2. Change the namespace to **Downloads**.
   `namespace VOD.Admin.Pages.Downloads`
3. Replace all occurrences of the **Video** entity and the **VideoDTO** with **Download** and **DownloadDTO**.
4. Change the text in the **Alert** property to *Created a new Download:* followed by the title of the download.
   `Alert = $"Created a new Download: {Input.Title}.";`
5. Save all files.

The complete code for the **CreateModel** class:

```
[Authorize(Roles = "Admin")]
public class CreateModel : PageModel
{
    #region Properties
    private readonly IAdminService _db;
    [BindProperty] public DownloadDTO Input { get; set; } =
        new DownloadDTO();
    [TempData] public string Alert { get; set; }
    #endregion

    #region Constructor
    public CreateModel(IAdminService db)
    {
        _db = db;
    }
    #endregion

    #region Actions
    public async Task<IActionResult> OnGetAsync()
    {
        try
        {
            ViewData["Modules"] = (await _db.GetAsync<Module,
                ModuleDTO>(true)).ToSelectList("Id", "CourseAndModule");
            return Page();
        }
```

```csharp
        catch
        {
            return RedirectToPage("/Index", new {
                alert = "You do not have access to this page." });
        }
    }

    public async Task<IActionResult> OnPostAsync()
    {
        if (ModelState.IsValid)
        {
            var id = Input.ModuleId;
            Input.CourseId = (await _db.SingleAsync<Module, ModuleDTO>(
                s => s.Id.Equals(id) && s.CourseId.Equals(0))).CourseId;
            var succeeded = (await _db.CreateAsync<DownloadDTO,
                Download>(Input)) > 0;

            if (succeeded)
            {
                // Message sent back to the Index Razor Page.
                Alert = $"Created a new Download: {Input.Title}.";

                return RedirectToPage("Index");
            }
        }

        // Something failed, redisplay the form.
        ViewData["Modules"] = (await _db.GetAsync<Module,
            ModuleDTO>(true)).ToSelectList("Id", "CourseAndModule");
        return Page();
    }
    #endregion
}
```

The Create Razor Page

1. Open the **Create** Razor Page in the *Downloads* folder (the *.cshtml* file).
2. Change the **ViewData** title to *Create Download*.
3. Change the content in the **form-group** <div> elements to display the values from the properties in the **Input** variable. Add and remove **form-group** <div> elements as needed.
4. Save all files.

The complete code for the **Create** Razor Page:

```
@page
@model CreateModel
@inject SignInManager<VODUser> SignInManager
@{
    ViewData["Title"] = "Create Download";
}

@if (SignInManager.IsSignedIn(User) && User.IsInRole("Admin"))
{
    <div class="row">
        <div class="col-md-8 offset-md-2">
            <h1>@ViewData["Title"]</h1>

            <partial name="_BackToIndexButtonsPartial" />
            <p></p>

            <form method="post">
                <div asp-validation-summary="All"
                    class="text-danger"></div>

                <div class="form-group">
                    <label asp-for="Input.Title"></label>
                    <input asp-for="Input.Title" class="form-control" />
                    <span asp-validation-for="Input.Title"
                        class="text-danger"></span>
                </div>
                <div class="form-group">
                    <label asp-for="Input.Url"></label>
                    <input asp-for="Input.Url" class="form-control" />
                    <span asp-validation-for="Input.Url"
                        class="text-danger"></span>
                </div>
                <div class="form-group">
                    <label asp-for="Input.Module"
                        class="control-label"></label>
                    <select asp-for="Input.ModuleId"
                        class="form-control"
                        asp-items="ViewBag.Modules"></select>
                </div>

                <button type="submit" class="btn btn-success">Create
                </button>
```

```
            </form>
        </div>
    </div>
}

@section Scripts {
    @await Html.PartialAsync("_ValidationScriptsPartial")
}
```

The EditModel Class

1. Open the **EditModel** class in the *Downloads* folder (the *.cshtml.cs* file).
2. Change the namespace to **Downloads**.
   `namespace VOD.Admin.Pages.Downloads`
3. Replace all occurrences of the **Video** entity and the **VideoDTO** with **Download** and **DownloadDTO**.
4. Replace the text in the **Alert** property to *Updated Download:* followed by the title of the download.
   `Alert = $"Updated Download: {Input.Title}.";`
5. Save all files.

The complete code for the **EditModel** class:

```
[Authorize(Roles = "Admin")]
public class EditModel : PageModel
{
    #region Properties
    private readonly IAdminService _db;
    [BindProperty] public DownloadDTO Input { get; set; } =
        new DownloadDTO();
    [TempData] public string Alert { get; set; }
    #endregion

    #region Constructor
    public EditModel(IAdminService db)
    {
        _db = db;
    }
    #endregion
```

```csharp
#region Actions
public async Task<IActionResult> OnGetAsync(int id, int courseId, 
int moduleId)
{
    try
    {
        ViewData["Modules"] = (await _db.GetAsync<Module, 
            ModuleDTO>(true)).ToSelectList("Id", "CourseAndModule");
        Input = await _db.SingleAsync<Download, DownloadDTO>(s =>
            s.Id.Equals(id) && s.ModuleId.Equals(moduleId) &&
            s.CourseId.Equals(courseId), true);
        return Page();
    }
    catch
    {
        return RedirectToPage("/Index", new {
            alert = "You do not have access to this page." });
    }
}

public async Task<IActionResult> OnPostAsync()
{
    if (ModelState.IsValid)
    {
        var id = Input.ModuleId;
        Input.CourseId = (await _db.SingleAsync<Module, ModuleDTO>(
            s => s.Id.Equals(id) && s.CourseId.Equals(0))).CourseId;
        var succeeded = await _db.UpdateAsync<DownloadDTO, 
            Download>(Input);

        if (succeeded)
        {
            // Message sent back to the Index Razor Page.
            Alert = $"Updated Download: {Input.Title}.";

            return RedirectToPage("Index");
        }
    }

    // Something failed, redisplay the form.
    // Reload the modules when the page is reloaded
    ViewData["Modules"] = (await _db.GetAsync<Module, 
        ModuleDTO>(true)).ToSelectList("Id", "CourseAndModule");
```

```
            return Page();
        }
        #endregion
}
```

The Edit Razor Page

1. Open the **Edit** Razor Page in the *Downloads* folder (the *.cshtml* file).
2. Change the **ViewData** title to *Edit Download*.
3. Change and remove the **form-group** <div> elements' contents to match the properties in the **Input** object.
4. Save all files.

The complete code for the **Edit** Razor Page:

```
@page
@model EditModel
@inject SignInManager<VODUser> SignInManager
@{
    ViewData["Title"] = "Edit Download";
}

@if (SignInManager.IsSignedIn(User) && User.IsInRole("Admin"))
{
    <div class="row">
        <div class="col-md-8 offset-md-2">
            <h1>@ViewData["Title"]</h1>

            <partial name="_BackToIndexButtonsPartial" />
            <p></p>

            <form method="post">
                <div asp-validation-summary="All"
                     class="text-danger"></div>

                <input type="hidden" asp-for="Input.Id" />

                <div class="form-group">
                    <label asp-for="Input.Title"></label>
                    <input asp-for="Input.Title" class="form-control" />
                    <span asp-validation-for="Input.Title"
                          class="text-danger"></span>
                </div>
```

```html
                <div class="form-group">
                    <label asp-for="Input.Url"></label>
                    <input asp-for="Input.Url" class="form-control" />
                    <span asp-validation-for="Input.Url"
                        class="text-danger"></span>
                </div>
                <div class="form-group">
                    <label asp-for="Input.Course"
                        class="control-label"></label>
                    <input asp-for="Input.Course" readonly
                        class="form-control" />
                </div>
                <div class="form-group">
                    <label asp-for="Input.Module"
                        class="control-label"></label>
                    <select asp-for="Input.ModuleId"
                        class="form-control"
                        asp-items="ViewBag.Modules"></select>
                </div>

                <button type="submit" class="btn btn-success">Save
                </button>
            </form>
        </div>
    </div>
}

@section Scripts {
    @await Html.PartialAsync("_ValidationScriptsPartial")
}
```

The DeleteModel Class

1. Open the **DeleteModel** class in the *Downloads* folder (the *.cshtml.cs* file).
2. Change the namespace to **Downloads**.
   `namespace VOD.Admin.Pages.Downloads`

3. Replace all occurrences of the **Video** entity and the **VideoDTO** with **Download** and **DownloadDTO**.
4. Replace the text in the **Alert** property to *Deleted Download:* followed by the title of the download.
   `Alert = $"Deleted Download: {Input.Title}.";`

5. Save all files.

24. The Remaining Razor Pages

The complete code for the **DeleteModel** class:

```
[Authorize(Roles = "Admin")]
public class DeleteModel : PageModel
{
    #region Properties
    private readonly IAdminService _db;
    [BindProperty] public DownloadDTO Input { get; set; } =
        new DownloadDTO();
    [TempData] public string Alert { get; set; }
    #endregion

    #region Constructor
    public DeleteModel(IAdminService db)
    {
        _db = db;
    }
    #endregion

    #region Actions
    public async Task<IActionResult> OnGetAsync(int id, int courseId,
    int moduleId)
    {
        try
        {
            Input = await _db.SingleAsync<Download, DownloadDTO>(s =>
                s.Id.Equals(id) && s.ModuleId.Equals(moduleId) &&
                s.CourseId.Equals(courseId), true);
            return Page();
        }
        catch
        {
            return RedirectToPage("/Index", new {
                alert = "You do not have access to this page." });
        }
    }

    public async Task<IActionResult> OnPostAsync()
    {
        int id = Input.Id, moduleId = Input.ModuleId,
            courseId = Input.CourseId;
```

```csharp
            if (ModelState.IsValid)
            {
                var succeeded = await _db.DeleteAsync<Download>(s =>
                    s.Id.Equals(id) && s.ModuleId.Equals(moduleId) &&
                    s.CourseId.Equals(courseId));

                if (succeeded)
                {
                    // Message sent back to the Index Razor Page.
                    Alert = $"Deleted Download: {Input.Title}.";

                    return RedirectToPage("Index");
                }
            }

            // Something failed, redisplay the form.
            Input = await _db.SingleAsync<Download, DownloadDTO>(s =>
                s.Id.Equals(id) && s.ModuleId.Equals(moduleId) &&
                s.CourseId.Equals(courseId), true);

            return Page();
        }
        #endregion
}
```

The Delete Razor Page

1. Open the **Delete** Razor Page in the *Downloads* folder (the *.cshtml* file).
2. Change the **ViewData** title to *Delete Download*.
3. Remove the **description** variable.
4. Change the contents of the <dd> and <dt> elements to match the properties in the **Input** object.
5. Save all files.
6. Start the **Admin** application and try the CRUD operations for the **Download** entity. Note the **Alert** messages.
7. Stop the application in Visual Studio.

The complete code for the **Delete** Razor Page:

```
@page
@model DeleteModel
@inject SignInManager<VODUser> SignInManager
@{ ViewData["Title"] = "Delete Download"; }

@if (SignInManager.IsSignedIn(User) && User.IsInRole("Admin"))
{
    <div class="row">
        <div class="col-md-8 offset-md-2">
            <h1>@ViewData["Title"]</h1>

            <partial name="_DeletePageButtons"
             model="@Model.Input.ButtonDTO" />

            <p></p>

            <dl class="dl-horizontal">
                <dt>@Html.DisplayNameFor(model => model.Input.Title)</dt>
                <dd>@Html.DisplayFor(model => model.Input.Title)</dd>
                <dt>@Html.DisplayNameFor(model => model.Input.Url)</dt>
                <dd>@Html.DisplayFor(model => model.Input.Url)</dd>
                <dt>@Html.DisplayNameFor(model => model.Input.Course)</dt>
                <dd>@Html.DisplayFor(model => model.Input.Course)</dd>
                <dt>@Html.DisplayNameFor(model => model.Input.Module)</dt>
                <dd>@Html.DisplayFor(model => model.Input.Module)</dd>
            </dl>

            <form method="post">
                <div asp-validation-summary="All"
                     class="text-danger"></div>

                <input type="hidden" asp-for="Input.Id" />
                <input type="hidden" asp-for="Input.Title" />
                <input type="hidden" asp-for="Input.CourseId" />
                <input type="hidden" asp-for="Input.ModuleId" />

                <button type="submit" class="btn btn-danger">Delete</button>
            </form>
        </div>
    </div>
}

@section Scripts {
    @await Html.PartialAsync("_ValidationScriptsPartial")
}
```

Summary

In this chapter, you implemented the rest of the Razor Pages needed in the administration application by reusing already created Razor Pages.

In the next section of the book, you will implement an API that you will call from the **Admin** project with **HttpClient** from the Razor Pages. Then you will secure the API with JSON Web Tokens (JWT).

Part 3:
API, HttpClient & JWT
How to Build and Secure an API

25. The API Project

Overview

In this chapter, you will create an API project with controllers that will communicate with the **AdminEFService** through the **IAdminService** interface injected through their constructors. You will then implement CRUD operations in the controllers by adding **Get**, **Put**, **Post**, and **Delete** actions that call methods in the **AdminEFService**.

Because the controllers all implement the same methods for different entities and they call the same generic methods, it will be very easy to copy the first controller as a template for the others and replace the entity and DTO classes. The exception is the **User** entity that uses the **UserService** service to perform its CRUD operations.

As an aside, in a real-world scenario, you probably wouldn't implement the creation of user accounts entirely in this fashion because it has security implications; here we do it to show how to use different services and to make all the menu links work in the **Admin** project. In an upcoming chapter, you will learn how to use JSON Web Tokens (JWTs) to better secure the back-end with authentication and authorization.

DTOs will transfer data between the API back-end and Admin front-end, and AutoMapper is used to transform the data from DTO to Entity and vice versa. Each entity has one DTO.

Technologies Used in This Chapter
1. **API** – The ASP.NET Core 2.2 API template that creates the API project.
2. **C#** – To write code in the Razor Pages code-behind methods.
3. **Services** – To communicate with the database.
4. **AutoMapper** – To map and transform data between types.
5. **Entity framework** – To perform CRUD operations in the database.

What Is HTTP, Response and Request?
The new Web API uses the same MVC framework as MVC applications. The controllers can answer requests for APIs and web pages. The API that you will create communicates over the HyperText Transfer Protocol (HTTP or HTTPS).

A Request sent over HTTP(S) contains three parts: a *verb* (what you want to do), *headers* (additional information), and *content* if any. The *verb* corresponds with the type of action you want to take; for instance, **Get**, **Put**, **Post**, and **Delete**. The headers can contain the length of the content and other information. Whether content is present or not is determined by the type of action you take; deleting an item does not require any information to be sent with the request since all information is available in the URL.

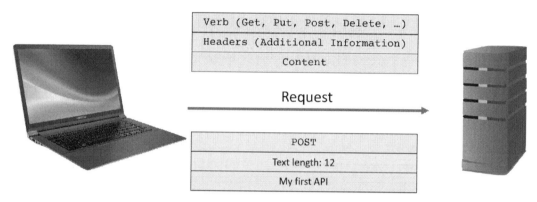

When the server completes its operation, a response is sent back, with a similar structure to the request; it has a *status code* that signals if the operation was successful or not, *headers* and *content* that may include information. In the image below the response returns with a status code of 201, which means that the API could create the item successfully. The content type *Text* specifies that text is being sent back with the response, and the content (body) of the message contains the text that was created and returned.

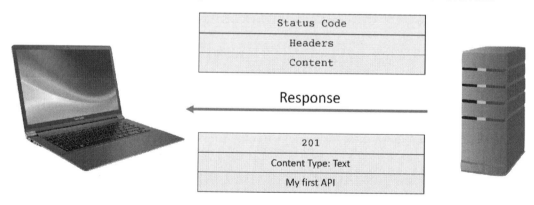

The API builds on top of this, so it is important to understand it. The main idea is that the server is stateless, which means that it doesn't maintain a constant connection and every request is a single roundtrip call. You will have to send all the information needed to complete a request within the header and content with every API call.

25. The API Project

When you make an API call, you need to provide a *verb* that specifies your intentions, what you want the server to do. The most common are: **Get**, which retrieves a resource, which can be a JSON file, an Entity Framework entity, or some other data; **Post**, which creates a new resource on the server; **Put**, which updates an entire existing resource that has been fetched earlier and now contains changes; **Patch**, which updates parts of an existing resource through a JSON Patch Document, sending only the changed data in the request; and **Delete**, which removes an existing resource. There are many more verbs that won't be covered in this chapter because they don't have any function in the API you are building.

We have talked about resources, but what are they? A resource can be a person, invoices, payments, products, and other things that can be represented by objects in the system, like entities and DTOs, that can be fetched, added, updated, and deleted.

Often, a resource is part of a context. That resource could be a single entity, like a person, but it could also be an invoice with related invoice items (an invoice without items doesn't make sense). So, keep in mind that a resource is not always a single entity. If you want to dig into this in more detail, you can look at Domain Driven Design (DDD).

The URIs are paths to the resources in your system, e.g., *api.yourserver.com/courses*. A query string transport a non-data element, such as a flag that specifies how many objects to return in a pagination scenario, or It could be a search string.

In this chapter, you will expand on what you have built in previous chapters and add an API that performs CRUD operations on the entities in the database. To achieve this, you will use services that you already have created and the Postman tool. In an upcoming chapter, you will use **HttpClient** to call the API from the Razor Pages in the **Admin** project.

Status Codes

To distinguish between successful and unsuccessful requests, the response that is sent back from the server as a result of your call will contain a status code. Status codes in the 200 range signals that the request was successful. Status codes in the 400 range signals that you made an error when making the request. Status codes in the 500 range signals that the server failed to fulfill your request. The table below shows the most common status codes. The ones that you really should pay attention to are **200 OK** (the request was successful); **201 Created** (the API created the resource); **400 Bad Request** (something was wrong with the request; a bad URI, for instance); **401 Unauthorized** (you are not logged in); **403 Forbidden** (you are logged in, but are not permitted to access the resource); **404**

Not Found (the resource isn't available); and **500 Internal Error** (The server could not fulfill the request, perhaps due to database failure).

Code	Description	Code	Description
200	OK	400	Bad Request
201	Created	401	Not Authorized
202	Accepted	403	Forbidden
302	Found	404	Not Found
304	Not Modified	405	Method Not Allowed
307	Temp. Redirect	409	Conflict
308	Perm. Redirect	500	Internal Error

Traditionally you returned these status codes from your API by wrapping the response in one of the built-in methods; this is still possible, but as you will see shortly, this is not necessary.

By adding the **[ApiController]** attribute to the controller class, you specify that this is an API controller that won't return HTML views or pages. One benefit of using this attribute is that it automatically performs data binding from the data in the body of the request to the receiving action's parameter data type, which means that you don't have to add the **[FromBody]** attribute to the parameters in the actions. If the body contains data that doesn't correspond to a property in the receiving type, that data will be ignored and lost.

When creating the action methods that receive the request and generate the response, you should decorate them with the appropriate verb attribute (even though it isn't strictly necessary in all scenarios, it is good practice). The most common attributes are: **HttpGet**, **HttpPost**, **HttpPut**, **HttpPatch**, and **HttpDelete**. Action methods can be named whatever you like if you apply the correct attributes to them. By studying the code below, you can glean that it is the method, not the class, that is the endpoint where the request ends up; a URI could be *http://localhost:6600/api/courses*; note that you don't add the name of the action method because the associated verb implies it.

The Route attribute can contain the name of the controller, or you can use square brackets to infer the controller's name from the class name.

25. The API Project

[Route("api/[controller]")].

By using **ActionResult<T>** instead of **IActionResult**, which is a commonly used return type, the API can reveal the data type the method is returning; use this with documentation tools to show the API's capabilities. Another benefit is that wrapping the response data with the **Ok** method no longer is necessary. ActionResult will infer the status code *200 OK* when the return type matches the generic data type; in other words, the returned object has the same type as the method's data type.

```
[Route("api/videos")]
[ApiController]
public class VideosController : ControllerBase
{
    [HttpPost]
    public async Task<ActionResult<VideoDTO>> Post(VideoDTO model)
    {
        try
        {
            if (model == null)
                return BadRequest("No entity provided");

            var course = await _db.GetAsync<Course>(model.CourseId);
            if (course == null)
                return NotFound("Could not find related entity");

            var entity = await _db.CreateAsync<VideoDTO>(model);
            if (entity == null)
                return BadRequest("Unable to add the entity");

            return Created(uri, entity);
        }
        catch
        {
            return StatusCode(StatusCodes.Status500InternalServerError,
                "Failed to add the entity");
        }
    }
}
```

What Is REST?

REST stands for *Representation State Transfer*, which means that the client data and server data should be separate from one another. It also means that the requests to the server are stateless and close the connection with every call. Cache requests for better performance, and use URIs to reach the server API. (You can read more about REST in Roy Fielding's doctoral dissertation that introduced the concept.)

There are possible problems with REST. One is that it is too difficult to adhere to REST completely; there is a dogma around it where some developers condemn APIs that are not 100% RESTful. Most developers adhere to the more pragmatic thought around REST — that it should be implemented to suit the goals of the project. It would be very cumbersome and time-consuming to build a completely RESTful API for every small application you create, where only a subset of REST is necessary. Most projects require you to be productive and move the project forward, not to be rigid and implement REST completely when it isn't needed or warranted.

Building a completely RESTful system can make it more maintainable in the long run, but the adherence to a principle versus the job you must do can make it backfire. To me, it's more important to use the necessary parts of REST such as statelessness, caching, and other things we have talked about than to implement it fully. Not everyone agrees with me on this.

Designing URIs

When you build the API, you should consider how to design the URIs. You can append a query string with a question mark after the URI.

Examples:

http://localhost:6600/api/courses/1/modules/2/videos
http://localhost:6600/api/courses/1/modules/2/videos/3
http://localhost:6600/api/courses/1/modules/2/videos/3?include=true

There is a relationship between the resource and the verb you use. Let's use the */Courses* endpoint as an example. When using the **Get** (read) verb with that endpoint, a list of all courses is sent back in the response. Use **Post** (create) to create a new resource. Use **Put** (update) to perform a batch update that updates several resources at the same time. Use **Delete** to delete a resource; you shouldn't be able to delete all resources with one request.

25. The API Project

Let's see what happens when we target a single item endpoint like */Courses/123*. **Get** (read) fetches the resource identified by the id *123* and sends it back in the response; **Post** (create) should return an error because it isn't possible to create a new resource while targeting an already existing resource; **Put** (update) updates the targeted resource; **Delete** removes the targeted resource from the data source.

The following table shows what should happen when sending a request.

Resource	Get (read)	Post (create)	Put (update)	Delete (remove)
/Courses	Get list	Create resource	Update Many	Remove Resource
/Courses/123	Get item	Error	Update item	Remove item

The following table shows what the response should contain (the returned data). Note that when making an update to a single resource, you can either send the updated item back with the response or only send back the status code; the reasoning is that the client already has all the updated information because it came to the API endpoint from the client.

Resource	Get (read)	Post (create)	Put (update)	Delete (remove)
/Courses	200 – OK A list of items	201 – Created The new item	400 – Bad Request No data	400 – Bad Request No data
/Courses/123	200 – OK A single item	400 – Bad Request No data	200 – OK The updated item/ status code only	200 – OK No data

The LinkGenerator Class

When building a RESTful API, you should return a link to the newly created resource within the response headers. In previous versions of ASP.NET Core, there wasn't an easy way to do this, and it often resulted in hard-coded strings for the URIs. In ASP.NET Core 2.2 and onward, you can inject a class named **LinkGenerator** into the controller's constructor and call one of the **Get** methods to generate the link from existing data, such as the controller name, the name of the **Get** action that fetches a single resource, and the id of the created resource. The **Created** method in the **Post** action returns the link with the new resource by adding it to the response headers.

```
var uri = _linkGenerator.GetPathByAction("Get", "Videos", new { id = id });
return Created(uri, entity);
```

Postman

In this chapter, you will use a tool called Postman to send raw HTTP requests to the API; in the next chapter, you will use **HttpClient** to call the API from the **Admin** UI.

You can download Postman at https://www.getpostman.com. It's a Chrome app, so it should work on any platform where ASP.NET Core works.

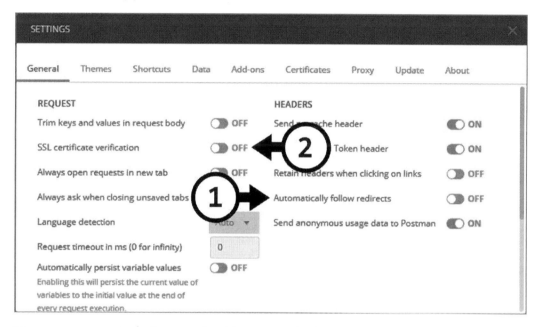

There are two settings that you should temporarily shut off when testing this API. The first is **SSL certificate verification**, which stops Postman from requesting an SSL certificate when calling over HTTPS; the second is **Automatically follow redirects**, which stops the API's routing system from redirecting to and displaying an error or login page. You find the settings under the **File-Settings** menu option.

To make it easier to call the API, you should assign a memorable port number for the API project in its settings in Visual Studio; you will do this when you create the **VOD.API** project.

25. The API Project

1. Open/close the history panel.
2. Request tabs. Click the **+** to add a new tab.
3. Select the *verb* you want to use when calling the API.
4. Enter the URI and query parameters here.
5. Click the **Body** tab and select the appropriate format of the body data (for this API, it will be the **Raw** option and **JSON** in the drop-down to the right of the options). Enter the JSON data in the text area below the toolbar.
6. Click the **Send** button to send the request to the API.
7. The response *status code* is displayed here. To inspect the response headers, you can click the **Headers** tab on the same toolbar.
8. The response area shows any returned data.

Adding the API Project

Adding the AutoMapper service changed with the release version 6.1.0 of the **AutoMapper.Extensions.Microsoft.DependencyInjection** NuGet package. In earlier versions, you called the **AddAutoMapper** method on the **service** object in the **ConfigureServices** method in the **Startup** class; in the 6.1.0 version, you pass in the mapped types to the **AddAutoMapper** method.

Example (6.0.0):
services.AddAutoMapper();

Example (6.1.0):
services.AddAutoMapper(typeof(Startup), typeof(Instructor), typeof(Course), typeof(Module), typeof(Video), typeof(Download));

1. Right click on the **Solution** node in the Solution Explorer and select **Add-New Project**.
2. Select the **ASP.NET Core Web Application** template and click the **Next** button.
3. Name the project *VOD.API* and click the **Create** button.
4. Select **.NET Core** and **ASP.NET Core 2.2** in the drop-downs.
5. Select the **API** project template and click the **Create** button.
6. Open the Project settings.
    a. Right click on the project's node in the Solution Explorer.
    b. Select the **Properties** option in the context menu.
    c. Click on the **Debug** tab to the left in the dialog.
    d. Change the URL in the App URL field to a memorable value, for instance, *6600*.
    e. Uncheck the **Enable SLL** option (don't forget to check it when you go to production).
    f. Above the URL settings, uncheck the **Launch Browser** option to keep Visual Studio from opening the browser when the **API** project starts.

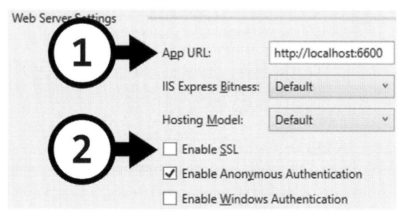

25. The API Project

7. Delete the *ValuesController.cs* file.
8. Add the **AutoMapper.Extensions.Microsoft.DependencyInjection** NuGet package to the **API** project.
9. Add a reference to the **Common** and **Database** projects.
10. Add the necessary service for handling database calls.
    ```
    services.AddDbContext<VODContext>(options =>
        options.UseSqlServer(
            Configuration.GetConnectionString("DefaultConnection")));
    ```
11. Add the necessary service to handle users and identity, such as roles.
    ```
    services.AddDefaultIdentity<VODUser>()
        .AddRoles<IdentityRole>()
        .AddEntityFrameworkStores<VODContext>();
    ```
12. Add a connection string that point to the database you created earlier in the *appsettings.json* file. You can copy it from one of the UI projects. Write the connection string on a single line.
    ```
    "ConnectionStrings": {
        "DefaultConnection":
            "Server=(localdb)\\mssqllocaldb;Database=VOD;
            Trusted_Connection=True;MultipleActiveResultSets=true"
    }
    ```
13. Open the **Startup** class and add the following services to the **ConfigureServices** method. The **IDbReadService** and **IDbWriteService** services are needed because the **AdminEFService** depend on them. The **IUserService** service will handle requests for user data. The **AddAutoMapper** method adds the AutoMapper service that is needed to map between types. Note that you need to pass in the type of the **Startup** class to the **AddAutoMapper** method if you use version 6.1.0 or greater of the **AutoMapper.Extensions.Microsoft.DependencyInjection** NuGet package.
    ```
    //services.AddAutoMapper(); // Version 6.0.0
    services.AddAutoMapper(typeof(Startup), typeof(Instructor),
        typeof(Course), typeof(Module), typeof(Video),
        typeof(Download)); // Version 6.1.0
    services.AddScoped<IDbReadService, DbReadService>();
    services.AddScoped<IDbWriteService, DbWriteService>();
    services.AddScoped<IAdminService, AdminEFService>();
    services.AddScoped<IUserService, UserService>();
    ```
14. Save the file and close the tab.

15. Right click on the **API** project in the Solution Explorer and select **Set as StartUp Project**.
16. Close and reopen the solution in Visual Studio.

Adding the Instructors Controller

The **Instructor** controller will handle requests for data related to instructors from the database using the **IAdminService** injected with an object from the **AdminEFService** class. In ASP.NET Core 2.2, the recommended way to create URI links is to inject the **LinkGenerator** into the constructor and call one of its **GetPathByXYZ** or **GetUriByXYZ** methods.

1. Add a new class named **InstructorsController** to the **Controllers** folder.
2. Add a constructor and Inject the **IAdminService** service and the **LinkGenerator** class into it. Store the injected objects in read-only class-level variables named **_db** and **_linkGenerator**.
3. Inherit the **ControllerBase** class and decorate the class with the **[ApiController]** attribute to specify that it is an API controller.
4. Add a **Route** attribute to specify the request Uri.
   ```
   [Route("api/instructors")]
   [ApiController]
   public class InstructorsController : ControllerBase
   ```

The code in the **InstructorsController** class so far:

```
[Route("api/instructors")]
[ApiController]
public class InstructorsController : ControllerBase
{
    #region Properties and Variables
    private readonly IAdminService _db;
    private readonly LinkGenerator _linkGenerator;
    #endregion
    #region Constructor
    public InstructorsController(IAdminService db, LinkGenerator
    linkGenerator)
    {
        _db = db;
        _linkGenerator = linkGenerator;
    }
    #endregion
}
```

Adding the Get Action Method

The **Get** action method should return a list of instructors, and if the Boolean **include** parameter is **true,** then its navigation properties should be filled. To be able to return status codes with the data, the return type should be **ActionResult**. Because the methods in the **IAdminService** are asynchronous, the **Get** method should return the **ActionResult** and the data as a **Task**. You can return the data without wrapping it in the **Ok** method by using a generic **ActionResult** with the correct data type; the data is assumed to be correct if it matches the data type.

The action methods should either return or receive objects of the **InstructorDTO** class because we don't want to use the entities directly.

1. Add a method named **Get** with a Boolean parameter named **include** with a default value of **false** to the class. Because the method calls other asynchronous methods, it should be decorated with the **async** keyword and return a **Task**. The task should wrap an **ActionResult<List<InstructorDTO>>**.
   ```
   [HttpGet()]
   public async Task<ActionResult<List<InstructorDTO>>> Get(bool include = false) { }
   ```

2. Add a try/catch-block to the method and return a *500 Internal Server Error* status code in the catch-block.
   ```
   return StatusCode(StatusCodes.Status500InternalServerError,
   "Database Failure");
   ```

3. In the try-block, return the result from calling the **GetAsync** method in the **IAdminService** instance with the **include** parameter's value. Specify the **Instructor** entity as the **TSource** type, and the **InstructorDTO** class as the **TDestination** type; **TDestination** determines the method's return type.
   ```
   return await _db.GetAsync<Instructor, InstructorDTO>(include);
   ```
4. Start the **API** application.
5. Start **Postman** and open a new tab.
6. Select the **Get** action in the drop-down to the left of the URI field.
7. Enter the *http://localhost:6600/api/instructors* URI into the text field and click the **Send** button.

Example of returned data from the **Get** action method:

```
[
    {
        "id": 1,
        "name": "John Doe",
        "description": "t amet, consectetur adipiscing elit",
        "thumbnail": "/images/Ice-Age-Scrat-icon.png",
        "buttonDTO": {
            "courseId": 0,
            "moduleId": 0,
            "id": 1,
            "userId": null,
            "itemId": "1"
        }
    },
    {
        "id": 2,
        "name": "Jane Doe",
        "description": "nsectetur adipiscing elit, sed do",
        "thumbnail": "/images/Ice-Age-Scrat-icon.png",
        "buttonDTO": {
            "courseId": 0,
            "moduleId": 0,
            "id": 2,
            "userId": null,
            "itemId": "2"
        }
    }
]
```

The complete code for the **Get** action method:

```
[HttpGet()]
public async Task<ActionResult<List<InstructorDTO>>> Get(bool include = false)
{
    try
    {
        return await _db.GetAsync<Instructor, InstructorDTO>(include);
    }
    catch
    {
        return StatusCode(StatusCodes.Status500InternalServerError,
```

```
        "Database Failure");
    }
}
```

Adding the Get Action Method for a Single Instructor

The **Get** action method should return a single instructor, and if the Boolean **include** parameter is **true,** then its navigation properties should be filled. The method must have an **id** parameter of type **int** because it returns a single instructor.

The methods should return a **Task<ActionResult<InstructorDTO>>**.

1. Copy the previous **Get** action method and paste in the copied code.
2. Change the return data type to **Task<ActionResult<InstructorDTO>>**.
3. Specify that the parameter is named **id** and is of type **int** in the **HttpGet** attribute.
   `[HttpGet("{id:int}")]`
4. Add an **int** parameter named **id**.
5. Delete the code in the try-block.
6. Call the **SingleAsync** method in the **IAdminService** and use a Lambda expression to pass in the **id**. Also, pass in the **include** parameter. Store the result in a variable named **dto**.
   `var dto = await _db.SingleAsync<Instructor, InstructorDTO>(s => s.Id.Equals(id), include);`
7. Return *404 Not Found* if EF can't find the instructor in the database.
   `if (dto == null) return NotFound();`
8. Return the instructor below the if-statement.
9. Start the **API** application.
10. Open a new tab in **Postman**.
11. Select the **Get** action in the drop-down to the left of the URI field.
12. Enter the *http://localhost:6600/api/instructors/1* URI, using one of the ids you got in the previous get, into the text field and click the **Send** button.

ASP.NET Core 2.2 MVC, Razor Pages, API, JSON Web Tokens & HttpClient

Example of returned data from the **Get** action method:

```
{
    "id": 1,
    "name": "John Doe",
    "description": "t amet, consectetur adipiscing elit",
    "thumbnail": "/images/Ice-Age-Scrat-icon.png",
    "buttonDTO": {
        "courseId": 0,
        "moduleId": 0,
        "id": 1,
        "userId": null,
        "itemId": "1"
    }
}
```

The complete code for the **Get** action method:

```
[HttpGet("{id:int}")]
public async Task<ActionResult<InstructorDTO>> Get(int id, bool include = false)
{
    try
    {
        var dto = await _db.SingleAsync<Instructor, InstructorDTO>(
            s => s.Id.Equals(id), include);

        if (dto == null) return NotFound();

        return dto;
    }
    catch
    {
        return StatusCode(StatusCodes.Status500InternalServerError,
            "Database Failure");
    }
}
```

Adding the Post Action Method

This **Post** action method should add a single instructor and return it and its URI in the request by calling the **Create** status method with the data. Use the **LinkGenerator** object to create the URI for the resource by sending in the name of the action and controller, and the id to it. The **Post** method should only have a parameter of the **InstructorDTO** type that receives the necessary data to create a new instructor.

The methods should return a **Task<ActionResult<InstructorDTO>>**.

1. Copy the previous **Get** action method and paste in the copied code.
2. Change the **HttpGet** attribute to **HttpPost**.
   [HttpPost]
3. Rename the method **Post** and replace the existing parameters with an **InstructorDTO** parameter named **model**.
4. Remove the code in the try-block.
5. Return *400 Bad Request* if the model is **null**.
   if (model == null) return BadRequest("No entity provided");
6. Call the **CreateAsync** method on the **_db** object and specify the **InstructorDTO** as the **TSource** and the **Instructor** entity as the **TDestination**. Store the returned id from the method in a variable named **id**. Pass in the **model** parameter to the method.
   var id = await _db.CreateAsync<InstructorDTO, Instructor>(model);
7. Use the returned id to fetch the newly created instructor by calling the **SingleAsync** method and store it in a variable named **dto**.
   var dto = await _db.SingleAsync<Instructor, InstructorDTO>(s => s.Id.Equals(id));
8. Return *400 Bad Request* if the API can't find the entity in the database.
   if (dto == null) return BadRequest("Unable to add the entity");
9. Use the **LinkGenerator** object to create a URI for the new instructor. Pass in the name of the **Get** action that returns a single instructor, the name of the controller, and the id of the created instructor. Store the URI in a variable named **uri**.
   var uri = _linkGenerator.GetPathByAction("Get", "Instructors", new { id });
10. Return the instructor and the URI with the **Create** status method; this will return the status code *201 Created* with the response data.
    return Created(uri, dto);
13. Change the error message in the catch-block to *Failed to add the entity*.
14. Start the **API** application and open a new tab in **Postman**.

15. Select the **Post** action in the drop-down to the left of the URI field.
16. Enter the *http://localhost:6600/api/instructors* URI into the text field.
17. Select the **Raw** option and **JSON (application/json)** in the drop-down, and enter JSON data for a new instructor in the **Body** tab.
    ```
    {
        "name": "Newt Newton",
        "description": "t amet, consectetur adipiscing elit",
        "thumbnail": "/images/newt.png"
    }
    ```
18. Add the **application/json** content type to the **Headers** section (**Key**: Content-Type and **Value**: application/json).
19. Click the **Send** button.

Example of returned data from the **Get** action method:

```
{
    "id": 43,
    "name": "Newt Newton",
    "description": "t amet, consectetur adipiscing elit",
    "thumbnail": "/images/newt.png",
    "buttonDTO": {
        "courseId": 0,
        "moduleId": 0,
        "id": 43,
        "userId": null,
        "itemId": "43"
    }
}
```

The complete code for the **Post** action method:

```
[HttpPost]
public async Task<ActionResult<InstructorDTO>> Post(InstructorDTO model)
{
    try
    {
        if (model == null) return BadRequest("No entity provided");

        var id = await _db.CreateAsync<InstructorDTO,
            Instructor>(model);
```

25. The API Project

```
            var dto = await _db.SingleAsync<Instructor, InstructorDTO>(
                s => s.Id.Equals(id));

            if (dto == null) return BadRequest(
                "Unable to add the entity");

            var uri = _linkGenerator.GetPathByAction("Get", "Instructors",
                new { id });

            return Created(uri, dto);
        }
        catch
        {
            return StatusCode(StatusCodes.Status500InternalServerError,
                "Failed to add the entity");
        }
    }
}
```

Adding the Put Action Method

This **Put** action method should update all the data for a single instructor and not return any content, only the **NoContent** status method.

The methods should return a **Task<IActionResult>**.

1. Copy the **Post** action method and paste in the copied code.
2. Change the **HttpPost** attribute to **HttpPut** and specify that it should take an id of **int** type in the URI.
   `[HttpPut("{id:int}")]`
3. Change the return type to **Task<IActionResult>** and add an **int** parameter named **id**.
   `public async Task<IActionResult> Put(int id, InstructorDTO model)`
4. Add an if-statement checking that the value of the **id** parameter and the **Id** property in the **model** object are identical below the first if-statement; if not, the status *400 BedRequest* should be returned.
   `if (!id.Equals(model.Id)) return BadRequest("Differing ids");`
5. Replace the rest of the code in the try-block with a call to the **AnyAsync** and store the result in a variable named **exists**; the variable will be **true** if EF finds the instructor.
   `var exists = await _db.AnyAsync<Instructor>(a => a.Id.Equals(id));`

6. Change the *400 Bad Request* status to *404 Not Found* if the exists variable is **false**.
   ```
   if (!exists) return NotFound("Could not find entity");
   ```
7. Call the **UpdateAsync** method in the **_db** object and return the status *204 No Content* by calling the **NoContent** method if the call is successful.
   ```
   if (await _db.UpdateAsync<InstructorDTO, Instructor>(model))
       return NoContent();
   ```
8. Return *400 Bad Request* below the catch-block.
   ```
   return BadRequest("Unable to update the entity");
   ```
9. Change the error message in the catch-block to *Failed to update the entity*.
10. Start the **API** application and open a new tab in **Postman**.
11. Select the **Put** action in the drop-down to the left of the URI field.
12. Enter the *http://localhost:6600/api/instructors/43* URI into the text field (use the id from the instructor you added with the post earlier).
13. Enter new JSON data for the instructor to update in the **Body** tab. Select the **Raw** option and **JSON (application/json)** in the drop-down.
    ```
    {
        "id": "43",
        "name": "Updated Newt Newton",
        "description": " Updated t amet, consectetur adipiscing elit",
        "thumbnail": "/images/updatednewt.png"
    }
    ```
14. Add the **application/json** content type to the **Headers** section (**Key: Content-Type** and **Value: application/json**).
15. Click the **Send** button.
16. Note that the response only contains the *204 No Content* status code.
17. Go back to the second **Get** tab and change the id in the URI to the id corresponding to the instructor you updated. Make sure that the request updated the instructor.

Example of returned data from the **Get** action after the **Put**:

```
{
    "id": 43,
    "name": "Updated Newt Newton",
    "description": " Updated t amet, consectetur adipiscing elit",
    "thumbnail": "/images/updatednewt.png",
```

```
    "buttonDTO": {
        "courseId": 0,
        "moduleId": 0,
        "id": 43,
        "userId": null,
        "itemId": "43"
    }
}
```

The complete code for the **Put** action method:

```
[HttpPut("{id:int}")]
public async Task<IActionResult> Put(int id, InstructorDTO model)
{
    try
    {
        if (model == null) return BadRequest("No entity provided");
        if (!id.Equals(model.Id)) return BadRequest("Differing ids");

        var exists = await _db.AnyAsync<Instructor>(a =>
            a.Id.Equals(id));

        if (!exists) return NotFound("Could not find entity");

        if (await _db.UpdateAsync<InstructorDTO, Instructor>(model))
            return NoContent();
    }
    catch
    {
        return StatusCode(StatusCodes.Status500InternalServerError,
            "Failed to update the entity");
    }

    return BadRequest("Unable to update the entity");
}
```

Adding the Delete Action Method

This **Delete** action method should remove a single instructor and not return any content using the **NoContent** status method.

The methods should return a **Task<ActionResult>**.

1. Copy the **Get** action method that returns a single instructor and paste in the copied code.
2. Change the **HttpPost** attribute to **HttpDelete**.
   ```
   [HttpDelete("{id:int}")]
   ```
3. Change the return type to **Task<IActionResult>** and remove the **include** parameter.
   ```
   public async Task<IActionResult> Delete(int id)
   ```
4. Replace the **SingleAsync** method call and the if-statement with a call to the **AnyAsync** method and an if-statement that returns *404 Not Found* if the result is **false**.
   ```
   var exists = await _db.AnyAsync<Instructor>(a => a.Id.Equals(id));
   if (!exists) return BadRequest("Could not find entity");
   ```
5. Replace the **return** statement with an if-statement that awaits the result from calling the **DeleteAsync** method in the **_db** object and return *204 No Content* by calling the **NoContent** method if the call is successful.
   ```
   if (await _db.DeleteAsync<Instructor>(d => d.Id.Equals(id)))
       return NoContent();
   ```
6. Return *400 Bad Request* below the catch-block.
   ```
   return BadRequest("Failed to delete the entity");
   ```
7. Change the error message in the catch-block to *Failed to delete the entity*.
8. Start the **API** application and open a new tab in **Postman**.
9. Select the **Delete** action in the drop-down to the left of the URI field.
10. Enter the *http://localhost:6600/api/instructors/43* URI into the text field (use the id from the instructor you added with the post earlier).
11. Add the **application/json** content type to the **Headers** section (**Key: Content-Type** and **Value: application/json**).
12. Click the **Send** button.
13. Note that the response only contains the *204 No Content* status code.
14. Go back to the second **Get** tab and change the id in the URI to the id corresponding to the instructor you deleted. Make sure that the request deleted the instructor (Postman displays a *404 Not Found* status code).

The complete code for the **Delete** action method:

```
[HttpDelete("{id:int}")]
public async Task<IActionResult> Delete(int id)
{
    try
    {
        var exists = await _db.AnyAsync<Instructor>(a =>
            a.Id.Equals(id));

        if (!exists) return BadRequest("Could not find entity");

        if (await _db.DeleteAsync<Instructor>(d => d.Id.Equals(id)))
            return NoContent();
    }
    catch
    {
        return StatusCode(StatusCodes.Status500InternalServerError,
            "Failed to delete the entity");
    }

    return BadRequest("Failed to delete the entity");
}
```

Adding the Courses Controller

The **Courses** controller will handle requests for data related to courses from the database using the **IAdminService** injected with an object from the **AdminEFService** class. In ASP .NET Core 2.2, the recommended way to create URI links is to inject the **LinkGenerator** into the constructor and call one of its **GetPathByXYZ** or **GetUriByXYZ** methods.

To speed up the process of adding the **Course** controller, you will copy and modify the **Instructors** controller and its action methods.

Modifying the Action Methods
1. Copy the *InstructorsController.cs* file and rename it *CoursesController.cs*.
2. Rename the class and its constructor **CoursesController** and replace the route URI with *api/courses*.
3. Replace all occurrences of the **Instructor** entity with the **Course** entity and **InstructorDTO** with **CourseDTO**.

4. Copy the code that calls the **AnyAsync** method and checks its result from the **Put** action and pastes it in below the first if-statement in the **Post** action. Change the **TSource** to **Instructor**.

```
var exists = await _db.AnyAsync<Instructor>(a =>
    a.Id.Equals(model.InstructorId));

if (!exists) return NotFound("Could not find related entity");
```

5. In the **Post** action, replace the name of the *Instructors* controller with *Courses* in the **GetPathByAction** method that generate the URI for the newly created entity.
6. In the **Post** action directly below the **CreateAsync** method call, return *400 Bad Request* if the id is less than 1; this indicates that the API was unable to create the entity.

```
if (id < 1) return BadRequest("Unable to add the entity");
```

7. Locate the **Put** action and add a second call to the **AnyAsync** method for the **Instructor** entity above the previous **AnyAsync** method call.

```
var exists = await _db.AnyAsync<Instructor>(a =>
    a.Id.Equals(model.InstructorId));

if (!exists) return NotFound("Could not find related entity");
```

8. Start the **API** application and call the action methods with **Postman**.

Example JSON response from a **Get** request without included data in Postman:

Note that the **instructor** and **modules** properties are **null**.

URI: *http://localhost:6600/api/courses/2*

```
{
    "id": 2,
    "imageUrl": "/images/course2.jpg",
    "marqueeImageUrl": "/images/laptop.jpg",
    "title": "Course 2",
    "description": "Lorem ipsum dolor",
    "instructorId": 2,
    "instructor": null,
    "modules": [],
    "buttonDTO": {
        "courseId": 0,
        "moduleId": 0,
        "id": 2,
        "userId": null,
```

25. The API Project

```
            "itemId": "2"
        }
}
```

Example JSON response from a **Get** request with included data in Postman:

Note that the **instructor** and **modules** properties have data.

URI: *http://localhost:6600/api/courses/2?include=true*

```
{
    "id": 2,
    "imageUrl": "/images/course2.jpg",
    "marqueeImageUrl": "/images/laptop.jpg",
    "title": "Course 2",
    "description": "Lorem ipsum dolor",
    "instructorId": 2,
    "instructor": "Jane Doe",
    "modules": [
        {
            "id": 3,
            "title": "Module 3",
            "courseId": 2,
            "course": "Course 2",
            "videos": [],
            "downloads": [],
            "courseAndModule": "Module 3 (Course 2)",
            "buttonDTO": {
                "courseId": 2,
                "moduleId": 0,
                "id": 3,
                "userId": null,
                "itemId": "3"
            }
        }
    ],
    "buttonDTO": {
        "courseId": 0,
        "moduleId": 0,
        "id": 2,
        "userId": null,
        "itemId": "2"
    }
}
```

ASP.NET Core 2.2 MVC, Razor Pages, API, JSON Web Tokens & HttpClient

Example JSON **Post** request object in Postman creating a course:

Send this object in the body of the **Post** request:

URI: *http://localhost:6600/api/courses*

```
{
    "imageUrl": "/images/course1.jpg",
    "marqueeImageUrl": "/images/laptop.jpg",
    "title": "New Course",
    "description": "Lorem ipsum dolor",
    "instructorId": 1
}
```

The **Post** response returns this object:

```
{
    "id": 51,
    "imageUrl": "/images/course1.jpg",
    "marqueeImageUrl": "/images/laptop.jpg",
    "title": "New Course",
    "description": "Lorem ipsum dolor",
    "instructorId": 1,
    "instructor": null,
    "modules": [],
    "buttonDTO": {
        "courseId": 0,
        "moduleId": 0,
        "id": 51,
        "userId": null,
        "itemId": "51"
    }
}
```

Example JSON **Put** request object in Postman creating a course:

Note that no JSON object is returned with the response when making a **Put** request; only the status code *204 No Content* is returned. You can check for the updated entity by making a **Get** request for it.

25. The API Project

Send this object in the body of the **Put** request:

URI: *http://localhost:6600/api/courses/51*

```
{
    "id": 51,
    "imageUrl": "/images/course1.jpg",
    "marqueeImageUrl": "/images/laptop.jpg",
    "title": "Updated Course",
    "description": "Updated description",
    "instructorId": 1
}
```

Example **Delete** request in Postman:

Note that no JSON object is posted in the body nor returned with the response when making a **Delete** request; only the status code *204 No Content* is returned. You can check that the API removes the entity from the database by making a **Get** request for the deleted entity; if the status *404 Not Found* is returned, then the entity was successfully removed.

URI: *http://localhost:6600/api/courses/51*

The complete code for the **CoursesController** class:

```
[Route("api/courses")]
[ApiController]
public class CoursesController : ControllerBase
{
    #region Properties and Variables
    private readonly IAdminService _db;
    private readonly LinkGenerator _linkGenerator;
    #endregion

    #region Constructor
    public CoursesController(IAdminService db,
        LinkGenerator linkGenerator)
    {
        _db = db;
        _linkGenerator = linkGenerator;
    }
    #endregion
```

```csharp
#region Actions
[HttpGet()]
public async Task<ActionResult<List<CourseDTO>>> Get(
bool include = false)
{
    try
    {
        return await _db.GetAsync<Course, CourseDTO>(include);
    }
    catch
    {
        return StatusCode(StatusCodes.Status500InternalServerError,
            "Database Failure");
    }
}

[HttpGet("{id:int}")]
public async Task<ActionResult<CourseDTO>> Get(int id,
bool include = false)
{
    try
    {
        var dto = await _db.SingleAsync<Course, CourseDTO>(s =>
            s.Id.Equals(id), include);

        if (dto == null) return NotFound();

        return dto;

    }
    catch
    {
        return StatusCode(StatusCodes.Status500InternalServerError,
            "Database Failure");
    }
}

[HttpPost]
public async Task<ActionResult<CourseDTO>> Post(CourseDTO model)
{
    try
    {
        if (model == null) return BadRequest("No entity provided");
```

```csharp
            var exists = await _db.AnyAsync<Instructor>(a =>
                a.Id.Equals(model.InstructorId));
            if (!exists) return NotFound(
                "Could not find related entity");

            var id = await _db.CreateAsync<CourseDTO, Course>(model);
            if (id < 1) return BadRequest("Unable to add the entity");

            var dto = await _db.SingleAsync<Course, CourseDTO>(s =>
                s.Id.Equals(id));

            if (dto == null) return BadRequest(
                "Unable to add the entity");

            var uri = _linkGenerator.GetPathByAction("Get", "Courses",
                new { id });

            return Created(uri, dto);
        }
        catch
        {
            return StatusCode(StatusCodes.Status500InternalServerError,
                "Failed to add the entity");
        }
    }
}

[HttpPut("{id:int}")]
public async Task<IActionResult> Put(int id, CourseDTO model)
{
    try
    {
        if (model == null) return BadRequest("Missing entity");
        if (!id.Equals(model.Id)) return BadRequest(
            "Differing ids");

        var exists = await _db.AnyAsync<Instructor>(a =>
            a.Id.Equals(model.InstructorId));

        if (!exists) return NotFound(
            "Could not find related entity");

        exists = await _db.AnyAsync<Course>(a => a.Id.Equals(id));
        if (!exists) return NotFound("Could not find entity");
```

```csharp
            if (await _db.UpdateAsync<CourseDTO, Course>(model))
                return NoContent();
        }
        catch
        {
            return StatusCode(StatusCodes.Status500InternalServerError,
                "Failed to update the entity");
        }

        return BadRequest("Unable to update the entity");

    }

    [HttpDelete("{id:int}")]
    public async Task<IActionResult> Delete(int id)
    {
        try
        {
            var exists = await _db.AnyAsync<Course>(a =>
                a.Id.Equals(id));

            if (!exists) return BadRequest("Could not find entity");

            if (await _db.DeleteAsync<Course>(d => d.Id.Equals(id)))
                return NoContent();
        }
        catch
        {
            return StatusCode(StatusCodes.Status500InternalServerError,
                "Failed to delete the entity");
        }

        return BadRequest("Failed to delete the entity");
    }
    #endregion
}
```

Adding the Modules Controller

The **Modules** controller will handle requests for data related to modules from the database using the **IAdminService** injected with an object from the **AdminEFService** class. In ASP.NET Core 2.2, the recommended way to create URI links is to inject the **LinkGenerator** into the constructor and call one of its **GetPathByXYZ** or **GetUriByXYZ** methods.

25. The API Project

To speed up the process of adding the **Modules** controller, you will copy and modify the **Courses** controller and its action methods. The URI should expand the previous URI with the course id and the modules route: *api/courses/{courseId}/modules*. The parameter name *courseId* must have a corresponding **int** parameter with the same name in all the action methods.

Modifying the Action Methods
1. Copy the *CoursesController.cs* file and rename it *ModulesController.cs*.
2. Rename the class and its constructor **ModulesController** and replace the route URI with *api/courses/{courseId}/modules*.
3. Replace all occurrences of the **Course** entity with the **Module** entity and **CourseDTO** with **ModuleDTO**.
4. Add an **int** parameter named **courseId** to all the action methods.
5. Add another **GetAsync** call to the first **Get** action above the **return** statement that fetches the modules matching the passed-in **courseId**.
   ```
   var dtos = courseId.Equals(0) ?
       await _db.GetAsync<Module, ModuleDTO>(include) :
       await _db.GetAsync<Module, ModuleDTO>(g =>
           g.CourseId.Equals(courseId), include);
   ```
6. If the **include** parameter is **false** in the **dtos** variable, then remove the data for the **Downloads** and **Videos** navigation properties in the collection of modules.
   ```
   if (!include)
   {
       foreach (var dto in dtos)
       {
           dto.Downloads = null;
           dto.Videos = null;
       }
   }
   ```
7. Return the fetched modules.
   ```
   return dto;
   ```
8. Repeat the previous three bullets for the second **Get** action but use the **SingleAsync** method instead. Also, check if the DTO is **null** above the already existing if-statement and return **BadRequest** if it is.
   ```
   var dto = courseId.Equals(0) ?
       await _db.SingleAsync<Module, ModuleDTO>(s =>
           s.Id.Equals(id), include) :
   ```

```
            await _db.SingleAsync<Module, ModuleDTO>(s =>
                s.Id.Equals(id) && s.CourseId.Equals(courseId), include);

        if (dto == null) return NotFound();
        if (!include)
        {
            dto.Downloads = null;
            dto.Videos = null;
        }
```

9. In the **Post** action, add an if-statement above the first if-statement that checks if the **courseId** parameter is 0 and assigns the value from the **model** object if it is.
   ```
   if (courseId.Equals(0)) courseId = model.CourseId;
   ```

10. In the **Post** action, add an if-statement below the other two if-statements at the beginning of the try-block that checks if the **courseId** parameter and the corresponding id in the **model** object aren't equal. If they differ, return *400 Bad Request*.
    ```
    if (!model.CourseId.Equals(courseId))
        return BadRequest("Differing ids");
    ```

11. In the **Post** action, change the parameter used in the Lambda expression for the **AnyAsync** method call from **model.InstructorId** to the **courseId** parameter and its type to **Course**.

12. In the **Post** action, add the **courseId** parameter to the Lambda expression for the **SingleAsync** method call.
    ```
    var dto = await _db.SingleAsync<Module, ModuleDTO>(s =>
        s.CourseId.Equals(courseId) && s.Id.Equals(id));
    ```

13. In the **Post** action, replace the name of the *Courses* controller with *Modules* and add the courseId parameter to the URI parameters in the **GetPathByAction** method that generate the URI for the newly created entity.
    ```
    var uri = _linkGenerator.GetPathByAction("Get", "Modules", new {
    id, courseId });
    ```

14. In the **Put** action, change the parameter used in the Lambda expression from **model.InstructorId** to the **courseId** parameter and the entity to **Course** for the **AnyAsync** method call.
    ```
    var exists = await _db.AnyAsync<Course>(a =>
        a.Id.Equals(courseId));
    if (!exists) return BadRequest("Could not find related entity");
    ```

25. The API Project

15. In the **Delete** action, add the **courseId** parameter to the two Lambda expressions.
    ```
    var exists = await _db.AnyAsync<Module>(a => a.Id.Equals(id) &&
        a.CourseId.Equals(courseId));
    ```

16. Copy the **AnyAsync<Module>** method call and its corresponding if-statement from the **Put** action and paste it in below the **AnyAsync** call in the **Delete** action.
    ```
    exists = await _db.AnyAsync<Module>(a => a.Id.Equals(id) &&
        a.CourseId.Equals(courseId));
    if (!exists) return BadRequest("Could not find entity");
    ```

17. Add the course id to the Lambda expression in the **DeleteAsync** method call.
    ```
    if (await _db.DeleteAsync<Module>(d => d.Id.Equals(id) &&
        d.CourseId.Equals(courseId))) return NoContent();
    ```

18. Start the **API** application and call the action methods with **Postman**.

Example JSON response from a **Get** request without included data in Postman:

Note that the **course**, **downloads**, and **videos** properties are **null**.

URI: *http://localhost:6600/api/courses/1/modules/1*

```
{
    "id": 1,
    "title": "Module 1",
    "courseId": 1,
    "course": null,
    "videos": null,
    "downloads": null,
    "courseAndModule": "Module 1 ()",
    "buttonDTO": {
        "courseId": 1,
        "moduleId": 0,
        "id": 1,
        "userId": null,
        "itemId": "1"
    }
}
```

ASP.NET Core 2.2 MVC, Razor Pages, API, JSON Web Tokens & HttpClient

Example JSON response from a **Get** request with included data in Postman:

Note that the **instructor** and **modules** properties have data.

http://localhost:6600/api/courses/1/modules/1?include=true

```
{
    "id": 1,
    "title": "Module 1",
    "courseId": 1,
    "course": "Course 1",
    "videos": [
    {
        "id": 1,
        "title": "Video 1 Title",
        "description": "orem ipsum dolor sit amet",
        "duration": 50,
        "thumbnail": "/images/video1.jpg",
        "url": "https://www.youtube.com/embed/BJFyzpBcaCY",
        "moduleId": 1,
        "courseId": 1,
        "course": "Course 1",
        "module": "Module 1",
        "buttonDTO": {
            "courseId": 1,
            "moduleId": 1,
            "id": 1,
            "userId": null,
            "itemId": "1"
        }
    }],
    "downloads": [
    {
        "id": 1,
        "title": "ADO.NET 1 (PDF)",
        "url": "https://some-url",
        "moduleId": 1,
        "courseId": 1,
        "course": "Course 1",
        "module": "Module 1",
        "buttonDTO": {
            "courseId": 1,
            "moduleId": 1,
            "id": 1,
            "userId": null,
```

25. The API Project

```
            "itemId": "1"
        }
    }],
    "courseAndModule": "Module 1 (Course 1)",
    "buttonDTO": {
        "courseId": 1,
        "moduleId": 0,
        "id": 1,
        "userId": null,
        "itemId": "1"
    }
}
```

Example JSON **Post** request object in Postman creating a module:

Send this object in the body of the **Post** request:

URI: *http://localhost:6600/api/courses/1/modules*

```
{
    "title": "New Module",
    "courseId": 1
}
```

The **Post** response returns this object:

```
{
    "id": 54,
    "title": "New Module",
    "courseId": 1,
    "course": null,
    "videos": [],
    "downloads": [],
    "courseAndModule": "New Module ()",
    "buttonDTO": {
        "courseId": 1,
        "moduleId": 0,
        "id": 54,
        "userId": null,
        "itemId": "54"
    }
}
```

Example JSON **Put** request object in Postman creating a module:

Note that no JSON object is returned with the response when making a **Put** request; only the status code *204 No Content* is returned. You can check that the entity was updated by doing a **Get** request for the updated entity.

Send this object in the body of the **Put** request:

URI: *http://localhost:6600/api/courses/1/modules/54*

```
{
    "id": 54,
    "title": "Updated Module",
    "courseId": 1
}
```

Example **Delete** request in Postman:

Note that no JSON object is posted in the body nor returned with the response when making a **Delete** request; only the status code *204 No Content* is returned. You can check that the API removes the entity from the database by making a **Get** request for the deleted entity; if the status *404 Not Found* is returned, then the entity was successfully removed.

URI: *http://localhost:6600/api/courses/1/modules/54*

The complete code for the **ModulesController** class:

```
[Route("api/courses/{courseId}/modules")]
[ApiController]
public class ModulesController : ControllerBase
{
    #region Properties and Variables
    private readonly IAdminService _db;
    private readonly LinkGenerator _linkGenerator;
    #endregion

    #region Constructor
    public ModulesController(IAdminService db, LinkGenerator linkGenerator)
    {
        _db = db;
        _linkGenerator = linkGenerator;
    }
    #endregion
```

```csharp
#region Actions
[HttpGet()]
public async Task<ActionResult<List<ModuleDTO>>> Get(int courseId,
bool include = false)
{
    try
    {
        var dtos = courseId.Equals(0) ?
            await _db.GetAsync<Module, ModuleDTO>(include) :
            await _db.GetAsync<Module, ModuleDTO>(g =>
                g.CourseId.Equals(courseId), include);

        if (!include)
        {
            foreach (var dto in dtos)
            {
                dto.Downloads = null;
                dto.Videos = null;
            }
        }

        return dtos;
    }
    catch
    {
        return StatusCode(StatusCodes.Status500InternalServerError,
            "Database Failure");
    }
}

[HttpGet("{id:int}")]
public async Task<ActionResult<ModuleDTO>> Get(int id, int courseId,
bool include = false)
{
    try
    {
        var dto = courseId.Equals(0) ?
            await _db.SingleAsync<Module, ModuleDTO>(s =>
                s.Id.Equals(id), include) :
            await _db.SingleAsync<Module, ModuleDTO>(s =>
                s.Id.Equals(id) && s.CourseId.Equals(courseId),
                    include);

        if (dto == null) return NotFound();
```

```csharp
            if (!include)
            {
                dto.Downloads = null;
                dto.Videos = null;
            }

            return dto;

        }
        catch
        {
            return StatusCode(StatusCodes.Status500InternalServerError,
                "Database Failure");
        }
    }

    [HttpPost]
    public async Task<ActionResult<ModuleDTO>> Post(int courseId, 
    ModuleDTO model)
    {
        try
        {
            if (courseId.Equals(0)) courseId = model.CourseId;
            if (model == null) return BadRequest("No entity provided");
            if (!model.CourseId.Equals(courseId))
                return BadRequest("Differing ids");

            var exists = await _db.AnyAsync<Course>(a =>
                a.Id.Equals(courseId));
            if (!exists)
                return NotFound("Could not find related entity");

            var id = await _db.CreateAsync<ModuleDTO, Module>(model);
            if (id < 1) return BadRequest("Unable to add the entity");

            var dto = await _db.SingleAsync<Module, ModuleDTO>(s =>
                s.CourseId.Equals(courseId) && s.Id.Equals(id));

            if (dto == null)
                return BadRequest("Unable to add the entity");

            var uri = _linkGenerator.GetPathByAction(
                "Get", "Modules", new { id, courseId });
```

```
            return Created(uri, dto);
    }
    catch
    {
        return StatusCode(StatusCodes.Status500InternalServerError,
            "Failed to add the entity");
    }
}

[HttpPut("{id:int}")]
public async Task<ActionResult<ModuleDTO>> Put(int id, int courseId,
ModuleDTO model)
{
    try
    {
        if (model == null) return BadRequest("No entity provided");
        if (!id.Equals(model.Id))
            return BadRequest("Differing ids");

        var exists = await _db.AnyAsync<Course>(a =>
            a.Id.Equals(courseId));
        if (!exists)
            return NotFound("Could not find related entity");

        exists = await _db.AnyAsync<Module>(a => a.Id.Equals(id));
        if (!exists) return NotFound("Could not find entity");

        if (await _db.UpdateAsync<ModuleDTO, Module>(model))
            return NoContent();
    }
    catch
    {
        return StatusCode(StatusCodes.Status500InternalServerError,
            "Failed to update the entity");
    }

    return BadRequest("Unable to update the entity");
}
```

```
    [HttpDelete("{id:int}")]
    public async Task<IActionResult> Delete(int id, int courseId)
    {
        try
        {
            var exists = await _db.AnyAsync<Module>(a =>
                a.Id.Equals(id) && a.CourseId.Equals(courseId));

            if (!exists) return BadRequest("Could not find entity");

            if (await _db.DeleteAsync<Module>(d => d.Id.Equals(id) &&
                d.CourseId.Equals(courseId))) return NoContent();
        }
        catch
        {
            return StatusCode(StatusCodes.Status500InternalServerError,
                "Failed to delete the entity");
        }

        return BadRequest("Failed to delete the entity");
    }
    #endregion
}
```

Adding the Videos Controller

The **Videos** controller will handle requests for data related to modules from the database using the **IAdminService** injected with an object from the **AdminEFService** class. In ASP .NET Core 2.2, the recommended way to create URI links is to inject the **LinkGenerator** into the constructor and call one of its **GetPathByXYZ** or **GetUriByXYZ** methods.

To speed up the process of adding the **Videos** controller, you will copy and modify the **Modules** controller and its action methods. The URI should expand the previous URI with the module id and the videos route: *api/courses/{courseId}/modules/{moduleId}/videos*. The parameters named *courseId* and *moduleId* must have a corresponding **int** parameter with the same names in all the action methods.

Modifying the Action Methods
1. Copy the *ModulesController.cs* file and rename it *VideosController.cs*.
2. Rename the class and its constructor **VideosController** and replace the route URI with *api/courses/{courseId}/modules/{moduleId}/videos*.

25. The API Project

3. Replace all occurrences of the **Module** entity with the **Video** entity and **ModuleDTO** with **VideoDTO**.
4. Add an **int** parameter named **moduleId** to all the action methods.
5. In the first **Get** action, add a comparison of the video entity's **ModuleId** property with the method's **moduleId** parameter to the second **GetAsync** method call.
   ```
   await _db.GetAsync<Video, VideoDTO>(g =>
       g.CourseId.Equals(courseId) &&
       g.ModuleId.Equals(moduleId), include);
   ```
6. In the first **Get** action, remove the if-block for the **include** parameter and all its content
7. In the second **Get** action, repeat the previous two bullets.
8. In the **Post** action, add an if-statement below the first if-statement that checks if the **moduleId** parameter is 0 and assigns the value from the **model** object if it is.
   ```
   if (moduleId.Equals(0)) moduleId = model.ModuleId;
   ```
9. In the **Post** action, add an if-statement below the other three if-statements at the beginning of the try-block that checks if the **Title** property in the **model** object is **null** or empty. You can call the **IsNullOrEmptyOrWhiteSpace** extension method on the **Title** property to check the value. Return *400 Bad Request* if it is **null** or empty.
   ```
   if (model.Title.IsNullOrEmptyOrWhiteSpace())
       return BadRequest("Title is required");
   ```
10. In the **Post** action, copy the **AnyAsync** method call and its corresponding if-statement and paste it in below the code you copied. Change the type to the **Module** entity and add the module id to the Lambda expression.
    ```
    exists = await _db.AnyAsync<Module>(a => a.Id.Equals(moduleId) &&
        a.CourseId.Equals(courseId));

    if (!exists) return BadRequest("Could not find related entity");
    ```
11. In the **Post** action, add the module id to the Lambda expression for the **SingleAsync** method.
    ```
    var dto = await _db.SingleAsync<Video, VideoDTO>(s =>
        s.CourseId.Equals(courseId) && s.ModuleId.Equals(moduleId) &&
        s.Id.Equals(id), true);
    ```

12. In the **Post** action, replace the name of the *Modules* controller with *Videos* and add the **moduleId** parameter to the URI's parameters in the **GetPathByAction** method that generate the URI for the newly created entity.
    ```
    var uri = _linkGenerator.GetPathByAction("Get", "Videos", new {
    id, courseId, moduleId });
    ```

13. In the **Put** action, add an if-statement below the other two if-statements at the beginning of the try-block that checks if the **Title** property in the **model** object is **null** or empty. You can call the **IsNullOrEmptyOrWhiteSpace** extension method on the **Title** property to check the value. Return *400 Bad Request* if it is **null** or empty.
    ```
    if (model.Title.IsNullOrEmptyOrWhiteSpace())
        return BadRequest("Title is required");
    ```

14. In the **Put** action, copy the **AnyAsync<Course>** method call and its corresponding if-statement and paste it in below the code you just copied. Replace the type with **Module** and add a check for the **moduleId** parameter.
    ```
    exists = await _db.AnyAsync<Module>(a => a.Id.Equals(moduleId) &&
        a.CourseId.Equals(courseId));

    if (!exists) return NotFound("Could not find related entity");
    ```

15. In the **Put** action, copy the previous **AnyAsync<Module>** method call and its corresponding if-statement and paste it in below the code you copied. Replace the **courseId** and **moduleId** parameters with their corresponding values in the **model** object.
    ```
    exists = await _db.AnyAsync<Module>(a =>
        a.Id.Equals(model.ModuleId) &&
        a.CourseId.Equals(model.CourseId));

    if (!exists) return NotFound("Could not find related entity");
    ```

16. In the **Delete** action, add checks for the **courseId** and **moduleId** to the Lambda expression for the **AnyAsync<Video>** and **DeleteAsync<Video>** method call.
    ```
    var exists = await _db.AnyAsync<Video>(a => a.Id.Equals(id) &&
        a.ModuleId.Equals(moduleId) && a.CourseId.Equals(courseId));

    if (!exists) return BadRequest("Could not find entity");

    if (await _db.DeleteAsync<Video>(d => d.Id.Equals(id) &&
        d.ModuleId.Equals(moduleId) && d.CourseId.Equals(courseId)))
            return NoContent();
    ```

17. Start the **API** application and call the action methods with **Postman**.

Example JSON response from a **Get** request without included data in Postman:

Note that the **course** and **modules** properties are **null**.

URI: *http://localhost:6600/api/courses/1/modules/1/videos/1*

```
{
    "id": 1,
    "title": "Video 1 Title",
    "description": "orem ipsum dolor sit amet",
    "duration": 50,
    "thumbnail": "/images/video1.jpg",
    "url": "https://www.youtube.com/embed/BJFyzpBcaCY",
    "moduleId": 1,
    "courseId": 1,
    "course": null,
    "module": null,
    "buttonDTO": {
        "courseId": 1,
        "moduleId": 1,
        "id": 1,
        "userId": null,
        "itemId": "1"
    }
}
```

Example JSON response from a **Get** request with included data in Postman:

Note that the **instructor** and **modules** properties have data.

URI: *http://localhost:6600/api/courses/1/modules/1/videos/1?include=true*

```
{
    "id": 1,
    "title": "Video 1 Title",
    "description": "orem ipsum dolor sit amet",
    "duration": 50,
    "thumbnail": "/images/video1.jpg",
    "url": "https://www.youtube.com/embed/BJFyzpBcaCY",
    "moduleId": 1,
    "courseId": 1,
    "course": "Course 1",
    "module": "Module 1",
```

```
    "buttonDTO": {
        "courseId": 1,
        "moduleId": 1,
        "id": 1,
        "userId": null,
        "itemId": "1"
    }
}
```

Example JSON **Post** request object in Postman creating a video:

This object is passed in the body of the **Post** request:

URI: *http://localhost:6600/api/courses/1/modules/1/videos*

```
{
    "title": "New Video Title",
    "description": "New Video Description",
    "duration": 100,
    "thumbnail": "/images/video1.jpg",
    "url": "https://www.youtube.com/embed/BJFyzpBcaCY",
    "moduleId": 1,
    "courseId": 1
}
```

The **Post** response returns this object:

```
{
    "id": 53,
    "title": "New Video Title",
    "description": "New Video Description",
    "duration": 100,
    "thumbnail": "/images/video1.jpg",
    "url": "https://www.youtube.com/embed/BJFyzpBcaCY",
    "moduleId": 1,
    "courseId": 1,
    "course": "Course 1",
    "module": "Module 1",
    "buttonDTO": {
        "courseId": 1,
        "moduleId": 1,
        "id": 53,
        "userId": null,
        "itemId": "53"
    }
}
```

Example JSON **Put** request object in Postman creating a video:

Note that no JSON object is returned with the response when making a **Put** request; only the status code *204 No Content* is returned. You can check for the updated entity by making a **Get** request for it.

Send this object in the body of the **Put** request:

URI: *http://localhost:6600/api/courses/1/modules/1/videos/53*

```
{
    "id": 53,
    "title": "Updated Video Title",
    "description": "Updated Video Description",
    "duration": 100,
    "thumbnail": "/images/video1.jpg",
    "url": "https://www.youtube.com/embed/BJFyzpBcaCY",
    "moduleId": 1,
    "courseId": 1
}
```

Example **Delete** request in Postman:

Note that no JSON object is posted in the body nor returned with the response when making a **Delete** request; only the status code *204 No Content* is returned. You can check that the API removes the entity from the database by making a **Get** request for the deleted entity; if the status *404 Not Found* is returned, then the entity was successfully removed.

URI: *http://localhost:6600/api/courses/1/modules/1/videos/53*

The complete code for the **VideosController** class:

```
[Route("api/courses/{courseId}/modules/{moduleId}/videos")]
[ApiController]
public class VideosController : ControllerBase
{
    #region Properties and Variables
    private readonly IAdminService _db;
    private readonly LinkGenerator _linkGenerator;
    #endregion
```

```csharp
#region Constructor
public VideosController(IAdminService db, LinkGenerator
linkGenerator)
{
    _db = db;
    _linkGenerator = linkGenerator;
}
#endregion

#region Actions
[HttpGet()]
public async Task<ActionResult<List<VideoDTO>>> Get(int courseId,
int moduleId, bool include = false)
{
    try
    {
        var dtos = courseId.Equals(0) ?
            await _db.GetAsync<Video, VideoDTO>(include) :
            await _db.GetAsync<Video, VideoDTO>(g =>
                g.CourseId.Equals(courseId) &&
                g.ModuleId.Equals(moduleId), include);

        return dtos;
    }
    catch
    {
        return StatusCode(StatusCodes.Status500InternalServerError,
            "Database Failure");
    }
}

[HttpGet("{id:int}")]
public async Task<ActionResult<VideoDTO>> Get(int id, int courseId,
int moduleId, bool include = false)
{
    try
    {
        var dto = courseId.Equals(0) ?
            await _db.SingleAsync<Video, VideoDTO>(s =>
                s.Id.Equals(id), include) :
            await _db.SingleAsync<Video, VideoDTO>(s =>
                s.Id.Equals(id) && s.CourseId.Equals(courseId) &&
                s.ModuleId.Equals(moduleId), include);
```

```csharp
            if (dto == null) return NotFound();

            return dto;
        }
        catch
        {
            return StatusCode(StatusCodes.Status500InternalServerError,
                "Database Failure");
        }
    }
}

[HttpPost]
public async Task<ActionResult<VideoDTO>> Post(int courseId,
int moduleId, VideoDTO model)
{
    try
    {
        if (courseId.Equals(0)) courseId = model.CourseId;
        if (moduleId.Equals(0)) moduleId = model.ModuleId;
        if (model == null) return BadRequest("No entity provided");
        if (!model.CourseId.Equals(courseId))
            return BadRequest("Differing ids");
        if (model.Title.IsNullOrEmptyOrWhiteSpace())
            return BadRequest("Title is required");

        var exists = await _db.AnyAsync<Course>(a =>
            a.Id.Equals(courseId));
        if (!exists)
            return NotFound("Could not find related entity");

        exists = await _db.AnyAsync<Module>(a =>
            a.Id.Equals(moduleId) && a.CourseId.Equals(courseId));
        if (!exists)
            return BadRequest("Could not find related entity");

        var id = await _db.CreateAsync<VideoDTO, Video>(model);
        if (id < 1) return BadRequest("Unable to add the entity");

        var dto = await _db.SingleAsync<Video, VideoDTO>(s =>
            s.CourseId.Equals(courseId) &&
            s.ModuleId.Equals(moduleId) && s.Id.Equals(id));
        if (dto == null)
            return BadRequest("Unable to add the entity");
```

```csharp
            var uri = _linkGenerator.GetPathByAction(
                "Get", "Videos", new { id, courseId, moduleId });

            return Created(uri, dto);
        }
        catch
        {
            return StatusCode(StatusCodes.Status500InternalServerError,
                "Failed to add the entity");
        }
    }

    [HttpPut("{id:int}")]
    public async Task<ActionResult<VideoDTO>> Put(int id, int courseId,
    int moduleId, VideoDTO model)
    {
        try
        {
            if (model == null) return BadRequest("No entity provided");
            if (!id.Equals(model.Id))
                return BadRequest("Differing ids");
            if (model.Title.IsNullOrEmptyOrWhiteSpace())
                return BadRequest("Title is required");

            var exists = await _db.AnyAsync<Course>(a =>
                a.Id.Equals(courseId));
            if (!exists)
                return NotFound("Could not find related entity");

            exists = await _db.AnyAsync<Module>(a =>
                a.Id.Equals(moduleId) && a.CourseId.Equals(courseId));
            if (!exists)
                return NotFound("Could not find related entity");

            exists = await _db.AnyAsync<Module>(a =>
                a.Id.Equals(model.ModuleId) &&
                a.CourseId.Equals(model.CourseId));
            if (!exists)
                return NotFound("Could not find related entity");

            exists = await _db.AnyAsync<Video>(a => a.Id.Equals(id));
            if (!exists) return NotFound("Could not find entity");

            if (await _db.UpdateAsync<VideoDTO, Video>(model))
```

```csharp
            return NoContent();
        }
        catch
        {
            return StatusCode(StatusCodes.Status500InternalServerError,
                "Failed to update the entity");
        }

        return BadRequest("Unable to update the entity");
    }

    [HttpDelete("{id:int}")]
    public async Task<IActionResult> Delete(int id, int courseId,
    int moduleId)
    {
        try
        {
            var exists = await _db.AnyAsync<Video>(a => a.Id.Equals(id)
                && a.ModuleId.Equals(moduleId)
                && a.CourseId.Equals(courseId));
            if (!exists) return BadRequest("Could not find entity");

            if (await _db.DeleteAsync<Video>(d => d.Id.Equals(id) &&
                d.ModuleId.Equals(moduleId) &&
                d.CourseId.Equals(courseId)))
                    return NoContent();
        }
        catch
        {
            return StatusCode(StatusCodes.Status500InternalServerError,
                "Failed to delete the entity");
        }

        return BadRequest("Failed to delete the entity");
    }
    #endregion
}
```

Adding the Downloads Controller

The **Downloads** controller will handle requests for data related to downloads from the database using the **IAdminService** injected with an object from the **AdminEFService** class. In ASP.NET Core 2.2, the recommended way to create URI links is to inject the **Link-Generator** into the constructor and call one of its **GetPathByXYZ** or **GetUriByXYZ** methods.

To speed up the process of adding the **Downloads** controller, you will copy and modify the **Videos** controller and its action methods. Replace *videos* with *downloads* in the URI: *api/courses/{courseId}/modules/{moduleId}/**downloads***.

Modifying the Action Methods

1. Copy the *VideosController.cs* file and rename it *DownloadsController.cs*.
2. Rename the class and its constructor **DownloadsController** and replace the route URI with *api/courses/{courseId}/modules/{moduleId}/downloads*.
3. Replace all occurrences of the **Video** entity with the **Download** entity and **VideoDTO** with **DownloadDTO**.
4. In the **Post** action, replace the name of the *Videos* controller with *Downloads* in the **GetPathByAction** method that generates the URI for the newly created entity.
5. Start the **API** application and call the action methods with **Postman**.

Example JSON response from a **Get** request without included data in Postman:

Note that the **course** and **module** properties are **null**.

URI: *http://localhost:6600/api/courses/1/modules/1/downloads/1*

```
{
    "id": 1,
    "title": "ADO.NET 1 (PDF)",
    "url": "https://some-url",
    "moduleId": 1,
    "courseId": 1,
    "course": "Course 1",
    "module": "Modeule 1",
    "buttonDTO": {
        "courseId": 1,
        "moduleId": 1,
        "id": 1,
        "userId": null,
        "itemId": "1"
    }
}
```

Example JSON response from a **Get** request with included data in Postman:

Note that the **instructor** and **modules** properties have data.

URI: *http://localhost:6600/api/courses/1/modules/1/downloads/1?include=true*

```
{
    "id": 1,
    "title": "ADO.NET 1 (PDF)",
    "url": "https://some-url",
    "moduleId": 1,
    "courseId": 1,
    "course": "Course 1",
    "module": "Modeule 1",
    "buttonDTO": {
        "courseId": 1,
        "moduleId": 1,
        "id": 1,
        "userId": null,
        "itemId": "1"
    }
}
```

Example JSON **Post** request object in Postman creating a download:

Send this object in the body of the **Post** request:

URI: *http://localhost:6600/api/courses/1/modules/1/downloads*

```
{
    "title": "New Download",
    "url": "https://new-url",
    "moduleId": 1,
    "courseId": 1
}
```

The **Post** response returns this object:

```
{
    "id": 25,
    "title": "New Download",
    "url": "https://new-url",
    "moduleId": 1,
    "courseId": 1,
    "course": "Course 1",
```

```
        "module": "Modeule 1",
        "buttonDTO": {
            "courseId": 1,
            "moduleId": 1,
            "id": 25,
            "userId": null,
            "itemId": "25"
        }
    }
}
```

Example JSON **Put** request object in Postman creating a download:

Note that no JSON object is returned with the response when making a **Put** request; only the status code *204 No Content* is returned. You can check the updated entity by making a **Get** request for it.

Send this object in the body of the **Put** request:

URI: *http://localhost:6600/api/courses/1/modules/1/downloads/25*

```
{
    "id": 25,
    "title": "Updated Download",
    "url": "https://updated-url",
    "moduleId": 1,
    "courseId": 1
}
```

Example **Delete** request in Postman:

Note that no JSON object is posted in the body nor returned with the response when making a **Delete** request; only the status code *204 No Content* is returned. You can check that the API removes the entity from the database by making a **Get** request for the deleted entity; if the status *404 Not Found* is returned, then the entity was successfully removed.

URI: *http://localhost:6600/api/courses/1/modules/1/downloads/25*

The complete code for the **DownloadsController** class:

```
[Route("api/courses/{courseId}/modules/{moduleId}/downloads")]
[ApiController]
public class DownloadsController : ControllerBase
{
```

25. The API Project

```
#region Properties and Variables
private readonly LinkGenerator _linkGenerator;
private readonly IAdminService _db;
private readonly IMapper _mapper;
#endregion

#region Constructor
public DownloadsController(IAdminService db, IMapper mapper,
LinkGenerator linkGenerator)
{
    _db = db;
    _mapper = mapper;
    _linkGenerator = linkGenerator;
}
#endregion

#region Actions
[HttpGet()]
public async Task<ActionResult<List<DownloadDTO>>> Get(int courseId,
int moduleId, bool include = false)
{
    try
    {
        return courseId.Equals(0) || moduleId.Equals(0) ?
            await _db.GetAsync<Download, DownloadDTO>(include) :
            await _db.GetAsync<Download, DownloadDTO>(g =>
                g.CourseId.Equals(courseId) &&
                g.ModuleId.Equals(moduleId), include);
    }
    catch
    {
        return StatusCode(StatusCodes.Status500InternalServerError,
            "Database Failure");
    }
}

[HttpGet("{id:int}")]
public async Task<ActionResult<DownloadDTO>> Get(int id,
int courseId, int moduleId)
{
    try
    {
```

```csharp
            var entity = courseId.Equals(0) || moduleId.Equals(0) ?
                await _db.SingleAsync<Download, DownloadDTO>(s =>
                    s.Id.Equals(id), true) :
                await _db.SingleAsync<Download, DownloadDTO>(s =>
                    s.CourseId.Equals(courseId) &&
                    s.ModuleId.Equals(moduleId) && s.Id.Equals(id),
                        true);

            if (entity == null) return NotFound();
            return entity;
        }
        catch
        {
            return StatusCode(StatusCodes.Status500InternalServerError,
                "Database Failure");
        }
    }

    [HttpPost]
    public async Task<ActionResult<DownloadDTO>> Post(DownloadDTO model,
    int courseId, int moduleId)
    {
        try
        {
            if (courseId.Equals(0)) courseId = model.CourseId;
            if (moduleId.Equals(0)) moduleId = model.ModuleId;
            if (model == null) return BadRequest("No entity provided");
            if (!model.CourseId.Equals(courseId))
                return BadRequest("Differing ids");

            if (model.Title.IsNullOrEmptyOrWhiteSpace())
                return BadRequest("Title is required");

            var exists = await _db.AnyAsync<Course>(a =>
                a.Id.Equals(courseId));

            if (!exists) return BadRequest(
                "Could not find related entity");

            exists = await _db.AnyAsync<Module>(a =>
                a.Id.Equals(moduleId) && a.CourseId.Equals(courseId));
            if (!exists) return BadRequest(
                "Could not find related entity");
```

```csharp
            var id = await _db.CreateAsync<DownloadDTO, Download>(
                model);

            if (id < 1) return BadRequest("Unable to add the entity");

            var dto = await _db.SingleAsync<Download, DownloadDTO>(s =>
                s.CourseId.Equals(courseId) &&
                s.ModuleId.Equals(moduleId) && s.Id.Equals(id), true);

            if (dto == null) return BadRequest(
                "Unable to add the entity");

            var uri = _linkGenerator.GetPathByAction("Get", "Downloads",
                new { courseId = dto.CourseId, moduleId = dto.ModuleId,
                    id = dto.Id });

            return Created(uri, dto);
        }
        catch
        {
            return StatusCode(StatusCodes.Status500InternalServerError,
                "Failed to add the entity");
        }
    }
}

[HttpPut("{id:int}")]
public async Task<IActionResult> Put(int courseId, int moduleId,
int id, DownloadDTO model)
{
    try
    {
        if (model == null) return BadRequest("Missing entity");
        if (!model.Id.Equals(id)) return BadRequest(
            "Differing ids");

        if (model.Title.IsNullOrEmptyOrWhiteSpace())
            return BadRequest("Title is required");

        var exists = await _db.AnyAsync<Course>(a =>
            a.Id.Equals(courseId));
        if (!exists) return BadRequest(
            "Could not find related entity");
```

```csharp
            exists = await _db.AnyAsync<Module>(a =>
                a.Id.Equals(moduleId) && a.CourseId.Equals(courseId));
            if (!exists) return BadRequest(
                "Could not find related entity");

            exists = await _db.AnyAsync<Module>(a =>
                a.Id.Equals(model.ModuleId) &&
                a.CourseId.Equals(model.CourseId));

            if (!exists) return BadRequest(
                "Could not find related entity");

            exists = await _db.AnyAsync<Download>(a => a.Id.Equals(id));
            if (!exists) return BadRequest("Could not find entity");

            if (await _db.UpdateAsync<DownloadDTO, Download>(model))
                return NoContent();
        }
        catch
        {
            return StatusCode(StatusCodes.Status500InternalServerError,
                "Failed to update the entity");
        }

        return BadRequest("Unable to update the entity");
    }

    [HttpDelete("{id:int}")]
    public async Task<IActionResult> Delete(int id, int courseId,
    int moduleId)
    {
        try
        {
            var exists = await _db.AnyAsync<Course>(g =>
                g.Id.Equals(courseId));
            if (!exists) return BadRequest(
                "Could not find related entity");

            exists = await _db.AnyAsync<Module>(g =>
                g.CourseId.Equals(courseId) && g.Id.Equals(moduleId));
            if (!exists) return BadRequest(
                "Could not find related entity");
```

```
                exists = await _db.AnyAsync<Download>(g =>
                    g.Id.Equals(id) &&
                    g.CourseId.Equals(courseId) &&
                    g.ModuleId.Equals(moduleId));

                if (!exists) return BadRequest("Could not find entity");

                if (await _db.DeleteAsync<Download>(d =>
                    d.Id.Equals(id) &&
                    d.CourseId.Equals(courseId) &&
                    d.ModuleId.Equals(moduleId))) return NoContent();
            }
            catch
            {
                return StatusCode(StatusCodes.Status500InternalServerError,
                    "Failed to delete the entity");
            }

            return BadRequest("Unable to update the entity");
        }
        #endregion
}
```

Summary

In this chapter, you built an API with multiple controllers that perform CRUD operations in the database. You then tested the API using the Postman tool.

In the next chapter, you will implement an **HttpClientFactory** service that will handle the **HttpClient** instances used when calling the API from the **AdminAPIService** service you will implement using the **IAdminService** interface. By using that interface, you ensure that all Razor Pages will continue to work without any refactoring.

You will use reflection to build the Uris needed to call the API from properties in generic types, objects, and Lambda expressions.

ASP.NET Core 2.2 MVC, Razor Pages, API, JSON Web Tokens & HttpClient

26. Calling the API With HttpClient

Overview

In this chapter, you will use the **IAdminService** interface to create a new service for the **HttpClient** that will call the API to perform CRUD operations in the database. By using the same interface that you used for the **AdminEFService** that communicates directly with the database, you can switch between them with one line of code and call the API for data; it also poses an interesting scenario where you will need to use reflection to find the id properties needed to make the API calls. True, you could create a new service with one specific method for each CRUD operation and controller in the API, but that would mean a massive refactoring of the Razor Pages, which can be relatively easily avoided by reusing the **IAdminService** interface.

Reflection into generic types poses a challenge when the CRUD methods have Lambda expressions; this means that you will have to tackle reflection for Lambda expressions, which is more involved than reflection for regular types.

The new **AdminAPIService** service will get injected with a **HttpClientFactoryService** service that contains all the HTTP CRUD methods that call the API; it also has a cancellation token that can be used to cancel one or more requests when making calls over HTTP with instances of the **HttpClient** class instead of using Entity Framework directly. The HTTP Client Factory service handles cancellation if implemented, but it's out of scope for this book.

There are several ways **HttpClient** can integrate with an API. Here we will focus on one that is a best practice by Microsoft, which uses an HTTP Client Factory released with ASP.NET Core 2.1.

Technologies Used in This Chapter

1. **API** – The API project performs CRUD operations in the database.
2. **C#** – To write code for the service and **HttpClient**.
3. **Reflection** – To find and use properties in generic types and objects.
4. **HttpClient** – Makes HTTP Requests to the API and receives responses.
5. **Services** – To communicate with the API.
6. **AutoMapper** – To map and transform data between types.
7. **Entity framework** – To perform CRUD operations in the database.

What is HttpClient?

HTTP is a request-response protocol between a client and a server, where the client requests information from the server and the server sends a response back with a status code and data. A web browser is such a client, but a more practical approach when building an API is to use a tool, such as Postman as you did in the previous chapter. In this chapter, you will use **HttpClient** to call the API from the Razor Pages in the **Admin** UI project.

In the previous chapter, you learned that the client, which in that scenario was Postman, can send HTTP Requests to the API on the server by specifying a *verb*, *headers*, and in some cases *content*.

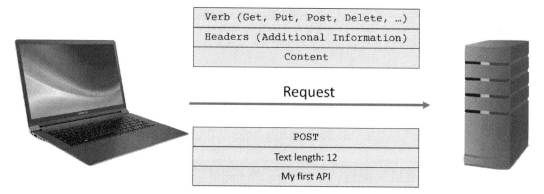

And that the server will send a response message back with a *Status Code*, *Content Headers*, and in some cases *data*.

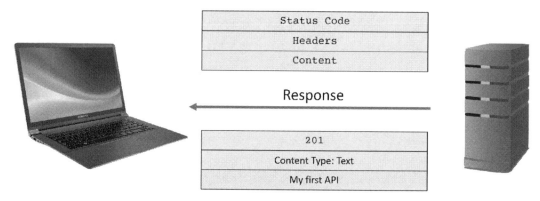

In this chapter you will use **HttpClient**, instead of Postman, to send requests and receive responses from the API on the server. It does this by using one or more message handlers, which are instances of the **HttpMessageHandler** class, that are executed by an instance of the **HttpClientHandler** class. Each message handler can opt to pass it to the next handler in the pipeline or send a response back; one such scenario is a caching handler that returns cached data if available. This pattern is called the Delegating Handler Pattern.

An all too familiar way of using the **HttpClient** in examples on the Internet is to wrap the creation of the instance in a **using** statement that will dispose of the object when finished; Microsoft does not recommend this because instances of the **HttpClient** are meant to be long-lived and reused. When disposing of an **HttpClient** instance, it disposes of the underlying **HttpClientHandler**, and closes its connection; this can lead to performance issues because reopening a connection takes time. In addition to that, you may run out of sockets to create a new connection because of the time it takes to free up the disposed of resources.

```
public class BadExample
{
    private HttpClient _httpClient = new HttpClient();
    public Example()
    {
        _httpClient.BaseAddress = new Uri("http://localhost:6600");
        _httpClient.Timeout = new TimeSpan(0, 0, 30);
    }

    public async Task Get()
    {
        // A using will create performance issues
        using (var httpClient = new HttpClient())
        {
            // Code to make a Get request
        }
    }
}
```

A better way to use the **HttpClient** is to let an instance of the **HttpClientFactoryService** class handle the creation and destruction of the instances, which is what you will learn in this chapter.

Another way to use **HttpClient** is to call one of its asynchronous methods, **GetAsync** in this example, which returns a **Task<HttpResponseMessage>** with the status code and data from the API. The method calls the **EnsureSuccessStatusCode** after the response has returned to ensure that the request throws an exception if unsuccessful.

```
public async Task Get()
{
    var courses = await _httpClient.GetAsync("api/courses");
    response.EnsureSuccessStatusCode();
    var content = await response.Content.ReadAsStringAsync();
    var courses = JsonConvert.DeserializeObject<IEnumerable<Course>>(
        content);
}
```

The data returned in the **response** variable's **Content** property isn't readable text; to get the data you must parse it into a string, byte array, or read it as a stream. You will use a stream later in this chapter. The **ReadStringAsync** method will return the data as a JSON object or array.

The JSON data deserializes into objects of the desired type with the **JsonConvert.DeserializeObject** method, which is in the **Newtonsoft.Json** namespace that requires the **Newtonsoft.Json** NuGet package to be installed.

But why did the API return JSON? It did so because it is the default content type for the API. It is not uncommon for an API to provide multiple content types such as JSON and XML. You can change the formatter used by configuring it for the **AddMvc** method in the **ConfigureServices** method in the **Startup** class, but you must remember to implement an XML de-serializer and ask for that format in the request headers.

```
services.AddMvc(options =>
{
    options.OutputFormatters.Insert(0, XmlSerializerOutputFormatter());
    options.InputFormatters.Insert(0, XmlSerializerInputFormatter(
        options));
}).SetCompatibilityVersion(CompatibilityVersion.Version_2_2);
```

HTTP Headers

You can send additional information with a request or response by adding it to its *Headers* section. A header value has a case-insensitive name followed by a colon and its value. If the value consists of multiple value parts, then separate them with commas.

```
Name: value
Name: value1, value2
```

26. Calling The API With HttpClient

The client provides request headers that contain data about the resource or the client itself. One example is the **Accept** header that tells the API which data type(s) the client wants the response to return in.

```
Accept: application/json
Accept: application/json, text/html
```

The response headers can contain information generated by the API, such as the **Content-Type** that tells the client how to deserialize the result.

```
Content-Type: application/json
```

It is best practice to provide the necessary headers because it improves reliability and is mandatory in a RESTful API.

The content negotiation mechanism (that determines the format(s) the client expects and the format(s) the server provides) depends on what **Accept** headers the request has and the **ContentType** header of the response.

You can add **Accept** headers by calling the **Add** method on the **DefaultRequestHeaders** collection of the **_httpClient** object in the constructor. It is best to clear the collection before adding your own headers.

```
_httpClient.DefaultRequestHeaders.Clear();
_httpClient.DefaultRequestHeaders.Accept.Add(
    new MediaTypeWithQualityHeaderValue("application/json"));
_httpClient.DefaultRequestHeaders.Accept.Add(
    new MediaTypeWithQualityHeaderValue("application/xml"));
```

Using multiple media types requires you to implement de-serializers for all scenarios; in the example above both JSON and XML are acceptable return types.

```
List<Course> courses;

if (response.Content.Headers.ContentType.MediaType ==
"application/json")
{
    courses = JsonConvert.DeserializeObject<List<Course>>(content);
}
else if (response.Content.Headers.ContentType.MediaType ==
"application/xml")
{
    var serializer = new XmlSerializer(typeof(List<Course>));
```

```
        courses = (List<Course>)serializer.Deserialize(
            new StringReader(content));
}
```

Note that the **Accept** headers will be the same for all requests when implementing the headers directly on the **HttpClient** instance in the constructor. A better way to implement the **Accept** headers and call the API is to use an instance of the **HttpRequestMessage** class.

```
public async Task Get()
{
    var request = new HttpRequestMessage(HttpMethod.Get, "api/courses");
    request.Headers.Accept.Add(
        new MediaTypeWithQualityHeaderValue("application/json"));

    var response = await _httpClient.SendAsync(request);
    response.EnsureSuccessStatusCode();

    var content = await response.Content.ReadAsStringAsync();
    var courses = JsonConvert.DeserializeObject<List<Course>>(content);
}
```

The preferred **SendAsync** method can handle any request as opposed to the **GetAsync**, **PostAsync**, **PutAsync**, and **DeleteAsync** shortcut methods. Important to note is that the shortcut methods don't set or send **Accept** headers; you assign them on **HttpClient** level, which might not be allowed or work in your solution; and assigning **Accept** headers for each call is required in a RESTful system. As you have learned earlier, assigning the headers on the **HttpClient** means that all requests will have the same headers, which means that you would have to dispose of the current **HttpClient** and create a new instance to change the **Accept** headers.

Using Streams to Improve Performance and Memory Usage

Why use streams? The main reason for using client-side streams is that it can enhance the performance because no in-between storage of the data is necessary, as it is when reading the data as a string; where all the data is temporarily stored in the client's memory until all the data has arrived in the response. The stream reads or writes the data as a sequence of bytes that bypasses the temporary storage that strings require.

26. Calling The API With HttpClient

Example of requesting data and reading the response as a string.

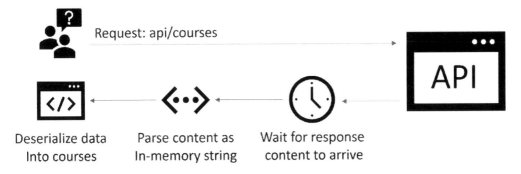

Example of requesting data and reading the response as a stream.

To use a stream, you create a **HttpRequestMessage** object, call the API with the **SendAsync** method, and check for a successful response. But instead of calling the **ReadAsStringAsync** to read the data as a string, you call the **RadAsStreamAsync** method and use a **StreamReader** object with **JsonTextReader** and **JsonSerializer** objects to read the data as a stream, bypassing the in-memory storage that a string requires.

```
var content = await response.Content.ReadAsStreamAsync();

using (var reader = new StreamReader(content))
{
    using (var jsonReader = new JsonTextReader(reader))
    {
        var jsonSerializer = new JsonSerializer();
        var courses = jsonSerializer.Deserialize<List<Course>>(
            jsonReader);
```

```
        // Do something with courses
    }
}
```

There is a huge drawback in the way the previous example with the stream treats data; all the data must arrive before the stream can begin to deserialize it. To improve the performance further, you can manipulate the **HttpCompletionMode** to begin streaming as soon as the response headers arrive instead of waiting until all data has arrived.

Because we only wait for the headers to arrive, the data can begin streaming as soon as it arrives. The only thing you must do for this to work is to pass in **HttpCompletionMode.ResponseHeadersRead** as a second parameter to the **SendAsync** method.

```
var response = await _httpClient.SendAsync(request, 
    HttpCompletionOption.ResponseHeadersRead);
```

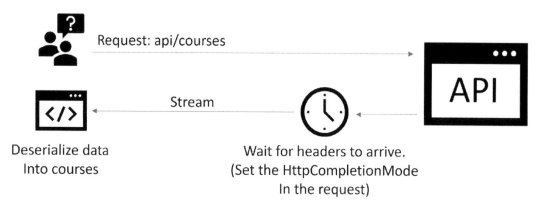

You can also use a stream when posting data to the API. To achieve this, you use a **MemoryStream** object to hold the serialized object that will be sent to the API and use a **StreamWriter** object to write the data into the **MemoryStream**. Remember to keep the stream open after the data has been written to the **MemoryStream** because it will be used later when posting the data to the API. Then use a **JsonTextWriter** with the **StreamWriter** to serialize the data into JSON with a **JsonSerializer** object. Don't forget to flush the text writer to ensure that the writer serializes all bytes.

26. Calling The API With HttpClient

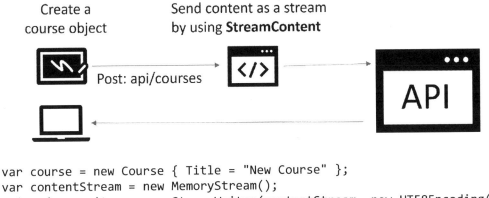

```
var course = new Course { Title = "New Course" };
var contentStream = new MemoryStream();
using (var writer = new StreamWriter(contentStream, new UTF8Encoding(),
1024, true))
{
    using (var jsonWriter = new JsonTextWriter(writer))
    {
        var jsonSerializer = new JsonSerializer();
        jsonSerializer.Serialize(writer, course);
        jsonWriter.Flush();
    }
}
```

When the data is in the **MemoryStream**, you must reset the stream to its start position to be able to read it when posting the data. Then you use an **HttpRequestMessage** object with its **HttpMethod** set to **Post** to call the API. As before, you must set the accept headers to *application/json* on the request object to tell the API to serialize the data to JSON. Then, create a **StreamContent** object that will be used to stream the **Course** object from the **MemoryStream** to the API. Use the **Content** property of the request object to assign the streamed content to its body and specify the **ContentType** as *application/json* to signal to the server that the data is in JSON format.

Call the **SendAsync** method on the **HttpClient** object and pass in the request object to the method. After ensuring a successful post, you can read the created object from the response with the **ReadAsStreamAsync** method, much like you have done before.

```
contentStream.Seek(0, SeekOrigin.Begin);

// Create a request object that will send the streamed data to the API.
using (var request = new HttpRequestMessage(HttpMethod.Post,
"api/courses"))
{
```

```csharp
        request.Headers.Accept.Add(new MediaTypeWithQualityHeaderValue(
            "application/json"));

    // Use a stream to read the course object from the MemoryStream.
    using (var streamContent = new StreamContent(contentStream))
    {
        // Add the course object tom the request's body content.
        request.Content = streamContent;
        request.Content.Headers.ContentType =
            new MediaTypeHeaderValue("application/json");

        // Post the streaming data to the API.
        var response = await _httpClient.SendAsync(request);
        response.EnsureSuccessStatusCode();

        // Get the created object from the response.
        using (response = await _httpClient.SendAsync(request,
        HttpCompletionOption.ResponseHeadersRead))
        {
            response.EnsureSuccessStatusCode();
            var content = await response.Content.ReadAsStreamAsync();

            using (var reader = new StreamReader(content))
            {
                using (var jsonReader = new JsonTextReader(reader))
                {
                    var jsonSerializer = new JsonSerializer();
                    var courses = jsonSerializer.Deserialize<Course>(
                        jsonReader);

                    // Do something with the course
                }
            }
        }
    }
}
```

You might encounter slower performance with streams in certain scenarios, but it is important to look at the big picture here; speed isn't everything. Memory usage is also important when creating temporary strings that requires the Garbage Collection to work harder. When the Garbage Collection is used excessively the memory can start to fill up. You should always strive to create as few objects as possible and release them to Garbage Collection as soon as possible.

There is one more thing we can do to improve the performance, and that is to use compression when sending data. To add compression, you add an **AcceptEncoding** property to the headers and specify the type of compression you want to use; **gzip** is available out-of-the-box.

```
request.Headers.AcceptEncoding.Add(
    new StringWithQualityHeaderValue("gzip"));
```

You also need to enable **gzip** compression when the **HttpClient** object is instantiated.

```
private HttpClient _httpClient = new HttpClient(new HttpClientHandler()
{ AutomaticDecompression = DecompressionMethods.GZip });
```

Supporting Cancellation

Canceling a request can be beneficial to performance in that long-running tasks can be stopped to free up resources that slow down or freeze the browser.

Because **HttpClient** is asynchronous and works with **Tasks**, canceling long-running requests is possible if, for instance, the visitor to the site navigates away from the page because it takes too long to load the information. Fetching a large resource can be canceled instead of it continuing in the background. Here, you will learn how to prepare the application for cancellation.

The application must handle two scenarios: the first is when you cancel the **Task** – when the user decides to leave the page or with some other means cancels the loading of a resource; the other handles timeouts gracefully.

A **CancellationTokenSource** holds a **CancellationToken** in its **Token** property; that token is passed to the methods, enabling the cancellation of their work; it handles all cancellation requests.

The **HttpClient** listens for cancellation requests and stops the running **Task**(s) if cancellation is triggered.

The **CancellationTokenSource** has two methods that can be used to cancel a request: the first is **Cancel** that, let's say, a button calls; the other is **CancelAfter** that cancels the request after a set amount of time.

```
var cancellationTokenSource = new CancellationTokenSource();
cancellationTokenSource.CancelAfter(3000);
```

After the time has elapsed, the method cancels the request and throws a **TaskCancelled-Exception**, which a try/catch-block handles with cleanup code in its catch-block.

Here, the **CancellationTokenSource** is instantiated on class-level to reuse its token in all methods that should implement cancellation; you can see that the **Get** method receives it as a parameter that the **SendAsync** method uses.

```
public class CancellationExample
{
    private HttpClient _httpClient = new HttpClient(
        new HttpClientHandler() { AutomaticDecompression =
            DecompressionMethods.GZip });

    private CancellationTokenSource cancellationTokenSource =
        new CancellationTokenSource();

    public CancellationExample()
    {
        _httpClient.BaseAddress = new Uri("http://localhost:6600");
        _httpClient.Timeout = new TimeSpan(0, 0, 30);
        _httpClient.DefaultRequestHeaders.Clear();
    }

    public async Task CallTheMethod()
    {
        cancellationTokenSource.CancelAfter(3000);
        await Get(cancellationTokenSource.Token);
    }

    public async Task Get(CancellationToken cancellationToken)
    {
        var request = new HttpRequestMessage(HttpMethod.Get,
            "api/courses");
        request.Headers.Accept.Add(
            new MediaTypeWithQualityHeaderValue("application/json"));
        request.Headers.AcceptEncoding.Add(
            new StringWithQualityHeaderValue("gzip"));

        try
        {
            using (var response = await _httpClient.SendAsync(request,
                HttpCompletionOption.ResponseHeadersRead,
                cancellationToken))
```

```
        {
            response.EnsureSuccessStatusCode();
            var content = await response.Content
                .ReadAsStreamAsync();

            using (var reader = new StreamReader(content))
            {
                using (var jsonReader = new JsonTextReader(reader))
                {
                    var jsonSerializer = new JsonSerializer();
                    var courses = jsonSerializer
                        .Deserialize<Course>(jsonReader);

                    // Do something with the course
                }
            }
        }
        catch (OperationCanceledException ex)
        {
            // Cleanup code and logging
        }
    }
  }
}
```

Using a HttpClientFactory

You have already learned that you shouldn't use a **using**-block with the **HttpClient** since it closes the underlying **HttpMessageHandler** and its connection, which can lead to performance issues and socket exhaustion. What you want to do is to keep the **HttpClient** and its connection open for multiple calls; the seemingly obvious solution would be to create a **static** instance of the **HttpClient**, but that is not advisable because it will retain its settings when you want them to change; for instance, when changing environment from development to production. It can also cause problems with the Azure Platform as a Service (PaaS) cloud services.

```
using (var httpClient = new HttpClient())
{
}
```

The best approach to solve these problems is to let a **HttpClientFactoryService** instance handle the creation and destruction of the **HttpClient** instances. The factory uses an **HttpMessageHandler** instance from a pool and manages their lifetimes instead of creating a new handler instance for each **HttpClient**.

Apart from solving socket exhaustion and DNS problems when switching environment, it also gives you a central location for naming and configuring **HttpClients**; for instance, when communicating with more than one API or microservice.

The project needs the **Microsoft.Extensions.Http** NuGet package, which already is referenced by ASP.NET Core to create a factory.

You can configure the **HttpClient(s)** that you want to use as named clients in the **ConfigureServices** method in the **Startup** class; here you can specify a base address, timeout, clear the request headers, and specify a decompression method. You can also create typed **HttpClients**, but that is beyond the scope of this book.

```
services.AddHttpClient("AdminClient", client =>
{
    client.BaseAddress = new Uri("http://localhost:6600");
    client.Timeout = new TimeSpan(0, 0, 30);
    client.DefaultRequestHeaders.Clear();
}).ConfigurePrimaryHttpMessageHandler(handler => new HttpClientHandler()
{
    AutomaticDecompression = System.Net.DecompressionMethods.GZip
});
```

Then you use dependency injection to receive an instance through the **IHttpClientFactory** interface that creates the **HttpClient(s)** and handles the pool of handlers.

```
public class HttpClientFactoryExample
{
    private readonly IHttpClientFactory _factory;
    private CancellationTokenSource cancellationTokenSource =
        new CancellationTokenSource();
```

```csharp
    public HttpClientFactoryExample(IHttpClientFactory factory)
    {
        _factory = factory;
    }

    public async Task Get(CancellationToken cancellationToken)
    {
        var httpClient = _factory.CreateClient("AdminClient");

        var request = new HttpRequestMessage(HttpMethod.Get,
            "api/courses");
        request.Headers.Accept.Add(new MediaTypeWithQualityHeaderValue(
            "application/json"));
        request.Headers.AcceptEncoding.Add(
            new StringWithQualityHeaderValue("gzip"));

        using (var response = await httpClient.SendAsync(request,
        HttpCompletionOption.ResponseHeadersRead, cancellationToken))
        {
            response.EnsureSuccessStatusCode();
            var content = await response.Content.ReadAsStreamAsync();

            using (var reader = new StreamReader(content))
            {
                using (var jsonReader = new JsonTextReader(reader))
                {
                    var jsonSerializer = new JsonSerializer();
                    var courses = jsonSerializer.Deserialize<Course>(
                        jsonReader);

                    // Do something with the course
                }
            }
        }
    }
}
```

Handling Errors

It's important to handle errors gracefully to keep the application from crashing. You can inspect the response's **IsSuccessStatusCode** property to see if an error has occurred. Inspect the response's **StatusCode** property to find out more about the error. You let the **EnsureSuccessStatusCode** method handle all other errors.

```csharp
using (var response = await httpClient.SendAsync(request,
HttpCompletionOption.ResponseHeadersRead, cancellationToken))
{
    if (!response.IsSuccessStatusCode)
    {
        if (response.StatusCode.Equals(HttpStatusCode.NotFound))
        {
            // Status Code: 404. Show error message to the user.
            return;
        }
        else if (response.StatusCode.Equals(
            HttpStatusCode.Unauthorized))
        {
            // Status Code: 401. Redirect to login.
            return;
        }

        response.EnsureSuccessStatusCode();
    }
}
```

Sometimes inspecting the status codes aren't enough; in those cases, you might have to read more information from the response body. One such scenario would be handling validation errors that can contain more information than only a status code.

```csharp
else if (response.StatusCode.Equals(HttpStatusCode.UnprocessableEntity))
{
    // Status Code: 422. Read response body.
    var errorStream = await response.Content.ReadAsStreamAsync();

    using (var reader = new StreamReader(content))
    {
        using (var jsonReader = new JsonTextReader(reader))
        {
            var jsonSerializer = new JsonSerializer();
            var courses = jsonSerializer.Deserialize(jsonReader);
            // Show error message
        }
    }
    return;
}
```

Adding the AdminAPIService and HttpClientFactoryService Classes

This **AdminAPIService** service class implements the same **IAdminService** interface as the previously added **AdminEFService** class, which saves some serious refactoring of the **Admin** Razor Pages. It also presents you with a very interesting scenario where you must use reflection with the generically defined methods to find out which id properties that should make up the URI; it is even more challenging because you need to inspect Lambda expressions to find out the properties involved.

The **AdminAPIService** must be injected with the **IHttpClientFactoryService** interface to receive an object of the **HttpClientFactoryService** class that will perform CRUD operations in the database by calling with the API.

1. Open the **Startup** class in the **Admin** project and locate the **ConfigureServices** and configure the *AdminClient* **HttpClient** service described earlier.
   ```
   services.AddHttpClient("AdminClient", client =>
   {
       client.BaseAddress = new Uri("http://localhost:6600");
       client.Timeout = new TimeSpan(0, 0, 30);
       client.DefaultRequestHeaders.Clear();
   }).ConfigurePrimaryHttpMessageHandler(handler =>
       new HttpClientHandler () {
       AutomaticDecompression = System.Net.DecompressionMethods.GZip
   });
   ```
2. Add a **public** class called **AdminAPIService** to the *Services* folder in the **Common** project. You add it to the **Common** project because it won't use the database directly.
3. Implement the **IAdminService** interface in the class; this should add its methods implemented with **NotImplementedException** exception to the class.
4. Add a new **public** empty interface named **IHttpClientFactoryService** to the *Services* folder in the **Common** project; you will add methods to the interface later.
   ```
   public interface IHttpClientFactoryService
   {
   }
   ```

5. Add a new **public** class named **HttpClientFactoryService** to the *Services* folder in the **Common** project and implement the empty **IHttpClientFactoryService** interface in it; you will add the methods from the interface as you add them.
   ```
   public class HttpClientFactoryService : IHttpClientFactoryService
   {
   }
   ```

6. Add a constructor to the **AdminAPIService** class and inject the **IHttpClientFactoryService** interface. Store the object in a variable named **_http**.
   ```
   private readonly IHttpClientFactoryService _http;
   ```
   ```
   public AdminAPIService(IHttpClientFactoryService http)
   {
       _http = http;
   }
   ```

7. Inject the **IHttpClientFactory** interface into the **HttpClientFactoryService** class to gain access to the methods you need to call the API over the HTTP protocol; this requires a reference to the **Microsoft.Extensions.Http** assembly.
   ```
   private readonly IHttpClientFactory _httpClientFactory;
   ```
   ```
   public HttpClientFactoryService(IHttpClientFactory httpClientFactory)
   {
       _httpClientFactory = httpClientFactory;
   }
   ```

8. Add a **CancellationTokenSource** variable to the **HttpClientFactoryService** class and instantiate it in the constructor.
   ```
   private CancellationTokenSource _cancellationTokenSource;
   ```

9. Add a **CancellationToken** variable to the class and assign the **Token** property from the **_cancellationTokenSource** object in the constructor. By adding the cancellation token to the class instead of inside the method, you can reuse it and can cancel many requests at the same time.
   ```
   private readonly CancellationToken _cancellationToken;
   ```

10. Open the **Startup** class in the **Admin** project and replace the **AdminEFService** class with **AdminAPIService** class in the **IAdminService** service declaration.
    ```
    services.AddScoped<IAdminService, AdminAPIService>();
    ```

11. In the **Startup** class, add a service declaration for the **IHttpClientFactoryService** interface and **HttpClientFactoryService** class.

26. Calling The API With HttpClient

```
    services.AddScoped<IHttpClientFactoryService,
    HttpClientFactoryService>();
```

12. Save all files.

The code in the **HttpClientFactoryService** class so far:

```
public class HttpClientFactoryService
{
    #region Variables
    private readonly IHttpClientFactory _httpClientFactory;
    private CancellationTokenSource _cancellationTokenSource;
    private readonly CancellationToken _cancellationToken;
    #endregion

    #region Constructor
    public HttpClientFactoryService(IHttpClientFactory
    httpClientFactory)
    {
        _httpClientFactory = httpClientFactory;
        _cancellationTokenSource = new CancellationTokenSource();
        _cancellationToken = _cancellationTokenSource.Token;
    }
    #endregion
}
```

The code in the **AdminAPIService** class so far:

```
public class AdminAPIService : IAdminService
{
    #region Properties
    private readonly IHttpClientFactoryService _http;
    #endregion

    #region Constructor
    public AdminAPIService(IHttpClientFactoryService http)
    {
        _http = http;
    }
    #endregion

    #region Methods
    public Task<bool> AnyAsync<TEntity>(Expression<Func<TEntity, bool>>
    expression) where TEntity : class
    {
```

```csharp
            throw new NotImplementedException();
        }

        public Task<int> CreateAsync<TSource, TDestination>(TSource item)
            where TSource : class where TDestination : class
        {
            throw new NotImplementedException();
        }

        public Task<bool> DeleteAsync<TSource>(Expression<Func<TSource,
        bool>> expression) where TSource : class
        {
            throw new NotImplementedException();
        }

        public Task<List<TDestination>> GetAsync<TSource, TDestination>(
        bool include = false)
        where TSource : class where TDestination : class
        {
            throw new NotImplementedException();
        }

        public Task<List<TDestination>> GetAsync<TSource, TDestination>(
        Expression<Func<TSource, bool>> expression, bool include = false)
        where TSource : class where TDestination : class
        {
            throw new NotImplementedException();
        }

        public Task<TDestination> SingleAsync<TSource, TDestination>(
        Expression<Func<TSource, bool>> expression, bool include = false)
        where TSource : class where TDestination : class
        {
            throw new NotImplementedException();
        }

        public Task<bool> UpdateAsync<TSource, TDestination>(TSource item)
            where TSource : class where TDestination : class
        {
            throw new NotImplementedException();
        }
        #endregion
}
```

Adding the HttpResponseException class

This exception class will be used to report errors from the API.

1. Add a new folder named *Exceptions* to the **Common** project.
2. Add a class named **HttpResponseException** to the *Exceptions* folder.
3. Inherit the **Exception** base class.
4. Add a **public** read-only property of type **HttpStatusCode** named **HttpStatusCode** to the class.
5. Add a **public** read-only property of type **object** named **ValidationErrors** to the class.
   ```
   public HttpStatusCode HttpStatusCode { get; }
   public object ValidationErrors { get; }
   ```
6. Add a constructor with parameters for HTTP status code, message, and validation errors.
   ```
   public HttpResponseException(HttpStatusCode status, string message, object validationErrors) : base(message)
   {
       HttpStatusCode = status;
       ValidationErrors = validationErrors;
   }
   ```
7. Now, add two more constructors with HTTP status code and message, and HTTP status code respectively.
8. Save the file.

The complete code for the **HttpResponseException** class:

```
public class HttpResponseException : Exception
{
    public HttpStatusCode HttpStatusCode { get; }
    public object ValidationErrors { get; }

    public HttpResponseException(HttpStatusCode status, string message, object validationErrors) : base(message)
    {
        HttpStatusCode = status;
        ValidationErrors = validationErrors;
    }
```

```
    public HttpResponseException(HttpStatusCode status, string message)
        : this(status, message, null)
    {
        HttpStatusCode = status;
    }

    public HttpResponseException(HttpStatusCode status)
        : this(status, string.Empty, null)
    {
        HttpStatusCode = status;
    }
}
```

Adding the StreamExtensions Class

This **static** class will contain extension methods for a **Stream** instance and will be used to serialize to and deserialize from JSON objects.

Serialize a JSON Object

This method will serialize JSON to a stream that can be used to send the request data to the API.

1. Add a **public static** class named **StreamExtensions** to the *Extensions* folder in the **Common** project.
2. Add an asynchronous method named **SerializeToJsonAndWriteAsync** that returns a **Task** and has six parameters.
   a. **stream** of type **Stream**; is the stream that the method works on.
   b. **objectToWrite** of type **T**; is the data to serialize.
   c. **encoding** of type **Encoding**; is the data encoding to use for the data.
   d. **bufferSize** of type **int**; determines how many bytes of the stream that will be processed at a time.
   e. **leaveOpen** of type **bool**; keeps the stream open after the initial **StreamWriter** disposes of it **true**.
   f. **resetStream** of type **bool**; restes the stream to position 0 after writing it if **true**.

```
public static async Task SerializeToJsonAndWriteAsync<T>(
    this Stream stream, T objectToWrite, Encoding encoding,
    int bufferSize, bool leaveOpen, bool resetStream = false) { }
```

3. Return exceptions if the **stream** or **encoding** parameters are **null**, or if it isn't possible to write to the stream.
   ```
   if (stream == null) throw new ArgumentNullException(
       nameof(stream));
   if (!stream.CanWrite) throw new NotSupportedException(
       "Can't write to this stream.");
   if (encoding == null) throw new ArgumentNullException(
       nameof(encoding));
   ```

4. Add a **using**-block for the **StreamWriter** that will serialize the data.
   ```
   using (var streamWriter = new StreamWriter(stream, encoding,
   bufferSize, leaveOpen)) { }
   ```

5. Add a **using**-block for the **JsonTextWriter** that uses the stream inside the previous **using**-block. It will convert the data to JSON (requires the **Newtonsoft.Json** NuGet package).
   ```
   using (var jsonTextWriter = new JsonTextWriter(streamWriter)) { }
   ```

6. Inside the second **using**-block, create an instance of the **JsonSerializer** and store it in a variable named **jsonSerializer** (requires the **Newtonsoft.Json** NuGet package).
   a. Call the **Serialize** method on the **jsonSerializer** object and pass in the **jsonTextWriter** instance to serialize the generic **objectToWrite** object.
   b. Flush the **jsonTextWriter** to make sure that all bytes will be serialized.
   ```
   var jsonSerializer = new JsonSerializer();
   jsonSerializer.Serialize(jsonTextWriter, objectToWrite);
   await jsonTextWriter.FlushAsync();
   ```

7. Below both **using**-blocks, add an if-block that checks if the stream should be reset to position 0.
   ```
   if (resetStream && stream.CanSeek)
       stream.Seek(0, SeekOrigin.Begin);
   ```

8. Save the file.

The complete code for the **SerializeToJsonAndWriteAsync** extension method:

```
public static async Task SerializeToJsonAndWriteAsync<T>(
this Stream stream, T objectToWrite, Encoding encoding, int bufferSize,
bool leaveOpen, bool resetStream = false)
{
    if (stream == null) throw new ArgumentNullException(nameof(stream));
    if (!stream.CanWrite) throw new NotSupportedException(
```

```csharp
        "Can't write to this stream.");
    if (encoding == null) throw new ArgumentNullException(nameof(
        encoding));

    using (var streamWriter = new StreamWriter(stream, encoding,
    bufferSize, leaveOpen))
    {
        using (var jsonTextWriter = new JsonTextWriter(streamWriter))
        {
            var jsonSerializer = new JsonSerializer();
            jsonSerializer.Serialize(jsonTextWriter, objectToWrite);
            await jsonTextWriter.FlushAsync();
        }
    }

    // Rest stream to position 0 after writing to the stream
    if (resetStream && stream.CanSeek) stream.Seek(0, SeekOrigin.Begin);
}
```

Deserialize From JSON to an Object of Generic Type

This method will deserialize the JSON response data sent from the API to the specified generic type.

1. Add a **public static** method named **ReadAndDeserializeFromJson<T>** that works on a **Stream** instance to the **StreamExtensions** class.
   ```csharp
   public static T ReadAndDeserializeFromJson<T>(this Stream stream)
   ```

2. Return exceptions if the **stream** is **null**, or if it isn't possible to read from the stream.
   ```csharp
   if (stream == null) throw new ArgumentNullException(
       nameof(stream));
   if (!stream.CanRead) throw new NotSupportedException(
       "Can't read from this stream.");
   ```

3. Add a **using**-block for the **StreamReader** that that will deserialize the JSON data into objects of the generic type **T**.
   ```csharp
   using (var streamReader = new StreamReader(stream,
       new UTF8Encoding(), true, 1024, false)) { }
   ```

4. Inside the previous **using**-block, add a **using**-block for the **JsonTextreader** that uses the stream to read JSON through the **stream** object.
   ```csharp
   using (var jsonTextReader = new JsonTextReader(streamReader)) { }
   ```

26. Calling The API With HttpClient

5. Inside the second **using**-block, create an instance of the **JsonSerializer** and store it in a variable named **jsonSerializer**.
   a. Call the **Deserialize<T>** method on the **jsonSerializer** object and pass in the **jsonTextReader** instance to convert the JSON data into objects of type **T**.
   b. Flush the **jsonTextWriter** to make sure that all bytes are serialized.

   ```
   var jsonSerializer = new JsonSerializer();
   return jsonSerializer.Deserialize<T>(jsonTextReader);
   ```

6. Save the file.

The complete code for the **ReadAndDeserializeFromJson<T>** extension method:

```
public static T ReadAndDeserializeFromJson<T>(this Stream stream)
{
    if (stream == null) throw new ArgumentNullException(nameof(stream));
    if (!stream.CanRead) throw new NotSupportedException(
        "Can't read from this stream.");

    using (var streamReader = new StreamReader(stream,
    new UTF8Encoding(), true, 1024, false))
    {
        using (var jsonTextReader = new JsonTextReader(streamReader))
        {
            var jsonSerializer = new JsonSerializer();
            return jsonSerializer.Deserialize<T>(jsonTextReader);
        }
    }
}
```

Deserialize From JSON to an Object Instance

This method will deserialize the JSON response data sent from the API into an **object** instance.

1. Add a **public static** method named **ReadAndDeserializeFromJson** that works on a **Stream** instance to the **StreamExtensions** class.
   ```
   public static object ReadAndDeserializeFromJson(this Stream stream)
   ```

2. Return exceptions if the **stream** is **null**, or if it isn't possible to read from the stream.

3. Add a **using**-block for the **StreamReader** that that will deserialize the JSON data into an instance of the **object** type.
4. Add a **using**-block for the **JsonTextreader** that uses the stream inside the previous **using**-block to read JSON through the **stream** object.
5. Inside the second **using**-block, create an instance of the **JsonSerializer** and store it in a variable named **jsonSerializer**.
6. Call the **Deserialize** method on the **jsonSerializer** object and pass in the **jsonTextReader** instance to convert the JSON data into an instance of the **object** type.
7. Save the file.

The complete code for the **ReadAndDeserializeFromJson** extension method:

```
public static object ReadAndDeserializeFromJson(this Stream stream)
{
    if (stream == null) throw new ArgumentNullException(nameof(stream));
    if (!stream.CanRead) throw new NotSupportedException(
        "Can't read from this stream.");

    using (var streamReader = new StreamReader(stream,
    new UTF8Encoding(), true, 1024, false))
    {
        using (var jsonTextReader = new JsonTextReader(streamReader))
        {
            var jsonSerializer = new JsonSerializer();
            return jsonSerializer.Deserialize(jsonTextReader);
        }
    }
}
```

Adding the HttpClientExtensions Class

This **static** class will contain extension methods for the **HttpClient** instance that the **HttpClientFactory** service will create. These methods will add necessary data to the headers and body of the request before it is sent to the API and then process the response.

You will add methods to this class as you add functionality to the **HttpClientFactory** class.

26. Calling The API With HttpClient

Create an Extension Method That Adds Request Headers

The request headers specify the required data format (*application/json*), adds a bearer token if a token is sent into the method though the **token** parameter, and specifies which compression method to use to minimize the size of the request's payload.

1. Add a **public static** class named **HttpClientExtensions** to the *Extensions* folder in the **Common** project.
2. Add a **private static** method named **CreateRequestHeaders** that returns a **HttpRequestMessage** and can be used on **strings**. The method should have two parameters; one for the HTTP method (Get, Put, Post, Delete) and one for the token with an empty string as its default value.
   ```
   private static HttpRequestMessage CreateRequestHeaders(this string
   uri, HttpMethod httpMethod, string token = "") { }
   ```
3. Add an **HttpRequestMessage** variable and pass the values from the **httpMethod** and **uri** parameters to its constructor.
   ```
   var requestHeader = new HttpRequestMessage(httpMethod, uri);
   ```
4. Use the **requestHeader** variable to add an **Accept** header for the *application/json* data format.
   ```
   requestHeader.Headers.Accept.Add(
       new MediaTypeWithQualityHeaderValue("application/json"));
   ```
5. Use the **requestHeader** variable to add an **Authorization** header with a *bearer* token for the token in the **token** parameter if it contains a value. You will add JWT authentication and authorization in an upcoming chapter.
   ```
   if (!token.IsNullOrEmptyOrWhiteSpace())
       requestHeader.Headers.Authorization =
           new AuthenticationHeaderValue("bearer", token);
   ```
6. Use the **requestHeader** variable to add an **AcceptEncoding** header for *gzip* compression if it is a **Get** request.
   ```
   if (httpMethod.Equals(HttpMethod.Get))
       requestHeader.Headers.AcceptEncoding.Add(
           new StringWithQualityHeaderValue("gzip"));
   ```
7. Return the **requestHeader** header object.

The complete code for the **CreateRequestHeaders** extension method:

```
private static HttpRequestMessage CreateRequestHeaders(this string uri, 
HttpMethod httpMethod, string token = "")
{
    var requestHeader = new HttpRequestMessage(httpMethod, uri);
    requestHeader.Headers.Accept.Add(
        new MediaTypeWithQualityHeaderValue("application/json"));

    if (!token.IsNullOrEmptyOrWhiteSpace())
        requestHeader.Headers.Authorization =
            new AuthenticationHeaderValue("bearer", token);

    if (httpMethod.Equals(HttpMethod.Get))
        requestHeader.Headers.AcceptEncoding.Add(
            new StringWithQualityHeaderValue("gzip"));

    return requestHeader;
}
```

Create an Extension Method That Serializes the Request Content

Because serializing data can improve performance, the request content, if available, will be serialized before adding it to the request.

1. Add a **private static** method named **SerializeRequestContentAsync** to the **HttpClientExtensions** class that return a **StreamContent** object wrapped in a **Task** and work with a generic type named **TRequest** that contains the content to serialize.
   ```
   private static async Task<StreamContent> 
   SerializeRequestContentAsync<TRequest>(this TRequest content) { }
   ```

2. Create a **MemoryStream** variable named **stream**.
   ```
   var stream = new MemoryStream();
   ```

3. Call the **SerializeToJsonAndWriteAsync** extension method you created earlier on the **stream** object to serialize the generic **TRequest** object to JSON. Pass in the content from the **content** parameter.
   ```
   await stream.SerializeToJsonAndWriteAsync(content, new 
   UTF8Encoding(), 1024, true);
   ```

4. Reset the stream to position 0 so that is can be read again.
   ```
   stream.Seek(0, SeekOrigin.Begin);
   ```

5. Create a **StreamContent** object for the stream and return it.
   ```
   return new StreamContent(stream);
   ```

6. Save all files.

The complete code for the **SerializeRequestContentAsync** method:

```
private static async Task<StreamContent>
SerializeRequestContentAsync<TRequest>(this TRequest content)
{
    var stream = new MemoryStream();
    await stream.SerializeToJsonAndWriteAsync(content,
        new UTF8Encoding(), 1024, true);
    stream.Seek(0, SeekOrigin.Begin);

    return new StreamContent(stream);
}
```

Create an Extension Method That Creates Request Content

The method adds request content data to the API request before sending it.

1. Add a **private static** method named **CreateRequestContent** to the **HttpClientExtensions** class that works on a **HttpRequestMessage** instance and has a generic **TRequest** parameter named **content**. It should return an instance of the **HttpRequestMessage** class wrapped in a **Task**.
   ```
   private static async Task<HttpRequestMessage>
   CreateRequestContent<TRequest>(this HttpRequestMessage
   requestMessage, TRequest content) { }
   ```

2. Assign the serialized content from the **content** parameter to the **Content** property of the **requestMessage** object; call the **SerializeRequestContentAsync** method to serialize the data.
   ```
   requestMessage.Content =
       await content.SerializeRequestContentAsync();
   ```

3. Add *application/json* as the content type to the header.
   ```
   requestMessage.Content.Headers.ContentType =
       new MediaTypeHeaderValue("application/json");
   ```

4. Return the **requestMessage** object.

ASP.NET Core 2.2 MVC, Razor Pages, API, JSON Web Tokens & HttpClient

The complete code for the **CreateRequestContent** method:

```
private static async Task<HttpRequestMessage>
CreateRequestContent<TRequest>(this HttpRequestMessage requestMessage,
TRequest content)
{
    requestMessage.Content =
        await content.SerializeRequestContentAsync();

    requestMessage.Content.Headers.ContentType =
        new MediaTypeHeaderValue("application/json");

    return requestMessage;
}
```

Create an Extension Method That Deserializes Response Data

This method will deserialize the response data that the API returns from a request.

1. Add a **private static** method named **DeserializeResponse** to the **HttpClientExtensions** class that works on a **HttpResponseMessage** instance and returns an instance of the **TResponse** type wrapped in a **Task**.
   ```
   private static async Task<TResponse> DeserializeResponse
   <TResponse>(this HttpResponseMessage response) { }
   ```

2. Call the **EnsureSuccessStatusCode** method on the **response** object to ensure that it doesn't have any errors.

3. Read the content of the **response.Content** property as a stream and store the result in a variable named **responseStream**.
   ```
   var responseStream = await response.Content.ReadAsStreamAsync();
   ```

4. Return the result from a call to the **ReadAndDeserializeFromJson** method on the stream to deserialize it into JSON of the specified generic **TResponse** type.
   ```
   return responseStream.ReadAndDeserializeFromJson<TResponse>();
   ```

5. Save the file.

The complete code for the **DeserializeResponse** method:

```
private static async Task<TResponse> DeserializeResponse<TResponse>(this
HttpResponseMessage response)
{
    response.EnsureSuccessStatusCode();
    var responseStream = await response.Content.ReadAsStreamAsync();
    return responseStream.ReadAndDeserializeFromJson<TResponse>();
}
```

Create an Extension Method That Throws an Exception Based on the Response Status Code

This method will check the response's status code and throw an **HttpResponseException** with a status message if an HTTP error has occurred. It can be called to ensure that a response has succeeded; it will throw an exception if the request was unsuccessful.

1. Add a **private static** method named **CheckStatusCodes** to the **HttpClientExtensions** class that works on a **HttpResponseMessage** instance and returns **Task**.
   ```
   private static async Task CheckStatusCodes(
       this HttpResponseMessage response) { }
   ```

2. Check if the response has an error with its **IsSuccessStatusCode** property and, if successful, calls the **EnsureSuccessStatusCode** method on the **response** object to be certain that no other errors have occurred.
   ```
   if (!response.IsSuccessStatusCode) { }
   else response.EnsureSuccessStatusCode();
   ```

3. Inside the previous if-block, add an **object** variable named **validationErrors** and assign **null** to it. Add a **string** variable named **message** and assign it an empty string.

4. Inside the previous if-block, add an if-block that checks for the *422 Unprocessable Entity* status code. If returning that status code, deserializing the response content for validation error messages is possible.
   ```
   if (response.StatusCode == HttpStatusCode.UnprocessableEntity)
   {
       var errorStream = await response.Content.ReadAsStreamAsync();
       validationErrors = errorStream.ReadAndDeserializeFromJson();
       message = "Could not process the entity.";
   }
   ```

5. Add else if-blocks for the most frequently returned errors (*400 Bad Request, 401 Unauthorized, 403 Forbidden, 404 Not Found*) and assign an appropriate message to the **message** variable.
6. Throw an **HttpResponseException** exception at the end of the if-block and pass in the **validationErrors** and **message** variables.
   throw new HttpResponseException(response.StatusCode, message, validationErrors);
7. Save the file.

The complete code for the **CheckStatusCodes** method:

```
private static async Task CheckStatusCodes(this HttpResponseMessage response)
{
    if (!response.IsSuccessStatusCode)
    {
        object validationErrors = null;
        var message = string.Empty;

        if (response.StatusCode == HttpStatusCode.UnprocessableEntity)
        {
            var errorStream =
                await response.Content.ReadAsStreamAsync();
            validationErrors = errorStream.ReadAndDeserializeFromJson();
            message = "Could not process the entity.";
        }
        else if (response.StatusCode == HttpStatusCode.BadRequest)
            message = "Bad request.";
        else if (response.StatusCode == HttpStatusCode.Forbidden)
            message = "Access denied.";
        else if (response.StatusCode == HttpStatusCode.NotFound)
            message = "Could not find the entity.";
        else if (response.StatusCode == HttpStatusCode.Unauthorized)
            message = "Not Logged In.";

        throw new HttpResponseException(response.StatusCode, message,
            validationErrors);
    }
    else
        response.EnsureSuccessStatusCode();
}
```

Implementing the GetAsync Method

This method will return a collection of DTO objects from the API using the **HttpClient-FactoryService** and the properties of the generic **TSource** type, which requires the use of reflection to inspect the type.

Find Id Properties From a Generic Type with Reflection

To figure out the ids that must be sent to the API to conform to the URI format you implemented in its controllers earlier, you need to extract them from the generic **TSource** type that defines the methods with reflection. The **TSource** type will be one of the entity classes that you used when creating the database, so it should contain the id properties needed.

```
public Task<List<TDestination>> GetAsync<TSource, TDestination>(bool
include = false) where TSource : class where TDestination : class { }
```

The found id properties are stored temporarily in a **Dictionary<string, object>** property named **_properties** for easy access. The property values in the collection will be 0 since they can't be determined from a generic type, but that doesn't matter since they won't be used in the API because all records will be returned from the database; they are only needed to create a valid URI.

```
Dictionary<string, object> _properties = new Dictionary<string,
object>();
```

1. Add a **Dictionary<string, object>** property named **_properties** to the **AdminAPIService** class and instantiate it.
2. Add a **private** parameter-less **void** method named **GetProperties<TSource>** to the **AdminAPIService** class.
   ```
   private void GetProperties<TSource>() { }
   ```
3. Inside the method, clear the **_properties** collection in the method.
   ```
   _properties.Clear();
   ```
4. Get the generic **TSource** type and store it in a variable named **type**.
   ```
   var type = typeof(TSource);
   ```
5. Call the **GetProperty** reflection method on the **type** variable to try to fetch the **Id**, **CourseId**, and **ModuleId** properties if they exist and store them in variables with the same names; if a property doesn't exist, its variable will contain **null**.
   ```
   var id = type.GetProperty("Id");
   var moduleId = type.GetProperty("ModuleId");
   var courseId = type.GetProperty("CourseId");
   ```

6. Check each property variable and add its name and the value 0 to the **_properties** collection if it exists. Note that the key name is in camel-case because the route ids for the controllers are in camel-case.
   ```
   if (id != null) _properties.Add("id", 0);
   if (moduleId != null) _properties.Add("moduleId", 0);
   if (courseId != null) _properties.Add("courseId", 0);
   ```
7. Add a try-block that surrounds the **NotImplementedException** in the **GetAsync** method that only has a **bool** parameter. Add a catch-block that throws the exception up the call chain.
8. Call the **GetProperties** method above the **throw**-statement in the try-block.
   ```
   GetProperties<TSource>();
   ```
9. Place a breakpoint on the row with the **NotImplementedException**.
10. Start the **Admin** application with debugging and click the **Instructor** card on the main page.
11. When the execution halts, inspect the **_properties** collection and add 0 to a key named for the **Id** property in the **Instructor** entity.
12. Stop the application in Visual Studio.

The complete code for the **GetProperties** method:

```
private void GetProperties<TSource>()
{
    _properties.Clear();
    var type = typeof(TSource);
    var id = type.GetProperty("Id");
    var moduleId = type.GetProperty("ModuleId");
    var courseId = type.GetProperty("CourseId");

    if (id != null) _properties.Add("id", 0);
    if (moduleId != null) _properties.Add("moduleId", 0);
    if (courseId != null) _properties.Add("courseId", 0);
}
```

The code in the **GetAsync** method, so far:

```
public Task<List<TDestination>> GetAsync<TSource, TDestination>(bool include = false) where TSource : class where TDestination : class
{
    try
    {
```

26. Calling The API With HttpClient

```
            GetProperties<TSource>();
            throw new NotImplementedException();
        }
        catch
        {
            throw;
        }
    }
}
```

Create a URI with the Generic Type and the Ids in the _properties Collection

To create a URI, you need to use the id names and values in the **_properties** collection and the name of the generic **TSource** type that defines the methods. Because the URI has the entity names and their ids, you need to send the values from the properties in the collection even if they are 0. The code you add to the **Get** actions later ignores 0 values.

Example route Uris:
api/instructors
api/courses
api/courses/{courseId}
api/courses/{courseId}/modules
api/courses/{courseId}/modules/{moduleId}
api/courses/{courseId}/modules/{moduleId}/videos

The **FormatUriWithoutIds<TSource>()** method should try to fetch the value for the **courseId** and **moduleId** keys in the collection and add their path to the URI if they exist and return the finished URI.

```
object courseId;
bool succeeded = _properties.TryGetValue("courseId", out courseId);
if (succeeded) uri = $"{uri}/courses/0";
```

1. Add a method named **FormatUriWithoutIds<TSource>** that returns a **string** to the **AdminAPIService** class.
   `private string FormatUriWithoutIds<TSource>() { }`
2. Add a **string** variable named **uri** with an initial value of *api* to the method.
3. Add two **object** variables named **courseId** and **moduleId** that will hold the values for the two keys with the same names in the **_properties** collection if they exist.
   ```
   string uri = "api";
   object moduleId, courseId;
   ```

4. Try to fetch the value for the **courseId** key in the collection and append its path to the **uri** variable if it exists.
   ```
   bool succeeded = _properties.TryGetValue("courseId", out courseId);
   if (succeeded) uri = $"{uri}/courses/0";
   ```
5. Repeat the previous bullet for the **moduleId** key in the collection.
6. Because all controller names are in plural form, you append the name of the **TSource** type with a trailing **s**.
   ```
   uri = $"{uri}/{typeof(TSource).Name}s";
   ```
7. Return the value in the **uri** variable.
8. Call the **FormatUriWithoutIds** method below the **GetProperties** method call in the **GetAsync** method in the **AdminAPIService** class and save the result in a variable named **uri**.
   ```
   string uri = FormatUriWithoutIds<TSource>();
   ```
9. Start the **Admin** application with debugging and click the **Instructor** card on the main page.
10. When the execution halts at the breakpoint, inspect the **uri** variable in the **GetAsync** method and make sure that it contains a valid URI.
11. Stop the application in Visual Studio.

The complete code for the **FormatUriWithoutIds** method:

```
private string FormatUriWithoutIds<TSource>()
{
    string uri = "api";
    object moduleId, courseId;

    bool succeeded = _properties.TryGetValue("courseId", out courseId);
    if (succeeded) uri = $"{uri}/courses/0";

    succeeded = _properties.TryGetValue("moduleId", out moduleId);
    if (succeeded) uri = $"{uri}/modules/0";

    uri = $"{uri}/{typeof(TSource).Name}s";

    return uri;
}
```

The code in the **GetAsync** method so far:

```
public Task<List<TDestination>> GetAsync<TSource, TDestination>(bool
include = false) where TSource : class where TDestination : class
{
    try
    {
        GetProperties<TSource>();
        string uri = FormatUriWithoutIds<TSource>();
        throw new NotImplementedException();
    }
    catch
    {
        throw;
    }
}
```

Calling the API

To call the API, you will add an asynchronous method named **GetListAsync** to the **IHttpClientFactoryService** interface and the **HttpClientFactoryService** class that calls the API over HTTP using the injected **IHttpClientFactory** instance.

The **GetListAsync** method should return a list of **TResponse** objects wrapped in a **Task** because the method is asynchronous and calls other asynchronous methods; it should also have tree **string** parameters named **uri**, **serviceName**, and **token**. The **uri** parameter will contain the URI from the **FormatUriWithoutIds** method call; the **serviceName** parameter will contain the name of the **HttpClient** that you have configured in the **Startup** class; the **token** parameter will be used in the next chapter when you implement authorization with JSON Web Tokens.

Because you might want to inspect the HTTP status code and validation errors when an exception has occurred, you will throw an **HttpResponseException** exception.

Adding the GetListAsync Extension Method in the HttpClientExtensions Class

1. Add a method named **GetListAsync** method that works on **HttpClient** objects to the **HttpClientExtensions** class. It should have two **string** parameters named **uri** and **token**; the latter will be used in the next chapter when you implement JWT tokens. It should also have a **CancellationToken** parameter named **cancellationToken** that can be used to cancel the current requests. The method should return a list of **TResponse** objects wrapped in a **Task**.

```
public static async Task<List<TResponse>> GetListAsync<TResponse>(
    this HttpClient client, string uri, CancellationToken 
    cancellationToken, string token = "") { }
```

2. Add a try/catch-block to the method and throw any exceptions up the call chain in the catch-block.
3. Call the **CreateRequestHeaders** extension method on the **uri** parameter in the try-block and pass in **HttpMethod.Get** to specify to call a **Get** action in the API. Also, pass in the token parameter with the token to use when implementing the token authorization in the next chapter. Store the returned request header in a variable named **requestHeaders**.
   ```
   var requestMessage = uri.CreateRequestHeaders(HttpMethod.Get, 
       token);
   ```
4. Add a **using**-block for the call to the **SendAsync** method (in the **HttpClient** service you configured in the **Startup** class) that calls the **Get** action method in the API. Pass in the **requestMessage** and **cancellationToken** variables and **HttpCompletionOption.ResponseHeadersRead** to specify that streaming the content can begin when the response headers have arrived from the API.
   ```
   using (var response = await client.SendAsync(requestMessage, 
   HttpCompletionOption.ResponseHeadersRead, cancellationToken)) { }
   ```
5. Inside the **using**-block, stream the response content to a variable named **stream**.
   ```
   var stream = await response.Content.ReadAsStreamAsync();
   ```
6. Inside the **using**-block, call the **CheckStatusCodes** method on the **response** variable to check for response errors.
   ```
   await response.CheckStatusCodes();
   ```
7. Inside the **using**-block, Call the **ReadAndDeserializeFromJson** method — that deserializes the stream content into a list of **TResponse** objects — and return the result.
   ```
   return stream.ReadAndDeserializeFromJson<List<TResponse>>();
   ```
8. Save all files.

26. Calling The API With HttpClient

The code for the **GetListAsync** extension method in the **HttpClientExtensions** class:

```
public static async Task<List<TResponse>> GetListAsync<TResponse>(
this HttpClient client, string uri, CancellationToken cancellationToken,
string token = "")
{
    try
    {
        var requestMessage = uri.CreateRequestHeaders(HttpMethod.Get,
            token);

        using (var response = await client.SendAsync(
        requestMessage, HttpCompletionOption.ResponseHeadersRead,
        cancellationToken))
        {
            var stream = await response.Content.ReadAsStreamAsync();
            await response.CheckStatusCodes();
            return stream.ReadAndDeserializeFromJson<List<TResponse>>();
        }
    }
    catch
    {
        throw;
    }
}
```

Adding the GetListAsync Method to the HttpClientFactoryService Class

1. Add a definition for the **GetListAsync** method to the **IHttpClientFactoryService** interface.
   `Task<List<TResponse>> GetListAsync<TResponse>(string uri, string serviceName, string token = "") where TResponse: class;`

2. Implement the method in the **HttpClientFactoryService** class and replace the **throw** statement with a try/catch-block where the catch throws any exceptions up the call chain.

3. Add the **async** keyword to the method to make it asynchronous.

4. Check that the **uri** and **serviceName** parameters aren't **null** or empty by calling the **IsNullOrEmptyOrWhiteSpace** extension method you added earlier inside the try-block. If any of them are **null** or empty, then throw a **HttpResponseException** exception with the status code *404 Not Found*.

```
        if (new string[] { uri, serviceName }.IsNullOrEmptyOrWhiteSpace())
            throw new HttpResponseException(HttpStatusCode.NotFound,
                "Could not find the resource");
```

5. Let the **HttpClientFactory** create an **HttpClient** instance and store it in a variable named **httpClient**. This object will make the call to the API.
   `var httpClient = _httpClientFactory.CreateClient(serviceName);`

6. Call the **GetListAsync** extension method on the **httpClient** object and pass in the value from the **uri**, **_cancellationToken** and the **token** variables and parameters. Return the result.

7. Save all files.

The complete code for the **GetListAsync** method in the **HttpClientFactoryService** class:

```
public async Task<List<TResponse>> GetListAsync<TResponse>(string uri,
string serviceName, string token = "") where TResponse : class
{
    try
    {
        if (new string[] { uri, serviceName }
            .IsNullOrEmptyOrWhiteSpace())
            throw new HttpResponseException(HttpStatusCode.NotFound,
                "Could not find the resource");

        var httpClient = _httpClientFactory.CreateClient(serviceName);
        return await httpClient.GetListAsync<TResponse>(uri.ToLower(),
            _cancellationToken, token);
    }
    catch
    {
        throw;
    }
}
```

Adding the GetAsync Method to the AdminAPIService Class

1. Go to the **GetAsync** method that you began implementing earlier in the **AdminAPIService** class and add the **async** keyword if you haven't already.
2. Remove the **NotImplementedException** exception.
3. Return the result from a call to the **GetListAsync** method on the **_http** object to call one of the API's **Get** actions. Pass in the **uri** parameter and append an

include parameter to it. Also, pass in the name of the **HttpClient** that you configured in the **Admin** project's **Startup** class.
```
return await _http.GetListAsync<TDestination>($"{uri}?include=
    {include.ToString()}", "AdminClient");
```
4. Save all files.
5. Start the **API** project and then the **Admin** project. Click the **Instructor** card. The **Index** Razor Page disiplays the instructors.
6. Stop the applications in Visual Studio.

The complete code for the **GetAsync** method in the **AdminAPIService** class:

```
public async Task<List<TDestination>> GetAsync<TSource,
TDestination>(bool include = false) where TSource : class where
TDestination : class
{
    try
    {
        GetProperties<TSource>();
        string uri = FormatUriWithoutIds<TSource>();
        return await _http.GetListAsync<TDestination>($"{uri}?include=
            {include.ToString()}", "AdminClient");
    }
    catch
    {
        throw;
    }
}
```

Implementing the SingleAsync Method

This method will fetch a single entity from the database by calling the **Get** action that has an id parameter and returns a DTO object in any of the API controllers.

To find out the ids to use in the URI when calling the API, you must use reflection to extract them from the Lambda expression passed in to the **GetProperties** method; this is trickier than finding ids in a generic type because recursion is involved when several ids are part of the Lambda.

The **GetProperties** method calls a method named **ResolveExpression** that picks apart the Lambda expression and uses recursion to fetch the left and right parts of each binary expression that contains an **and** (&&) operator. For each left and right expression, the

GetExpressionProperties method is called to extract the property and value from the expression.

If you want to deepen your knowledge about reflection and Lambda expressions, then the *LiteDB NoSQL Document Store* is an excellent example you can browse on GitHub. You can find the code here: *https://github.com/mbdavid/LiteDB*.

Each part of the Lambda has a left and a right part, where the left is a **MemberExpression** that contains the name of the property in the Lambda comparison and a **ConstantExpression** that holds the comparison value.

Consider the following Lambda expression; its left part is the **FirstName** property, and its right part is the name *Luke*.

```
p => p.FirstName.Equals("Luke")
```

This expression would only have one **BinaryExpression**.

```
LambdaExpression
{
    Body = BinaryExpression
    {
        Left = BinaryExpression
        {
            NodeType = Equal,
            Left = MemberExpression
            {
                Member.Name = "FirstName"
            },
            Right = ConstantExpression
            {
                Value = "Luke"
            }
        }
    }
}
```

Consider the following Lambda expression that has two parts; its left part is the **BinaryExpression** for the **FirstName** property and its right part is another **BinaryExpression** for the **LastName** property.

```
p => p.FirstName.Equals("Luke") && p.LastName.Equals("Skywalker")
```

An **AndAlso** node type combines the two **BinaryExpressions**.

```
LambdaExpression
{
    Body = BinaryExpression
    {
        Left = BinaryExpression
        {
            NodeType = Equal,
            Left = MemberExpression
            {
                Member.Name = "FirstName"
            },
            Right = ConstantExpression
            {
                Value = "Luke"
            }
        },
        Right = BinaryExpression
        {
            NodeType = Equal,
            Left = MemberExpression
            {
                Member.Name = "LastName"
            },
            Right = ConstantExpression
            {
                Value = "Skywalker"
            }
        }
    }
}
```

Consider the following Lambda expression that has three parts; its left part is a **Binary-Expression** with a left **BinaryExpression** part for the **FirstName** property and a right **BinaryExpression** part for the **LastName** property; the third expression is the right **Binary-Expression** part of the first **BinaryExpression** for the **Age** property.

```
p => p.FirstName.Equals("Luke") && p.LastName.Equals("Skywalker") &&
p.Age < 50
```

An **AndAlso** node type combines the two **BinaryExpressions**. The outer left **BinaryExpression** contains two other **BinaryExpressions** for the **FirstName** and **LastName** properties, and the outer right **BinaryExpression** contains the **Age** property.

```
LambdaExpression
{
    Body = BinaryExpression
    {
        NodeType = AndAlso,
        Left = BinaryExpression
        {
            NodeType = AndAlso,
            Left = BinaryExpression
            {
                NodeType = Equal,
                Left = MemberExpression
                {
                    Member.Name = "FirstName"
                },
                Right = ConstantExpression
                {
                    Value = "Luke"
                }
            },
            Right = BinaryExpression
            {
                NodeType = Equal,
                Left = MemberExpression
                {
                    Member.Name = "LastName"
                },
                Right = ConstantExpression
                {
                    Value = "Skywalker"
                }
            }
        },
        Right = BinaryExpression
        {
            NodeType = LessThan,
            Left = MemberExpression
            {
                Member.Name = "Age"
            },
```

```
            Right = ConstantExpression
            {
                Value = 50
            }
        }
    }
}
```

As you can see from the examples, recursion will be necessary to find all the properties and values in the Lambda expression. Let's make it a little easier by restricting the Lambda expression to use **and** (&&) to combine the individual property expressions and the **Equals** method to compare the values of the property and the comparison value. Note that == and **Equals** are evaluated differently by the logic, so to be consistent, you will only implement the code for the **Equals** method.

The GetExpressionProperties Method

This method picks apart a single expression and finds the property name with the **MemberExpression** object and the value with the **ConstantExpression** object.

```
NodeType = Equal,
Left = MemberExpression
{
    Member.Name = "FirstName"
},
Right = ConstantExpression
{
    Value = "Luke"
}
```

This **void** method should have an **Expression** parameter that will contain a single expression from the Lambda expression; an expression for one property comparison, for example: p.FirstName.Equals("Luke")

1. Add a **void** method named **GetExpressionProperties** that has an **Expression** parameter to the **AdminAPIService** class.
   `private void GetExpressionProperties(Expression expression) { }`

2. Cast the expression parameter to **MethodCallExpression** and store it in a variable named **body**. You need to do this to get access to its **Arguments** collection.
   `var body = (MethodCallExpression)expression;`

3. Fetch the first argument from the body object's **Arguments** collection.
   ```
   var argument = body.Arguments[0];
   ```
4. Add an if-block that checks that the argument is a **MemberExpression**.
   ```
   if (argument is MemberExpression) { }
   ```
5. Inside the if-block, cast the argument to **MemberExpression** and store it in a variable named **memberExpression**.
   ```
   var memberExpression = (MemberExpression)argument;
   ```
6. Cast the **memberExpression.Member** property to **FieldInfo** and call the **GetValue** to fetch the value; cast the **memberExpression.Expression** property to a **ConstantExpression** object and pass in its **Value** property to the **GetValue** method. Store the result in a variable named **value**; this is the value inside the **Equals** method in the expression.
   ```
   var value = ((FieldInfo)memberExpression.Member).GetValue(
       ((ConstantExpression)memberExpression.Expression).Value);
   ```
7. Add the property name and value to the **_properties** collection. The name is stored in the **memberExpression.Member.Name** property.
   ```
   _properties.Add(memberExpression.Member.Name, value);
   ```
8. Save all files.

The complete code for the **GetExpressionProperties** method:

```
private void GetExpressionProperties(Expression expression)
{
    var body = (MethodCallExpression)expression;
    var argument = body.Arguments[0];

    if (argument is MemberExpression)
    {
        var memberExpression = (MemberExpression)argument;
        var value = ((FieldInfo)memberExpression.Member).GetValue(
            ((ConstantExpression)memberExpression.Expression).Value);

        _properties.Add(memberExpression.Member.Name, value);
    }
}
```

The ResolveExpression Method

This method picks apart a Lambda expression and finds its expressions and calls the **GetExpressionProperties** method to resolve the properties with reflection.

Inspect the node type for each expression to find out the type of expression; if it contains an **and** (&&) operator for instance, and if it calls the **ResolveExpression** method for each expression, left and right. You can, of course, check for other expression types such as **or** (||) if you like, but it's not necessary for this solution.

1. Add a **void** method named **ResolveExpression** to the **AdminAPIService** class that has an **Expression** parameter.
   ```
   private void ResolveExpression(Expression expression) { }
   ```
2. Add a try/catch-block to the method where the catch-block throws any exceptions up the call chain.
3. Add an if-block inside the try-block that checks if **and** (&&) is part of the expression.
   ```
   if (expression.NodeType == ExpressionType.AndAlso) { }
   ```
4. Inside the if-block, cast the expression to **BinaryExpression** and store it in a variable named **binaryExpression**.
   ```
   var binaryExpression = expression as BinaryExpression;
   ```
5. Use recursion to call the **ResolveExpression** method for both the left and right side of the expression. In this example the first name is the left expression and the last name the right: p => p.FirstName.Equals("Luke") && p.LastName.Equals("Skywalker")

   ```
   ResolveExpression(binaryExpression.Left);
   ResolveExpression(binaryExpression.Right);
   ```
6. Add an else if-block that checks if the expression is a **MethodCallExpression** expression.
   ```
   else if (expression is MethodCallExpression) { }
   ```
7. Fetch the properties of the expression inside the else if-block by calling the **GetExpressionProperties** method and pass in the **expression** variable.
   ```
   GetExpressionProperties(expression);
   ```
8. Save all files.

The complete code for the **ResolveExpression** method:

```
private void ResolveExpression(Expression expression)
{
    try
    {
        // And: x.Age < 50 && x.FirstName == "Luke"
        if (expression.NodeType == ExpressionType.AndAlso)
        {
            var binaryExpression = expression as BinaryExpression;
            ResolveExpression(binaryExpression.Left);
            ResolveExpression(binaryExpression.Right);
        }
        else if (expression is MethodCallExpression)
        {
            GetExpressionProperties(expression);
        }
    }
    catch
    {
        throw;
    }
}
```

The GetProperties<TSource> Method for Lambda Expressions

This method will find the properties and their values in a Lambda expression and store them in the **_properties** dictionary collection.

1. Add a **void** method named **GetProperties<TSource>** to the **AdminAPIService** class that has an **Expression<Func<TSource, bool>>** parameter that will receive the Lambda expression to search for properties and their comparison values.
   ```
   private void GetProperties<TSource>(Expression<Func<TSource, bool>> expression) { }
   ```
2. Add a try/catch-block to the method where the catch-block throws any exceptions up the call chain.
3. Inside the try-block, cast the **expression** variable to **LambdaExpression** and store it in a variable named **lambda**.
   ```
   var lambda = expression as LambdaExpression;
   ```
4. Clear the **_properties** dictionary.

26. Calling The API With HttpClient

5. Call the **ResolveExpression** method with the expression in the **lambda.Body** property.
   `ResolveExpression(lambda.Body);`

6. Fetch the name of the generic **TSource** type and store the name in a variable named **typeName**.
   `var typeName = typeof(TSource).Name;`

7. Use the value in the typeName variable to check that the name isn't *Instructor* or *Course*, which corresponds to one of the two top-level entities **Instructor** and **Course**. Also, check that the **courseId** property isn't already in the **_properties** dictionary collection. If the expression is **true**, then add the **courseId** property with the value 0; this is necessary because there must always be a course id available in the collection to create a correct URI if the URI isn't for a top-level route.
   ```
   if (!typeName.Equals("Instructor") && !typeName.Equals("Course")
   && !_properties.ContainsKey("courseId"))
       _properties.Add("courseId", 0);
   ```

8. Save all files.

The complete code for the **GetProperties<TSource>** method:

```
private void GetProperties<TSource>(Expression<Func<TSource, bool>> expression)
{
    try
    {
        var lambda = expression as LambdaExpression;

        _properties.Clear();

        ResolveExpression(lambda.Body);

        var typeName = typeof(TSource).Name;
        if (!typeName.Equals("Instructor") &&
            !typeName.Equals("Course") &&
            !_properties.ContainsKey("courseId"))
                _properties.Add("courseId", 0);
    }
    catch { throw; }
}
```

The SingleAsync<TSource, TDestination> Method

This method will fetch a single entity from the database by calling the API and returning it as a DTO object. The **TSource** type is the entity type to fetch, and the **TDestination** type is the DTO type to return from the API.

1. Locate the **SingleAsync<TSource, TDestination>** method in the **AdminAPIService** class.
2. Add a try/catch-block around the **NotImplementedException** exception in the method where the catch-block throws any exceptions up the call chain.
3. In the try-block, call the **GetProperties** method and pass in the **expression** parameter to it above the **NotImplementedException** exception. GetProperties(expression);
4. Place a breakpoint on the **NotImplementedException** exception and start the **API** and **Admin** projects with debugging.
5. Click on the **Instructor** card on the **Index** page.
6. Click the **Edit** button for one of the instructors.
7. When the execution halts on the breakpoint, inspect the **_properties** collection to ensure that the **id** property and its value is in the collection.
8. Stop the applications in Visual Studio.

The code, so far, for the **SingleAsync<TSource, TDestination>** method:

```
public async Task<TDestination> SingleAsync<TSource, TDestination>(
Expression<Func<TSource, bool>> expression, bool include = false)
where TSource : class where TDestination : class
{
    try
    {
        GetProperties(expression);
        throw new NotImplementedException();
    }
    catch
    {
        throw;
    }
}
```

26. Calling The API With HttpClient

The FormatUriWithIds<TSource> Method

This method will format a URI for the **TSource** entity type and include its properties and their values in the URI.

1. Add a parameter-less **string** method named **FormatUriWithIds<TSource>** to the **AdminAPIService** class.
   ```
   private string FormatUriWithIds<TSource>() { }
   ```
2. Add a **string** variable named **uri** and assign the text *api* to it, which is the beginning of the API route for the desired action based on the **TSource** type.
3. Add three **object** variables named **id**, **moduleId**, and **courseId** that will hold the value for each property if found in the **_properties** collection.
4. Try to fetch the courseId property from the **_properties** collection by calling the **TryGetValue** on the **_properties** collection. If the collection contains the property, then append the */courses* route and the **courseId** property value to the **uri** variable.
   ```
   bool succeeded = _properties.TryGetValue("courseId",
        out courseId);
   if (succeeded) uri = $"{uri}/courses/{courseId}";
   ```
5. Repeat the previous bullet for the **moduleId** and **id** properties. If the id property is missing, then add the entity name suffixed with *s*.
6. Return the value in the **uri** variable from the method.
7. Call the **FormatUriWithIds<TSource>** method below the **GetProperties** method call in the **SingleAsync** method.
   ```
   string uri = FormatUriWithIds<TSource>();
   ```
8. Place a breakpoint on the **NotImplementedException** exception if you removed it earlier and start the **API** and **Admin** projects with debugging.
9. Click on the **Instructor** card on the **Index** page.
10. Click the **Edit** button for one of the instructors.
11. When the execution halts on the breakpoint, inspect the **uri** variable and make sure that it contains a valid URI. Example URI: *api/Instructors/2*.
12. Stop the applications in Visual Studio.

The complete code for the **FormatUriWithIds<TSource>** method:

```
private string FormatUriWithIds<TSource>()
{
    string uri = "api";
    object id, moduleId, courseId;

    bool succeeded = _properties.TryGetValue("courseId", out courseId);
    if (succeeded) uri = $"{uri}/courses/{courseId}";

    succeeded = _properties.TryGetValue("moduleId", out moduleId);
    if (succeeded) uri = $"{uri}/modules/{moduleId}";

    succeeded = _properties.TryGetValue("id", out id);
    if (id != null)
        uri = $"{uri}/{typeof(TSource).Name}s/{id}";
    else
        uri = $"{uri}/{typeof(TSource).Name}s";

    return uri;
}
```

The code, so far, for the **SingleAsync<TSource, TDestination>** method:

```
public async Task<TDestination> SingleAsync<TSource, TDestination>(
Expression<Func<TSource, bool>> expression, bool include = false)
where TSource : class where TDestination : class
{
    try
    {
        GetProperties(expression);
        string uri = FormatUriWithIds<TSource>();
        throw new NotImplementedException();
    }
    catch
    {
        throw;
    }
}
```

26. Calling The API With HttpClient

The GetAsync<TResponse, TRequest> Extension Method in the HttpClientExtensions Class

This method will call the API and deserialize the response object.

1. Open the **HttpClientExtensions** class and copy the **GetListAsync** method and rename the copy **GetAsync**.
2. Add another generic type named **TRequest** to the method definition.
3. Add a **TRequest** parameter named **content** to the left of the **token** parameter.
4. Change the return type of the **GetAsync** method to a single instance.
   ```
   public static async Task<TResponse> GetAsync<TResponse, TRequest>(
   this HttpClient client, string uri, CancellationToken
   cancellationToken, TRequest content, string token = "")
   ```
5. Below the **requestMessage** variable, call the **CreateRequestContent** method on the **requestMessage** variable and pass in the **content** parameter to it if the **content** parameter has a value.
   ```
   if (content != null) await requestMessage.CreateRequestContent(
       content);
   ```
6. Change the return type to a single instance for the **ReadAndDeserializeFromJson** method call.
7. Save all files.

The complete code for the **GetAsync<TResponse, TRequest>** extension method:

```
public static async Task<TResponse> GetAsync<TResponse, TRequest>(
this HttpClient client, string uri, CancellationToken cancellationToken,
TRequest content, string token = "")
{
    try
    {
        var requestMessage = uri.CreateRequestHeaders(HttpMethod.Get,
            token);

        if (content != null)
            await requestMessage.CreateRequestContent(content);

        using (var response = await client.SendAsync(
        requestMessage, HttpCompletionOption.ResponseHeadersRead,
        cancellationToken))
        {
            var stream = await response.Content.ReadAsStreamAsync();
```

```
            await response.CheckStatusCodes();
            return stream.ReadAndDeserializeFromJson<TResponse>();
        }
    }
    catch
    {
        throw;
    }
}
```

The GetAsync<TSource> Method in the HttpClientFactoryService Class

This method will format a URI for the **TSource** entity type and include its properties and their values in the URI.

1. Open the **IHttpClientFactoryService** interface and copy the **GetListAsync** method and rename the copy **GetAsync**.
2. Change the return type of the **GetAsync** method to a single instance.
   `Task<TResponse> GetAsync<TResponse>(string uri, string serviceName, string token = "") where TResponse : class;`
3. Open the **HttpClientFactoryService** class and copy the **GetListAsync** method and rename it **GetAsync**.
4. Rename the **GetListAsync** method call at the end of the try-block **GetAsync** and add **string** type to the method definition and **null** for the **content** parameter (the **string** type is arbitrary because it is left unused in this scenario).

The complete code for the **GetAsync** method in the **HttpClientFactoryService** class:

```
public async Task<TResponse> GetAsync<TResponse>(string uri, string serviceName, string token = "")
{
    try
    {
        if (new []{ uri, serviceName }.IsNullOrEmptyOrWhiteSpace())
            throw new HttpResponseException(HttpStatusCode.NotFound,
                "Could not find the resource");

        var httpClient = _httpClientFactory.CreateClient(serviceName);

        return await httpClient.GetAsync<TResponse, string>(
            uri.ToLower(), _cancellationToken, null, token);
    }
```

26. Calling The API With HttpClient

```
        catch
        {
            throw;
        }
}
```

Calling the API

This method will format a URI for the **TSource** entity type and include its properties and their values in the URI.

1. Open the **SingleAsync** method in the **AdminAPIService** class.
2. Replace the **NotImplementedException** code with a call to the **_http.GetAsync** method to call the API and pass in the **uri** parameter's value appended with the **include** parameter and specify the name of the **HttpClient** service you configured in the **Startup** class.
   ```
   return await _http.GetAsync<TDestination>($"{uri}?include=
       {include.ToString()}", "AdminClient");
   ```
3. Add the **async** keyword to the **SingleAsync** method if you haven't already.
4. Remove or disable any breakpoints and start the **API** and **Admin** projects.
5. Click on the **Instructors** card.
6. Click the **Edit** button for one of the instructors. The **Edit** Razor Page displays the instructor's data.
7. Click the **Back to List** button and then click the **Delete** button for one of the instructors. The **Delete** Razor Page displays the instructor's data. Don't click the red **Delete** button on the **Delete** page.
8. Stop the applications in Visual Studio.

The complete code for the **SingleAsync** method in the **AdminAPIService** class:

```
public async Task<TDestination> SingleAsync<TSource, TDestination>(
Expression<Func<TSource, bool>> expression, bool include = false)
where TSource : class where TDestination : class
{
    try
    {
        GetProperties(expression);
        string uri = FormatUriWithIds<TSource>();
        return await _http.GetAsync<TDestination>($"{uri}?include=
            {include.ToString()}", "AdminClient");
    }
```

```
        catch
        {
            throw;
        }
}
```

Implementing the PostAsync Method
This method will create a new entity in the database by calling the **Post** action in one of the API controllers with a DTO object in the post's body content.

The PostAsync<TRequest, TResponse> Extension Method in the HttpClientExtensions Class
This extension method will call the API and deserialize the response object.

1. Open the **HttpClientExtensions** class and add a new **async static** method named **PostAsync** defined by the two generic **TResponse** and **TRequest** types that return a DTO of the **TResponse** type. The API creates an object of type **TRequest**. The method should work on the **HttpClient** service you registered in the **Startup** class and have a **string** parameter named **uri**, a **TRequest** parameter named **content**, which is the content used to create the record in the database, a **CancellationToken** parameter named **cancellationToken**, and a **string** parameter named **token** for the JWT token you will add in the next chapter.
   ```
   public static async Task<TResponse> PostAsync<TRequest,
   TResponse>(this HttpClient client, string uri, TRequest content,
   CancellationToken cancellationToken, string token = "") { }
   ```
2. Add a try/catch-block in the method where the catch-block throws any exceptions up the call chain.
3. In the try-block, add a **using**-block that calls the **CreateRequestHeaders** extension method that you created earlier to add header information to the **HttpRequestMessage** that calls the **Post** action in the API.
   ```
   using (var requestMessage = uri.CreateRequestHeaders(
   HttpMethod.Post, token)) { }
   ```
4. Inside the previous **using**-block, add another **using**-block that calls the **CreateRequestContent** extension method you created earlier on the **requestMessage** variable to add the object from the **TRequest** parameter.
   ```
   using ((await requestMessage.CreateRequestContent(content))
           .Content) { }
   ```

26. Calling The API With HttpClient

5. Inside the previous **using**-block, add another **using**-block that calls the **SendAsync** method in the **HttpClient** service you configured in the **Startup** class and saves the returned **HttpResponseMessage** object in a variable named **responseMessage**. Pass in the **requestMessage** object, the completion option set to **ResponseHeadersRead**, and the cancellation token.
   ```
   using (var responseMessage = await client.SendAsync(
       requestMessage, HttpCompletionOption.ResponseHeadersRead,
       cancellationToken)) { }
   ```

6. Inside the previous **using**-block, call the **CheckStatusCode** extension method you created earlier to check if there are any response errors.
   ```
   await responseMessage.CheckStatusCodes();
   ```

7. Call the **DeserializeResponse** extension method you created earlier to convert the JSON response object into a **TResponse** object below the **CheckStatusCode** method call.
   ```
   return await responseMessage.DeserializeResponse<TResponse>();
   ```

8. Save all files.

The complete code for the **PostAsync<TResponse, TRequest>** extension method in the **HttpClientExtensions** Class:

```
public static async Task<TResponse> PostAsync<TRequest, TResponse>(
this HttpClient client, string uri, TRequest content, CancellationToken
cancellationToken, string token = "")
{
    try
    {
        using (var requestMessage = uri.CreateRequestHeaders(
        HttpMethod.Post, token))
        {
            using ((await requestMessage.CreateRequestContent(
            content)).Content)
            {
                using (var responseMessage = await client.SendAsync(
                requestMessage, HttpCompletionOption.ResponseHeadersRead,
                cancellationToken))
                {
                    await responseMessage.CheckStatusCodes();
                    return await responseMessage.DeserializeResponse
                        <TResponse>();
                }
```

```
            }
        }
    }
    catch
    {
        throw;
    }
}
```

The PostAsync<TRequest, TResponse> Method in the HttpClientFactoryService Class

This method will create an instance of the **HttpClient** service you configured in the **Startup** class and use the **PostAsync** extension method you just created to call the API and create the record in the database.

1. Open the **IHttpClientFactoryService** interface and copy the **GetAsync** method and rename the copy **PostAsync**.
2. Add a **TRequest** type to the method and constrain it to classes.
3. Add a **TRequest** parameter named **content** as the method's first parameter; this will contain the object to persist to the database.
   ```
   Task<TResponse> PostAsync<TRequest, TResponse>(TRequest content,
   string uri, string serviceName, string token = "") where
   TResponse: class where TRequest: class;
   ```
4. Implement the method in the **HttpClientFactoryService** class.
5. Copy all code in the **GetAsync** method and replace the **throw**-statement in the **CreateAsync** method with it.
6. Replace the **httpClient.GetAsync** method call with **httpClient.PostAsync** and pass in the **content** parameter as its second value.
   ```
   return await httpClient.PostAsync<TRequest, TResponse>(
       uri.ToLower(), content, _cancellationToken, token);
   ```
7. Add the **async** keyword to the **PostAsync** method if you haven't already.
8. Save all files.

26. Calling The API With HttpClient

The complete code for the **PostAsync<TResponse, TRequest>** method in the **HttpClientFactoryService** class:

```
public async Task<TResponse> PostAsync<TRequest, TResponse>(TRequest
content, string uri, string serviceName, string token = "") where
TResponse : class where TRequest: class
{
    try
    {
        if (new string[] { uri, serviceName }
            .IsNullOrEmptyOrWhiteSpace())
            throw new HttpResponseException(HttpStatusCode.NotFound,
                "Could not find the resource");

        var httpClient = _httpClientFactory.CreateClient(serviceName);
        return await httpClient.PostAsync<TRequest, TResponse>(
            uri.ToLower(), content, _cancellationToken, token);
    }
    catch
    {
        throw;
    }
}
```

The GetProperties<TSource>(TSource source) Method for Objects

This method will find the properties and their values in an object with reflection and store them in the **_properties** dictionary collection.

1. Add a **void** method named **GetProperties<TSource>** to the **AdminAPIService** class that has a **TSource** parameter named **source** that will contain the object to search for properties and their values.
   `private void GetProperties<TSource>(TSource source) { }`
2. Add a try/catch-block to the method where the catch-block clears the **_properties** collection and throws any exceptions up the call chain.
3. Inside the try-block, clear the **_properties** collection.
4. Try to fetch the **Id**, **CourseId**, and **ModuleId** properties and store them in variables named **idProperty**, **courseProperty**, and **moduleProperty**. If a variable isn't **null**, then the property was found and is stored in the variable.
   ```
   var idProperty = source.GetType().GetProperty("Id");
   var moduleProperty = source.GetType().GetProperty("ModuleId");
   var courseProperty = source.GetType().GetProperty("CourseId");
   ```

5. If the **idProperty** isn't **null,** then fetch its value and store it in the **_properties** collection with the key **id** if it is greater than 0.
```
if (idProperty != null)
{
    var id = idProperty.GetValue(source);
    if (id != null && (int)id > 0) _properties.Add("id", id);
}
```
6. Repeat the previous bullet for the **courseProperty** and **moduleProperty** properties and name the keys **courseId** and **moduleId** (note the camel-case).
7. Save all files.

The complete code for the **GetProperties<TSource>(TSource source)** method:

```
private void GetProperties<TSource>(TSource source)
{
    try
    {
        _properties.Clear();
        var idProperty = source.GetType().GetProperty("Id");
        var moduleProperty = source.GetType().GetProperty("ModuleId");
        var courseProperty = source.GetType().GetProperty("CourseId");

        if (idProperty != null)
        {
            var id = idProperty.GetValue(source);
            if (id != null && (int)id > 0) _properties.Add("id", id);
        }

        if (moduleProperty != null)
        {
            var moduleId = moduleProperty.GetValue(source);
            if (moduleId != null && (int)moduleId > 0)
                _properties.Add("moduleId", moduleId);
        }

        if (courseProperty != null)
        {
            var courseId = courseProperty.GetValue(source);
            if (courseId != null && (int)courseId > 0)
                _properties.Add("courseId", courseId);
        }
    }
}
```

```
        catch
        {
            _properties.Clear();
            throw;
        }
}
```

Calling the API

This method will call the API to create a resource in the database based on the entity type that defines the **CreateAsync** method. The method will return the id of the created resource.

1. Copy the code in the **SingleAsync** method in the **AdminAPIService** class.
2. Replace the **NotImplementedException** code in the **CreateAsync** method with the copied code.
3. Add the **async** keyword to the method if you haven't already.
4. Replace the **TSource** type with **TDestination** for the **FormatUriWithIds** method call.
5. Replace the **expression** parameter with the **item** instance in the **GetProperties** method call.
6. Replace the **return** statement with a call to the **PostAsync** method in the **HttpClientFactoryService** service. Note that **TRequest** and **TResponse** defining the called method are the same **TSource** type (the same DTO class) because the API will receive and return objects with the same DTO; this is not the case if you implement the API to receive one type and return another type.
   ```
   var response = await _http.PostAsync<TSource, TSource>(item, uri, "AdminClient");
   ```
7. Use reflection to fetch and return the value of the **Id** property of the returned **TSource** object.
   ```
   return (int)response.GetType().GetProperty("Id")
       .GetValue(response);
   ```
8. Save all files.
9. Start the **API** and **Admin** projects and click on the **Instructor** card.
10. Click the **Create New** button and fill out the form, then click the **Create** button.
11. The **Index** Razor Page displays the new instructor.
12. Close the application in Visual Studio.

The complete code for the **CreateAsync** method in the **AdminAPIService** class:

```
public async Task<int> CreateAsync<TSource, TDestination>(TSource item) 
where TSource : class where TDestination : class
{
    try
    {
        GetProperties(item);
        string uri = FormatUriWithIds<TDestination>();
        var response = await _http.PostAsync<TSource, TSource>(item, 
            uri, "AdminClient");
        return (int)response.GetType().GetProperty("Id")
            .GetValue(response);
    }
    catch
    {
        throw;
    }
}
```

Implementing the UpdateAsync Method

This method will update an existing entity in the database by calling the **Put** action in one of the API controllers with a DTO object in the put's body content.

The PutAsync<TRequest , TResponse> Extension Method in the HttpClientExtensions Class

This method will call the API and deserialize the response object.

1. Open the **HttpClientExtensions** class and copy the **PostAsync** method and rename the copy **PutAsync**.
2. Change **HttpMethod.Post** to **HttpMethod.Put** for the **CreateRequestHeaders** method call.

26. Calling The API With HttpClient

The complete code for the **PutAsync<TRequest, TResponse>** extension method in the **HttpClientExtensions** class:

```
public static async Task<TResponse> PutAsync<TRequest, TResponse>(this 
HttpClient client, string uri, TRequest content, CancellationToken 
cancellationToken, string token = "")
{
    try
    {
        using (var requestMessage = 
            uri.CreateRequestHeaders(HttpMethod.Put, token))
        {
            using ((await requestMessage.CreateRequestContent(content))
            .Content)
            {
                using (var responseMessage = await client.SendAsync(
                    requestMessage, HttpCompletionOption.ResponseHeadersRead,
                    cancellationToken))
                {
                    await responseMessage.CheckStatusCodes();
                    return await responseMessage
                        .DeserializeResponse<TResponse>();
                }
            }
        }
    }
    catch
    {
        throw;
    }
}
```

The PutAsync<TRequest, TResponse> Method in the HttpClientFactoryService Class

This method will call the **Put** action in one of the API controllers and return the response from the API call.

1. Open the **IHttpClientFactoryService** interface and copy the **PostAsync** method and rename the copy **PutAsync**.
2. Implement the **PutAsync** method in the **HttpClientFactoryService** class.
3. Add the **async** keyword to the method if you haven't already.

4. Copy the code in the **PostAsync** method in the **HttpClientFactoryService** class and replace the **NotImplementedException** code in the **PutAsync** method with the copied code.
5. Replace the **httpClient.PostAsync** method call with a call to the **httpClient.PutAsync** method.
6. Save all files.

The complete code for the **PutAsync<TRequest, TResponse>** method in the **HttpClientFactoryService** class:

```
public async Task<TResponse> PutAsync<TRequest, TResponse>(TRequest
content, string uri, string serviceName, string token = "") where
TResponse : class where TRequest : class
{
    try
    {
        if (new string[] { uri, serviceName }
            .IsNullOrEmptyOrWhiteSpace())
            throw new HttpResponseException(HttpStatusCode.NotFound,
                "Could not find the resource");

        var httpClient = _httpClientFactory.CreateClient(serviceName);

        return await httpClient.PutAsync<TRequest, TResponse>(
            uri.ToLower(), content, _cancellationToken, token);
    }
    catch
    {
        throw;
    }
}
```

Calling the API

This method will format a URI for the **TSource** entity type and include its properties and their values in the URI that calls the **Put** action method in the API.

1. Copy the code in the **CreateAsync** method in the **AdminAPIService** class.
2. Replace the **NotImplementedException** code in the **UpdateAsync** method with the copied code.
3. Add the **async** keyword to the method if you haven't already.

4. Change the **return** statement to return **true** in the try-block and **false** in the catch-block.
5. Replace the call to **_http.PostAsync** with a call to **_http.PutAsync**.
6. Save all files.
7. Start the **API** and **Admin** projects and click on the **Instructor** card.
8. Click the **Edit** button and change some values in the form, then click the **Save** button.
9. The **Index** Razor Page displays the updated instructor's information.
10. Close the application in Visual Studio.

The complete code for the **UpdateAsync<TSource , TDestination>** method in the **AdminAPIService** class:

```
public async Task<bool> UpdateAsync<TSource, TDestination>(TSource item)
where TSource : class where TDestination : class
{
    try
    {
        GetProperties(item);
        string uri = FormatUriWithIds<TDestination>();
        var response = await _http.PutAsync<TSource, TSource>(item, uri,
            "AdminClient");
        return true;
    }
    catch {
        return false;
    }
}
```

Implementing the DeleteAsync Method

This method will delete a record in the database by calling the **Delete** action in one of the API controllers.

The DeleteAsync Extension Method in the HttpClientExtensions Class

This method will call the API and de-serialize the response object.

1. Open the **HttpClientExtensions** class and copy the **PutAsync** method and rename the copy **DeleteAsync**.
2. Remove the **TRequest** and **TResponse** generic types from the method.
3. Remove the **TRequest content** parameter.

4. Replace the **TResponse** return type with the **string** type.
5. Remove the **using**-block for the **CreateRequestContent** method. A delete shouldn't have any data in its body; an id should be enough, which the URI provides.
6. Replace the **HttpMethod.Put** with **HttpMethod.Delete**.
7. Replace the **DeserializeResponse** method call with a call to the **ReadStringAsync** method on the response's **Content** property.
   `return await responseMessage.Content.ReadAsStringAsync();`
8. Save all files.

The complete code for the **DeleteAsync** extension method in the **HttpClientExtensions** class:

```
public static async Task<string> DeleteAsync(this HttpClient client,
string uri, CancellationToken cancellationToken, string token = "")
{
    try
    {
        using (var requestMessage = uri.CreateRequestHeaders(
        HttpMethod.Delete, token))
        {
            using (var responseMessage = await client.SendAsync(
            requestMessage, HttpCompletionOption.ResponseHeadersRead,
            cancellationToken))
            {
                await responseMessage.CheckStatusCodes();
                return await responseMessage.Content
                    .ReadAsStringAsync();
            }
        }
    }
    catch
    {
        throw;
    }
}
```

The DeleteAsync Method in the HttpClientFactoryService Class

This method will create an instance of the **HttpClient** service you configured in the **Startup** class and call the **DeleteAsync** method in the **HttpClientExtensions** class that calls the API.

1. Open the **IHttpClientFactoryService** interface and definition for a **DeleteAsync** method that returns a **string** wrapped in a **Task**.
    a. Copy the parameters from the **GetListAsync** method and add them to the **DeleteAsync** definition.

    ```
    Task<string> DeleteAsync(string uri, string serviceName, string token = "");
    ```

2. Implement the **DeleteAsync** method in the **HttpClientFactoryService** class.
3. Add the **async** keyword to the method if you haven't already.
4. Copy the code in the **GetListAsync** method in the **HttpClientFactoryService** class and replace the **throw**-statement with it in the **DeleteAsync** method.
5. Replace the **httpClient.GetListAsync** method call with a call to the **httpClient.DeleteAsync** method and remove the **TResponse** generic type.

    ```
    return await httpClient.DeleteAsync(uri.ToLower(),
        _cancellationToken, token);
    ```

6. Save all files.

The complete code for the **DeleteAsync** method in the **HttpClientFactoryService** class:

```
public async Task<string> DeleteAsync(string uri, string serviceName,
string token = "")
{
    try
    {
        if (new string[] { uri, serviceName }
            .IsNullOrEmptyOrWhiteSpace())
            throw new HttpResponseException(HttpStatusCode.NotFound,
                "Could not find the resource");

        var httpClient = _httpClientFactory.CreateClient(serviceName);
        return await httpClient.DeleteAsync(uri.ToLower(),
            _cancellationToken, token);
    }
    catch
    {
        throw;
    }
}
```

Calling the API

This method will format a URI for the **TSource** entity type and include its properties and their values in the URI that is used to call the API.

1. Copy the code in the **UpdateAsync** method in the **AdminAPIService** class and replace the **NotImplementedException** code it in the **DeleteAsync** method with the copied code.
2. Add the **async** keyword to the method if you haven't already.
3. Replace the **item** parameter in the **GetProperties** method call with the **expression** parameter.
4. Replace the generic **TDestination** type with the generic **TSource** type for the **FormatUriWithIds** method call.
5. Replace the **_http.PutAsync** method call with a call to the **_http.DeleteAsync** method and remove the **TSource** generic type and the item parameter.
   ```
   var response = await _http.DeleteAsync(uri, "AdminClient");
   ```
6. Save all files.
7. Start the **API** and **Admin** projects and click on the **Instructor** card.
8. Click the **Delete** button and change some values in the form, then click the **Delete** button.
9. The **Index** Razor Page no longer displays the instructor.
10. Now, test the CRUD operations for courses, modules, videos, and downloads.
11. Close the application in Visual Studio.

The complete code for the **DeleteAsync** method in the **AdminAPIService** class:

```
public async Task<bool> DeleteAsync<TSource>(Expression<Func<TSource,
bool>> expression) where TSource : class
{
    try
    {
        GetProperties(expression);
        string uri = FormatUriWithIds<TSource>();
        var response = await _http.DeleteAsync(uri, "AdminClient");
        return true;
    }
    catch { return false; }
}
```

Summary

In this chapter, you have learned how to use reflection to find properties and their values from generic types, objects, and Lambda expressions.

You have also learned how to build two services that use extension methods to call the API to perform CRUD operations.

In the next chapter, you will learn how to create JSON Web Tokens (JWT) and use them to secure the API with authorization and authentication. You will use the JWTs in subsequent calls to the API.

ASP.NET Core 2.2 MVC, Razor Pages, API, JSON Web Tokens & HttpClient

27. JSON Web Tokens (JWT)

Overview
In this chapter, you will use JSON Web Tokens (JWT) to authenticate and authorize users and give them access to the API controllers and their actions based on claims and policies. JWT is an industry standard for security tokens that you will use to grant access to the API's resources, and by extension, the data in the database.

A JWT is a small self-contained token (a JSON string) that contains credentials, claims, and other information as needed to authenticate the token and authorize access to resources based on the claims. The goal of a JWT is to pass information from a client to the server (the API) and use that information without needing to look up information in a data store.

Technologies Used in This Chapter
1. **API** – The API project performs CRUD operations in the database.
2. **Service** – To implement a token service.
3. **C#** – To create the service.
4. **JSON Web Tokens (JWT)** – To authorize access in the API.
5. **Claims and Policies** – To authorize users and grant access to controller actions.

The JWT Structure
A JWT has three sections: a header that specifies the algorithm used to encrypt the JWT data and the token type, which often is *JWT*.

```
{
    "alg":"HS256",
    "typ":"JWT"
}
```

A payload with information that the server may need.

```
{
    "sub":"0123456789",
    "name":"John Doe",
    "admin":true
}
```

The third part is an encrypted signature that ensures that the token is valid.

ASP.NET Core 2.2 MVC, Razor Pages, API, JSON Web Tokens & HttpClient

The token is generated by the server for each user and then sent to the server from the client with every request to authorize access to resources based on the claims in the token; the claims are part of the encrypted token's payload.

The three parts of the token are encoded with **Base64Encode** and separated by periods (.). The signature is a hash of the header, payload, and a secret stored on the server; if the signature is invalid, the token as a whole is invalid.

Encrypted signature:

```
HMACSH256(
    Base64UrlEncode(header) + "." + Base64UrlEncode(payload),
    SECRET
)
```

Complete token:

```
    Base64Encode(header) + "." +
    Base64Encode(payload) + "." +
    Base64Encode(SECRET)
```

Base64Encode(header).Base64Encode(payload).Base64Encode(signature)

Example Token:

eyJhbGciOiJIUzI1NiIsInR5cCI6IkpXVCJ9.eyJzdWIiOiIxMjM0NTY3ODkwIiwibmFtZSI6IkpvaG4gRG9lIiwiaWF0IjoxNTE2MjM5MDIyfQ.SflKxwRJSMeKKF2QT4fwpMeJf36POk6yJV_adQssw5c

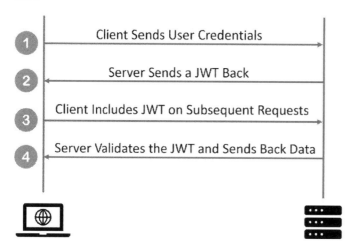

27. JSON Web Tokens (JWT)

1. The client sends user credentials (username and password) to the server to generate a JWT token, which will be used to authorize the user on subsequent calls.
2. The server generates a token based on the verified user's roles and/or claims, and other information, and sends the token to the client.
3. The client then sends that token as a *bearer* token in all request headers when calling the API. The API controlers or actions should have authorization implemented.
4. The server validates the token, and if valid, grants access based on the claims listed in the token. The most common reason for an invalid token is that it has expired and needs to be regenerated.

Creating the JWT

The first step in authorization with JWTs is to be able to generate and return them with a response when calling an API action. The second step is to secure the API using claims and policies, which you will do in an upcoming section.

To create a separation of concerns and to make the code more readable, you will create a service named **TokenService** in the API project that will contain all the code needed to create and verify a token. Inject the service into the controller of the **TokenController** class that can be called to generate and fetch tokens.

Adding the TokenDTO Class

To have all the information about a token in one container, you will create a class named **TokenDTO** that will encapsulate the JWT and its expiration date and expose that information through properties. To make it easier to see if the token has expired, a property named **TokenHasExpired** will return **true** or **false** based on the difference between the current date and the expiration date in the token.

1. Open the **Common** project and add a **public** class named **TokenDTO** to the *DTOModels* folder.
2. Add a **public string** property named **Token** with an empty string as its default value.
3. Add a **public DateTime** property named **TokenExpires** and assign the value **default** to it.

4. Add a **public** read-only **bool** property named **TokenHasExpired** that returns **true** if the token has its default value and **false** if the token's expiration date and time are in the future.
   ```
   public bool TokenHasExpired { get { return TokenExpires == default
   ? true : !(TokenExpires.Subtract(DateTime.UtcNow).Minutes > 0); }}
   ```
5. Add one empty constructor (that uses the default values) and one that has a **string** parameter named **token** and a **DateTime** parameter named **expires** and assign them to their corresponding properties inside the constructor.

The complete code for the **TokenDTO** class:

```
public class TokenDTO
{
    public string Token { get; set; } = "";
    public DateTime TokenExpires { get; set; } = default;
    public bool TokenHasExpired
    {
        get
        {
            return TokenExpires == default ? true :
                !(TokenExpires.Subtract(DateTime.UtcNow).Minutes > 0);
        }
    }

    public TokenDTO(string token, DateTime expires)
    {
        Token = token;
        TokenExpires = expires;
    }

    public TokenDTO()
    {
    }
}
```

Adding the TokenService Service

Let's begin by adding the token service that will generate and fetch tokens; it has two **public** methods named **GenerateTokenAsync** and **GetTokenAsync**. The **GenerateToken-Async** method will call three helper methods named **GetClaims**, **CreateToken**, and **AddTokenToUser** to implement separation of concerns and make the code more readable.

27. JSON Web Tokens (JWT)

Adding the ITokenService Interface
1. Open the **API** project and add a folder named *Services*.
2. Add a **public** interface named **ITokenService** to the *Services* folder.
3. Add a definition for an asynchronous method named **GenerateTokenAsync** that has a **LoginUserDTO** parameter named **loginUserDTO** and returns a **TokenDTO** instance wrapped in a **Task**.
4. Copy the previous method and rename the copy **GetTokenAsync** and add another **string** parameter named **userId**.

The complete code for the **ITokenService** interface:

```
public interface ITokenService
{
    Task<TokenDTO> GenerateTokenAsync(LoginUserDTO loginUserDto);
    Task<TokenDTO> GetTokenAsync(LoginUserDTO loginUserDto,
        string userId);
}
```

Adding the TokenService Class
1. Add a **public** class named **TokenService** to the *Services* folder in the **API** project.
2. Implement the **ITokenService** interface in the class.
3. Add a constructor and inject the **IConfiguration** and **IUserService** services and store the instances in variables named **_configuration** and **_user**. The **IConfiguration** interface is in the **Microsoft.Extensions.Configuration** namespace.
4. Add a service configuration for the **ITokenService** interface to the **Startup** class in the API project. Recreate the service instance each time an instance is requested; to achieve this, you use the **AddTransient** service registration method.
   ```
   services.AddTransient<ITokenService, TokenService>();
   ```

The code, so far, for the **TokenService** class:

```
public class TokenService : ITokenService
{
    #region Properties
    private readonly IConfiguration _configuration;
    private readonly IUserService _users;
    #endregion
```

```
#region Constructors
public TokenService(IConfiguration configuration,
IUserService userService)
{
    _configuration = configuration;
    _users = userService;
}
#endregion

#region Token Methods
public async Task<TokenDTO> GetTokenAsync(LoginUserDTO loginUserDto,
string userId)
{
    throw new NotImplementedException();
}

public async Task<TokenDTO> GenerateTokenAsync(LoginUserDTO
loginUserDto)
{
    throw new NotImplementedException();
}
#endregion
}
```

Fetching the User's Claims

Because the token will include the claims for the user, you will add a **private** method to the **TokenService** class that fetches the logged-in user's claims. The claims will be used later to authorize the user when calling the API. Claims are more granular than roles, which are better suited if you use broad authorization with roles such as *Admin*. Claims, on the other hand, can implement detailed authorization for small tasks, such as separate claims for reading, writing, deleting, or updating resources through a controller's actions. This private method should not be added to the interface because it is a helper method that only is called internally in the **TokenService** class.

1. Add a **private** method named **GetClaims** to the **TokenService** class that has a **VODUser** parameter named **user** and a **bool** parameter named **includeUser-Claims**. The latter parameter determines if the user's claims should include the token with the default claims. The method should return a list of **Claim** objects.
    ```
    private List<Claim> GetClaims(VODUser user,
        bool includeUserClaims) { }
    ```

27. JSON Web Tokens (JWT)

2. Create a collection of **Claim** objects with the most common claims: user name, email, and a unique id.
   ```
   var claims = new List<Claim>
   {
       new Claim(JwtRegisteredClaimNames.Sub, user.UserName),
       new Claim(JwtRegisteredClaimNames.Email, user.Email),
       new Claim(JwtRegisteredClaimNames.Jti, Guid.NewGuid().ToString())
   };
   ```
3. Add the user's claims to the previous collection if the **includeUserClaims** parameter is **true**. Don't add the **Token** and **TokenExpires** claims because then the old claim and expiration date will be added to the new token, making it bloated with old information.
   ```
   if (includeUserClaims)
       foreach (var claim in user.Claims)
           if (!claim.Type.Equals("Token") &&
               !claim.Type.Equals("TokenExpires")) claims.Add(claim);
   ```
4. Return the claims collection from the method.
5. Save all files.

The complete code for the **GetClaims** method:

```
private List<Claim> GetClaims(VODUser user, bool includeUserClaims)
{
    var claims = new List<Claim>
    {
        new Claim(JwtRegisteredClaimNames.Sub, user.UserName),
        new Claim(JwtRegisteredClaimNames.Email, user.Email),
        new Claim(JwtRegisteredClaimNames.Jti,
            Guid.NewGuid().ToString())
    };

    if (includeUserClaims)
        foreach (var claim in user.Claims)
            if (!claim.Type.Equals("Token") &&
                !claim.Type.Equals("TokenExpires")) claims.Add(claim);

    return claims;
}
```

Creating the Token

Creating the token involves encryption using a secret key and other information stored in the *appsettings.json* file (or other more secure storage). The **CreateToken** method should receive the list of claims the **GetClaims** method generated and return an instance of the **TokenDTO** class containing the new token. This **private** method should not be added to the interface because it is a helper method used internally in the **TokenService** class.

An instance of the **JwtSecurityToken** class is used to create a token object containing the necessary information to generate the finished token.

```
var jwtToken = new JwtSecurityToken (
    issuer: "http://csharpschool.com",
    audience: "http://csharpschool.com",
    notBefore: now,
    expires: now.AddDays(duration),
    claims: claims,
    signingCredentials: credentials
);
```

- **Issuer**: this property specifies the domain that the token originated from. This value can be set to **null** if the token is used within the same domain.
- **audience**: this property specifies the domain of the intended audience.
- **notBefore**: this property specifies the earliest date and time you can use the token.
- **expires**: this property specifies when the token expires.
- **claims**: this property holds a list of claims associated with the user.
- **signingCredential**: this property holds the encrypted secret key.

1. Open the *appsettings.json* file in the API project and add a long string to a property named **SigningSecret** containing the secret that will be used to verify that the token is authentic and originated from the application's server. Also, add a property named **Duration** that determines how long a new token will be valid.
   ```
   "Jwt": {
     "SigningSecret": "A-VeRy-LonG-AnD-seCUre-StrInG",
     "Duration": 10 // minutes, days, or ...
   }
   ```

27. JSON Web Tokens (JWT)

2. Add a **private** method named **CreateToken** to the **TokenService** class that takes a list of claims and returns an instance of the **TokenDTO** class.
   ```
   private TokenDTO CreateToken(IList<Claim> claims) { }
   ```
3. Add a try/catch-block where the catch throws any exception up the call chain.
4. In the try-block, use the configuration service injected through the constructor to fetch the secret key and then convert it to an 8-bit unsigned integer array.
   ```
   var signingKey = Convert.FromBase64String(
       _configuration["Jwt:SigningSecret"]);
   ```
5. Use symmetric encryption to encrypt the secret key (the same secret and encryption will be used later when authenticating the token). Here, we use **HMACSHA256** that computes a Hash-based Message Authentication Code (HMAC) by using the SHA256 hash function. This hash will then be compared to the hashed key from the server when a user tries to access the API with the token.
   ```
   var credentials = new SigningCredentials(
       new SymmetricSecurityKey(signingKey),
       SecurityAlgorithms.HmacSha256Signature);
   ```
6. Fetch the token duration from the *appsettings.json* file and the current date and time.
   ```
   var duration = int.Parse(_configuration["Jwt:Duration"]);
   var now = DateTime.UtcNow;
   ```
7. Use the gathered information to create a token object.
   ```
   var jwtToken = new JwtSecurityToken
   (
       issuer: "http://your-domain.com",
       audience: "http://audience-domain.com",
       notBefore: now,
       expires: now.AddDays(duration),
       claims: claims,
       signingCredentials: credentials
   );
   ```
8. Create an instance of the **JwtSecurityTokenHandler** class and use it to create the token. Then return the token as a **TokenDTO** object.
   ```
   var jwtTokenHandler = new JwtSecurityTokenHandler();
   var token = jwtTokenHandler.WriteToken(jwtToken);
   return new TokenDTO(token, jwtToken.ValidTo);
   ```

9. Save all files.

The complete code for the **CreateToken** method:

```
private TokenDTO CreateToken(IList<Claim> claims)
{
    try
    {
        var signingKey = Convert.FromBase64String(
            _configuration["Jwt:SigningSecret"]);

        var credentials = new SigningCredentials(
            new SymmetricSecurityKey(signingKey),
            SecurityAlgorithms.HmacSha256Signature);

        var duration = int.Parse(_configuration["Jwt:Duration"]);
        var now = DateTime.UtcNow;

        var jwtToken = new JwtSecurityToken
        (
            issuer: "http://csharpschool.com",
            audience: "http://csharpschool.com",
            notBefore: now,
            expires: now.AddDays(duration),
            claims: claims,
            signingCredentials: credentials
        );

        var jwtTokenHandler = new JwtSecurityTokenHandler();
        var token = jwtTokenHandler.WriteToken(jwtToken);
        return new TokenDTO(token, jwtToken.ValidTo);
    }
    catch
    {
        throw;
    }
}
```

Update the UserService to Handle Claims

Because the user's claims should be stored and removed when the user is processed, you need to add that functionality to the methods in the **UserService** class.

27. JSON Web Tokens (JWT)

1. Open the **UserDTO** class in the **Common** project and add a **TokenDTO** property named **Token**.
   ```
   public TokenDTO Token { get; set; }
   ```
2. Open the **UserService** class in the **Database** project.
3. Locate the **GetUsersAsync**, **GetUserAsync**, and **GetUserByEmailAsync** methods and add a **TokenDTO** instance to the **Token** property of the **UserDTO** object and instantiate it with data from the **Token** and **TokenExpires** fields of the user instance.
   ```
   Token = new TokenDTO(user.Token, user.TokenExpires),
   ```
4. Locate the **UpdateUserAsync** method and an if-block that checks if the token contains data below the code that assigns the email.
   ```
   if (user.Token != null && user.Token.Token != null &&
   user.Token.Token.Length > 0) { }
   ```
5. Inside the if-block, add the token and expiration to the corresponding fields in the database.
   ```
   dbUser.Token = user.Token.Token;
   dbUser.TokenExpires = user.Token.TokenExpires;
   ```
6. Create new claims for the token and the expiration date; the new claims will be used if the current claims don't contain these claims.
   ```
   var newTokenClaim = new Claim("Token", user.Token.Token);
   var newTokenExpires = new Claim("TokenExpires",
       user.Token.TokenExpires.ToString("yyyy-MM-dd hh:mm:ss"));
   ```
7. Fetch all the user's claims to a variable named **userClaims** and use the collection to find the **Token** and **TokenExpires** claims if they exist.
   ```
   var userClaims = await _userManager.GetClaimsAsync(dbUser);
   var currentTokenClaim = userClaims.SingleOrDefault(c =>
       c.Type.Equals("Token"));
   var currentTokenClaimExpires = userClaims.SingleOrDefault(c =>
       c.Type.Equals("TokenExpires"));
   ```
8. Add the new claim if the **currentTokenClaim** is missing or replace the current claim with the new claim if it exists. Do the same for the **currentTokenClaimExpires** claim.
   ```
   if (currentTokenClaim == null)
       await _userManager.AddClaimAsync(dbUser, newTokenClaim);
   else
       await _userManager.ReplaceClaimAsync(dbUser,
           currentTokenClaim, newTokenClaim);
   ```

```
if (currentTokenClaimExpires == null)
    await _userManager.AddClaimAsync(dbUser, newTokenExpires);
else
    await _userManager.ReplaceClaimAsync(dbUser,
        currentTokenClaimExpires, newTokenExpires);
```

9. Below the **isAdmin** variable, add a **Claim** variable named **adminClaim** with the key from the **admin** variable and the value **true**.
   ```
   var admin = "Admin";
   var isAdmin = await _userManager.IsInRoleAsync(dbUser, admin);
   var adminClaim = new Claim(admin, "true");
   ```

10. Remove the *Admin* role and claim if the user is an admin in the database, but the **UserDTO** object that will update the database says that the user no longer is an admin.
    ```
    if (isAdmin && !user.IsAdmin)
    {
        // Remove Admin Role
        await _userManager.RemoveFromRoleAsync(dbUser, admin);

        // Remove Admin Claim
        await _userManager.RemoveClaimAsync(dbUser, adminClaim);
    }
    ```

11. Add the user to the *Admin* role and claim if the user is an admin in the **UserDTO** object that will update the database but not in the database.
    ```
    else if (!isAdmin && user.IsAdmin)
    {
        // Add Admin Role
        await _userManager.AddToRoleAsync(dbUser, admin);

        // Add Admin Claim
        await _userManager.AddClaimAsync(dbUser, adminClaim);
    }
    ```

12. Locate the **DeleteUserAsync** method and fetch and remove the user's claims below the code that removes the user's roles.
    ```
    var userClaims = _db.UserClaims.Where(ur =>
        ur.UserId.Equals(dbUser.Id));

    _db.UserClaims.RemoveRange(userClaims);
    ```

13. Locate the **GetUserAsync** method that returns a **VODUser** object wrapped in a **Task** and include the user's claims if the **includeClaims** parameter is **true**.

27. JSON Web Tokens (JWT)

```
    if (includeClaims) user.Claims =
        await _userManager.GetClaimsAsync(user);
```

The complete code for the **GetUsersAsync** method:

```
public async Task<IEnumerable<UserDTO>> GetUsersAsync()
{
    return await _db.Users
        .OrderBy(u => u.Email)
        .Select(user => new UserDTO
        {
            Id = user.Id,
            Email = user.Email,
            Token = new TokenDTO(user.Token, user.TokenExpires),
            IsAdmin = _db.UserRoles.Any(ur =>
                ur.UserId.Equals(user.Id) &&
                ur.RoleId.Equals(1.ToString()))
        }
        ).ToListAsync();
}
```

The complete code for the **UpdateUserAsync** method:

```
public async Task<bool> UpdateUserAsync(UserDTO user)
{
    var dbUser = await _db.Users.FirstOrDefaultAsync(u =>
        u.Id.Equals(user.Id));
    if (dbUser == null) return false;
    if (string.IsNullOrEmpty(user.Email)) return false;

    dbUser.Email = user.Email;

    #region Create new token here
    if (user.Token != null && user.Token.Token != null &&
        user.Token.Token.Length > 0)
    {
        // Add token to the user in the database
        dbUser.Token = user.Token.Token;
        dbUser.TokenExpires = user.Token.TokenExpires;

        // Add token claim to the user in the database
        var newTokenClaim = new Claim("Token", user.Token.Token);
        var newTokenExpires = new Claim("TokenExpires",
            user.Token.TokenExpires.ToString("yyyy-MM-dd hh:mm:ss"));
```

```csharp
        // Add or replace the claims for the token and expiration date
        var userClaims = await _userManager.GetClaimsAsync(dbUser);
        var currentTokenClaim = userClaims.SingleOrDefault(c =>
            c.Type.Equals("Token"));
        var currentTokenClaimExpires = userClaims.SingleOrDefault(c =>
            c.Type.Equals("TokenExpires"));

        if (currentTokenClaim == null)
            await _userManager.AddClaimAsync(dbUser, newTokenClaim);
        else
            await _userManager.ReplaceClaimAsync(dbUser,
                currentTokenClaim, newTokenClaim);

        if (currentTokenClaimExpires == null)
            await _userManager.AddClaimAsync(dbUser, newTokenExpires);
        else
            await _userManager.ReplaceClaimAsync(dbUser,
                currentTokenClaimExpires, newTokenExpires);
    }
    #endregion

    #region Admin Role and Claim
    var admin = "Admin";
    var isAdmin = await _userManager.IsInRoleAsync(dbUser, admin);
    var adminClaim = new Claim(admin, "true");

    if (isAdmin && !user.IsAdmin)
    {
        // Remove Admin Role
        await _userManager.RemoveFromRoleAsync(dbUser, admin);

        // Remove Admin Claim
        await _userManager.RemoveClaimAsync(dbUser, adminClaim);
    }
    else if (!isAdmin && user.IsAdmin)
    {
        // Add Admin Role
        await _userManager.AddToRoleAsync(dbUser, admin);

        // Add Admin Claim
        await _userManager.AddClaimAsync(dbUser, adminClaim);
    }
    #endregion
```

```
    var result = await _db.SaveChangesAsync();
    return result >= 0;
}
```

The complete code for the **DeleteUserAsync** method:

```
public async Task<bool> DeleteUserAsync(string userId)
{
    try
    {
        // Fetch user
        var dbUser = await _userManager.FindByIdAsync(userId);
        if (dbUser == null) return false;

        // Remove roles from user
        var userRoles = await _userManager.GetRolesAsync(dbUser);
        var roleRemoved = await _userManager.RemoveFromRolesAsync(
            dbUser, userRoles);

        // Remove the user's claims
        var userClaims = _db.UserClaims.Where(ur =>
            ur.UserId.Equals(dbUser.Id));
        _db.UserClaims.RemoveRange(userClaims);

        // Remove the user
        var deleted = await _userManager.DeleteAsync(dbUser);
        return deleted.Succeeded;
    }
    catch
    {
        return false;
    }
}
```

The complete code for the **GetUserAsync** method:

```
public async Task<VODUser> GetUserAsync(LoginUserDTO loginUser, bool
includeClaims = false)
{
    try
    {
        var user = await _userManager.FindByEmailAsync(loginUser.Email);
```

```
            if (user == null) return null;

            if(loginUser.Password.IsNullOrEmptyOrWhiteSpace() &&
                loginUser.PasswordHash.IsNullOrEmptyOrWhiteSpace())
                    return null;

            if (loginUser.Password.Length > 0)
            {
                var password =
                    _userManager.PasswordHasher.VerifyHashedPassword(user,
                        user.PasswordHash, loginUser.Password);

                if (password == PasswordVerificationResult.Failed)
                    return null;
            }
            else
            {
                if (!user.PasswordHash.Equals(loginUser.PasswordHash))
                    return null;
            }

            // Include the user's claims
            if (includeClaims) user.Claims =
                await _userManager.GetClaimsAsync(user);

            return user;
        }
        catch
        {
            throw;
        }
    }
}
```

Adding the Token to the User

This method will add the token to the user in the database.

1. Add a **private** method named **AddTokenToUserAsync** to the **TokenService** class that takes a **string** parameter named **userId** and an instance of the **TokenDTO** class named **token**, and returns a **bool** wrapped in a **Task**.
2. Fetch the user as a **UserDTO** named **userDTO** by calling the **GetUserAsync** method on the **_user** service object.
3. Add the token and expiration date to the **userDTO** object.

27. JSON Web Tokens (JWT)

4. Return the result from a call to the **UpdateUserAsync** method on the **_user** service object and pass it the **userDTO** object as data.
5. Save all files.

The complete code for the **AddTokenToUserAsync** method:

```
private async Task<bool> AddTokenToUserAsync(string userId, TokenDTO token)
{
    var userDTO = await _users.GetUserAsync(userId);
    userDTO.Token.Token = token.Token;
    userDTO.Token.TokenExpires = token.TokenExpires;

    return await _users.UpdateUserAsync(userDTO);
}
```

Generate the Token and Add It to the User

1. Locate the **GenerateTokenAsync** method in the **TokenService** class.
2. Add the **async** keyword to the method to enable asynchronous method calls.
3. Replace the **throw**-statement with a try/catch-block where the catch throws all exceptions up the call chain.
4. In the try-block, fetch the user by calling the **GetUserAsync** with the **LoginUserDTO** object and **true** for fetching the user's claims.
   ```
   var user = await _users.GetUserAsync(loginUserDto, true);
   ```
5. Throw an **UnauthorizedAccessException** exception if the user doesn't exist.
   ```
   if (user == null) throw new UnauthorizedAccessException();
   ```
6. Fetch the user's claims and store them in a variable named **claims**.
   ```
   var claims = GetClaims(user, true);
   ```
7. Create a new token containing the user's claims.
   ```
   var token = CreateToken(claims);
   ```
8. Add the token to the user and throw a **SecurityTokenException** exception if unsuccessful.
   ```
   var succeeded = await AddTokenToUserAsync(user.Id, token);
   if (!succeeded) throw new SecurityTokenException(
       "Could not add a token to the user");
   ```
9. Return the token from the method.
10. Save all files.

The complete code for the **GenerateTokenAsync** method:

```
public async Task<TokenDTO> GenerateTokenAsync(LoginUserDTO
loginUserDto)
{
    try
    {
        var user = await _users.GetUserAsync(loginUserDto, true);

        if (user == null) throw new UnauthorizedAccessException();

        var claims = GetClaims(user, true);

        var token = CreateToken(claims);

        var succeeded = await AddTokenToUserAsync(user.Id, token);
        if (!succeeded) throw new SecurityTokenException(
            "Could not add a token to the user");

        return token;
    }
    catch
    {
        throw;
    }
}
```

Fetching a User's Token

This method will fetch the user's token data from the database and return it as a **TokenDTO** object.

1. Locate the **GetTokenAsync** method in the **TokenService** class.
2. Add the **async** keyword to the method to enable asynchronous method calls.
3. Replace the **throw**-statement with a try/catch-block where the catch throws exceptions up the call chain.
4. In the try-block, fetch the user by calling the **GetUserAsync** with the **LoginUserDTO** object and **true** for fetching the user's claims.
   ```
   var user = await _users.GetUserAsync(loginUserDto, true);
   ```

27. JSON Web Tokens (JWT)

5. Throw an **UnauthorizedAccessException** exception if the user doesn't exist or the **userId** parameter differs from the **Id** property of the **LoginUserDTO** object.
   ```
   if (user == null) throw new UnauthorizedAccessException();

   if (!userId.Equals(user.Id))
       throw new UnauthorizedAccessException();
   ```

6. Return a new **TokenDTO** object with the data from the fetched user.
   ```
   return new TokenDTO(user.Token, user.TokenExpires);
   ```

7. Save all files.

The complete code for the **GetTokenAsync** method:

```
public async Task<TokenDTO> GetTokenAsync(LoginUserDTO loginUserDto,
string userId)
{
    try
    {
        var user = await _users.GetUserAsync(loginUserDto, true);

        if (user == null) throw new UnauthorizedAccessException();

        if (!userId.Equals(user.Id))
            throw new UnauthorizedAccessException();

        return new TokenDTO(user.Token, user.TokenExpires);
    }
    catch
    {
        throw;
    }
}
```

Adding the TokenController Class

Now that you have created the service needed to create and fetch JWT tokens, it's time to add a controller that will use the service to create and return a JWT for a user. The controller will have the route *api/token* and use an injected instance of the **ITokenService** that you created in the previous section.

It will have an asynchronous **Post** action named **GenerateTokenAsync** that has a **LoginUserDTO** parameter and returns a **TokenDTO** wrapped in an **ActionResult**, which enables it to return status codes with the data or as errors if something goes wrong.

555

It should also have an asynchronous **Get** action named **GetTokenAsync** that has a **LoginUserDTO** parameter and a **string** parameter named **userId**; like the **GenerateTokenAsync** method, this method should return a **TokenDTO** wrapped in an **ActionResult**.

Adding the GenerateToken Action

1. Add a new class named **TokenController** to the *Controllers* folder in the API project and inherit from the **ControllerBase** class.
2. Add the **ApiController** and **Route** attributes; the route should be *api/token*.
3. Add a constructor and inject the **ITokenService** service and store it in a variable named **_tokenService**.
   ```
   [Route("api/token")]
   [ApiController]
   public class TokenController : ControllerBase
   {
       private readonly ITokenService _tokenService;

       public TokenController(ITokenService tokenService)
       {
           _tokenService = tokenService;
       }
   }
   ```
4. Add an asynchronous **Post** action named **GenerateTokenAsync** that has a **LoginUserDTO** parameter and returns a **TokenDTO** wrapped in an **ActionResult**.
   ```
   [HttpPost]
   public async Task<ActionResult<TokenDTO>> GenerateTokenAsync(
   LoginUserDTO loginUserDto) { }
   ```
5. Add a try/catch-block where the catch-block returns the *Unauthorized* status code by calling the method with the same name.
6. Inside the try-block, call the **GenerateTokenAsync** method in the **TokenService** and store the token in a variable named **jwt**.
   ```
   var jwt = await _tokenService.GenerateTokenAsync(loginUserDto);
   ```
7. Return the *Unauthorized* status code if the **jwt.Token** property is **null**.
   ```
   if (jwt.Token == null) return Unauthorized();
   ```
8. Return the token from the method.
9. Save all files.

27. JSON Web Tokens (JWT)

Adding the GetToken Action

1. Add an asynchronous **Get** action named **GetTokenAsync** that has a **LoginUserDTO** parameter and a **string** parameter named **_userId** and returns a **TokenDTO** wrapped in an **ActionResult**.
   ```
   [HttpGet("{userId}")]
   public async Task<ActionResult<TokenDTO>> GetTokenAsync(string
   userId, LoginUserDTO loginUserDto) { }
   ```
2. Add a try/catch-block where the catch-block returns the *Unauthorized* status code by calling the method with the same name.
3. Inside the try-block, call the **GetTokenAsync** method in the **TokenService** and store the token in a variable named **jwt**.
   ```
   var jwt = await _tokenService.GetTokenAsync(loginUserDto, userId);
   ```
4. Return the *Unauthorized* status code if the **jwt.Token** property is **null**.
   ```
   if (jwt.Token == null) return Unauthorized();
   ```
5. Return the token from the method.
6. Save all files.

The complete code for the **TokenController** class:

```
[Route("api/token")]
[ApiController]
public class TokenController : ControllerBase
{
    private readonly ITokenService _tokenService;

    public TokenController(ITokenService tokenService)
    {
        _tokenService = tokenService;
    }

    [HttpPost]
    public async Task<ActionResult<TokenDTO>> GenerateTokenAsync(
    LoginUserDTO loginUserDto)
    {
        try
        {
            var jwt = await _tokenService.GenerateTokenAsync(
                loginUserDto);

            if (jwt.Token == null) return Unauthorized();
```

```csharp
            return jwt;
        }
        catch
        {
            return Unauthorized();
        }
    }

    [HttpGet("{userId}")]
    public async Task<ActionResult<TokenDTO>> GetTokenAsync(
        string userId, LoginUserDTO loginUserDto)
    {
        try
        {
            var jwt = await _tokenService.GetTokenAsync(loginUserDto,
                userId);

            if (jwt.Token == null) return Unauthorized();

            return jwt;
        }
        catch
        {
            return Unauthorized();
        }
    }
}
```

Testing the TokenController
1. Start the **API** project and Postman.
2. Open a new tab in Postman and select **POST** in the drop-down to the left of the URI field.
3. Enter the *http://localhost:6600/api/token* URI in the text field.
4. Click the Headers link and add a **Content-Type** header for *application/json*.
5. Click the **Body** link and enter a valid user. You can get the email and password hash from the **AspNetUsers** table. Remember that the **GenerateTokenAsync** action requires values for the properties in the **LoginUserDTO** class. The **password** property can be empty because the **passwordHash** property has a value and only one of them is required.

```
{
    "email": "a@b.c",
    "password": "",
    "passwordHash": "AQAAAAEAACcQAAAAEAkM1F+B3zl1exnwsmFC61k8"
}
```

6. Click the **Send** button. A token should be returned to Postman.

```
{
    "token": "eyJhbGciOiJodHRwOi8vd3d3LncLCJqdGkiOiJhYzhkMWQ3MC
             .eyJzdWIiOiJhQGIuYyIsImVtYWlsIjoiYUBiLmMiLCJqdGkiO
             .ZSFIe9cR9p9I6AglEwdaONaZ10MMderB0MLZSFIe9cR9p9I6A",
    "tokenExpires": "2019-05-05T11:23:16Z",
    "tokenHasExpired": false
}
```

7. You can check that the token and expiration claims were successfully added to the user by examining the **Token** and **TokenExpires** fields for the user in the **AspNetUsers** table and the user's claims in the **AspNetUserClaims** table.
8. Open a new tab in Postman and select **GET** in the drop-down to the left of the URI field.
9. Enter the URI with the user id in the text field *http://localhost:6600/api/token/88f17367-d303-4383-a54e-ec15e86e532e*. You can get the user id, email, and password hash from the **AspNetUsers** table
10. Click the Headers link and add a **Content-Type** header for *application/json*.
11. Copy the body from the **Post** tab and switch to the **Get** tab. Paste in the copied user object in the **Body**.
12. Click the **Send** button. Postman receives the created token.
13. Stop the application in Visual Studio.

Securing the API

Now that you have learned how to generate and store the JWTs, it's time to secure the API by configuring JSON Web Token authentication and use the claims in the JWT to configure authorization policies that can be used to secure controllers and actions.

Adding Authorization with Claims and Policies

To secure the API with authorization, you must make sure that the new users have one or both of the *VODUser* and *Admin* claims that will determine their access to the API's controllers and actions. Use the claims when configuring policies in the **Startup** class and when securing the controllers and actions with the **Authorize** attribute. The code below shows how to configure a policy for the *Admin* claim. The first string is the name of the policy; the second is the name of the claim, and the third is the value the claim must have to give access to the protected resource.

```
services.AddAuthorization(options =>
{
    options.AddPolicy("Admin", policy => policy.RequireClaim("Admin",
        "true"));
});
```

The code below shows how to add authorization to a controller or action with the *Admin* policy.

```
[Authorize(Policy = "Admin")]
```

Add the *VODUser* claim when registering a new user with one of the **Admin** or **UI** sites. Add the *Admin* claim when registering a new user with the **Admin** site or added or removed based on the **Is Admin** checkbox on the **Edit** Razor Page; you have already added the code for the **Is Admin** checkbox in the **UpdateUserAsync** method in the **UserService** class. The *Admin* role should also be added to new users when registered with the **Admin** site; this role gives the user access to the **Admin UI** and has nothing to do with authorization in the API.

Now, you will add the claims and role in the **Register** Razor Pages for the **Admin** and **UI** sites. You should immediately see that the role has been added to the new user because the cards on the **Index** Razor Page in the **Admin UI** will only be visible if the user has the *Admin* role. You can check that the claims have been added by looking in the **AspNetUsers** and **AspNetUserClaims** tables.

```
var identityResult = await _userManager.AddClaimAsync(user,
    new Claim("VODUser", "true"));
```

1. Open the *Register.cshtml.cs* file in the **Admin** project.
2. Locate the if-block that checks the **result.Succeeded** property and add both claims to the user at the beginning of the if-block. You could log a message for a successfully added claim.
   ```
   var identityResult = await _userManager.AddClaimAsync(user,
       new Claim("VODUser", "true"));
   ```

```
if (identityResult.Succeeded) _logger.LogInformation(
    "Added the VODUser Claim to the User.");

identityResult = await _userManager.AddClaimAsync(user,
    new Claim("Admin", "true"));

if (identityResult.Succeeded) _logger.LogInformation(
    "Added the Admin Claim to the User.");
```

3. Add the role below the claims.
   ```
   identityResult = await _userManager.AddToRoleAsync(user, "Admin");

   if (identityResult.Succeeded) _logger.LogInformation(
       "Added the Admin Role to the User.");
   ```
4. Open the *Register.cshtml.cs* file in the **UI** project.
5. Locate the if-block that checks the **result.Succeeded** property and add the *VODUser* claim to the user at the beginning of the if-block; users registered with the **UI** project should not have the *Admin* claim. You could log a message for a successfully added claim.
   ```
   var identityResult = await _userManager.AddClaimAsync(user,
       new Claim("VODUser", "true"));

   if (identityResult.Succeeded) _logger.LogInformation(
       "Added the VODUser Claim to the User.");
   ```
6. Start the **API** and **Admin** projects and click the **Instructors** card; the **Index** Razor Page should list all instructors.
7. Stop the application in Visual Studio.
8. Add the **Authorize** attribute with a policy named *Admin* to the **InstructorsController** class.
   ```
   [Authorize(Policy = "Admin")]
   ```
9. Start the **API** and **Admin** projects and click the **Instructors** card; the API throws the following exception: **System.InvalidOperationException:** *'The AuthorizationPolicy named: 'Admin' was not found.'*. The reason for this exception is that you haven't configured the policy in the **Startup** class yet.
10. Stop the application in Visual Studio.
11. Open the Startup class in the API project and add the policies to the **ConfigureServices** method.
    ```
    services.AddAuthorization(options =>
    {
        options.AddPolicy("VODUser", policy =>
            policy.RequireClaim("VODUser", "true"));
    ```

```
            options.AddPolicy("Admin", policy =>
                policy.RequireClaim("Admin", "true"));
        });
```

12. Start the **API** and **Admin** projects and click the **Instructors** card; The **Index** Razor Page displays the following error message above the cards. The reason for this error is that you have added authorization to the **InstructorsController** but the user JWT token is unverified, and therefore the user hasn't been authenticated and can't be authorized based on the claims in the token.

    > You do not have access to this page. ×

13. Click the **Courses** card; the **Index** Razor Page should display the courses.
14. Stop the application in Visual Studio.
15. Add the same **Authorize** attribute you used with the **InstructorsController** to all other controllers in the **API** project except the **TokenController** that should be available to anonymous users.

Adding JWT Authentication

Now that the **API's** controllers have authorization, the next step is to activate authentication using the JWT token. You have only added authorization for the *Admin* claim, but you can easily add authorization for the *VODUser* claim.

Replace the default **Identity**-based authentication with the JWT Bearer authentication scheme to add JWT token-based authentication for the user's token; you do this by adding new default authentication options. The **DefaultAuthenticateScheme** option activates JWT token authentication, and the **DefaultChallengeScheme** option prompts the user to sign in.

```
services.AddAuthentication(options =>
{
    options.DefaultAuthenticateScheme =
        JwtBearerDefaults.AuthenticationScheme;
    options.DefaultChallengeScheme =
        JwtBearerDefaults.AuthenticationScheme;
})
```

When the default authentication scheme is defined, you must configure the JWT Bearer options. You do this by chaining on the **AddJwtBearer** method; this will make the authentication look for a JWT token in the headers of the API call.

27. JSON Web Tokens (JWT)

The same secret key that was used to create the token must be hashed with the same algorithm and added to the configuration to ensure that the token is valid.

There's no set way to configure the bearer token authentication; you must determine the correct validation options based on your API. The settings below have loose security settings where neither the issuer nor the audience is validated. The **ValidateLifetime** property specifies whether the expiration should be validated; the **ValidateIssuerSigningKey** determines whether to evaluate the signing key in the **IssuerSigningKey** property; the **ClockSkew** property specifies the value for the earliest correct date and time; the **RequireHttpsMetadata** determines whether HTTPS is required to call the API.

```
.AddJwtBearer(options =>
{
    var signingKey = new SymmetricSecurityKey(Convert.FromBase64String(
        Configuration["Jwt:SigningSecret"]));

    options.TokenValidationParameters = new TokenValidationParameters
    {
        ValidateIssuer = false,
        ValidateAudience = false,
        ValidateLifetime = true,
        ValidateIssuerSigningKey = true,
        IssuerSigningKey = signingKey,
        ClockSkew = TimeSpan.Zero
    };
    options.RequireHttpsMetadata = false;
});
```

You also need to add the authentication middleware above the **AddMvc** middleware in the **Configure** method in the **Startup** class.

```
app.UseAuthentication();
```

1. Open the **Startup** class in the **API** project and add the previously described code to the **ConfigureServices** method above the **Authorization** configuration you added earlier and the middleware to the **Configure** method.
2. Start the **API** and **Admin** projects and click the **Users** card. You need to remove the *Admin* role and add it again to add the *Admin* claim.
3. Edit the user and remove the tick in the **Is Admin** checkbox and click the **Save** button.
4. Edit the user and add a tick in the **Is Admin** checkbox and click the **Save** button.

5. Click the **Instructors** card; the **Index** Razor Page displays the same error message as before above the cards on the **Index** Razor Page. The reason for this error is that you are trying to call the API without a JWT token.

> You do not have access to this page. ✕

6. Open the **AspNetUser** table and copy the token from the **Token** field. Note that you might have to generate a new token with Postman if it has expired.
7. Open Postman and open a new **Get** tab and add the URI to the **Instructors** controller *http://localhost:6600/api/instructors*.
8. Add a **Content-Type** header for *application/json*.
9. Click the **Send** button. No data is returned with the response, only a *401 Unauthorized* status code, which means that the user is unauthenticated by the JWT bearer token security in the API.
10. Add an **Authorization** header and add the word **Bearer** followed by the token as its value to send the **Bearer** authentication token with the request.
    ```
    Bearer  iJodHRwOi8vd3d3LnczLm9yZy8yMDAxLzA0L3htbGRzaWctbW9yZSNobW
            .IiOiJhQGIuYyIsImVtYWlsIjoiYUBiLmMiLCJqdGkiOiJhYzhkMWQ3MC
            .7SRsoF9OLZSFIe9cR9p9I6AglEwdaONaZ10MMderB0M
    ```
11. Click the **Send** button again; now the list of instructors should be returned with the response and the status code should be *200 OK*.
12. Stop the application in Visual Studio.

Adding the JWT Token to the HttpClient API Calls

Now that you have established that the JWT token authentication and authorization works, it's time to add the token to the **HttpClient** API calls from the **Admin** application.

Let's add a new service that has three methods for creating, fetching and checking the JWT token from the **Admin** application. The **CreateTokenAsync** will call the API's **CreateToken-Async** to generate a new token for the logged-in user. The **GetTokenAsync** method will fetch the token from the logged-in user's claims and if possible, create an instance of the **TokenDTO** with the fetched data, otherwise the **GetTokenAsync** action in the API will be called to fetch the user's token. The **CheckTokenAsync** method will fetch the user's token and check its expiration date; if the token has expired, the **CreateTokenAsync** method in the service is called to create a new token.

27. JSON Web Tokens (JWT)

The **CreateTokenAsync** and **GetTokenAsync** methods must be added to the **HttpClientFactoryService** to be able to call the API with the **HttpClient** service you configured in the **Admin** project's **Startup** class.

Adding the CreateTokenAsync Method to the HttpClientFactoryService

1. Add a new method definition for a method named **CreateTokenAsync** to the **IHttpClientFactoryService** interface. The method should have four parameters: **user** of type **LoginUserDTO**, **uri** of type **string**, **serviceName** of type **string**, and **token** of type **string**. The method should return a **TokenDTO** instance wrapped in a **Task**.
   `Task<TokenDTO> CreateTokenAsync(LoginUserDTO user, string uri, string serviceName, string token = "");`
2. Implement the method in the **HttpClientFactoryService** class and add the **async** keyword to make it asynchronous.
3. Copy the code in the **PostAsync** method and paste it into the **CreateTokenAsync** method.
4. Replace the **TRequest** and **TResponse** types with **LoginUserDTO** and **TokenDTO** and the **content** parameter with **user** parameter for the **PostAsync** method call.
5. Save all files.

The complete code for the **CreateTokenAsync** method:

```
public async Task<TokenDTO> CreateTokenAsync(LoginUserDTO user, string uri, string serviceName, string token = "")
{
    try
    {
        if (new string[] { uri, serviceName }
            .IsNullOrEmptyOrWhiteSpace())
            throw new HttpResponseException(HttpStatusCode.NotFound,
                "Could not find the resource");

        var httpClient = _httpClientFactory.CreateClient(serviceName);
        return await httpClient.PostAsync<LoginUserDTO, TokenDTO>(
            uri.ToLower(), user, _cancellationToken, token);
    }
    catch
    {
        throw;
    }
}
```

Adding the GetTokenAsync Method to the HttpClientFactoryService

1. Copy the **CreateTokenAsync** method definition in the **IHttpClientFactoryService** interface and rename the copy **GetTokenAsync**.
   Task<TokenDTO> GetTokenAsync(LoginUserDTO user, string uri, string serviceName, string token = "");
2. Implement the method in the **HttpClientFactoryService** class and add the **async** keyword to make it asynchronous.
3. Copy the code in the **GetAsync** method and paste it into the **GetTokenAsync** method.
4. Replace the **TResponse** and **string** types that define the **GetAsync** method with **TokenDTO, LoginUserDTO**.
5. Save all files.

The complete code for the **GetTokenAsync** method:

```
public async Task<TokenDTO> GetTokenAsync(LoginUserDTO user, string uri,
string serviceName, string token = "")
{
    try
    {
        if (new[] { uri, serviceName }.IsNullOrEmptyOrWhiteSpace())
            throw new HttpResponseException(HttpStatusCode.NotFound,
                "Could not find the resource");

        var httpClient = _httpClientFactory.CreateClient(serviceName);
        return await httpClient.GetAsync<TokenDTO, LoginUserDTO>(
            uri.ToLower(), _cancellationToken, null, token);
    }
    catch
    {
        throw;
    }
}
```

Adding the IJwtTokenService Interface

1. Add a new interface named **IJwtTokenService** to the *Services* folder in the **Common** project.
2. Add a definition for a parameter-less asynchronous method named **CreateTokenAsync** that returns an instance of the **TokenDTO** class wrapped in a **Task**.

27. JSON Web Tokens (JWT)

3. Add a definition for a parameter-less asynchronous method named **GetTokenAsync** that returns an instance of the **TokenDTO** class wrapped in a **Task**.
4. Add a definition for an asynchronous method named **CheckTokenAsync** that takes an instance of the **TokenDTO** class and returns an instance of the **TokenDTO** class wrapped in a **Task**.
5. Save all files.

The complete code for the **IJwtTokenService** interface:

```
public interface IJwtTokenService
{
    Task<TokenDTO> CreateTokenAsync();
    Task<TokenDTO> GetTokenAsync();
    Task<TokenDTO> CheckTokenAsync(TokenDTO token);
}
```

Adding the JwtTokenService Class

1. Add a **public** class named **JwtTokenService** to the *Services* folder in the **Common** project.
2. Inject a constructor with the **IHttpClientFactoryService** that you created earlier to make **HttpClient** calls to the API; the **UserManager** to get access to the logged-in user; the **IHttpContextAccessor** to get the logged-in user's id from its claims.
3. Implement the **IJwtTokenService** interface.
4. Add the **async** keyword to the methods to make them asynchronous.
5. Save all files.

The code, so far, for the **JwtTokenService** class:

```
public class JwtTokenService : IJwtTokenService
{
    #region Properties
    private readonly IHttpClientFactoryService _http;
    private readonly UserManager<VODUser> _userManager;
    private readonly IHttpContextAccessor _httpContextAccessor;
    #endregion
```

```csharp
    #region Constructor
    public JwtTokenService(IHttpClientFactoryService http,
    UserManager<VODUser> userManager, IHttpContextAccessor
    httpContextAccessor)
    {
        _http = http;
        _userManager = userManager;
        _httpContextAccessor = httpContextAccessor;
    }
    #endregion

    #region Token Methods
    public async Task<TokenDTO> CreateTokenAsync()
    {
        throw new NotImplementedException();
    }

    public async Task<TokenDTO> GetTokenAsync()
    {
        throw new NotImplementedException();
    }

    public async Task<TokenDTO> CheckTokenAsync(TokenDTO token)
    {
        throw new NotImplementedException();
    }

    #endregion
}
```

Implementing the CreateTokenAsync Method
1. Replace the **NotImplementedException** code with a try/catch-block that returns a default **TokenDTO** instance in the catch-block to the **CreateTokenAsync** method.
2. Inside the try-block, fetch the user id with the **_httpContextAccessor** object.
   ```
   var userId = _httpContextAccessor.HttpContext.User
        .FindFirst(ClaimTypes.NameIdentifier).Value;
   ```
3. Fetch the user with the **_userManager** object using the user id.
   ```
   var user = await _userManager.FindByIdAsync(userId);
   ```

27. JSON Web Tokens (JWT)

4. Use the data from the fetched user object to create an instance of the **LoginUserDTO** class that you need to call the **CreateTokenAsync** action method in the API.
   ```
   var tokenUser = new LoginUserDTO { Email = user.Email,
       Password = "", PasswordHash = user.PasswordHash };
   ```

5. Call the **CreateTokenAsync** action method in the API on the **_http** object and store the returned token in a variable named **token**.
   ```
   var token = await _http.CreateTokenAsync(tokenUser,
       "api/token", "AdminClient");
   ```

6. Return the token from the method.
7. Save all files.

The complete code for the **CreateTokenAsync** method in the **JwtTokenService** class:

```
public async Task<TokenDTO> CreateTokenAsync()
{
    try
    {
        var userId = _httpContextAccessor.HttpContext.User
            .FindFirst(ClaimTypes.NameIdentifier).Value;

        var user = await _userManager.FindByIdAsync(userId);

        var tokenUser = new LoginUserDTO { Email = user.Email,
            Password = "", PasswordHash = user.PasswordHash };

        var token = await _http.CreateTokenAsync(tokenUser,
            "api/token", "AdminClient");

        return token;
    }
    catch
    {
        return default;
    }
}
```

Implementing the GetTokenAsync Method

1. Replace the **NotImplementedException** code with a try/catch-block that returns a default **TokenDTO** instance in the catch-block to the **GetTokenAsync** method.
2. Inside the try-block, fetch the user id with the **_httpContextAccessor** object.
   ```
   var userId = _httpContextAccessor.HttpContext.User
       .FindFirst(ClaimTypes.NameIdentifier).Value;
   ```
3. Fetch the user with the **_userManager** object using the user id.
   ```
   var user = await _userManager.FindByIdAsync(userId);
   ```
4. Fetch the user's claims with the **_userManager** object and store them in a variable named **claims**.
   ```
   var claims = await _userManager.GetClaimsAsync(user);
   ```
5. Use the collection in the **claims** variable to fetch the user's **Token** and **TokenExpires** claims and store them in variables named **token** and **date**.
   ```
   var token = claims.Single(c => c.Type.Equals("Token")).Value;
   var date = claims.Single(c =>
       c.Type.Equals("TokenExpires")).Value;
   ```
6. Try to parse the expiration date into a valid **DateTime** object and store the result in a variable named **expires**.
   ```
   DateTime expires;
   var succeeded = DateTime.TryParse(date, out expires);
   ```
7. If the date could be parsed and the token contains a value, then return a **TokenDTO** instance with the values from the user's claims. You can call the **IsNullOrEmptyOrWhiteSpace** extension method you created earlier to check if the token contains a value.
   ```
   if (succeeded && !token.IsNullOrEmptyOrWhiteSpace())
       return new TokenDTO(token, expires);
   ```
8. If the parse was unsuccessful, then create an instance of the **LoginUserDTO** class and call the **GetTokenAsync** action method in the API.
   ```
   var tokenUser = new LoginUserDTO { Email = user.Email,
       Password = "", PasswordHash = user.PasswordHash };

   var newToken = await _http.GetTokenAsync(tokenUser,
       $"api/token/{user.Id}", "AdminClient");
   ```
9. Return the fetched token from the method.
10. Save all files.

27. JSON Web Tokens (JWT)

The complete code for the **GetTokenAsync** method in the **JwtTokenService** class:

```
public async Task<TokenDTO> GetTokenAsync()
{
    try
    {
        var userId = _httpContextAccessor.HttpContext.User
            .FindFirst(ClaimTypes.NameIdentifier).Value;

        var user = await _userManager.FindByIdAsync(userId);
        var claims = await _userManager.GetClaimsAsync(user);
        var token = claims.Single(c => c.Type.Equals("Token")).Value;
        var date = claims.Single(c =>
            c.Type.Equals("TokenExpires")).Value;

        DateTime expires;
        var succeeded = DateTime.TryParse(date, out expires);

        // Return token from the user object
        if (succeeded && !token.IsNullOrEmptyOrWhiteSpace())
            return new TokenDTO(token, expires);

        // Return token from the API
        var tokenUser = new LoginUserDTO { Email = user.Email,
            Password = "", PasswordHash = user.PasswordHash };

        var newToken = await _http.GetTokenAsync(tokenUser,
            $"api/token/{user.Id}", "AdminClient");

        return newToken;
    }
    catch
    {
        return default;
    }
}
```

Implementing the CheckTokenAsync Method
1. Replace the **NotImplementedException** code with a try/catch-block that returns a default **TokenDTO** instance in the catch-block to the **CheckTokenAsync** method.
2. Inside the try-block, add an if-block that checks that the token hasn't expired.
    `if (token.TokenHasExpired) { }`

3. Inside the if-block, try to fetch the token by calling the **GetTokenAsync** method in the same service and replace the token in the method's **token** parameter.
   `token = await GetTokenAsync();`
4. Inside the if-block, add an if-statement that checks if the token has expired and calls the **CreateTokenAsync** method in the same service if it has; replacing the token in the **token** parameter.
   `if (token.TokenHasExpired) token = await CreateTokenAsync();`
5. Below the outermost if-block, return the token from the method.
6. Open the **Startup** class in the **Admin** project and add a service configuration for the **IJwtTokenService** service.
   `services.AddScoped<IJwtTokenService, JwtTokenService>();`
7. Save all files.

The complete code for the **CheckTokenAsync** method in the **JwtTokenService** class:

```
public async Task<TokenDTO> CheckTokenAsync(TokenDTO token)
{
    try
    {
        if (token.TokenHasExpired)
        {
            token = await GetTokenAsync();
            if (token.TokenHasExpired) token = await CreateTokenAsync();
        }

        return token;
    }
    catch
    {
        return default;
    }
}
```

Adding the Token to the AdminAPIService

Inject **IJwtTokenService** into the **AdminAPIService** and pass the token methods with each API call.

1. Open the **AdminAPIService** class in the *Services* folder in the **Common** project.
2. Inject the **IJwtTokenService** into the constructor and store the instance in a variable named **_jwt**.

27. JSON Web Tokens (JWT)

3. Add a **TokenDTO** variable named token to the class and instantiate it.
   `TokenDTO token = new TokenDTO();`
4. Open the **GetAsync** method and check the token below the **FormatUriWithoutIds** call by calling the **CheckTokenAsync** method in the **_jwt** service. Store the returned token in the **token** variable you added to the class.
   `token = await _jwt.CheckTokenAsync(token);`
5. Add the token in the **token.Token** property to the **GetListAsync** API method call.
   `return await _http.GetListAsync<TDestination>($"{uri}?include={include.ToString()}", "AdminClient", token.Token);`
6. Repeat the previous two bullets for the **SingleAsync**, **CreateAsync**, **DeleteAsync**, and **UpdateAsync** methods.
7. Save all files.
8. Start the API and the **Admin** application and perform CRUD operations for the different entities to make sure that the JWT authentication and authorization works.

Summary

In this chapter, you learned how to create JSON Web Tokens (JWTs) and how to secure the API with JSON Bearer Token authentication and claims based policy authorization that uses claims from the JWT.

I truly hope that you enjoyed the book and have learned a lot. Please leave a review on Amazon so that other readers can make an informed decision based on your and other readers' thoughts about the book.

Regards,

Jonas Fagerberg

ASP.NET Core 2.2 MVC, Razor Pages, API, JSON Web Tokens & HttpClient

Other Books and Courses by the Author

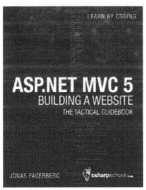 

ASP.NET Core 2.0 – MVC & Razor Pages

ASP.NET Core 1.1 – Building a Website

ASP.NET Core 1.1 – Building a Web API

ASP.NET MVC 5 – Building a Website

C# for Beginners

Online Courses and Free Content by the Author
You can find online courses and free content at https://www.csharpschool.com.

Made in the USA
Columbia, SC
28 July 2019